The Twenty-First-Century Parson's Handbook

The Twenty-First-Century Parson's Handbook

A Guide for Anglican Liturgy and Parish Ministry in the Prayer Book Catholic Tradition

JARED C. CRAMER

WIPF & STOCK · Eugene, Oregon

THE TWENTY-FIRST-CENTURY PARSON'S HANDBOOK
A Guide for Anglican Liturgy and Parish Ministry in the Prayer Book Catholic Tradition

Copyright © 2025 Jared C. Cramer. All rights reserved. Except for brief quotations in critical publications or reviews, no part of this book may be reproduced in any manner without prior written permission from the publisher. Write: Permissions, Wipf and Stock Publishers, 199 W. 8th Ave., Suite 3, Eugene, OR 97401.

Wipf & Stock
An Imprint of Wipf and Stock Publishers
199 W. 8th Ave., Suite 3
Eugene, OR 97401

www.wipfandstock.com

PAPERBACK ISBN: 979-8-3852-0527-1
HARDCOVER ISBN: 979-8-3852-0528-8
EBOOK ISBN: 979-8-3852-0529-5

01/28/25

Unless otherwise noted, all Scripture quotations are from New Revised Standard Version Bible with the apocrypha. Copyright © 1989 by the National Council of the Churches of Christ in the United States of America. Used by permission. All rights reserved worldwide.

For Marion J. Hatchett, of Blessed Memory

"The rubrics of the Book of Common Prayer exist to protect the laity from the whims and eccentricities of their clergy."
—Marion J. Hatchett

Contents

Acknowledgments ix

Preface xvii

Introduction 1

1 The Chancel, Nave, and Their Furniture 36
2 The Holy Table and Its Furniture 64
3 Colors, Vestments, and Ornaments 85
4 Vestries and Sacristies 131
5 General Principles of Ceremonial 143
6 The Daily Office 178
7 The Great Litany 204
8 Processions 208
9 Introduction to Communion 219
10 Holy Communion, the Simple Form 246
11 Holy Communion in Detail 250
12 Holy Baptism 269
13 Catechism and Confirmation 283
14 The Solemnization of Matrimony 301
15 Confession, Unction, and Last Rites 317
16 The Burial of the Dead 334
17 Notes on the Seasons 346

Appendix 1: The Most Common Rubrical Violations 377

Appendix 2: A Litany of Saints for the Episcopal Church 382

Bibliography 387
Index 395

Acknowledgments

THOUGH MY INITIAL EXPLORATION of the Anglican tradition of Christianity was theological (at least to my mind at the time), very quickly I discovered that the liturgy of the church fed my soul in a profound, deep, and meaningful way. Raised in the Churches of Christ (a cappella), I grew up with a profound appreciation for the power of worship to shape us. What I discovered in the Episcopal Church, however, was a formation in worship that was deeper, honed by centuries of practice, and one that reached into every nook and cranny of my soul.

My first note of gratitude, then, is to the Episcopal Church that first welcomed me in when I was exploring this tradition nearly twenty years ago: the Church of the Heavenly Rest in Abilene, Texas. The priest at that church (now the bishop of the Episcopal Diocese of Northwest Texas, the Rt. Rev. J. Scott Mayer) kindly led me as I explored a tradition whose theology and worship were different than my own . . . and yet, the emphasis on the centrality of baptism and Eucharist alongside of a rich tradition of hymnody, I would discover, fulfilled many of the longings and ideals implanted in me by my upbringing.

As I was looking at places to do my Anglican formation in seminary, my friend, now the Rev. Dr. Jesse W. Abell, encouraged me to look at the University of the South in Sewanee, Tennessee, where he was finishing his own seminary formation at the time. I had not even considered that school and am grateful he nudged me. As you will read below, Sewanee became a tremendously important part of my formation journey. I distinctly remember when both of us, as students, were in the library of one of the seminary professors at Sewanee. Jesse handed me a copy of *The Parson's Handbook*. He told me it was an essential book and I needed to get a copy of my own. Little did he know how much Percy Dearmer's work, especially that handbook, would shape my own future, academically and pastorally. I'm grateful.

ACKNOWLEDGMENTS

The professor of liturgics while I was at Sewanee (now the dean of the seminary, the Very Rev. James F. Turrell) was on sabbatical when I arrived and so my first classes in church music and liturgy were taught by Marion J. Hatchett, one of the framers of the 1979 prayer book, not to mention the *Book of Occasional Services* and *The Hymnal 1982*. I had always done well in school, graduating with my bachelor of science in biblical studies *summa cum laude* and then graduating with my master of divinity with academic honors. My very first liturgy assignment for Marion was graded a *D*. I thereby learned that, though I had affection for the prayer book, I had never read it as closely as I should have. It was Marion who taught me in class the essentiality of the rubrics (including the quote attributed to him at the beginning of this book, a statement that he would repeat regularly). In particular, he taught how the rubrics exist to affirm all orders of ministry and ensure that the entire community has a role in the worship of the people of God. He also took a personal interest in me (as he had with so many students over the course of his career), inviting me over for cigarettes and scotch and, eventually, dinner as well. It was in his kitchen, as his wife was working on a risotto, that my wife first whispered in my ear that she loved me. In many ways, I am the priest I am—and the person I am—because of his wisdom, insights, and kindness. I miss him dearly but I'm sure he is enjoying the heavenly choirs of angels (perhaps even encouraging them to give shape-note singing a try).

After James Turrell returned from sabbatical, he taught another liturgics practicum for us, one that was eminently helpful in its own way. (While Marion's stories were stellar, his focus was more on the history and ideas of liturgical worship at that point in his life, and we needed some more practical advice, like how to say mass.) James Turrell was also an excellent teacher and aptly ensured we all knew how to execute the liturgies of the prayer book well and faithfully. After I was ordained, he helpfully responded to several of my frantic emails when I could not remember how exactly to do something as a new cleric. His insistence upon the quality of worship—no matter the style—has stuck with me.

My first cure[1] was at Historic Christ Church in Alexandria, Virginia, a traditionally low-church parish where I would celebrate Eucharist in a blue cassock and surplice. (Blue was thought to be the American patriotic color best used as a corollary to the red that is used for cassocks

---

1. The term "cure of souls" (*cura animarum*) is one of the traditional descriptors of pastoral ministry and, in our day of overly programmatic or therapeutic understandings of ministry, the parson would do well to recover it.

ACKNOWLEDGMENTS

in royal peculiar chapels in England.) I longed, though, to be further trained in the catholic tradition of Anglicanism and the Rev. Nathan J. A. Humphrey, then an associate at St. Paul's, K Street, in Washington, DC, kindly took me under his wing. He enabled me to become an honorary assistant of that parish and to learn from the riches of the Anglo-Catholic tradition. A version of his customary from St. Paul's, K Street (much edited over the past fifteen years) remains the basis for the customary I currently use at my parish. I'm grateful for the many things Nathan taught me, especially to cover your clerical collar properly with an amice and not to tie the girdle in such a way that your stomach hangs over it when you are older and, shall we say, less lean than you were in your twenties.

For the past fourteen years, I have been blessed to serve as the rector of St. John's Episcopal Church in Grand Haven, Michigan, my hometown. The people of St. John's called me when I was only twenty-eight years old, telling me that they weren't anxious about calling a young priest because they wanted a rector who would grow with them. I believe I have grown immeasurably over these years with them, and I am grateful for their kindness and patience. They are not an Anglo-Catholic parish, and so they also have been the place where I have sought to understand how to maintain the ideals of a prayer-book-catholic approach to worship in a church that doesn't have the three sacred minsters or use an eastward facing altar. I am particularly grateful for those brave souls who accepted my invitation to serve as the first vergers of the parish and who worked with me to build the customary we use as a community: Nancy Collins, Ron Lindquist, Debbie Wakerkley, and Chuck Wibert. Ron and Chuck have since died and joined the worship of heaven. Chuck, in particular, though, along with Debbie, was the longest serving verger until congestive heart failure caused him to step into verger emeritus status. He cared deeply for the worship of the church, loved the ministry of verger, and is buried at the verger's position at the outdoor altar he and his wife, Betty, gave to the parish to place in our memorial garden. We're currently working on pulling together what is needed to use that altar for outdoor worship and I look forward to standing there to celebrate Eucharist, knowing Chuck is nearby—as he should be. I'm grateful as well for those who later joined those initial four in service: Jane Freedberg, Bob Harsha, Lauren Wegner, Fr. Daniel Snyder, Kathy Harris, Robert Babcock, Cathryn Marshall, Rob Andersen, Melissa Branderhorst, and Thomas Johnstone. Each of them has brought distinct gifts and insights to the service of the church and has blessed me.

ACKNOWLEDGMENTS

I'm grateful as well to the insights I learned when I returned to Sewanee for their doctor of ministry program. After an initial focus in the area of spirituality I found myself drawn more and more to questions of liturgy. I'm grateful to the Rt. Rev. J. Neil Alexander, former dean of the School of Theology, and once more, James Turrell, for helping me understand the structure of ritual better, particularly as it relates to the rites of Christian initiation. Similarly, Bishop Alexander helped me in a later course, along with the Rev. Dr. Melissa M. Hartley, associate university chaplain at Sewanee, develop a stronger sense of liturgical time and how that influences the celebration of our liturgical rites. The Rev. Dr. Benjamin King, now dean of the chapel and the Duncalf-Villavoso Professor of Church History at the Episcopal Seminary of the Southwest, served as one of the readers for my final doctoral project on Percy Dearmer. Dr. King helped me situate Dearmer's work in the context of the Oxford movement and Ritualism (both of which Dearmer was, of course, a product of, as much as he reacted against them at times). Similarly, James Turrell served as my second reader for that doctoral project, helping me keep the work in conversation with the best of current liturgical theology and practice. I'm grateful to them both.

As I approached the completion of this current work, I reached out to several people I trusted for their own insights and advice when it came to how one might take a book written one hundred years ago on Anglican worship and rewrite it for our own time. Several of them offered numerous suggestions, which are incorporated in these pages. I'm grateful to Robert McCormick, organist and director of music at Good Shepherd Episcopal in Rosemont, Pennsylvania, for his advice on questions of music as well as sound Anglo-Catholic practice from his vantage point on the organ bench at several excellent churches in that tradition.

Richard Pryor III serves as the creative editor of *Earth and Altar* and is currently a student in the area of church history and ecumenics at Princeton Theological School. I first met Richard while we were both alternate deputies at General Convention. In addition to solid advice on many aspects of this book, Richard kept me apprised of the developments of the General Convention that occurred while I worked on this book.

Derek Olsen's interest in things medieval, monastic, and liturgical was invaluable in several sections (including when he quibbled with Dearmer in areas like liturgical colors). It was Derek who kindly pointed out to me at a conference I once organized that I shouldn't have separated the presentation of the bread and wine from the offerings of the

ACKNOWLEDGMENTS

people, according to the rubrics of the church. Though I fear I found myself mostly annoyed in the moment of stress, I later repented and even changed my own practice in the parish. He regularly invites me and the rest of the church to take our prayer book more seriously, and his book *Inwardly Digest: The Prayer Book as a Guide to a Spiritual Life* remains one of my favorites to use in the parish, especially with those seeking to go deeper in their own spiritual lives.

Our current assisting bishop in the Episcopal Diocese of Western Michigan and the Episcopal Diocese of Eastern Michigan (soon to be the Episcopal Diocese of the Great Lakes), the Rt. Rev Gladstone "Skip" Adams provided helpful feedback from the perspective of a bishop. Trevor Floyd, my most trusted vendor when it comes to anything I need liturgically, gave helpful advice on many aspects of the sections on vestments and hangings. May his company, Trevor W. Floyd & Co., get much more work; their vestments and church furnishing are of a quality not often seen in our time.

Two liturgists also read this work and provided helpful feedback, critique, and encouragement. The Rev. Matthew S. C. Olver, PhD, who serves as the affiliate professor of liturgics and pastoral theology at Nashotah House was a tremendous encouragement and help to me. The Very Rev. Patrick Malloy, PhD, who serves as dean of the Cathedral Church of St. John the Divine in New York City also provided helpful advice and encouragement. If my book on prayer-book-catholic worship is too much, please feel free to discard it and instead purchase his book *Celebrating the Eucharist: A Practical Ceremonial Guide for Clergy and Other Liturgical Ministers*. If you follow his advice, your worship will be a rich and full experience of the best of the prayer book tradition.

Finally, when I was a young priest, the Rev. J. L. Anthony Parker, then rector of St. John's-in-the-Village in Baltimore, Maryland, invited me to the American Sarum Conference in 2010 at Bronxville, New York. I was a new rector and could not afford the conference on my own, and Anthony offered to pay my way, noting other clerics did this for him when he was young and the day would come when I would do it for others. The conference was fascinating and was also my first experience with the old "English Use" tradition. Anthony also encouraged me to take Dearmer seriously not only as an historical figure but as someone who could be a guide for worship in our own time. In addition to giving me regular advice as a new rector, Anthony kindly read this book

ACKNOWLEDGMENTS

and gave me several suggestions to strengthen the work. I hope the final product pleases him.

I would also note my gratitude to George Callihan who was, once more, tremendously helpful at several points during the path of shepherding this through to completion. In particular, I am grateful for George's patience as I worked with those listed above to garner feedback and try to make this book as strong and helpful as as possible. I'm also grateful to the careful and detailed work of my copyeditor, Brittany McComb. In addition to being an excellent copyeditor (who, among other things, helpfully cured me of my allergy of too many semicolons in early twentieth century prose), Brittany was indefatigable in ensuring everything was sourced properly—not always an easy task for a book that is being rewritten a hundred years after its last edition. Her intelligence, keen eye, and helpful suggestions to make the writing clearer to the reader were invaluable. Savanah N. Landerholm did wonderful work in typesetting the text and ensuring the design was true to the original handbook while also meeting the best of current publishing standards. I deeply appreciate her patience as I made final edits to make the book as strong as possible. As always, working with George, Brittany, Savanah, and everyone at Wipf and Stock has been a lovely experience.

When I began this book nearly a year ago, I did not think it would take this long to complete it. However, thanks to all those mentioned (and those whose names I am currently forgetting), I have a fair amount of pride in the book you hold in your hands. I wish I had been given a resource like this as a new priest. Whether or not you find yourself, like me, in the tradition of a prayer book catholic, I do think it will be helpful to you.

However, I would not have been able to spend the extra time on the book were it not for the patience and support of my wife, Bethany, and our daughter, Lucille. In particular, I'm grateful for the time Lucille spent playing—popping into my office with cards, notes, cootie-catchers, and questions—while I was trying to bring this manuscript to completion. Lucille, as you grow up, I hope you know you are never an intrusion or interruption in daddy's work. You are each and every day a gift. And I owe you a day at Michigan's Adventure very soon. Bethany, I owe you a dinner at Ruth's Chris (and very likely a weeklong vacation where I never open my laptop once). They both give so much to the church in so many ways: Bethany, baking communion bread and helping to run the live stream of our worship, and Lucille, by taking on the job of crucifer as we came out of the pandemic, even though she was just five years old, because someone needed to carry the cross, and she was one of the few children regularly there in those early days back in church. They both remind me regularly that the best of worship is when it truly is the cooperative act of the entire community of believers. And the beauty of worship pales in comparison to the beauty of their love. Thank you.

Whatever in this book is helpful is likely due to something Dearmer wrote a hundred years ago or an insight I gleaned from those mentioned in these acknowledgments. Anything that falls short is due to my own imperfection. While I doubt this new version of the handbook will go through twelve editions, I do hope that it is helpful and that the recovery of the prayer book catholic tradition of worship I have sought in this book will continue to inform the church so that our worship can be a beautiful offering to God.

Jared+
The Feast of St. Augustine of Hippo, Bishop and Theologian, †430

Preface

When the first *Parson's Handbook* was published in 1899, Dearmer wrote, "The object of this Handbook is to help, in however humble a way, towards remedying the lamentable confusion, lawlessness, and vulgarity which are conspicuous in the Church at this time." By the time he published the twelfth and final edition in 1932, he found himself able to write, "A consistent Anglican use is now established and understood in every part of the world." He wrote, therefore, with a sense that many of his goals had been reached and could be seen in all corners of Anglicanism.

In preparing this update to Dearmer's work, I have sought to strike a delicate balance. I began the work with the exact text of the twelfth edition and worked through it from start to finish. In some sections, only a light update of language and approach was needed to bring it in line with contemporary scholarship and practice. A good example of that sort of section is chapter one, where there is information on the various items in a parish church. In other sections, the information and advice needed to be updated and almost entirely rewritten afresh. A good example of that would be the sections on funerals, weddings, and the catechism.

My attempt throughout, though, has been to articulate what I would call a consistent "prayer book catholic" approach to priestly ministry. By prayer book catholic, I mean an approach to church that is in accord with the established norms of our church and also authentic to the long and rich history of the traditions of Anglican Christianity, a tradition I do find peculiar and particular (in the best meaning of those words) among the various traditions of the Christian faith. In doing so, I have sought to keep my revisions true to the basic ideals of Dearmer's work, not only in the *Parson's Handbook* but throughout his significant breadth of writing. I sought to articulate those ideals in my previous book on Dearmer.[2] They are, briefly:

1. Fidelity to the Book of Common Prayer
2. Reverence for beauty and art
3. Simplicity over elaborate ceremonial
4. Upholding the cooperative worshiping community as essential
5. Worship that is authentic and true to its context
6. Liturgical spaces designed and used with attention to liturgical scholarship
7. Thoughtful and dignified movement
8. Worship that is attentive to concerns of justice and ethics
9. Discussing liturgy with a distinct sense of humor

My previous book laid out how these principles may be found throughout Dearmer's work, and it would be a helpful companion to the parson who seeks to understand the context, tradition, and framework that stands behind this new version of *The Parson's Handbook*.

On that final and ninth point, I am aware of the well-worn adage of the difference between a terrorist and a liturgist: sometimes you can negotiate with a terrorist. While inflexibility is indeed a hallmark of a good deal of liturgical opinion (albeit, often much more among the clergy than among liturgical scholars), this reality should be held gently. On one side, it is meet and right to have sound liturgical principles that neither bend nor break but provide a foundation from which liturgical decisions can be made. On the other side, none of us can honestly claim to know perfectly what the best and perfect liturgical decision is in every circumstance (as much as it pains me to acknowledge this!). Thus, it is wise to know why you believe what you believe, to hold that belief with an equal amount of conviction and curiosity, and to have a fair sense of humor about the whole matter. In the end, it is grace that saves us, not liturgical perfection. And, as it says on the sign I posted in the vesting sacristy of my own parish to remind me, "The greatest mistake one can make in liturgy is to worry too much about making a mistake—don't miss God with us."

---

2. Cramer, *Percy Dearmer Revisited*.

PREFACE

One way that Dearmer balanced the need for sound liturgical principles (and better liturgical practice than he found in his own time) with the fussiness of far too many supposed liturgists was to write with a very specific tone. He paired an elegant Victorian-style prose with an acerbic wit. As much as is possible, I have sought to preserve that tone in this volume. While I am certain that I cannot construct prose of the same beauty as Dearmer, I have done my best. And I do believe one of the aspects of Dearmer's work that made it a delight to read (whether or not you always agreed with him!) was his distinct sense of humor. So, for example, when writing about the person who reads the Gospel, he once wrote,

> It is right that the gospeller should be preceded to the chancel step by the epistoler (carrying the book) and the clerk, who will then stand on his right and left, facing him as he reads. When people thought that the north was inhabited by evil spirits, there was perhaps some meaning in the reader turning in that direction; but now that we know it to be inhabited by Scotsmen, the gesture seems uncalled for.[3]

That final sentence is far from essential to the point he is making and yet it gives you a sense of the twinkle in the eye with which Dearmer offered his views. At times I have moderated Dearmer's sardonic tone, particularly where scholarship has shifted. At other times, I have sought to adopt it, particularly where I think the church in our own time has lost sight of the essential principles of worship.

As one reads the twelfth edition of his handbook, it was clear that he believed that the "Deposited Book" represented the best of what had come to be understood about the liturgical traditions and rites of Anglicanism. The Deposited Book, in many ways, was a realization of the aspirations of the liberal catholic wing of the church, but was a revision that failed when it was put to the House of Commons—not once but twice—because of Protestant evangelicals and nonconformists who feared what they perceived as creeping Catholicism. But the book was deeply important to Dearmer. He was a part of one of the first committees to work on the revision process in England.[4] This is actually one of the places where his connection to Charles Gore in the area of liturgy is most clearly seen. Dearmer and Gore were both part of the fifteen member committee. Gore also served as president of the Alcuin Club, a group

---

3. Dearmer, *Short Handbook*, 42–43.
4. Spinks, "Prayer Book 'Crisis,'" 240.

"founded with the object of promoting the study of the History and use of the Book of Common Prayer." Dearmer served as the club's secretary and treasurer.[5] The Alcuin Club's proposals, to which both Gore and Dearmer contributed, represented the views of more moderate Anglo-Catholics and were essential to the work on the Deposited Book. When the final version of the 1928 book failed to be authorized, Dearmer was deeply disappointed.[6]

Strangely enough, the twelfth edition of his handbook was published as referring to the Deposited Book as though many of its principles would still come to fruition. Despite its failure of authorization in parliament, he still hoped that the revisions, occurring after the controversies of the nineteenth and early twentieth centuries, could yet produce a prayer book that would be truly reflective of the beauty of the Anglican heritage and based upon sound liturgical scholarship. He believed that a new book could offer an inclusive approach that could draw together the various parties and streams in the Church of England, "not fearing freedom because there is freedom in Nonconformity, nor beauty because there is beauty in the rest of Christendom."[7] Above all, he longed for the church finally to move past the polemics of the prior age and become "simple in her teaching as the Gospels are simple, and pure in heart as they are pure."[8]

Despite these hopes, a new revision of the Church of England's prayer book never did come to pass after the failures of 1928. Four years after publishing the twelfth edition of his book, Dearmer himself died at the age of sixty-nine, after having served five years as a canon at Westminster Abbey (an appointment that was opposed by the dean, William Foxley Norris).[9] A thirteenth edition of his *Parson's Handbook* was later published in 1965 by a pupil, Cyril Pocknee, but it never captured the attention of the average clergyperson in the same way Dearmer's previous editions had. Over time, the handbook faded into obscurity in much of the church, a curious volume sometimes passed down from a retired cleric to one newly ordained but no longer understood to be the rich resource for liturgy and ministry it had once been.

In the 1979 American Prayer Book, the average parson is faced with quite a different ecclesial and liturgical landscape than was the case

---

5. Kiraz, *Memorial Services*, i.
6. Spinks, "Prayer Book 'Crisis,'" 241.
7. Dearmer, *Story*, 131.
8. Dearmer, *Story*, 132.
9. Nan Dearmer, *Life of Dearmer*, 99.

PREFACE

for Dearmer one hundred years ago. We have experienced the rise and culmination of the liturgical movement both in the reforms of Vatican II (some of which are increasingly contested today among our Roman Catholic siblings) and in our own prayer book (more on that below). We exist in an entirely different relationship to society, not relying on congress to pass revisions to our own prayer book. Furthermore, in the United States, the Episcopal Church never retained the ornaments rubric—that governing feature and source of so much controversy in nineteenth and early twentieth-century Anglicanism and a focus of many of Dearmer's own arguments in the original *Parson's Handbook*. And, as one considers Dearmer's confident statement at the outset of the twelfth edition of his handbook, it is doubtful if the "consistent Anglican use" was ever truly established worldwide, at least not in the way Dearmer optimistically wished for near the end of his own life.

That said, I do believe that there are principles of Anglican worship that are held in common by the churches across our communion. And these principles of worship go far beyond aesthetics, touching to the heart of the Christian faith as it has been understood and practiced in the Anglican tradition. These principles are not merely affections for all things English and old, but they are principles that get to the heart of what we believe about the practice of Christianity as heirs of the Anglican tradition. Indeed, as Dearmer himself noted time and again, "doctrine follows ceremonial, and loyalty is evoked by visible emblems."[10]

There are two principles that stand at the base of *The Parson's Handbook*, from the first edition in 1899 and through all subsequent texts. Both of these principles have brought home the importance of ceremonial, even to those who might have originally found themselves to be indifferent. The first of these is the divine character of beauty. Dearmer believed that beauty was just as necessary to a well-lived life as truth and, more importantly, that worship that is aesthetically bad is also untrue to the Divinity who is worshiped. For that reason, worship that lacks beauty can be a sort of idolatry since it is directed to an object that is not the supreme Artist of the world, the Artist whose beauty called into being all things that exist.

The more extreme low-church wing of the Church of England had furthered a divide in the church from beauty and art for explicit and

---

10. Dearmer, *Parson's Handbook*, v.

theological reasons. As Dearmer believed was so often the case, they took a fair criticism too far:

> The Puritans (like St. Bernard) felt that the vision of God was obscured by decorative display. It is true also that excess of ornament is a real danger, and that beauty itself is lost when the need of simplicity and sincerity are forgotten. But there was also the insanity of a wild reaction, a kind of Romanism turned inside out. Because the Roman Catholic Church (in common with the whole of Christendom up to the 16th century) acted on the obvious truth that beauty is a good thing, the growing Puritan party paid Rome the compliment of embracing ugliness for her sake.[11]

For Dearmer, beauty and art were not only important or helpful aspects of Christian worship, but they were also essential. This was the foundation of his approach to liturgy throughout his life, not only a mere question of taste but one that arose from his theological beliefs. "If you ask me, 'How can art be a necessary part of the worship of God, if its motive is beauty?' I reply, 'Because beauty is the manifestation of the Father; and this is precisely what modern Christianity has forgotten.'"[12] In Dearmer's view, beauty is a particular mode of God's revelation. The incarnation of the Son is the fundamental ground of all divine revelation, but Dearmer believed that beauty was its own further manifestation of the divine life. For that reason, beauty and art are not only essential to the church, but they are also essential to a life fully lived.

The second principle has already been mentioned—that doctrine follows ceremonial. Here, the principle is just as essential even if it may also be misunderstood. After all, there is a perception that Dearmer's works on ceremonial existed primarily for a polemical purpose. That is, some might say that Dearmer was only interested in fighting against romanizing tendencies in Anglican worship—and isn't that concept outmoded in an ecumenical age?

In fact, it is true that the twentieth century saw a fundamental and ecumenical shift in the worship of the Christian church across denominations and traditions. A variety of streams, some reaching back as far as the sixteenth century, coalesced to form what would become known as the liturgical movement.[13] This movement brought together liturgi-

---

11. Dearmer, *Story*, 81.
12. Dearmer, *Art*, 7.
13. For a description of the roots behind the movement, see Fenwick and Spinks,

cal scholars from across denominations focused on the renewal of the worship of the church, particularly through the return to biblical and patristic sources. After Vatican II, and subsequent shifts in other Christian traditions, the worship of believers throughout Christianity became more unified in approach, structure, and principles.

At the same time, any good ecumenist will tell you that ecumenical dialogue is best furthered not by simply wiping away the peculiarities of each tradition but instead by a deeper understanding and appreciation of one's own tradition alongside of the traditions of others. In fact, it is only with such an understanding that we can intelligently and thoughtfully interact with the traditions of others. This is true just as much in the area of liturgy as it is in the areas of history and theology.

Though names like John Mason Neale (1818–66), W. H. Frere (1863–1938), and Massey Shepherd (1913–90) are better known when it comes to central figures in the development of Anglican liturgy and the liturgical movement itself, Percy Dearmer also had a significant impact upon the worship life of the Anglican Communion. Dearmer operated at a time when the heat of the Ritualist controversy was finally beginning to die down and he was, thus, able to engage that movement critically, particularly placing it within the context of late nineteenth and early twentieth-century Anglican worship. Furthermore, it must be remembered that the early shape of the liturgical movement in England was mediated through the leaders of the Ritualists—alongside the leaders in the Christian Socialist Movement.[14] Dearmer brought together both streams and created something new, an "English Use" approach to liturgy that might also be called "Prayer Book Catholic," hence my own adoption of that phrase to guide this revision of his handbook.

The challenge came to Anglicans in Dearmer's time to set themselves in order by coming up with a coherent and authentic Anglican approach to liturgy, rooted firmly in the tradition of English catholicity and neither reaching to Rome in imitation nor fearing the historical liturgical traditions of our own tradition and church in an unthinking anti-Catholic bias. In Dearmer's time, those who could not bring themselves to face the truth that there is no need either to follow a foreign tradition or fear the authentic traditions of our own church, drifted by inevitable logic into worse positions. The result was that the battle became a grave obstacle to

---

Worship in Transition, 13–21.

14. See the argument made for these two key sources in Fenwick and Spinks, *Worship in Transition*, 39–40.

the peace of the church, alienating the laity and giving new power to the attack on the church from abroad.

Unfortunately, Dearmer's longing for a unified Anglican approach to worship that is based upon the prayer book and is attentive to the principles of beauty and ceremony remains on the horizon even today. In our own time, with the 1979 prayer book having passed its fortieth year of use, we have a very odd situation. While the prayer book is widely praised in our church as one of the greatest of the Anglican tradition, has been memorialized by the General Convention, and is seen as the summit of the work of the liturgical movement as found in the Anglican tradition in the United States . . . praise does not lead to obedience. This fact bears repeating: praise does not lead to obedience.

Some, having grown tired with the liturgies in the book, have taken to crafting their own. Others, confident that we have "evolved" past quaint ideas like the prayer book's insistence that baptism properly precedes communion, have taken to rejecting the standards of our book—even when those standards have been upheld by several General Conventions of this church. Even worse, bishops who are supposed to be guardians and shepherds of the faith have formally authorized violations of this standard and doctrinal teaching. Indeed, the episcopal authorization of disloyalty to the prayer book and the General Convention is just as great a problem on the left of our church as it is on the right. On both sides, the rights of the laity (as a whole, not just in one locale) to have a voice in the doctrine, discipline, and worship of the church have been abrogated.

One lives in hope that a new loyalty to the prayer book and the best of Anglican tradition may yet be recovered. Or, if the time has indeed arrived for a revision to the prayer book, that such a revision will be done carefully, with the conservatism that is the hallmark of Anglican liturgy paired with the insistence that beautiful and true worship must be recognizable to those who participate in it. When the rich and loyal traditions of Anglican worship are practiced by those who are well trained and obedient to the church, the world will see that there is open to Christendom a way, free from the tottering obscurantisms of the past, as Christian in the light of beauty as in its goal of truth.

It is my own hope that this revision of Dearmer's handbook will be a welcome voice from our own past into the much-needed conversations of today.

Introduction

"The divine beauty, whereby the outward draperies of nature are sacraments of the unseen, is fresh and spontaneous, and has a certain breadth of simplicity which combines an infinity of parts in a whole that can be readily understood."[1] So began Dearmer's introduction to his handbook, and the truth of this statement transcends the years that passed since it was first published. A true understanding of the power of simple, beautiful liturgical art in the celebration of the sacraments of the church stands at the base of the prayer book catholic tradition.

The art of public worship attempts to secure some reflection of God's nature while it expresses the adoration of God by humanity. But, like all arts, it has its technique and its limitations. This is true even of services without a liturgical framework (which are not within the province of this book). Nonliturgical services of worship are of great importance in their own traditions, and they have their own technique, more subtle, one that is learned more implicitly through experience than explicitly through training in specific forms. Those who desire to offer liturgical worship (which is the province of this book) have to build their art upon liturgical science and to abide by principles and rules which they have limited power to alter. They have to concern themselves with a multitude of details, which give to the uninitiated an effect of elaboration.

It should, therefore, be stated at the outset (as Dearmer himself stated consistently throughout the various publications of his *Parson's Handbook*) that the particular and several details are not meant to proclaim an elaborate ceremonial as the writer's ideal for worship in the Anglican tradition. Rather, the details are themselves inevitable, partly because students often want them, partly for the reason that this writer is not laying down laws of his own, and partly because they belong to the

---

1. Dearmer, *Parson's Handbook*, 1.

nature of a subject that is both slightly hampered and greatly helped by authority and tradition.

Only the church acting officially has the authority to abolish and to simplify. Such authoritative simplification is certainly needed from time to time, as the preface to the prayer book reminds us. And, because unintelligent accretion has always been the vice of religious ceremonial, details are often added that come to be regarded as of sacred obligation as the generations pass. In the end, though, these details can even wind up undermining the significance and the beauty of the original rite. Therefore, as the prayer book preface reminds us, our Anglican tradition always seeks "to keep the happy mean between too much stiffness in refusing, and too much easiness in admitting variations in things once advisedly established."[2]

Even through the twelfth edition of *The Parson's Handbook*, Dearmer longed for the bishops of the church, as a part of their historic teaching office and their position as the chief priests of their diocese, to issue directions for public worship. He hoped they would act with the advice of liturgical scholars and offer the directions for the voluntary acceptance of clergy and laity. For good or ill, the vast majority of the bishops of the Anglican tradition have not been keen on taking on this responsibility. Indeed, in the Episcopal Church, those bishops who have attempted such specific ceremonial instruction have generally not found their guidelines well received. In the place of such direction from the bishops, there have been a succession of liturgical handbooks and manuals, each offering the advice of the author for the proper execution of the liturgies of the church, usually focusing on one part of the life of the parish church.[3] And thus, though in some ways there are common threads in the worship of our church, when it comes to the question of what constitutes authentically Anglican liturgy, disorder and personal preference (along with liturgical practices that are confused or simply unpleasant) seem at times to reign supreme—particularly when some of our bishops encourage liturgical formulations that run counter to the rubrics of our prayer book. Indeed, it is a sad truth that few diocesan liturgies express the height and power of prayer book liturgy, focused instead on the passing whims of those few people put in charge who seem to believe their liturgical innovations

2. *1979 Book of Common Prayer*, 9.

3. Some of the best of the most recently published include the recent series from Church Publishing, Turrell's *Celebrating the Rites of Initiation*, Alexander's *Celebrating Liturgical Time*, and Malloy's *Celebrating the Eucharist*.

are an improvement upon the worship of the church as laid down by all orders of ministry through an authorized Book of Common Prayer. We can do better.

THE THREE PARTIES OF OUR CHURCH, AND THEIR EFFECT UPON OUR LITURGY

Neither disorder nor the neglect of aesthetic are normal things. They came into the Anglican tradition through definite historical causes and produced what may be described as three parties: low, moderate, and high, with two wild wings we may be content to call "very low" and "very high," respectively. The low party, in Dearmer's time, wished to retain the later Hanoverian peculiarities, which, whatever they were, never claimed to be in accordance with the prayer book. All of this has changed, of course, in the hundred some years since Dearmer wrote the first—and even the final—revision of *The Parson's Handbook*. That said, the current low party in America often recalls the days when churches were full at the height of modern Christendom in the middle of the twentieth century and see a return to the lower liturgy of that time as a way of reviving the popular appeal of religion. What they fail to realize is that the churches may have been fuller of people but that was to do with societal expectations—not because those crowds who attended were deeply committed to the way of Christ and the worship of the triune God. In Dearmer's time, he criticized the subsequent revivals of the late nineteenth century, insisting that they left the church weaker than it was before. Having seen the confluence of the rise of evangelical revivalist Christianity and its intersection with Christian nationalism, it seems that his own criticism that revivalism may inflame emotions but does not provoke discipleship remains well placed. Rather, a better renewal is needed to make the church strong again.

In our own day, the spirit of the low party remains evident in two distinct groups. First, there are those truly faithful and traditional evangelical Anglicans. These are those who wish to do away with what they see as the pomp and circumstance of modern Anglican liturgy. They see the many successes of the high party—the adoption of altar hangings, candles, chasubles, and the like—as errors that distract from the plain worship of the church. Though there is something to be said for the low evangelical tradition, I will not be the one to speak in its favor. I am, for good or ill, precluded to do so by my own beliefs in the historic beauty of Anglican worship. That said, as long as their worship remains obedient to our prayer book and thoughtful in its execution, I wish them all God's blessings as another faithful part of the body of Christ.

At the same time, I would suggest that the spirit of the low party also rests with a second group, one that is relatively new within our church—those who seem to thrive on a spirit of innovation. Like their low party forebears, the innovators see much of the tradition of the church in worship as an obstacle to be overcome so that their own sense of what is best may rise to the top. It is certainly true that the 1979 Book of Common Prayer is not a perfect book. However, the Innovators do not even see it as a book to which they owe allegiance. Rather, they see the prayer book as an amiable resource placed upon the shelf—rather like an uncle of whom you are rather fond but do not take too seriously.

Instead of devotion to the prayer book tradition of Anglican liturgy, the innovators cherish creative liturgies. They import the liturgical practices of other provinces of our communion, often without regard to the cultural contexts from which those practices arose. They comfortably cast aside the carefully constructed prayers of the church—even in baptismal liturgies—in favor of their own latest favorite turn of phrase or clever point. They feel comfortable ignoring rules of the prayer book and the church (like the requirement of only the baptized being admitted to Communion, despite the repeated refusal of the General Convention of this church to authorize their innovation). Time and again, their individual consciences and theological beliefs stand over and against the authority of the laity across the church who had a voice in the prayer book norms to which we must hold. Thus—as Marion Hatchett so often warned—in churches where these lawless clergy serve, the worship by the people is made subject to the whims and eccentricities of the clergy. Though they claim to reject clericalism, often eschewing titles and insisting upon being called by their first name, their belief that they can serve as the sole arbiter of liturgy—despite the rubrics of the prayer book—demonstrates that the voice of the laity throughout the church bears only little influence, if any, upon the way they conduct liturgy.

The moderate party in the Anglican tradition used to seek that excellent spirit of compromise, which sometimes ended in a combination of the errors of the two extremes of low and high. However, like the low party, they were frankly lawless. They based their liturgical principles most often upon what caused the least amount of consternation

INTRODUCTION

and conflict in their congregations. Unfortunately, this means they often inherited remarkably bad liturgical practices but, in the name of moderation, refused to curb them. Whereas in the innovators the creativity and opinions of the clergy were the highest authority, in the moderate party the last person to complain in the priest's office was usually the actual liturgical authority in the parish. The rubrics and ideals of the prayer book are left to one side just as much by the moderate, much to the dismay of many faithful Anglicans.

All of this has made it difficult for either to blame the high, or the very high, who had often been called "Ritualists" (would that they had always deserved the name!) for the current lack of coherence and faithfulness in the worship of our church. The object of the high party was at first the very reverse of insubordination: they wished only to obey the prayer book in all its rubrics. Most specifically, they took their stand on what was known as the ornaments rubric of the 1662 prayer book... but it is here that many modern Episcopalians will immediately find themselves lost.

Thus, let's put a pin in the conversation about the various parties of our church so that we might have an excursus on that rubric—along with Dearmer's interpretation and its function in Anglican liturgy in the nineteenth and twentieth century. In the end, this will be quite helpful for understanding the development of the high and very high party, and especially the Ritualists with whom Dearmer disagreed so strongly. After all, much of his original book came out of that disagreement with those who claimed to offer truly catholic liturgy in his own time. Though the ornaments rubric no longer holds sway in much of the Anglican Communion, the history behind its controversy remains instructive.

AN EXCURSUS ON THE ORNAMENTS RUBRIC IN DEARMER'S THOUGHT AND ANGLICAN PRACTICE

The early Ritualists of the 1860s began their changes by using the ornaments rubric as a clause that could cover a multitude of adaptations in practice, including the restoration of eucharistic vestments and vested altars with candles upon them. The ornaments rubric was an opening rubric, placed directly before the beginning of morning prayer in the 1559 Book of Common Prayer, which stated,

And here is to be noted that the minister at the time of the communion, and at all other times in his ministration, shall use such ornaments in the church as were in use by authority of Parliament in the second year of the reign of King Edward the Sixth according to the Act of Parliament set in the beginning of this book.[4]

No small amount of ink has been spent in arguing whether this rubric means the more medieval ornaments common before the changes later in the Edwardian era or if, in actuality, it was insisting upon a more minimalist view of ornaments from the 1549 Book of Common Prayer that came into practice late in the reign of King Edward.

"And the chancels shall remain as they have done in times past."[5]

4. 1559 *Book of Common Prayer*, 2.

5. 1549 *Book of Common Prayer*, 1. Frontispiece. From a drawing by A. Stratton, ARIBA, and G. Lucas, ARIBA (1906). A typical chancel of fully developed English Gothic architecture with its furniture, showing the arrangement that the prayer book rubrics were designed to continue and that should be in use now, allowances being made for varying styles of architecture. The altar stands under the normal large east window, which is here flanked by figures of saints. The altar is vested in an embroidered frontlet and a paneled frontal of rich material; on it stand two candlesticks and two cushions; it is enclosed by the riddels on either side, which hang from rods, a candle being carried at the end of each rod. The dorsal in this case takes the form of a sculptured reredos richly colored and gilt, the central figure representing Christ in majesty. This reredos might be covered with a dorsal of tapestry in ferial seasons and should be

INTRODUCTION

A significant portion of Dearmer's work was engaged in understanding and arguing for a particular interpretation of this rubric. Indeed, the subject covers nearly twenty pages of the introduction to the final and twelfth edition of *The Parson's Handbook*.[6] Though some might believe that the elimination of this rubric would solve all the fuss and controversy regarding the ornaments in worship, Dearmer disagreed. He noted, "In America there is no Ornaments Rubric, but the difficulties are there nonetheless, and ceremonial vagaries is an acuter form."[7] Further, Dearmer argued that since it was retained in the 1662 Book of Common Prayer, it remains an important rubric for Church of England clerics. He argued that it is the only direction given in the prayer book with regard to what the priest is to wear when conducting services.[8] Further, he insisted, "The Ornaments Rubric is in fact the 'interpretation clause of the Prayer Book.' It covers all the rubrics which are to follow. Through it alone can they be obeyed."[9] For all these reasons, it is important to acknowledge some of Dearmer's own views on this rubric. Though the rubric itself is not in force in today's Episcopal Church, a brief examination of Dearmer's work with the question will be helpful in understanding positions he took throughout his life when it came to the question of vestments and the ornaments of the church.

On an historical note, Dearmer argues that though the interpretation of this rubric is clear to the Anglicans of his time, the reason it was not followed in many churches was because of the liturgical tolerance of the Church of England. He notes that

> the Puritans were merely non-conforming churchmen, who continued to communicate at their parish churches, and were almost as much opposed to the idea of schism as the high

---

covered with white linen in Lent. The altar stands on three steps, which are carpeted. On the pavement are the two standards. In the north wall is a richly decorated aumbry. The credence stands against the south wall, prepared for the service, with the chalice and paten, ewer and basin, towel, canister and cruets lying on it. West of the credence is the piscina with a shelf, and west of the piscina the priest's and deacon's sedilia are seen. Wooden rails, covered in this case with housing cloths, stand on the communion step. The housing cloth, no longer in use, was laid over the rail so that those who came forward to receive would place their hands under the cloth, the sacrament being placed directly in the mouth. It also was meant to catch the host if it was inadvertently dropped by the priest.

6. Dearmer, *Parson's Handbook*, 16–37.
7. Dearmer, *Public Worship*, 113–14.
8. Dearmer, *Parson's Handbook*, 16.
9. Dearmer, *Parson's Handbook*, 17.

churchmen themselves. Therefore, every effort had to be made to allow them latitude until the fury should be overpast.[10]

Thus, the bishops were selective in their enforcement of (what Dearmer believed was) the full meaning of the rubric, hoping to keep the Puritans fully within the bounds of the Church of England. As Dearmer argues, "The bishops found their hands full with trying to enforce the use of the surplice alone, at a time when a large number of clergy insisted on ministering in a cloak, sleeveless jacket, or a horseman's coat."[11]

Ornaments of the Chancel and of the Ministers[12]

At the Savoy Conference in 1661, following the Restoration of Charles II, there was an attempt to reconcile the divergent streams within the Church of England. There, the Puritans formally objected

---

10. Dearmer, *Parson's Handbook*, 17–18.
11. Dearmer, *Parson's Handbook*, 20.
12. Fifteenth century. Brit. Mus. MS. Add. 16997. Priest in scarlet chasuble, with narrow gold Y-shaped orphreys; deacon, kneeling, in scarlet dalmatic, with narrow gold orphreys; subdeacon or clerk in albe without tunicle, both hold candles. Rulers in scarlet copes with golden hoods kneel in midst of choir; two boys in sleeved rochets kneel by lectern; clergy in the stalls. Altar with blue frontal and upper frontal, gold frontlet; two candles on altar, two on brackets projecting from the dorsal, and two held by the ministers; hanging pyx under green canopy above the altar.

to the rubric, desiring "that it may be wholly left out."[13] The bishops rejected this and Dearmer noted that they even retained it on its own page, by itself, something later printers changed from the original edition. He argued that they retained the rubric in the hope that, though the Commonwealth had destroyed many of the ornaments of the church, the slightly less reformed practice would be maintained. He believed the practice affirmed by the ornaments rubric was that which would have been found in 1548 (the second year of Edward's reign, according to Dearmer's argument),[14] before the changes of even the 1549 prayer book would have taken place. Following this rubric would result in ornaments that would at least be acceptable to those more conservative and Protestant streams in the Church of England. And, Dearmer believed, this was a specific act of restoration, given that the Edwardian prayer book (which eliminated many of these ornaments) was itself not in use until the third year of Edward's reign. Furthermore, he argues, "That the Rubric ordered the ornaments of that Book, including the chasuble, was frankly admitted even in the eighteenth century, when the use of the chasuble would have been unthinkable."[15] It was not a rubric well followed, but Dearmer believed that the intent of the rubric was clear when one looked at it historically.

However, unlike the Ritualists, Dearmer did not argue for a militant line on this question. He insisted that when the older ornaments were to be used, it should be with tolerance, moderation, and a loyalty to the use of the Church of England and not the practices of Rome (more on that further on in this introduction). Dearmer also insisted that a faithful English use should be based upon an examination of the whole Church of England and not, as some had argued, upon the curiosities of the use at Salisbury Cathedral alone. What was needed was a faithful approach to ornaments based upon actual historical English practice.[16]

---

13. Dearmer, *Parson's Handbook*, 23.

14. Dearmer, *Parson's Handbook*, 24–32. In his specific argument for the dating, he writes, "The second year of Edward VI was, beyond any doubt, from Jan. 28, 1548 to Jan. 27, 1549. The First Prayer Book received the authority of Parliament in the last week of that year, Jan. 21, 1549, but the Act itself fixes the day on which it is to come into use as the Whitsunday following, June 9, 1549, or if it might be had sooner, then three weeks after a copy had been procured. So that the First Prayer Book could not possibly have been anywhere in use until some weeks (at the very earliest) after the *third* year of Edward VI had begun." *Parson's Handbook*, 27.

15. Dearmer, *Parson's Handbook*, 25.

16. Dearmer, *Parson's Handbook*, 36–37.

As the work of the Ritualists grew and advanced, their interpretation of the rubric broadened. For Richard Littledale, every aspect of the Roman Catholic Missal that had not been abolished by Henry VIII or Edward VI remained lawful unless there was a specific statement in the prayer book forbidding its use—silence permitted all things, he believed.[17]

Older high churchmen rejected this interpretation. They believed the changes of the Ritualist clergy were just as bad a violation of the rubrics of the prayer book as the excesses of the evangelical movement. The older high churchmen had sought a renewal of conformity to the rubrics, one that they believed had even garnered acceptance among those in the low church party. They believed progress had been made in restoring unity to the worship of the church and now the Ritualists were destroying that very uniformity, using the ornaments rubric as a way to upend the ideals of the worship of the prayer book. As Nockles notes, "Ritualism represented the logical outcome of the sectarian tendency in Tractarianism to pursue that which was deemed catholic even at the expense of submission to episcopal authority."[18]

Dearmer's argument with regard to the ornaments rubric became less important as *The Parson's Handbook* went through further revisions. As he himself noted in the twelfth edition, the proposed (but failed) Book of Common Prayer of 1928 had added a new rubric: "For the avoidance of all controversy and doubtfulness, it is hereby prescribed that, notwithstanding anything that is elsewhere enjoined in any Rubric or Canon, the Priest in celebrating the Holy Communion shall wear either a surplice with stole or with scarf and hood, or a white albe plain with vestment or cope." Dearmer continued, observing "there can be few reasonable men who will not accept this as the end of a demoralizing controversy."[19]

Here ends the excursus.

THE THREE PARTIES OF OUR CHURCH, CONTINUED

It was in the second half of the nineteenth century that a division began in the high party as the Ritualists developed and changed focus. Some believed that, given their claim to be a part of the catholic church, "they

---

17. Nockles, *Oxford Movement*, 216.
18. Nockles, *Oxford Movement*, 217.
19. Dearmer, *Parson's Handbook*, 31–32.

could not fail to be influenced by developments within Roman Catholicism and to feel themselves to be in competition with Roman Catholics when it came to ritual innovations."[20] Others, however, sought to find a way of affirming the catholic heritage and basis of Anglican worship without looking to Rome for a model. Dearmer came from this second stream and eventually became a leading voice for an approach to Anglican worship that was a middle way—neither Roman nor Protestant (that is, based wholly in the Reformation)—but thoroughly Anglican, an approach that drew its principles from English Christianity before Reformation times.

The ideals of *The Parson's Handbook* are founded upon the clause in the preface to the Book of Common Prayer that is clear that national churches have the authority to order their worship in ways that are appropriate to their context and needs. Dearmer insisted that this was entirely in keeping with the precedents of the catholic church throughout history—despite, one would assume, the movements towards Roman uniformity during the Middle Ages. He continued, "She has furthermore declared her strong adherence to the best of antiquity; and therefore distinctively Roman practices, which are mainly of seventeenth, eighteenth, or nineteenth-century growth, are doubly opposed to the standard which she sets up."[21] That is, the ancient practices of the Church of England—including, as well, those present in the early sixteenth century—should provide the resources from which Anglican worship is developed. When Anglicans draw instead from Roman practices that have developed on their own after the Reformation, they are importing ideas and customs that have no root in Anglicanism.

Thus, specific Roman practices that had become bound up with ideas of what high church liturgy needed to be should actually be rejected by the good prayer book catholic. For example, "The idea that an altar is incomplete (or 'Protestant') without a cross needs to be strenuously combated."[22] In other areas, he rejected Roman importations not only as inauthentic to Anglicanism but also, ironically enough, inauthentic to good Roman liturgy: "Such things as lace albes and fiddle-back chasubles cannot in fact be classed as Roman but simply as a decadent form of art."[23] Throughout his work, he sought to reject areas where Roman

20. Yates, *Anglican Ritualism in Victorian Britain*, 66.
21. Dearmer, *Parson's Handbook*, 33.
22. Dearmer, *Parson's Handbook*, 86.
23. Dearmer, *Ornaments*, 48. Dearmer goes on to underscore this point by quoting

liturgical choices were being used in Anglican liturgy, often with those who imported them not understanding the history and theology behind the practice they used.

On this, I'm reminded of a story Marion Hatchett told while I was in one of his classes. He visited a parish where, during the administration, a dutiful acolyte would hold a paten underneath the minister's hand when the bread was distributed, lest a crumb fall to the ground. However, upon reaching the end of the altar rail, the acolyte turned the paten on its side, gave it a good knock to clean anything off and onto the floor, and then resumed the practice once more. Someone had clearly seen this practice in another church and adopted it without regard to the meaning or even the purpose behind it.

Unfortunately, the prelates of those early days of the Ritualist movement were not conversant with the question of the ornaments rubric, nor were they always themselves prepared to obey the prayer book. They allowed some of the clergy of the high party to be prosecuted before courts. They were, in fact, caught unawares by the new desire for more color and action in ceremonial, and were unable to lead at a time when wise leadership was acutely needed. Consequently the "ritualistic" clergy were sometimes forced to disobey the bishops in order that they might obey the prayer book.

From this confusion there grew up in many places a spirit of confirmed lawlessness; and some of those who had begun by taking their stand on the ornaments rubric ended by denying it in favor of the customs of a foreign church—that of Rome—till they seemed almost to agree with their former opponents. They advocated that such ornaments as were in use in Anglican churches in the second year of Edward's reign were not the ones to be used but, rather, those in use currently in the Roman tradition should be adopted!

In the introduction to the original *Parson's Handbook* there were some words about preachers in sweated surplices and cassocks pointing to a cheap cross upon an evilly produced altar, all unconscious of the social misery involved in the making of such ornaments. Largely owing to a long campaign of the Christian Social Union in the nineteenth and twentieth centuries, the conditions for making liturgical pieces had been greatly improved, and the meanly made furniture also, produced by

---

a lecture that Monseigneur Batiffol gave (in Dearmer's words, "quite daringly") at an Ecclesiastical Art Exhibition in France, wherein he pleads for a return to more ancient forms of vestments in the Roman Church.

INTRODUCTION

underpaid labor, had often been replaced by something better. And so, these sections were eventually omitted in later editions.

Yet it is troubling knowing that the advent of the internet and the global economy have brought about a reversion in churches in the practice of purchasing vestments and liturgical items that may not have been made under fair and just working traditions, much less made to be beautiful and of heirloom quality. Furthermore, the multiplicity in options has often resulted in purchases that are quite contrary to the historic beauty of Anglican worship. The worst offenses in this category often come from the more inexpensive supply houses of the Roman tradition.

The best way for a priest to avoid the evils of sweated vestments or ugly purchases is to rely upon quality supply houses in the Anglican tradition and to consult broadly as well with those in the parish community who have at least skill, if not actual training, on matters of art and beauty. One thinks that many a horrid chasuble purchase could have been avoided if the well-meaning priest would have first simply asked the opinion of someone in the parish who had a sense of taste and style. One of the greatest gifts of Dearmer's handbook to the church was that he encouraged relationships with true liturgical artists. In our own time, there are several that the parson should consult. Skilled artists like Trevor Floyd[24] and Davis d'Ambly[25] come to mind as excellent resources for vestments that are well made and with an eye towards true art and beauty. Trevor Floyd's ability to work with a variety of parish styles and budgets, while still insisting that quality should never be sacrificed, is unparalleled. Similarly, Davis d'Ambly is perhaps one of the greatest liturgical artists of our time. For full shops, Watts & Co. is one of the best in the Anglican tradition, having recently rescued and restored the venerable J. Wippel & Co. The Holy Rood Guild, though sponsored by Trappists in the Roman Catholic tradition, also has excellent staff for custom designs.

The alienation of artists, musicians, and of the literary world from the church must indeed cease. Dearmer longed for this in his own time, and we must work for it in our own. In the absence of true artists and musicians, the latest fad or the preference of the current generation in power will always result in worship that falls short of good Anglican standards. Indeed, the problem before us now is not so much the reconciliation of religion with science, but its reconciliation with art. Most of

---

24. See his work at his website (https://trevorfloyd.com/).

25. See his work at his website, Liturgical Art (https://www.liturgicalartist.com/about.php).

the tawdry stupidity or stuffy gloom of our churches, most of the bad ceremonial—whether static, bustling, or convulsive—is due to the decline of art in the church, or to the senseless imitation of those meretricious ornaments, both of the church and its ministers, with which ignorant and indiscreet persons have ruined the ancient beauty of Roman Catholic churches abroad. We, who have the noble standard of the prayer book for our guide, are saved from that barbarous degradation of Christian worship many Roman Catholics now also lament.

These errors, deficiencies, prejudices, and distortions—along with the pervading atmosphere of bad hymns—have continually alienated our young people and furthered a continued decline in candidates for the ministry. One has to look no further than the *Hymnal Revision Feasibility Study*, published by the Church Pension Group, where the demographic group with the strongest opposition to hymnal revision was clergy who were twenty-nine or younger![26] The cure to all of this is to be found in loyal obedience to lawful authority; and that obedience can only become spontaneous and effective when lawful authority is informed by liturgical understanding and a sound aesthetic. Such obedience, both to the prayer book and to authority, is solemnly promised by all the clergy in the Declaration of Conformity:

> I solemnly declare that I do believe the Holy Scriptures of the Old and New Testaments to be the Word of God, and to contain all things necessary to salvation; and I do solemnly engage to conform to the doctrine, discipline, and worship of the Episcopal Church.

In the original version of the declaration used in the Church of England, the candidate also declared,

> I assent to the Thirty-nine Articles of Religion, and to the Book of Common Prayer, and of Ordering of Bishops, Priests and Deacons; I believe the doctrine of the Church of England, as therein set forth, to be agreeable to the Word of God.

Two principles are here set forth, as Archbishop Frederick Temple once pointed out. In the first place, the Anglican Tradition in the 1662 prayer book does not press doctrinal conformity to her own distinctive formulas beyond the point of a general acceptance or "assent." Even in the current form of the declaration found in the Episcopal Church's prayer book,

---

26. Price et al., *Hymnal Revision*, 20.

the declaration is to believe in the Scriptures and that they contain all things necessary to salvation—not that all things in them are necessary to salvation.

And yet, note what has persisted throughout the centuries: an understanding that, when it comes to the ritual and worship of the church, there is to be no compromise. Thus, the candidate quite literally *solemnly* pledges to conform to the doctrine, discipline, and worship of the Episcopal Church. When it comes to doctrine, the definition is explained in title IV of the canons as "the basic and essential teachings of the Church and is to be found in the Canon of Holy Scripture as understood in the Apostles and Nicene Creeds and in the sacramental rites, the Ordinal and Catechism of the Book of Common Prayer."[27] This is, of course, a rather broad and generous understanding of doctrine, which promotes a healthy diversity of doctrinal beliefs. And yet, beyond this broad understanding of doctrine there remains a deep commitment expected of those being ordained that they will indeed live out with great humility their vows to the discipline and worship of the Episcopal Church. Because, despite the breadth of our church when it comes to doctrine, the discipline and worship of the Episcopal Church is clearly laid out. The discipline of our church can be found primarily in the canons and the worship of our church can be found primarily in the prayer book (though there are, of course, instances where one informs the other).

Freedom to think, freedom to discuss, and freedom to develop are necessary to the very existence of life and truth in a church. But for the priest to omit or radically to alter the common services of that church is fatal to the Christian fellowship. It robs the people of their rights.

It is true that different degrees of elaboration are legitimate, and indeed necessary. One parish may have simpler ornaments or ceremonial, just as one may have simpler music than another. In many parishes, for instance, a simple form of Eucharist is needed—a service in which the music is restricted perhaps to a few easy hymns, the ornaments to the plainest vestments, and the ceremonial to the necessary actions. In some where the services of a priest are not available on a weekly basis, the simple and beautiful liturgy of morning prayer can be laid out as our morning sacrifice to God, wherein we hear God's word and respond with our petitions. Simplicity is far from the enemy—and when compared

---

27. Episcopal Church, *Canons* (2022), §IV.2.

with an excess of overwrought ritual, which distracts people from the God they are there to worship, simplicity may at times be preferred.

But how seldom has a simple service been seen that was at once law abiding and consistent, reverent, devout, and dignified? What wanton diversities of ritual and ceremonial, what gross exaggerations of party differences, what strange substitutes of our own imagining, have been put forward in the place of the order of the prayer book! To provide varying degrees of the same thing is both lawful and expedient; but it is neither lawful nor expedient to introduce or to continue irreconcilable and indefensible divergences—many of them created in the twentieth-century, an age great in literature, science, reform, and invention, but an age also when forms and ideals of art were deconstructed and when religion was often expressed in the form of the lowest common denominator. Indeed, it may be argued that religion's greatest obstacles today are some of the poorer liturgical art, ceremonial, and the so-called "modern" hymnody of the past few decades.

A book would be required to reveal the breach that was made in the popular traditional religion during the nineteenth and twentieth centuries and to show why it has so seriously alienated the people. That breach began earlier than either the Tractarian movement, and their Ritualist successors in Dearmer's time, or that of the new innovator party of our own time. No matter the party, however, all have taken an approach that was offensive to the body of Christ, as the clergy violently changed the character of the services—often without sufficient regard for the rights of the laity.

Throughout this, in each generation, the bewildered people were told that their old customs were wrong and that they ought to do things the way the priest now told them to—even though that priest could not turn to a page in the prayer book to support the changes themselves. The religion of the common people has, in all history, rested on traditional customs; and even now the tradition remains broken. The people have not been reconciled, and further attempts at change—particularly when it is the next clever idea of the priest instead of the gathered discernment of the community—will only result in further alienation.

Indeed, this clergy-centric approach is seen most clearly in the blood that has been spilt in countless churches to pull altars away from the wall (though this requirement exists nowhere in our own prayer book, much less in the actual documents of Vatican II, for those who persist in looking to Rome for direction in Anglican liturgy). Ironically, this change was actually a singularly important move towards further clericalization of the liturgy. Compare that battle with the number (or, more accurately, the profound lack) of clergy who have fought valiantly for the restoration of a full immersion baptismal font—something actually expected by our prayer book and present in our own early Anglican tradition. I daresay a survey of our parishes will show battles about altars have been far more common (and successful) than battles for the restoration of the full-immersion liturgical font. Clergy have fought the first battle and not the latter because their attention has been far too focused on where they stand and not sufficiently focused on the baptismal identity and authority of the people of God.

Though the gift of the 1979 Book of Common Prayer was in many ways the fullest manifestation of the highest ideals and principles of liturgy and Anglican devotion in its time, it is unfortunate that in many places public worship did not develop gradually and naturally to a full use of that prayer book system. In some mysterious way, antiquarianism, or the love of innovation simply for the sake of something new, or just plain clericalism led the clergy of all parties astray and turned them at times into ruthless liturgical leaders, so that all the hopes and all the devoted labors of the previous generations have not recovered the old confidence and sense of community.

Indeed, the developments in worship following the COVID-19 pandemic, when for many their experience of worship became something one watched on YouTube while sipping a cup of coffee, make it ever more necessary to have fellowship in our services, to restore a sense of the liturgy as the corporate work of the laity and clergy together—a beautiful, sacred, and tangible offering to God.

The general remedy in the realm of public worship is to consider the people and to get back to the prayer book. For the church of the Anglican tradition has, as Bishop E. S. Talbot once said, "A mind of her own; a mind and therefore a character, a temperament, a complexion; and of this mind the Prayer Book is the main and representative expression."[28] We shall best discover that mind and complexion if we go straight to the church's authorized standards. After all, it is not truly ritual but ceremonial changes that disturb the people, as all history shows. If the authorized rite is done with care and wisdom, the people will find themselves reconnected to the God of their ancestors.

---

28. Cited by Dearmer, *Parson's Handbook*, 10.

Consider the Bible upon which the prayer book is based, and which in fact forms so large a part of the prayer book services. Now the careful directions as to ornaments and vestments in the Pentateuch are familiar to every student of biblical studies, and there is no hint that the principle of such worship was dropped under the new covenant.[29] Our Lord attended the services of the temple, and no word of censure escaped his lips when it came to the rite and ritual itself. He was very far from ignoring the subject, for no one ever laid more stress upon the dangers of formalism and the obsession over minutiae, which besets priestly castes; he condemned ceremoniousness but had no hard word against ceremonial. Indeed, he protected the worship of the temple against profane interruption, driving out not those who adorned it with ceremonial but those who dishonored it with commercialism.

Next, consider the title page of the prayer book, where one might expect to find a succinct description of its contents:

> The
> Book of
> Common Prayer
> and Administration of the Sacraments
> and Other Rites
> and Ceremonies of the Church
> Together with The Psalter or Psalms of David
> According to the use of
> The Episcopal Church

The prayer book contains then the ordinary services of the catholic church, in accordance with the ancient right of each national church to frame its own use of the historic rites and ceremonies. Thus, our prayer book sets forth the use of the Episcopal Church.

Next, consider the preface of the book itself. The preface of the prayer book was little changed from the first book in 1549, its minor revision in 1552, and the restored book of 1559 that stands at the base of Anglicanism. It was also little changed in the next century in 1604, a revision that was eventually abolished during the English Civil War and was then restored in 1662. This 1662 book, with a preface remarkably similar after

---

29. "The Church," says our twentieth article, "hath power to decree Rites or Ceremonies," but not "to ordain anything that is contrary to God's Word written," although, as the seventh article points out, the Mosaic law as touching ceremonies and rites is not binding upon Christian men. The Bible reveals a true principle; it embodies a universal human instinct for beauty in worship under the divine guidance.

one hundred years of upheaval, remains the official book of the Church of England. It was this book, of course, which formed the basis and starting point for the first American prayer book. Indeed, much of the language of the 1662 prayer book is also used in the preface of the first American prayer book—the preface still printed today in the 1979 edition. These prefaces together provide excellent reasons for their respective revisions. Both prefaces are careful to point out that "the middle way between two extremes" had been taken—the middle way, that is, between "too much stiffness in refusing" and "too much easiness in admitting any variation" from the former book. They also mention, among other improvements made, sometimes for the better direction of clergy and at other times to conform to changing circumstances (for example, the change in prayers for civic leaders required due to the American Revolution).

The 1662 prayer book goes on to note other changes, ones that mark the basis for the Anglican tradition of prayer book worship. These changes are actually taken from the first prayer book of 1549 and so truly do stand at the base of reformed Anglican worship. The first preface, titled "Concerning the Service of the Church," is an adaptation of the preface to the reformed Breviary of Cardinal Quignon, which it follows in all essentials.[30] This breviary—which, interestingly enough, given its use in our prayer book, is a book on daily prayers, not Holy Eucharist—was published with the connivance of Pope Paul III in 1535. That it should have been the model of our church's first introduction to the Book of Common Prayer illustrates the ideal of the English bishops: to use words that will survive the distortion of party use—at once catholic and evangelical. It was a liberal ideal as well, inspired by the Renaissance and the New Learning of Erasmus, Colet, and Warham. "Concerning the Service of the Church" does not deal with ceremonial but with the practical question of restoring the lectionary and Psalter to their ancient thoroughness and simplicity in accordance with the "godly and decent order of the ancient Fathers." Four times in this short preface is the example of the ancient Fathers invoked: in accordance with their example, the language is to be that which is understood by the people; untrue, uncertain, and superstitious readings are to be dropped, and nothing is to be read that is not in Scripture, or "agreeable to the same." This is the most important of our prefaces, because it stood alone at the head of the first prayer

---

30. This work was wonderfully and laboriously done by Frank Edward Brightman in his two-volume work *The English Rite*, first published by Rivingtons in 1915 and 1921, and most recently published in its second revised edition in 1970.

book and has been with us ever since. It concludes with a reference to the bishop who is to "take order for the quieting and appeasing" of any doubts that may arise, "so that the same order be not contrary to anything contained in this Book."[31]

The third preface of the 1662 prayer book, "Of Ceremonies, Why Some Be Abolished and Some Retained," is also probably by Cranmer. In the first book it was placed at the end and was followed by a section titled "Certain Notes," which ordered the use of the vestments to be mentioned later, and allowed for the omission of the *Gloria in excelsis*, creed, and other parts in the old way. The ceremonies it speaks of as abolished could not have been the use of those vestments; nor, when the preface was written, could they have been such as are given in that book, nor those which were allowed in that book, "kneeling, crossing, holding up of hands, knocking upon the breast, and other gestures." There is indeed no hint of any revolutionary change in ceremonial, though there is a wholesome reminder of the fact that "Christ's Gospel is not a ceremonial law." It is assumed throughout that only those ceremonies have been changed which the rites and rubrics of the book have altered, dropped, or superseded.

And it was not ceremonial beauty that was abolished, but certain ceremonies, some of which, indeed, "at the first were of godly intent and purpose devised" but had "at length turned to vanity and superstition." It is precisely, by the way, for these reasons that practices have been over and over again abolished in the Roman Church itself, where yet "undiscreet devotion" still works much havoc. Some, by "the great excess and multitude of them," had become an intolerable burden; but "the most weighty cause of the abolishment of certain Ceremonies was, that they were so far abused" by the "superstitious blindness" of the ignorant and the "unsatiable avarice" of those who traded on it, such "that the abuses could not well be taken away, the thing remaining still."[32] So, then, even those ceremonies which have been abolished were of godly intent originally, or at the worst due to undiscreet devotion and a zeal without knowledge, and were not removed in mere wantonness but because of certain abuses that had fastened inseparably upon them.

This does not suggest a destruction of beauty in worship. Even this is further safeguarded in the next paragraph, by a cutting reply to those who wanted "innovations and newfangledness"—"surely where the old

---

31. *1662 Book of Common Prayer*, 6.
32. *1662 Book of Common Prayer*, 6–8.

may be well used, there they cannot reasonably reprove the old only for their age, without betraying of their own folly." Indeed, so conservative is this preface that it does not hesitate to declare that innovations ("as much as may be with true setting forth of Christ's religion") are "always to be eschewed." Lamentably, this wise and conservative principle when it comes to worship is currently quite far from the current zeitgeist of our church. Every successive General Convention has proposals for tinkering and adding new liturgies and prayers when all that is truly needed is for people to draw deeply from the authorized rites and liturgies our church has already put into place.

After a happy apology for the retained ceremonies that they are "neither dark nor dumb," the preface concludes with the significant declaration that, while we claim our right to an English use, "we condemn no other nations," a remark which shows how far the spirit of the prayer book is removed from the censorious intolerance that once abounded on both sides. And this English use, Dearmer noted, had been adapted gently by his American siblings in the Episcopal Church to reflect our own national culture. It also flows through into other contextualized and culturally adapted prayer books. Two excellent examples are *An Anglican Prayer Book* (from the Anglican Church of Southern Africa) and *A New Zealand Prayer Book / He Karakia Mihinare o Aotearoa* (from the Anglican Church in Aotearoa, New Zealand, and Polynesia). Both books reflect a distinct cultural identity in the church in which they are approved. It remains unfortunate that some in the Episcopal Church continue to engage in cultural appropriation by drawing from those books without respecting their distinct cultural context. One wonders what makes someone think that the New Zealand book is so superior to our own, except perhaps that it is foreign, and some seem always to search for novelty, even at the cost of honoring cultural traditions that are not our own to use. The same could be said for many of the faux-Celtic liturgies constantly making their way around the church. Now, if anyone truly wishes to restore the richness of Celtic spirituality to Anglicanism, they should reach first for the older penitentials rather than the latest book with a Celtic knot on the cover.

From the prefaces, the 1662 prayer book takes us to the kalendar,[33] with its careful provision for the reading of the Bible, where we find, as we

---

33. The use of a *k* in the spelling of kalendar is to distinguish an ecclesiastical kalendar, which is marked by feasts, fasts, and church seasons, from a secular calendar, which measures the movement of the earth around the sun and the moon around the

should expect, a simplification that contains all the main features of the old order, purified of mythical accretions. There are the seasons, the great feasts, and the saints' days, broadly classified in two divisions. Unfortunately, this part of the 1979 prayer book has become the source of much confusion, sometimes because of a lawless unwillingness of the clergy to follow the directions of the book and other times because of the strange modern desire, seemingly, to return to the older medieval kalendars filled with so-called saints whose lives—though admirable—do not have at their base a manifestation of the power of the grace of God, through the paschal mystery, to change actual people in lived history. But, the principles of the book itself remain clean and clear, even if the application of section five in the scheme below has at times become difficult in practice.

In the 1979 prayer book, there are now five divisions of days within the life of the church:

1. There are seven *principal feasts*, all of which the prayer book expects will be observed on their actual day with a celebration of Holy Eucharist. The careful reader would do well to note that the Feast of All Saints may be celebrated on the Sunday following November 1, but that this is only allowed as an extra observance "in addition to its observance on the fixed date."[34]

2. The next class of feasts are *feasts of our Lord*, falling into two categories. First, *all Sundays are understood as feasts of our Lord* and, thus, should be observed with the celebration of Holy Eucharist as the principal act of worship. There are three further fixed feasts of our Lord (Holy Name, Presentation, and Transfiguration), which would take precedence on a Sunday observance if the feast happened to fall on a Sunday. On pp. 996–1000, the prayer book daily office lectionary also sets the feasts of our Lord apart by providing special propers for the eve of the feasts.

3. The kalendar then turns to *holy days*. As the first-class notes, these do not rank above a Sunday and, so, "are normally transferred to the first convenient open day within the week" when they fall on one. The first set of holy days are the seven "other feasts of our Lord," which are appointed to fixed days, three of which were noted above as being able to take precedence on a Sunday.[35] Of these seven feasts, two are the traditional Marian feasts (Annunciation and Visitation), one is the observance of the forerunner of our Lord (St. John the Baptist), one is an additional

---

earth. Both come from the original Latin word "kalendrium."

34. *1979 Book of Common Prayer*, 15.
35. *1979 Book of Common Prayer*, 16.

INTRODUCTION

incarnational feast (Holy Name), and the remaining two commemorate events which broaden our understanding of the paschal mystery (Transfiguration and Holy Cross). In addition to these, the prayer book gives "other major feasts" that share the class of a holy day. Propers are given for the eve of the dedication of a church, the eve of the patronal feast of the church, and the eve of feasts of apostles and evangelists, in general.[36] However, by not giving specific propers for each of the eves of the feasts of evangelists and apostles, but instead generic options, they are set apart from the higher classed "other feasts of our Lord." The kalendar does give permission for feasts of our Lord and other major feasts to be transferred to a weekday. However, for the cleric who may be slow to understand or obstinate of will, the rubrics also make clear, once more, that this allowance does not apply to principal feasts.

4. Christians in the Episcopal Church are then enjoined to *days of special devotion*. These are days observed by special acts of discipline and self-denial. They include Ash Wednesday, the weekdays of Lent and Holy Week (excepting, of course, the celebration of the Annunciation, if that occurs in Lent). They also include Good Friday and (much to the surprise of the Episcopalian who actually reads this page) all other Fridays of the year (excepting those that fall in Christmastide, Eastertide, or on a feast of our Lord).

5. Finally, there are *days of optional observance*. This includes days listed in the prayer book for that purpose and also would include the days listed in whichever sanctorale is currently approved by the General Convention. Over recent years, there has been a lamentable amount of confusion in this area. In 2018, the Standing Commission on Liturgy and Music (SCLM) sought to mitigate that confusion by presenting to the General Convention a new version of *Lesser Feasts and Fasts*, one that would finally supplant the confusion created by *Holy Women, Holy Men* and its successor *A Great Cloud of Witnesses*. The Committee tasked with this project rejected the SCLM's proposal and instead proposed a massive confusion by adding all people ever authorized into one new kalendar. The House of Deputies strongly rejected this folly, instead approving an authorization of the 2018 version of *Lesser Feasts and Fasts*. Unfortunately, though, a few bishops of the church disliked the way Lesser Feasts and Fast 2018 created a new sanctorale and also included a section of other supplemental observances. It is interesting that the objection of the

---

36. *1979 Book of Common Prayer*, 1001.

bishops was that they found this confusing—because their clergy (who actually are the ones who make use of this on a regular basis) did not find the 2018 proposal confusing when they approved its authorization. Regardless, the bishops chose also to authorize the continued use of the *Lesser Feasts and Fasts 2006* and also to "commend the continued availability" of *A Great Cloud of Witnesses 2015*.[37] All of this seems to have been resolved by the 2022 General Convention, which authorized a new version of *Lesser Feasts and Fasts* as the authoritative sanctorale for days of optional observance. Of course, the propensity to muck about in the sanctorale will likely continue and one hopes careful consideration of who is properly included, given our church's understanding of sanctity in the life of the baptized, will guide the way.

Thus, the 1979 Book of Common Prayer invites those who loyally follow it to center their life and their year upon the paschal mystery of Christ's dying and rising—particularly as that mystery is revealed in its own way through the seven principal feasts. Further, it enjoins upon all a faithful adherence to the celebration of that mystery on Sundays and other major feasts and, for those who are able, the other holy days. The days of special devotion flow from that kalendrical center, inviting the faithful to acts of devotion that seek to form our own lives after a deeper engagement with the paschal mystery. Days of optional observance are then provided for saints who have patterned their own lives on the paschal mystery in ways that are inspiring, true, and manifold in nature.

All of this focus on the kalendar at the start and introduction is needed to make clear the heart of Anglican worship. It is not found in curious customs or eccentricities, nor even in specific ornaments and forms. Rather, the heart of our worship must always be an attentive engagement with the paschal mystery, an offering of ourselves in union with Christ to God and a celebration of the sacraments of grace. The rest of our worship in the Anglican tradition—the forms, structures, vestments, and ornaments—should all further that aim. When they begin to distract from it, they should be discarded quickly so that focus on Christ may return to the fore.

From the kalendar of the church, the 1662 preface turns to the question of how morning and evening prayer are to be said along with two rubrics that greatly concerned questions of ceremonial in Dearmer's time. The requirement that "Chancels shall remain as they have done in

---

37. Episcopal Church, *79th General Convention*, 679.

times past" and the above-noted ornaments rubric, which has already been discussed sufficiently.[38] Though the clear insistence on the arrangement of the chancel in 1662 is much desired by some clergy, the 1979 American book provides no such explicit comfort, and we are left to imply the proper arrangement of worship space, given the rubrics of the current American prayer book.

That said, a few more words about the ornaments of the ministers may be helpful here at the start. For convenience we may classify the ornaments of the ministers under three heads. These heads come from Dearmer's explication of the ornaments rubric, but they remain helpful for understanding the classification of vestments and other ornaments in the Anglican tradition, along with the weight and import of their use:

A. Vestments mentioned in the first prayer book;

B. Other ornaments mentioned in that book;

C. Ornaments both of the church and the ministers either (1) implied in the book, or (2) in lawful use under its provisions.

The vestments mentioned in the first prayer book include the plain white albe, worn with either the chasuble (called simply "a vestment" in that book) or the cope. There are also albes worn with tunicles for Communion and albes or surplices worn with a cope or hood for non-eucharistic liturgies. Furthermore, for a bishop, there is the albe or the rochet (generally, in Anglican use, a bishop's form of surplice), worn with either a cope or chasuble. The bishop also has the pastoral staff. All these vestments are found in the first prayer book and have the full weight of Anglican tradition behind their use.

There are other ornaments of the church mentioned in the first prayer book. These are generally not contentious in use and include the Bible, the prayer book, alms box, corporal (called a corporas in the first book), the Lord's table, chalice and paten, font, chrisom (baptismal gown), choir door, bell, chair, and pulpit. Additionally, the first book spoke of the Book of Homilies, but that is no longer a part of the worship of the Episcopal Church.

Certain other ornaments were implied in the first book. These would include the credence, vessels for wine, water, chrism, and other oil, along with the vessels needed to carry Holy Communion to those who were ill

---

38. To view the ornaments rubric in the first form it appeared in the prayer book, see *1549 Book of Common Prayer*, 2.

or infirm. The lectern, reading pew, and litany desk may also be inferred given their use in the first book. Furthermore, clerks and choristers likely wore garments of some sort (Dearmer suspects a rochet or surplice, with copes on grand occasions). There is also evidence of the black scarf, or tippet, before and after 1549 in portraits of Warham, Cranmer, and Parker.

Interestingly, the chimere that is often worn over the rochet by bishops was not mentioned in the first book or any other thereafter. It was originally a part of the bishop's civil dress. Archbishop Parker put it on, together with tippet, immediately after his consecration in 1549. He also wore a cope with regularity. However, as Puritan feelings increased in the Church of England, he gave up the use of the cope. The chimere was first used liturgically by Archbishop Parker when he preached before the queen in 1573. It seems to have been first used in conducting services during the reign of James I. The earliest effigy of a bishop in rochet, chimere, and tippet (without a cope or mantle) is Bishop Guest in 1577 at Salisbury.

The fair linen for the Lord's table must have been in use in 1549, and it is mentioned in our present prayer book. Also in use in 1549 likely would have been the frontal, which is ordered with the fair linen by canon 82;[39] along with reredoses, dorsals, and other hangings. We must also assume that the altar cross was in use in some places under the first prayer book. However, it is nowhere mentioned. Though it was quite unusual on the high altar before the Reformation, it was rarely seen on other altars. The altar cross indeed was merely the head of the processional cross, which was dropped into a base upon the altar when the procession was over—so we must include the processional cross as well, though it can also be defended on the analogy of other ornaments carried in procession. Such are the virges, maces, and wands, carried from time immemorial by vergers, churchwardens, and others.

The truth is that no society can be rigidly bound to the past. But loyalty to the past is as necessary in the art of public worship as in any other art, especially when the art of the past is as noble as it is in the case of Anglican worship. Altar lights are a good example of the interpretation of the ornaments rubric by a living tradition. They are not mentioned or implied in the first prayer book, though they must have been in pretty general use at the time, and they were used through Elizabeth's reign, in the teeth of much Puritan opposition, down to the present day. And if

---

39. Church of England, *Canons* (1604), no. 82.

there were two lights upon the altar, then, on the same principle, standards carried by acolytes are certainly in the tradition as well.

Incense is on a different footing. Its use for sweetening the church has never been disallowed. The fact that incense is prominent in the Bible is doubtless the main reason why it was not given up and was defended and used by divines like George Herbert, Lancelot Andrewes, and John Cosin. Indeed, it did not pass out of use until sometime in the eighteenth century and was soon revived by others in the nineteenth. The simple method of using the incense, the method used for half the Christian era, can hardly be called overly ceremonial. Some might consider it far more beautiful than the fumigatory gesticulations of the later Latin rules. Simple also must have been the use in the royal chapel under Elizabeth and Charles I, and that of coronations after the Restoration. Its use today in the normal parish will depend upon several factors—including sound teaching on its history, an engagement in conversation with the laity, and an attentiveness to the reality that some do have an allergic reaction to the smoke (or, more usually, the fumes from quick-light charcoal). If the highest quality pure nard Frankincense is used along with high-quality coals (coconut charcoal is not only free of additives but also is a sustainable product), and the censer is often and properly cleaned, the cause for irritation will certainly dissipate significantly. That said, the wise parson will always ensure that whenever incense is used there are also opportunities for celebration that do not include incense. The only exception to this pastoral rule would be in those parishes where its constant use is expected and is a strong part of the tradition of the local community.

How, then, should all the vestments and other ornaments of the church be used?

First, they must be used in tolerance. We can minimize party spirit, instead of exaggerating it as in the past, by our ceremonial. Those, for instance, who dislike the chasuble have a special duty not to be dismal, and those who use it, not to be aggressive in ornament or design.

Second, they should be used with moderation. There are churches that endeavor to follow the prayer book use, and yet they discredit this use by excess of ornament and ceremonial and by the crowding of servers in a small space. *Caput artis est decere quod facias.*[40]

---

40. In his *De Oratore*, Cicero writes, "The chief thing in any art you may practise is that you do only the one you are fit for." Cicero, *On the Orator*, 1.29, quoted in Wood, *Dictionary*, 97.

Third, they should be used with loyalty to the rich Anglican tradition from whence we come. Here there is much more to be said. The noble trinity of order, freedom, and beauty, which is our Anglican heritage, is still sometimes violated by the perversities of self will. Factions and fancies still abound, though they are condemned in this very connection in documents that stand at the base of the Anglican tradition—namely, by the thirty-fourth article,[41] by the preface, "Of Ceremonies," in the first book,[42] and indeed by every catholic authority. The "public and common order" belongs of right to the whole body of the faithful, and if it is tampered with by the individual fancies of clerics, it must, in the nature of things, be gradually and inevitably degraded.

The public and common order of our worship should neither be judged nor amended by referring to the court or liturgical rules or formularies of Rome, which has no authority in this communion. Indeed, the practices of the Roman Church can only be followed here by a violent exercise of that private judgment, which is amusingly and ironically Protestant, under whatever name it may disguise itself. Our church has declared again and again her right to order her own ceremonies—and in this she has all catholic precedent on her side. She has furthermore declared her strong adherence to the best of antiquity; therefore distinctively Roman practices (most of which are of much more modern tradition than our own!) are doubly opposed to the standard she sets up. Our solemn promises at ordination make any rejection of our own traditional practices in favor of those from another communion utterly impossible for us.

Nor indeed, are we better off by following medieval Salisbury. In many respects the rules of this particular cathedral were altered by the generations that came between their enactment and the second year of Edward VI, and also by the rubrics of the 1662 prayer book, which book expressly declares that as regards "saying and singing" (upon which depends a good deal of our ceremonial) there should be—not the use of Sarum or of any other diocese—but one national English use.[43]

---

41. "Whosoever, through his private judgment, willingly and purposely, doth openly break the Traditions and Ceremonies of the Church, which be not repugnant to the Word of God, and be ordained and approved by common authority, ought to be rebuked openly." *1979 Book of Common Prayer*, 874.

42. "The appointment of the which order pertaineth not to private men: Therefore no man ought to take in hand nor presume to appoint or alter any public or common order in Christ's Church, except he be lawfully called and authorized thereunto." *1549 Book of Common Prayer*, 122–23.

43. "And where heretofore, there hath been great diversity in saying and singing in

INTRODUCTION

This does not lessen the high value of the Sarum books in interpreting our own rubrics, but it must never be forgotten that all the ceremonies of a magnificent cathedral cannot be applicable to a parish church. Indeed, we know that they were never so applied. A great deal of harm has been done by the thoughtless use of the word "Sarum," when the statements of the prayer book should have led us to say "English" or "Anglican." This has been especially the case in the matter of colors, which are dealt with in a section of this handbook. It is not to the Rome or Paris of the twentieth century, nor is it to the Salisbury of the fourteenth, that the ornaments rubric referred Anglicans to in Dearmer's time but to the England of 1548. And if some priests break the Rubric in favor of Rome, they must not be surprised if others break it in favor of Geneva. Similarly, in our own time, we should look carefully to the traditions of Anglican worship and come up with an approach to colors that resonates with our own traditions and with the current authorized prayer book.

Fourth, the ornaments must be used as they are intended within the prayer book. Some may have interpreted this to mean that, where there are no services in the prayer book for certain ornaments, the old services must be revived. But this is an impossible view. Rather, old services should be revived when doing so would further the engagement of the people in the paschal mystery, when it would kindle their devotion and strengthen their will. Once revived, with proper permission from the ecclesiastical authority, then the appropriate ornaments may be considered.

Lastly, the ornaments must be used in the traditional way. The prayer book is generally regarded with a strong bias in one direction or another, for our minds have been twisted by the party struggles that weakened the Christian religion and nearly broke the church. Even now, we are not yet free of these party struggles; many indeed still submit their minds to the slow poison of party newspapers, blogs, and Facebook pages. Further, well-endowed societies and other organizations still exist to sharpen the old weapons and maintain the old illusions.

But a moment's thought will make it clear that the prayer book requires us to travel beyond our prejudices. We are to interpret it, not from a Victorian anymore than from an Elizabethan, Caroline, or Hanoverian point of view, not from the view of the liberal progressive tradition anymore than from the conservative tradition. Rather, we are to interpret

---

churches within this realm: some following Salisbury use, some Herford use, same the use of Bangor, some of York, and some of Lincoln: Now from henceforth, all the whole realm shall have but one use." *1662 Book of Common Prayer*, 6.

it from the view of Scripture, the early church, and the broad Anglican tradition that began with Christians who were at once desirous of reform and conversant with the old ceremonial.

There is a wise saying attributed to Thomas à Kempis—which, had it been remembered, would have averted many a disastrous misunderstanding of Holy Scripture—that says the Bible must be read in the same spirit in which it was written. May we not say that the same principle, if applied to the prayer book, would have averted much of the former falling away and much of the latter chaos of ill-directed revival? The prayer book was written partly by primitive Christians and Christians from the Middle Ages and partly by those who translated and compiled it—skilled ritualists like Cranmer, who used many of the older ornaments and had an intimate knowledge of the older tradition.

The prayer book does not pretend to be a complete directory. Like its immediate predecessors, the medieval missals, it is meager in its ceremonial directions, leaving much to ancient custom. It can easily be proved both in the prayer book and in the Sarum Missal that certain things have to be done for which there is no direction given. Furthermore, there were good reasons why its ceremonial should be quietly left to tradition, as it was. Too complete an array of rubrics in the 1662 prayer book would have led to schism, and schism was more dreaded than disobedience in those days.

Before 1662, the Puritans, as we have seen, were nonconformists in the strict and only correct manner of that word, in the meaning which they themselves gave to it. After that date nonconformity was still allowed among those Anglicans who remained in communion with the church but did not properly interpret or follow the rubrics. This sort of nonconformity was allowed for the sake of peace and comprehension. Thus, it was that nonconformity became a tradition in the church. Curiously enough, today many Christians who are popularly considered to be especially Anglican are modern nonconformists in exactly the same sense as were the Puritans of the Elizabethan and Jacobean era.

This comprehensive tolerance of nonconformity to the church's rubrics was wise and just. At the same time, the history of the eighteenth century shows that it was carried too far. The history of the seventeenth century shows that it was not able to avert the schism it was designed to prevent. The history of the twentieth century showed how this comprehensive tolerance was able to hold together a church battered by sweeping societal change—at least until that tolerance began to give way to the bitter battles of the later twentieth and early twenty-first century.

INTRODUCTION

Regardless, that comprehensive tolerance saved the church from being swamped by Puritanism, and by either conservative or liberal forces, in those hard times. Our comprehensive tolerance has kept the bulk of our communion together—at least when that tolerance has run the day. And for those who are dismayed by the tolerance and worry about the result upon the church, the history of our own times shows that such nonconformity is bound gradually to disappear as soon as the old prejudices begin to die a natural death. This curious lax administration, through four centuries of perfectly definite laws, is a monument to Anglican indifference to logic; but it is also a monument of that profound and practical common sense that is the peculiar characteristic of Anglicans.

And yet, in our own time, something must be done that will help reestablish in the Episcopal Church a type of service such as the prayer book contemplates, a service unequaled in Christendom for dignity, beauty, and reverence while also being entirely intelligible to the people. Something must be done both to satisfy the consciences of those who cannot be content with mere nonconformity and to establish the ceremonial of the future on a sound foundation.

No individual, or unauthorized committee of individuals, has any right to dictate in such a matter. Yet much may be done in the way of suggestion. For in the great majority of cases it is now certain on what lines a committee of experts would decide. Some things that are now common will no doubt have to be altered; but, as these grew up during the infancy of liturgical science and are due either to ignorance or to a rather wanton exercise of private judgment, it is far better that they should be altered at once.

As for this handbook, I can only say that I have tried to follow the insights and ideals of Percy Dearmer and apply them to our own time and place as best as I could. I have also consulted the most trustworthy and acknowledged contemporary authorities and avoided giving my own private opinion except in small practical matters independent of ceremonial. I have tried to make it clear when it is only my own opinion that is offered. I have also tried to be entirely faithful to the principles that are stated in this introduction.

There are numerous places where, given the space of one hundred years since Dearmer's final edition of the *Handbook*, I have needed to stray from his original advice. I hope I have done that by applying the principles of prayer book catholicity to the current ecclesial context of the priest. One example of this adaptation is the use of the subdeacon.

Dearmer could not have foreseen the abolishment of the subdiaconate in 1972 with the *motu proprio Ministeria Quaedam*.[44] While Anglicans are not, of course, bound by decisions the bishop of Rome may make with regard to the ministers of the church, this decision was a part of the larger liturgical movement of the time. Furthermore, this role was not retained in the orders of the clergy when the Church of England separated from Rome in the sixteenth century (though there were always churches that retained the liturgical function and assigned it to a lay person).

A corollary development of the liturgical movement was the increased role the laity were given in the worship of the church. In the current prayer book of the Episcopal Church, it is clear that several rights and privileges are reserved for the laity and should not be usurped by the clergy. Additionally, as our canons have developed, forming structure around the theology of the prayer book, the lay person who assists with the distribution of Communion has become a minister under license from the bishop. First called a "lay eucharistic minister," our current canons refer instead to a "eucharistic minister."[45]

Thus, for those who may wish to retain the older rites and traditions, the most natural approach would be to assign the eucharistic minister many of the duties which had once been assigned to a subdeacon. The prayer book catholic will likely have great concern to use the language of the prayer book and our church's canons here and to call that person a eucharistic minister. Some churches, having retained the language of subdeacon, may very well choose to continue that terminology. Regardless, a lay person who has undergone significant training and who vests appropriately can serve aptly in this role and enable the rites of today to exist in a clean alignment with the rites of the historic catholic tradition of English Christianity. Given the changes and shifts in other parts of Christendom, the use of the three sacred ministers of priest, deacon, and a eucharistic minister vested and functioning as the older minister of subdeacon has become nearly a distinctly Anglican use, as witnessed by dozens of English cathedrals.

Everyone who writes about ceremonial is certain to be subject to one of two forms of criticism: either one's directions are too minute or they are not minute enough.

---

44. Paul VI, *Ministeria Quaedam*.
45. Episcopal Church, *Canons* (2022), §III.4.6

INTRODUCTION

The answer to the first objection is plain in a practical book of this kind. No one is bound to follow them—it is safer, therefore, to give too many directions than too few. Half an hour with a blue pencil will reduce the ceremonial to the required simplicity, but faults of omission would take much longer to rectify.

Furthermore, there is undoubtedly a right and a wrong way of doing most things, and therefore it is just as well to do things in the right way. For, unless one has an unusually large share of instinctive grace and tact, one will otherwise be in danger of making oneself, and also the service one is conducting (which is more important), appear uncouth, strange, or ridiculous.

Ceremonial directions often appear at first sight to be overly minute. But all the manners of our everyday life are governed by rules quite as elaborate. It is just that, having been instructed in them from our earliest childhood, we do not notice them. Let anyone write out a paper of directions for the conduct of a proper dinner party and that person will find these far outdistance the most meticulous ceremonies ever held in a church. Yet those who simplify too much the ceremonial of the dinner table become obnoxious in their behavior.

The ancient traditions are not extravagant. Rather, they are restraints upon private extravagance. They are, like those of society, the result of the accumulated experience of many centuries. They were chosen because they were found to make the service run without hitch or possibility of accident and to give a measure of grace and dignity even to those who are naturally awkward. How much of the old catholic ceremonial has been retained, even among those who are most opposed to ceremonies, will be clear to anyone who compares the worship of the barest church with that of a place of worship with no such traditions.

One need not go far to notice how many of the clergy and other church officials do, as a matter of fact, stand in very great need of a few elementary lessons in deportment. Such lessons are needed in all civilized society—not to make one stiff or ceremonious but to prevent one being stiff, to make one natural and unaffected. Indeed, the doings of some of the "ritualistic" clergy that cause offense are really their own private ideas of what is reverent and seemly, and not those of church tradition, which are essentially moderate and subdued.

On the other hand, what would be thought of a state function, if those who took part in it behaved like a Victorian cathedral choir? Yet one might expect as much trouble to be given to the service of the church as to that of the State. To those at the opposite extreme, who may urge that my suggestions are not minute enough, I would reply that my object has simply been to carry through the services of our church, as they stand, with the ornaments that are appropriate.

It is clear from the tenor of the prayer book that a simplification of ceremonial was intended. Therefore, it is not necessary in a book of this sort to work in every old ceremony, whether there is a place for them or not. Furthermore, it must be remembered that much of the ceremonial that we see is not taken from our own traditions but from foreign sources. If even the old "ceremonies" are convicted by our prayer book of great excess and multitude, much more must those of later continental ritualists be out of the question for us. The mind of the prayer book indubitably is to simplify rites and ceremonies without detracting either from their grace, significance, or richness. The prayer book wisely considers that Anglicanism is its own tradition, one that has arisen and is practiced differently in every province and country of our communion. Therefore, we "condemn no other nations"; we have no right to impose upon ourselves or upon others that bondage to fresh minutiae of ceremonial the ecclesiastics of some other countries or traditions, rightly or wrongly, now consider needful.

I am hopeful that an increase in the beauty of worship will continue to grow till there is not a single form of religion left that discards the almost universal human instinct for the beauty of ceremonial worship. Yet it also appears certain that freedom will also be a mark of the future rather than strict ceremonial uniformity. We need not regret this tendency, for such uniformity never was obtained in the time when the church was at peace. Its attempted enforcement, in Rome or elsewhere, is a sign that the church catholic is divided.

This book must not, therefore, be taken as the attempt of an unauthorized person to dictate to his siblings in Christ. Whether they conform little or much or altogether is a matter for them to settle with their own consciences. I have only tried to show what it is that our church requires and what the best of our tradition would invite. The requirements of the church leave many degrees of ceremonial open to us, even within the limits of strict conformity. But, whether the ceremonial used is little or much, the services of our church should at least be conducted on the legitimate lines, if only that they may be freed from what is anomalous, irreverent, tawdry, or grotesque.

Beautiful, authentic worship, in which all the people participate in the best tradition of the church is our goal—because when that is achieved, the end will not be the most recent clever turn of phrase or liturgical hijinks. Rather, the end will be none other than the vision of God, even as that vision is reflected in the face of your sibling in Christ.

1

The Chancel, Nave, and Their Furniture

IN PLANNING A NEW church, or considering a renovation to an existing space, a few words should be said about the orientation of the nave, chancel, and sanctuary of the building, as there has been much confusion over the years with regard to the proper principles at work in these important decisions.

Dearmer's first love was art and architecture, and it wasn't until near the end of his time in Oxford that he turned to a sense of calling to holy orders.[1] By the time Dearmer was active in ministry, the impact of a group known as the Cambridge Camden Society was felt throughout the Church of England. This group, later known as the Ecclesiological Society, was founded in 1839 by undergraduates at Trinity College, Cambridge, including the great Anglo-Catholic priest and hymn writer, John Mason Neale. Their goal was to revive Gothic architecture and liturgical practices in the Church of England as a part of the broader Oxford Movement. The ideals of this society can be found throughout Dearmer's various editions of *The Parson's Handbook*.

In 1994, the Church Building Fund published a slender booklet entitled *The Church for Common Prayer: A Statement on Worship Space for the Episcopal Church*.[2] Developed alongside of the Episcopal Church's Standing Commission on Liturgy on Church Music, Standing Liturgical Commission,

---

1. See Beeson, "Master of Ceremonies," 98–103. You can see much of Dearmer's continued interest in art and architecture in his small book *Christianity and Art*, as well as in *The Cathedral Church of Wells* and *The Cathedral Church of Oxford*, especially engaging the architecture on pp. 20–86 and 27–56, respectively.

2. Fulton et al., *Church for Common Prayer*.

the Association of Diocesan Liturgy and Music Commissions, and Associated Parishes for Liturgy and Mission, it represents the best thinking of its own time for how a worship space could best be designed and laid out in accordance with the ideals of the 1979 Book of Common Prayer. Many churches constructed or renovated since that time have followed these ideals (though, it must be acknowledged, far too many parsons were either unaware or uninterested in this book, often putting other priorities like the increase of seating ahead of liturgical concerns).

In general, this book assumes the neo-Gothic layout many Episcopal Churches have inherited, as this is, particularly, the architectural style most often preferred by those who find themselves in the prayer book catholic tradition of the church. However, the ideals of this book should be easy to apply to any liturgical space (and might even provide an opportunity for conversation between parson and the people regarding what slight changes should be made to a liturgical space to make it more conducive to the worship of God in the Anglican tradition). Though it is generally the case that the building always wins, this is not an axiom to be humbly accepted. Through careful and collaborative work and conversation, any church structure can be a place where the worship of God can take place in the beauty of holiness and according to the rubrics and ideals of our prayer book.[3]

THE NAVE AND CHANCEL

It should be remembered that it is not essential, although it is generally convenient, for the chancel to be raised one or perhaps two steps above the nave. In most old churches there is only a difference of one step; in others chancel and nave are on the same level. In some churches in England (though rarely in America) there is even a descent of one step into the chancel. A step up makes it easier for the service to be heard and seen. At the same time, to pile up the chancel at a great height above the nave is an innovation that causes many inconveniences. A church is not a theater, and it is not necessary or even advisable that all the action in the chancel should be displayed with great prominence. To do so gives the impression that worship is a show one is watching as opposed to the corporate action of the gathered community. Especially where space is

---

3. For a more fulsome discussion, as well as helpful advice in how to use a liturgical space in accordance with the rubrics and ideals of the prayer book, see Malloy, *Celebrating the Eucharist*, 32–46.

limited, the fact must be borne in mind that each step reduces the size of the floor. There are many churches where the ministers at the altar have no room to move because the architect has sacrificed everything to perching them upon as many steps as possible.

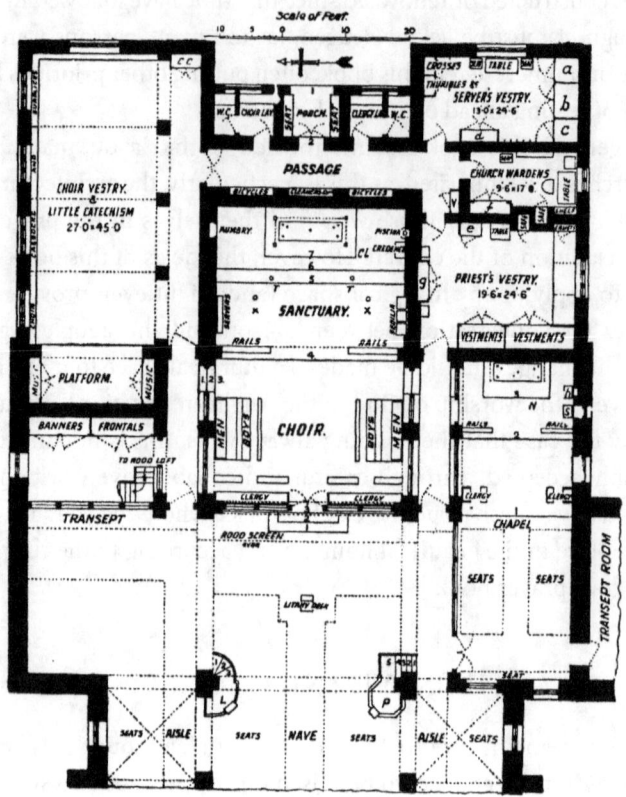

Index to Plan

(The first bay only of the Nave is shown. A Transept Room is suggested at the south transept, as a subsidiary church room, suitable for general purposes, for a tea-room, for classes or other meetings, and suitable also for a Sunday Kindergarten—when the Nave would be occupied by the Great, and the Choir Vestry by the Little Catechism, or their equivalents. The Choir Vestry, with its Platform and Aisle, would be used for the Easter Vestry and other large meetings.)

Numbers represent steps.
1, 2, 3. (Under Rood Screen) Chancel steps.
4. (In Sanctuary) Communion step.
x, x. Standard candlesticks.
T, T.   Usual position of Taperers (o o, their candlesticks).
5. Subdeacon's step. ⎱ The figures
6. Deacon's step.   ⎰ show the usual
CL. Position of Clerk. ⎱ position of the
7. Foot-pace.   ⎰ ministers.
L. Lectern.
P. Pulpit.
CC. Cupboard for children's material.

a, b, c. Servers' cupboards, for Albes, &c.
d. Sacristan's store cupboard.
f. Churchwardens' cupboard for books.
V. Verger's cupboard.
e. Parson's cupboard for Cassocks, &c.
g. Cupboard for Surplices and Albes.
In Priest's Vestry, a press, with drawers, under the window.
3 in Chapel, foot-pace.
N in Chapel, normal position of server.
2 In Chapel, Communion step.
h in Chapel, Credence.
S in Chapel, Sedile for minister.

Dearmer's Plan for a Modern Chancel and Chapel, with Vestries[4]

4. 1913. By Vivian H. King, associate of the Royal Institute of British Architects (ARIBA). Showing a typical and convenient disposition of the east end of a modern

The chancel should not be crowded with benches and desks, which has a very bad effect, but should be kept as open as possible. In small chancels it is certainly best not to have a surpliced choir so that only stalls for the clergy and a few seats for servers are needed. Whatever choir there is can then be accommodated in a gallery with the organ, which will increase reverence, economize space, and improve the quality of the singing. Or, alternatively, in absence of a rear gallery, singers may sit in last pews of the congregation to assist with the singing of the service then come to the chancel steps to offer any anthems during the liturgy. However, a choir (at least in the form so many clergy and lay leaders think of one) is not nearly as essential as so many seem to assume. A few words on this question might be helpful.

It is necessary to combat the idea that surpliced choirs are indispensable to a well-conducted service. They sometimes are useful and sometimes the reverse, actually. Particularly for many small churches, the struggle to keep the choir roster full requires significant energy for an ideal that is a rather modern innovation in the average congregation. Furthermore, too much focus on the choir can distract from the musical education of the congregation. In particular, for smaller congregations, some training in singing and music for the congregation can produce a much more vibrant service than the half-hearted singing of the congregation led by a too small choir that adds little to the liturgy. In general, we should seek less for noise and more for music. If there is a choir, the quality of the music is essential even if that means that the braver choirmasters should refuse choristers who cannot sing. In this approach, many churches will be content with a quartet or two chanters to lead the singing and chant the alternate verses of the psalms and anthems. Furthermore, we may well hope that most churches will come to realize the profound educational value of good music and the demoralizing effect of that which is bad.

Before the Reformation many churches had no choirs at all. There were often choirs in churches that had convenient chancels, and there were cantors as well (called "rulers" in the Sarum Use)[5] who had seats in the midst of the choir in imitation of the cathedrals. We learn also, from an interesting passage in the Sarum Customary, that provision was made for such an imitation of the cathedral use in parish churches: the

---

parish church, which can be varied to suit different requirements.

5. Pearson, *Sarum Missal in English*, xxv.

choristers could stand in front of the choir stalls, while other clergy could occupy the stalls behind them, just as they do still in some churches today.[6] We are not, of course, bound by medieval precedent. When surpliced choirs were introduced in more modern times, it was often with the understanding that they were "high church." This was a mistaken idea, and the result has often put an undue burden upon smaller congregations. This idea being disposed of, then, we must judge surpliced choirs by their fruits—musical, artistic, and devotional. Congregations should choose leaders and musical artists for their music who meet those ends, knowing that a surpliced choir is not the only way music has historically been offered in the liturgy and it is far from the only way it can best be offered in our own time.

The stalls for the clergy often nowadays face north and south. Dearmer argued in the successive editions of his handbook that clergy stalls should properly be "returned" and all face east. He fundamentally rejected the idea that they should face west (i.e., face the people, as in many contemporary church arrangements). Dearmer argued that having the clergy stalls in line with the choir was actually a modern innovation and that precedent was in favor of returning them, even in small parish churches, to face the altar. Dearmer believed there were several good reasons for this approach, insisting that, among the great practical advantages, the devotions of the clergy are assisted, the clergy are prevented from staring at the people, and unruly choristers are kept under better control.[7]

Regardless of the arrangement of the stalls, in a parish with multiple clergy, they should sit in order with the rector of the parish occupying the decani stall, the first on the south side; the senior assistant curate having that of the precentor (cantoris), the first on the north side; the second assistant curate would sit in the second stall on the decani side; and other clergy and choristers would similarly sit in order on both sides with the senior being farthest from the altar, subject of course to musical and other considerations. In most churches, however, there is only a priest and, if fortunate, a deacon or assisting priest. In those cases, the celebrant (whether rector or assisting priest) should take the seat on the south side, closest to the altar. The deacon should properly be seated to the right of the celebrant. Assisting clergy may then be seated in choir alternating

---

6. Pearson, *Sarum Missal in English*, xxv–xxvi.
7. Dearmer, *Parson's Handbook*, 48.

between north and south sides. (And, as Malloy rightly notes, at no point should the clergy and ministers be seated directly in front of the altar, obscuring the altar's role as the focal point for our worship of God.)[8]

A second shelf for keeping books will be useful in all the stalls, and divisions should be made so as to keep each person's books separate. Where there are cantors or leaders of the choir, these will need a lectern and stools in the midst of the chancel. Often a moveable one will work nicely. Choristers should not be required to sit crowded together; closeness should be due to the needs of musical art and not the space into which a group is placed. In the case of small chancels, the floor space may sometimes be increased by forgoing desks and supplying only a simple row of chairs with kneeling cushions that can be pulled out when needed.

No wood or metal work that can possibly come in the way should have sharp edges or corners, nor should anyone be allowed to drive a nail into the stalls for the purpose of fixing decorations—these points should be made particularly clear in the policies for weddings (and even funerals at times), but the point should also be made for those who decorate the church for festive occasions (e.g., for the greening of the church at the end of Advent before the first services of Christmas). When decorations are used for festal occasions, care should be taken so that they can be removed without leaving unsightly tacks or nails, which can furthermore become a hazard during the rest of the year.

LIGHTS AND CANDLES

To best highlight the beauty of the altar, it should be kept in a quiet light and soft LED bulbs in both the chancel and altar area will be appreciated by worship ministers who used to have to sweat under the glare of strong traditional electric lights. Oil lamps are to be avoided, as they contribute towards spoiling and dirtying everything in the church if they are not regularly trimmed and cared for.

Gas or electric lights on the altar itself are intolerable. Liturgical companies have successfully convinced many modern parishes to switch to candles with oil wicks, resulting in the fact that the skills needed for

---

8. Malloy, *Celebrating the Eucharist*, 39. Though, as he notes on the same page, an exception to this rule may be made for pontifical rites where the bishop presides while sitting in a cathedra in front of the altar. But even then, a proper faldstool is far preferable to the "bishop's chair" so many church supply warehouses convinced churches to buy in recent centuries.

tending to proper beeswax candles are often absent in most churches. Though true beeswax candles are always preferred (and can be quite practical, once one learns how to use them well), the newer oil wick candles are an acceptable substitute that may regrettably be permitted, with one clear exception. The paschal candle should never be a plastic tube with an oil wick. This convention eliminates entirely the meaning and power of the blessing of the new paschal candle at the Great Vigil of Easter as well as the experience of watching the candle slowly burn down throughout the year when it is brought out once more for baptisms and funerals.

Similarly, if a church is to use the modern devotion of an Advent wreath, traditional candles are to be preferred so that the differences in heights during the succeeding weeks of Advent can give a sense of the passage of time—though, it must be explicitly noted that devotions at the lighting of these candles (outside of the Lucenarium in the prayer book's order of worship for evening, which would not be used on a Sunday morning anyway) are wholly unneeded and contrary to the rubrics of our church.[9]

All other lighting, whether in nave or choir, should be of as simple and unobtrusive in nature as possible. As a general rule lights (particularly those at lecterns, pulpits, or ambos) should not be set at any great height, but as near as possible to the places where they are wanted for shedding light on the books.

THE ROOD

If the chancels are to be as they were "in times past" (see the excursus on the ornaments rubric in the introduction to this book for the import of that phrase), we now face a reality in the modern church where few chancels bear any resemblance to the historic chancels of times past. While it was thought that the removal of roodscreens and the creation of open chancels with free standing altars symbolized the breaking down of the barriers of clericalism, this has not been the case. Indeed, we have discovered that no matter the architecture of a space, a clericalist parson remains just as stubbornly clericalist. What is needed is less innovation in architecture and more attention to formation (including formation of character) of clergy if the church is going to resolve problems of priests who simply do not know how to function in their role with grace and a collaborative spirit.

9. "When the Advent Wreath is used in the worshiping community at morning services, the appropriate number of candles on the wreath are lighted, without prayer or ceremony, with the other candles." *Book of Occasional Services*, 20.

THE CHANCEL, NAVE, AND THEIR FURNITURE

Within the Rood Screen (Fifteenth Century)[10]

Indeed, a return to the traditional liturgical structure of nave, chancel, and sanctuary, with the chancel and sanctuary separated from the nave with a rood,[11] gives a balance, dignity, and beauty to any liturgical space. Thus, we must certainly stand out against the strange and persistent dislike some have for the rood. Nothing can well be more impressive than the

10. 1835. Priest in gold chasuble (Y-shaped orphreys of red and gold) with gold stole and apparels; clerk in cassock and hood; clergy in surplices, one wearing a black cope and one with almuce on his head; mourners, some in black and some in brown cloaks and hoods. Altar on two steps with frontal of dark blue, powdered with gold stars, reredos with the crucifixion; hanging pyx above the altar under white canopy; herse cloth of blue, figured with gold, bearing a red and gold cross; six or more herse lights; rood loft, showing the back of the rood, with a lectern. The view is across the choir from south to north.

11. The word "rood" is an archaic word for pole derived from Old English and was the only Old English word used for the instrument of our Lord's death. See Oakley, "Pity and Glory," para. 5. Beginning in the eleventh century, the word "cross" gradually replaced "rood," though rood was maintained for this specific piece of architecture into our own time.

use of a true rood—one large cross or crucifix, and that alone, usually with the figures of St. Mary and St. John placed on either side of the rood, and sometimes other figures as well. There can furthermore be no doubt that the most appropriate position theologically, as well as the most impressive for the rood or cross, is the ancient place on the chancel screen or, when there is no screen, on a beam running across the chancel arch. The use of one single rood to gather the attention of the people also encourages a greater reserve in the use of a multiplicity of crucifixes, which should not be dotted about the church in the way one sometimes sees.

Furthermore, if done with care and beauty, then we can even let go of the prejudice against rood screens, a prejudice which is not authentic to our church and was imported because of the prejudices of Puritans and modern Roman Catholics. The rood loft was a common place also for the organ and for musicians. If used, it should be a substantial structure, resting on its beams and on the open screen below it. I do not think there is any difference of opinion among artists as to the great value of a well-designed rood screen. It should not, of course, be solid except in cathedral and collegiate churches, but, solid or open, it gives the most splendid opportunity to the sculptor and painter. The screen should ideally be of stone or wood (generally the same material as the church is constructed from) and not a mere iron grating. At the same time, it must not block out the high altar nor hide the occupants of the stalls in a parish church.

THE ORGAN

There are many good ways of placing the organ. To block up a chapel with it is a bad way. For larger organs some kind of loft should, if possible, be built. Organ pipes should be silvered, gilt, or left their natural color, which is a very good one; the decorations one generally sees on them are unnecessary and can become an unpleasant distraction (with the additional note that these sorts of decorations will not likely age well over time, unless meticulously cared for). In our time, there are fewer and fewer organ builders and those who have persisted are quite knowledgeable and skilled. They should be consulted, lest an architect unknowingly do damage to the musical offerings of the church by not properly designing the space for the instrument (or the instrument for the space).

Most would agree that the best arrangement, both for music and for ceremonial, in many churches, is the old-fashioned one of a west gallery with the choir. The choristers can still take part in processions before going up into the gallery, and by singing from behind the people, they can greatly encourage the singing of the entire congregation. Furthermore, it continues the ideal that the choir is not performing a concert the people are watching, but (facing the same direction as the people—towards the altar) they are offering their own musical gifts in worship to God alone, with the people having the blessed gift of overhearing the offering when an anthem or psalmody is sung by the choir alone. At the same time, in choirs with child choristers, an argument may be made that the chancel choir arrangement is superior for ensuring the children feel engaged in the liturgy itself. Careful consideration of the benefits and drawbacks of each approach is needed. Regardless of the position, if the congregation is trained to understand that actively listening (including to those singing behind them) is a participatory act of worship, much can be gained.

THE PULPIT, LECTERN, OR AMBO

The pulpit was ordered by canon 83 of the Church of England to be "provided in every church," and to be "comely and decent" and "seemly kept."[12] It may be in almost any part of the church, the usual place being at the side of the nave. My own opinion is that the south side is the best for everyone who is not left handed, since the preacher who is right handed, having the freer side towards the people, is able to speak right across the church with more ease and self-command.

A Sermon[13]

12. Church of England, *Canons* (1604), no. 83.
13. *Introduction to the Sacrament*, by Launcelot Addison, dean of Lichfield, fifth

It is curious to notice how few modern pulpits are well placed or adequately fitted. Often, they are pushed too far back or too much to the side of the church. Sometimes, of late years, expensive and very ugly stone pulpits have been set up. Of course, a really good stone pulpit is an excellent thing; but a wooden one has these great advantages—that it is warm, smooth, and clean to the preacher's hand; that it furnishes a church, giving it warmth and color; and that it can be more easily moved. If an immovable stone pulpit is to be built, a small platform should first be put together, and carefully tried in different positions. It should be moved about until the spot is found where gestures become easiest and unstrained and from which the largest part of the congregation can see the preacher. It will generally be found that the same place will be best for both purposes. In the case, for instance, of a church with two aisles, if the pulpit be brought well away from the pier arches, it will often be found not only that the acoustics are much improved but also that the preacher can see (and consequently be seen by) a far larger proportion of those who sit in the aisles. In a church with no aisles, the pulpit should not be stuck against the wall. If it instead projects into the church, the preacher will not only find it easier to speak but also to move, having no longer the fear of hitting the wall.

As for height, I would suggest that for the smallest church the floor of the pulpit be no lower than the shoulders of the people when they are sitting down. In a large church the pulpit may well be twice as high, but attention should be paid to acoustics, audio technology, and the use of a sounding board may be advised.

In the pulpit itself everything should be avoided that tends to make a preacher nervous or awkward. The steps to the pulpit are often better behind and out of sight, but in this case, there should be a door, or at least a wooden bar, so that the occupant need not fear the fate of Eli. The sides of the pulpit should not be so low down that the hands dangle helplessly; English people (and Episcopalians) as a rule find their hands rather in the way, and they will speak much better, and avoid fingering their garments much more, if they can rest their hands quite comfortably on the sides of the pulpit. I would therefore suggest thirty-eight to forty

---

edition, 1693. Preacher in priest's gown of the original shape the sleeves up to the rest and not tucked up to the elbow (compare with the illustration of "Priest in Official Habit" on p. 101 of this book). The altar is still of the same type as before the Reformation with frontal and dorsal, and two lighted candles standing on it. An alms-basin rests against the dorsal, over which are the tables of the Decalogue.

inches as a convenient height for parsons of average size; it is best to err on the side of height. Where the sides of the pulpit are too low, a rounded wooden rail can easily be fitted on to them, and it can very often be made to look well. The rail gives a rest for the fingers, it makes gesture more ready (the hands not having to be lifted so high), and at the same time it leaves the top of the pulpit (which should be at least four or five inches broad) quite free for books. Every pulpit should also have a shelf with a little ledge, large enough to hold the books, a box of tissues, and a glass of water. This also helps to prevent the preacher hanging over the pulpit. For the books, there should be space for the preacher's prayer book and perhaps a Bible, if desired. These books should not be too large to be put conveniently on the shelf, since anything that is in danger of tumbling over adds to the constraint of the preacher.

There should be a cushion or desk at the pulpit for those who use a manuscript (which, truth be told, should be most preachers, especially those who are under the illusion that the congregation enjoys the parson rambling on with no structure to the homily). This desk should not be made of cheap, shaky metal with thin edges. It should be substantial, with rounded edges that do not cut the hands. It should be firm, and readily adjustable both as to height and slope. It should also be removable—the clergy of a church sometimes forget that visiting preachers may be seriously inconvenienced by the presence or by the absence of a desk. Metal may sometimes be used instead of wood. But here, as elsewhere, it is well to remember that there is nothing particularly ecclesiastical or sacred about brass. It is better to cover the desk with a cloth, but there is no order that such cloths should follow the color of the seasons; the pulpit is not an altar, and its hangings may be chosen with a view to with a view to permanent use. The only significant time the cloth should be replaced is during Lent, when it should be another color and material, particularly if the Lenten array is used. The desk should look across to the opposite corner of the church, and not due west; in some churches the preacher is only heard properly when facing a particular spot, and the desk has to be fixed so as to put the preacher at the proper angle.

A round hole should be made in the top of the pulpit, or in the shelf, to hold a small clock (the atomic ones are excellent and the batteries last for quite long). This is important even if there is a clock in the church, for some preachers are shortsighted. In most small churches a plain round clock on the west gallery or wall will also be a convenience. Regardless, the congregation will often have cause to be grateful if there is a clock within sight of the preacher.

The question of sounding boards depends upon the acoustic properties of the church. Sometimes a panel or curtain behind the preacher may be an assistance; it also serves to rest the eyes of the congregation. A hanging round the front of the pulpit, covering the sides but not the base, may often hide a multitude of architectural sins.

In nothing are pulpits more badly managed than in the method of lighting. It may be laid down as an axiom that the lights should be reduced during the sermon; for this disposes the congregation to listen and not to stare about, rests their eyes, purifies the atmosphere, lessens the heat, spares the decorations, and reduces expense. Therefore, the pulpit must have an independent supply of light of its own. Modern computerized dimmers make this quite an easy addition in almost all churches. This light should not be supplied by two unguarded candles on the shelf, unless the preacher is absolutely determined to court martyrdom. Even then, however, when preachers find themselves placed so near the fire, they take such care to avoid it that they remain throughout their discourse as impassive as statues. When the candles are guarded, the preacher is equally under restraint; for there is fear of breaking the glass, and the fear of being ridiculous makes the preacher awkward. No candle-bracket of any sort or kind on the shelf, or within possible reach of the preacher, is tolerable.

Whatever light is used on the desk itself, it must be completely shaded. What is wanted is a flood of light on the desk and a clear light on the preacher, with no visible bulb at all. This can be easily obtained (1) by a bracket (if one can be fixed nearly over the pulpit desk) with a shaded light. If a silk shade is used it must be quite plain; red, or green, or dark yellow are good colors, lined with white. Concealed lights can also be arranged above the preacher, with separate switches so that the strength of the light can be varied. A well-designed lectern can be similarly treated. Lamps need to be lacquered, as otherwise they are difficult to clean.

The lectern may be beautiful or ugly, artistic or commercial, according to the spirit of the people who provide it. It can be cheap or dear, of wood or metal, according to their means; but it may be something other than a brass eagle without any offense against orthodoxy. Indeed, this type of lectern was not invented for reading the lessons at all but for the Epistle and Gospel, or for the use of the chanters. One thing is essential to the lectern: that the desk be of a convenient height and angle and not come between the reader's head and the congregation. From the platform to the lower edge of the desk, four feet is a good height. There is plenty of ancient precedent for much higher lecterns, but they were used for singing the service in the choir, and not for reading to the people. Like the pulpit, the lectern should be placed where the voice is best heard; for the older rubric of the 1662 prayer book (as well as common sense) orders that the reader shall so stand "as he may best be heard of all such as are present."[14] It may be on the opposite side to the pulpit, and not too near the chancel. It should stand on a platform at least a foot above the floor of the nave and should, if possible, not be on a lower level than the choir.

It is increasingly the case that a separate pulpit and lectern are not used and instead a singular ambo is preferred for both purposes.[15] The word comes from the Greek word ἄμβων and means "step" or "elevation."[16] Since the fourth century, it was common for a raised platform to be used for the reading or chanting of the Epistle and Gospel. In the Eastern tradition, this word refers to the projection directly in front of the doors of the iconostasis and is the place from which the deacon reads the Gospel, says the litanies, and from which the priest gives the dismissal during the divine services. As liturgy developed in the West, two ambos were used to distinguish between the Epistle and the Gospel, with the Epistle ambo placed at the southern side of the chancel and the Gospel ambo at the northern side. It was from this division that the modern practice of a lectern for the first several readings and a pulpit for the sermon developed—but in modern days, when the Gospel is often read from the midst of the people, the connection is broken, and the modern use sometimes gives the appearance of the pulpit being the province of the clergy compared to the lectern, which is then seen as the province of the laity.

This development in recent years of a singular ambo does an excellent job of unifying the proclamation of God's word, both by laity and clergy, whether it be from the Hebrew Bible, the Greek Epistles, the Gospels, or (God helping) the homily itself. In the case of the use of a singular ambo, the other directions above should still be heeded so that it is functional, beautiful, and an aid instead of a distraction in worship.

All lecterns may be draped with a cloth (of any color). Bookmarkers are a convenience but not an ecclesiastical ornament, needing a particular treatment. To change them with the seasons is unnecessary and rather

---

14. *1662 Book of Common Prayer*, 12.

15. An example of an argument for this approach may be found in Galley, *Ceremonies*, 5.

16. Liddell and Scott, *Greek-English Lexicon*, 74.

damaging to the book. Red or blue are good colors. Reverence would suggest a sparing use of these and similar things, of crosses and other very sacred symbols. Lectern cloths are among the ornaments of the rubric, and often they will greatly improve the appearance of a lectern. The usual pattern is, however, not a good one. The lectern cloth should be a strip of handsome material, as wide as the desk, and long enough to hang not only over the front but over the desk to a longer distance down the back. Cloths of this sort are better fringed at the ends, and sometimes also at the sides. They certainly need not follow the color of the seasons, though they may be put away in Lent and either replaced by white linen cloths, or the lectern may be left bare. Of all things of this kind, it is well to bear in mind it is better to spend a fair sum on one of good material than to waste the same amount on four or five cheap ones. Only the frontal and vestments need to be changed with the season.

THE FONT

The font, according to the canons of the Church of England, should be of stone (though in the United States, where there has never been a similar requirement, wood is often used, particularly in smaller churches) and, "set in the ancient usual place," i.e., near the church door.[17] This was again insisted on by the bishops at the Savoy Conference.[18] Though Dearmer insisted that the font was never, in England, placed in a special chapel or baptistry, this is not correct when the archeological record is considered. Lambert found that many of the early fonts in ancient England actually were separated from the church, in a building adjacent to the church.[19]

As the rubric in our baptismal service orders the font to be filled afresh at each baptism, a drain is necessary, or a removable bowl from which the water may be reverently emptied before a service where new water will be blessed. The Puritan practice of putting "pots, pails, or bason" in the font to hold the water was steadily condemned by our bishops from Parker downwards.[20] The font should have a cover, which may be a simple lid or an architectural feature. Covers to fonts are constantly ordered from the time of St. Edmund of Canterbury to as late a date as

---

17. Church of England, *Canons* (1604), no. 81.
18. Buchanan, *Savoy Conference*, 55.
19. Lambert, *Christians and Pagans*, 24–27.
20. Dearmer, *Parson's Handbook*, 61.

that of Cosin. Care should be taken at festivals, if the font is decorated, to keep the top of it clear; but when the font is ornamental in itself, it is better not to decorate it. A linen cloth was used to cover the water in the font long after the Reformation and may still be an entirely appropriate choice for a church without an expensive font cover.

It should be noted that baptism by immersion is the preferred form in the 1979 Book of Common Prayer, even if few clergy have been as eager to work for that architectural change as they were to wrest altars away from walls. The Didache of the late first or early second century prefers "living" (or running) water, in which the candidate is submerged or immersed.[21] Lambert suggests that immersion (pouring water over the heard of a standing candidate, as is often seen in iconography of Christ's baptism) was the more common practice in ancient England than submersion (dipping the candidate beneath the waters).[22]

Even as late as the ninth century Council of Chelsea, when infant baptism had clearly become the dominant mode, canon 11 of that council insisted that when infants are baptized, the presbyters "should not pour holy water on the heads of infants. Rather, let them be immersed (*mergantur*) in the font, in the way that the Son of God offered through himself as an example to all who believe, when he was immersed (*mergantus*) three times in the River Jordan."[23] It was not until the eleventh and twelfth centuries that stone fonts in churches became the standard.[24] Over the course of this time, the stone fonts themselves had developed, moving from basins on the floor, to basins mounted upon legs, to basins mounted upon single pedestals, increasingly higher as the possibility of adult baptism became correspondingly increasingly unlikely.[25]

Despite the aforementioned preference for submersion or immersion in the current prayer book, the architecture and existing fonts of many churches (not to mention the common Christian resistance to change in liturgical practice) has resulted in that practice not being

---

21. Milavec, *Didache*, 19. In addition to the Didache, see also Justin, *First Apology*, 1.61; Davies, *Setting of Baptism*, 2

22. Lambert, *Christians and Pagans*, 24.

23. The Latin is "Sciat etiam presbyterii, quando sacram baptismum ministrant, ut non effundant aquam sanctum super capita infantuum, sed semper mergantur in acria; sicut exemplum præbuit per Semetipsum Dei Filius omni credentit, quando esset ter mergatus in undis Jordanis." Haddon and Stubbs, *Councils and Ecclesiastical Documents*, 584. Translated by Thomas Williams in personal correspondence.

24. Blair, *Anglo-Saxon Society*, 462.

25. Bond, *Fonts*, 31–32.

widely adopted. Many newly constructed churches include full submersion baptistries, but these are often seen as cost (and space) prohibitive to install in existing congregations. However, the more traditional English practice of a sunken well, at least one foot deep and a few feet wide, would not require as significant an architectural change as the installation of a full submersion baptistery. Perhaps a recovery of this ancient form could ease the practical question of how our regular liturgical practice can best be brought in line with the ideals of our prayer book.

THE PEWS

Pews are by no means a Protestant invention, and in some ways they are better than chairs. They should, however, always be low (not more than two feet eight inches high), and the alleys both in aisles and the nave should be much wider than is usual. There are a good many old churches in England and the United States that show the medieval arrangement of low pews. They are like separate islands of low woodwork, with two in the nave and one in each aisle, and plenty of open space at the west end. To leave thus wide alleys, and a clear bay at the west where the font or baptismal pool stands, is a great help to the architecture of the church and gives room for the proper management of processions. Movable chairs can always be added when necessary. Increasingly churches are moving towards the use of chairs instead of pews as it makes the worshipping space more flexible for the community. This is a fine development—so long as the quality of the chairs is befitting of divine worship. Poorly made chairs in worship communicate the level of value placed upon this part of a congregation's life, and when the clergy are given fine chairs while the people sit in wobbly or ugly chairs, the message about the value of the baptized in worship is quite clear. If chairs are used, the line of each row of chairs may then be marked by brass-headed nails in the floor at either end, so that proper placement can be remembered for whenever the chairs are rearranged or moved for a special event.

When it comes to kneeling, overly high hassocks harbor dirt and prevent proper kneeling. The sloping boards also, high and narrow, which one sometimes sees, make it almost impossible to kneel. The most common practice in many churches is the use of kneelers affixed to the pew in front of the worshipper. These have the benefit of convenience in coming down and then being tucked away when not needed, but they also have the occasional problem of the raucous noise created when many of them go up and down at once (or when an unsuspecting worshipper accidentally lets one fall). Another convenient arrangement is for moderately thick pads to be hung by a hook opposite each seat or kept underneath the seat in front of the worshipper to be pulled out when needed. Kneeling is discouraged by benches or chairs being put too close together, so adequate space must be given. Whatever is chosen, the parson should test the kneeling accommodation and apply the golden rule to it.

PICTURES AND IMAGES

Pictures and images are legal in the Church of England and very well accepted in most Episcopal Churches these days. In the Church of England, it is required (and perhaps wisely considered on this side of the pond) that they not commemorate "feigned miracles," and are not abused by superstitious observances, but are for a memorial only.[26] Their destruction in the early days of the English Reformation was an act of lawless violence, and their use has never been entirely discontinued.

Dearmer had strong views against the use of the stations of the cross in parish churches, believing that they existed outside of the authorities of the Church of England and were kept in proportion in Roman Catholic churches by the multitude of other pictures, images, and shrines. He noted that in the average Anglican congregation, if the stations are the only artwork displayed, they can give an undue prominence to one part of our Lord's life. (He was further concerned that they commemorate traditional moments that have no true grounding in Scripture.)[27]

While much of what Dearmer said remains important to consider, the case is rather different now. The stations of the cross are an authorized rite in the *Book of Occasional Services*, and said book also includes a Scriptural version of them for the more cautious parson. Thus, the setting up of the stations in an Episcopal Church is wholly reasonable. It should also be noted, however, that they need not be installed permanently but could also be hung in the church during the seasons of Lent and Passiontide to help focus our attention only during those sacred days.

Furthermore, Dearmer's points about the approach remain key. In particular, the stations should be considered along with all other art used

---

26. Bray, "Elizabethan Injunctions," 305.
27. Dearmer, *Parson's Handbook*, 62.

in the church to ensure that undue attention is not given to our Lord's passion, crucifixion, and burial while the rest of his life (indeed, the rest of the life of the entire church) is visually absent. The parson would also be wise to consult those trained in design, art, and aesthetics to ensure that the stations chosen are of the proper size and fit well with the space in which they are hung.

Photographs do not look well in a church, and such things should be used very sparingly. Pictures with color are wanted—not copies but original paintings if possible. In our own day, prints of artwork, which are reasonable reproductions (and which do not look as though they came off a home printer or poster shop), can be had with some careful work at finding a good purveyor. When purchasing a print from a living artist, it is essential to ensure the purveyor is paying the artist and not merely copying the work. Well-made icons do much to add to the experience of a worship space, while also offering a method of prayer and devotion under the proper tutelage. However, many with a love for the Byzantine have been content with cheaply made icons that have no place in this tradition, which is arguably the richest and longest tradition of art in Christian worship. Hand-written icons are much to be preferred, particularly when they were written with prayer according to the tradition of the church. The placing of pictures, icons, or art on the walls, along with the placement of statues, requires much judgment. The choice of pictures indeed lays a solemn responsibility upon the parson, for many who see them will have their ideas of the Christian religion formed or modified by what they see. They may, for instance, form the impression that weak sentimentality or theatrical self-consciousness, is the religion of Christendom. On the other hand, they may learn to see in them sincerity, depth, and strength.

OTHER ITEMS IN THE NAVE AND CHANCEL

For the practice of the reconciliation of a penitent (commonly known as confession—which is only one part of the actual rite), there is a tradition in England of something known as "shriving pews." The astute reader will recognize in that word our own term for the Tuesday before Ash Wednesday, Shrove Tuesday. This comes from the Old English word "to shrive," which means "to forgive." However, the shape of shriving pews is not fully known, and so they cannot be restored. Some of the more catholic parishes had at one time set up confessional boxes, as used to be common in Roman Catholicism. However, the use of such boxes now often unnecessarily arouses prejudice and is also not in keeping even with the practices of even the Roman Church since the Second Vatican Council. It is also unneeded to put little curtains or crucifixes at the place where confessions are heard.

The prayer book does not contemplate routine and mandated confession, but clergy should remind the people of the principles laid down in the Exhortation, that when they find themselves burdened, they should avail themselves of a discrete and understanding priest.[28] The best place for the rite to be practiced is often with the penitent kneeling at the altar rail while the priest sits within the rail, either perpendicular to the penitent or both facing east. This makes it clear that the confession is given to God and that the priest is merely "listening in" on behalf of the church in order to provide encouragement, godly counsel, and to pronounce God's absolution upon the penitent.

One or more alms-boxes should be placed near the doors of the church, clearly marked "For the Poor" or "For the Parish's Ministry." These can provide an option for giving when people are not in attendance in worship. A handsome placard near them should also include a link and QR Code, along with any other instructions for giving online. In an age where fewer and fewer people carry cash (much less a checkbook), the parish that does not offer an easy method of online giving is telling the majority of people that their money is not truly needed. When alms boxes are used, they are often made of a rather flimsy wood screwed to the wall. As a result, they offer great temptations to any thief with tools and are used as an argument against open churches. It is a matter of common sense that a box containing money in a public place (for the church is a public place) should be very strong. The old boxes that have come down to us are formidable-looking things, heavily bound with iron. At the present day we can do even better. Small iron alms boxes, similar in construction to a small metal safe, can be obtained from any manufacturer of safes. They should be cemented or otherwise well-secured into the wall. The key for opening them should be kept in a secure place but not a place so secure that it will require a scavenger hunt later to retrieve people's gifts.

---

28. *1979 Book of Common Prayer*, 316–17.

Open boxes for parish magazines, leaflets, and tracts will also be needed, and a letterbox (glazed in front) for communications addressed to the clergy. In town churches it is most desirable to have a rack with good tracts and a moneybox (and a sign for how gifts may be made online) underneath. Such tracts should be scrupulously honest and free from all party bias or the parson's reputation for truthfulness will suffer. The Forward Movement in the Episcopal Church has done much good in restoring the tract tradition and is worthy of praise for that fact.

Notice boards should be well designed and kept very neatly. Therefore, each corner of each notice should be pinned down with a drawing-pin, with a stock of spare pins being kept near. Where there are several boards, it is a good plan to keep one for notices of the week, another in a less conspicuous position for notices of a more permanent character, and another for finance. A card announcing when and where the clergy can be seen and another for the names of the sick and departed for whom the prayers of the congregation are desired can hardly be dispensed with in a town parish.

Hymn boards are still useful, even in the days of service leaflets, and can provide another place where one can find the next hymn without the need of fumbling through a bulletin. Sometimes there is not enough room on them when there are processions or extra hymns. Ample space should be given at the top for the numbers of the psalms, if possible. A very convenient type is a reversible hymn board hung out from a bracket, so that the morning hymns can be on one side of it and the evening hymns on the other. It may be made like an oblong signboard and painted in rich colors. Hymn-boards should not be hung against pillars, responds, or screens. A verger or sacristan is generally the best person to look after them.

Devotional books for private reading are an admirable institution in a church; they encourage people to make use of the parish, besides assisting meditation and helping to dissipate prejudice. The Bible and other books were formerly kept on a desk for folk to read, but more can surely be done. The custom of keeping books in church had come in as early as 1488, and in the seventeenth century devotional books were common in church. A small bookcase may be hung near the west end or in a parish hall and supplied with a good selection of books, stamped with the name of the church. Separate books of the Bible with commentaries by present-day scholars, English religious classics, and some of the best poetry (such as Wordsworth, Donne, and Eliot) are suitable, as are new books, if they represent sound learning and are free from party spirit. Missionary magazines and the reports of any work in which the people are especially interested may also be kept on a shelf or table and then bound up from year to year.

Chapels, when used, should be enclosed by some kind of open screen with doors. A chapel needs an altar with a footpace and a credence, all of which may be smaller than those belonging to the chancel and sanctuary. Chapels ought properly to be fitted with stalls and separated by screens from the rest of the church. If, however, they are not so arranged, it is often best to use the chancel for the daily prayer services or for weekday offerings of Holy Eucharist.

There should always be benches set up in the church yard or porch. An open wire door to let air into the church is useful in the summer, and the porch itself should have gates. Many people seem to have an idea that they are not wanted in church and are shy of entering. It is therefore, in town churches, really important to put outside the church door a notice to the effect that "all are welcome."

The vergers should have a cupboard in some convenient part of the church where the gowns and maces or virges may be kept, along with hangings to indicate pews that are reserved for funerals or weddings. Either there or in the altar guild's sacristy alms bags may be kept, along with additional hymnbooks and suchlike things.

Signs outside with the name of the church are too often left to the curious decorative ideas of the local builder (or, unfortunately, ignored entirely). It is generally best that the service board should be white with its lettering in black of a broad and simple character, such as any decent craftsperson will execute—indeed the better class of local decorator can often produce tolerable lettering if told that it must be a plain kind and devoid of flourishes. (The Episcopal Church has a style guide that the wise parson will heed, even if, at times, it may be ignored in the interest of tradition and manners; thankfully, the guide does not have the same force of rubrics as the prayer book, and those are already ignored too much in the church.) The church's sign should give the times of services, along with information on the clergy and the church's website. A church without a website in this day and age might as well be a museum uninterested in visitors.

The parish church belongs to the people not only during service time but all through the day. It is not the parson's private property. The parson is merely one of the trustees for it and has a duty is to keep it at the people's service. It is really inexcusable to exclude them from it at any time of the day. Some parsons keep the outer doors of the church only half open, as if they wished to hide the fact that it is used as a Christian house of prayer. Now this half-open door is the sign among many businesses that closing time has come, and no one is expected to enter. Others only open a door that is out of sight. But if all the doors are kept freely open, it is safer than it would be with only one entrance; for a thief would have to keep a watch at all the entrances. As a matter of fact, thieves generally find it safer, for this reason, to break into a locked church. But the church is a public place, and therefore sacristies should be closed, valuables should be kept under lock and key, and reasonable precautions should be taken not to leave temptation in the way of a chance passerby. The best safeguard is for the church to be well used. Indeed, it is remarkable how few precautions are found necessary abroad. The people will gradually learn to use the church, if they are given the chance and not prevented from saying their prayers by the ungodly churlishness of the parson. It is more important that the church should be open than that it should be adorned with valuable things.

Every church should have at least two bells, though even with only one, a church need not be a public nuisance. No single bell, or couple of bells, should be rung for more than a minute or so; even three minutes is too long. The only exception to this rule would be churches that have sufficient bells for traditional change ringers. In that case, the beauty of the offering enables true bell ringing that can resound from the church. If there is only one bell in a church, it is much better only to ring two dozen strokes at fixed periods; this has the additional advantage of giving definite signals to clergy and choir. For instance, they might be rung ten minutes before the service, and again five minutes before (for the admission of the choir), and lastly, one minute before. It is well also to remember that bell hangers know how to hang bells and brick them in so that the sound is hardly heard in houses quite near the church, while it is carried upwards and away and heard in far places, mellowed by the distance.

Gothic architecture is most beautiful when it is true; the Victorian imitations of it hardly ever were. At the same time, it was only in use during four centuries of the Christian era and is therefore not more ecclesiastical than other forms of architecture. In the Gothic period, as in all other times, the church builders simply used the current style that was in use for secular buildings as well. The parson therefore should not try to tie down the architect to any popular idea as to what is ecclesiastical—which is, indeed, just the reverse of the whole Gothic spirit. Shoddy Gothic is the most hideous of all architecture, because *corruptio optimi pessima*.[29] In medieval, as in all other Christian times, architecture and all forms of decoration were free, although symbolism was so intensely appreciated. Even frontals and vestments were made without any regard to the supposed ecclesiastical character of their materials, with birds, beasts, flowers, and heraldic devices being freely used. Because the significance of symbolism was so well understood, sacred devices were used sparingly and with definite intention.

Special "ecclesiastical" materials only came in, even abroad, during the nineteenth century and were due mainly to commercial reasons and the rage for cheapness, because the constant use of a few stock patterns saved the shopkeepers the trouble of thinking. They soon convinced their customers that the materials on which they made the most profit were particularly suitable for use in church. Because of this reality, the judicious parson will take the time to find out true artists and workshops where items are made well, with quality materials, and where those creating them are justly compensated. Cheaply made church furnishings purchased from the internet that come from a questionable provenance when it comes to working conditions simply will not do.

Sound masonry is most necessary, even from the aesthetic point of view. A good architect's work is spoiled if nothing is asked of the builder but a low tender. The only advantage of this cheap building is that it tumbles down after a generation or two, and so the world is rid of it.

In dealing with old churches a very heavy responsibility rests upon the parson to protect such portions as have survived the ravages of one's predecessors. Much damage has been done to liturgical spaces in the name of innovation and an inability to keep from rearranging the furniture. The following rules issued by the Church Building Society will secure the parson against some of the worst evils: "Old masonry must not be reworked, scraped or scoured in a way which will remove the surface of the stone. Rubble walls ought not to be stripped of their ancient plaster,

---

29. This Latin phrase, roughly translated as "the corruption of the best is the worst of all" is a Socratic notion (see, for example, Xenophon, *Memorabilia*, 4.1.3). The phrase was important to St. Gregory the Great's warning of the consequences when those in great authority fall into corruption. The phrase was also a favorite of Ivan Dominic Illich, an Austrian Roman Catholic priest who renounced his orders in 1976, after twenty-five years of ministry, because of his conflicts with the Vatican over numerous issues including church bureaucracy, education, colonial missionary enterprises, and questions related to birth control and divorce. See Cayley, *Ivan Illich*.

internal or external, but the plaster should be repaired or renewed if it needs it. Old carpentry and joiner's work which has been painted may have the paint cleaned off so that the wrought surface is not injured, but no woodwork is to be scraped, stained, oiled, or varnished."[30]

White distemper is one of the most valuable aids to the beauty of church interiors, as architects and other artists well know; and the notion that the whitening of our old churches was due to the Puritans has no foundation. The whitewash was there before—coat after coat of it is constantly found on medieval stonework; all the iconoclasts ever did was to paint over any pictures with the white that already covered the rest of the interior. The old builders would no more have left brick or stonework bare on church walls than they would have left it in houses: they plastered their interiors and whitened them. This whitening brings out the lines of the architecture and forms a beautiful setting for the hangings, ornaments, and paintings, whereas brick makes the use of bright color almost impossible—hence the cold uncolored reredoses of the present day.

Altars, reredoses, and other centers of ornament should be richly colored, but the interior itself should be made white; stenciling is only an improvement when used with great reserve and by an exceptionally competent artist; it is safer to avoid it and also to avoid the temptation to color moldings and ribs, which is even more disastrous. This may seem stern counsel, but it will be found that the entire whitening of walls and vaults at once brings out the richness of good color and gilding elsewhere. So evident is this that, when it is done, everyone appreciates it.

The walls should be completely whitened, right up to the glass of the windows, and so should the tracery and arches: half the beauty is lost if the stonework round arches, etc., is left uncovered. Distemper can easily be spoiled both by blueness on the one hand and by muddiness (the "stone color" so called, beloved of builders) on the other—it should be bright and pure, and mellowness soon develops. The utmost toning that is safe is as follows: ordinary whitening and size, to which is added a certain amount of black (enough to make the mixture look fairly gray in the pail), the tone being warmed by a little ochre or venetian red, added to take off the greyness. But best of all is pure unmixed white; and in smoky towns especially, nothing should be added.

---

30. Dearmer, *Parson's Handbook*, 69.

THE CHANCEL, NAVE, AND THEIR FURNITURE

THE DUTY OF CHURCHWARDENS

The duty of churchwardens is to see that the building and property of the church, and all contained therein, is maintained in a good and perfect state and for that purpose to make all such repairs as may from time to time be necessary. They should be careful that they do not by any neglect lay upon their successors a heavy expenditure. It is convenient for the wardens to divide their duties, and this has long been the custom in the Episcopal Church. And, thus, the senior warden often deals with the finance, the charities, assisting with administrative questions, while the junior warden focuses more on the building. In some parishes and dioceses, they are referred to as the rector's warden and the people's warden, respectively, and there is no harm to this custom so long as clergy and people feel fully represented by both. However, the junior warden's care should not be focused on the building alone but should include care of the fabric, organ, fittings, monuments, bells, ventilation, heating, lighting, and of the churchyard with its fences, paths, and gates. Some of these duties may be delegated to the others in the church, but a single person having overall responsibility is helpful.

The supervision of those who clean the parish is an important part of the oversight of the vestry and parson and the junior warden is well-advised to form a strong relationship with whatever volunteers or staff are tasked with this work. They must see that those responsible keep the pavements, windowsills, etc., clean. Care should be given to brushing and cleaning the mats and kneeling pads. They must also see that all carved work is cleaned sparingly and with the greatest care. Sometimes carved stone may need to be washed and wiped, but it should never be rubbed or scrubbed. Stalls, seats, and pews should be wiped with a damp cloth to remove the dust. Books and kneelers should be neatly arranged. The remoter parts of the church, such as the rood loft, the ringing loft, and furnace or boiler room, should be periodically visited with a keen eye to dirt and cobwebs. As far as possible, lights should be upgraded to the newer LED models, which throw far less heat at the choir and ministers, but care should be given to choose a warm temperature and not the harsh and bright blue light of an operating room. The organ will suffer serious damage unless it is cleaned from time to time, as well as regularly maintained and tuned by qualified organ technicians, a matter about which the organist should be consulted. Such vigilance as this will have its effect upon the health and comfort of the congregation and upon their attachment to the church.

Supervision is also needed over the ventilation and heating of the church. In churches without air conditioning (a reality in the northern parts of the country that always seems to shock those in the southern parts), the windows—and in summer the doors also—should be opened between the services, and special care must be given on hot days to keeping the air fresh and cool by opening more windows than usual. For those with full heating and cooling systems, a smart thermostat to which the parson and verger have access will be appreciated when the temperature in the nave becomes unexpectedly uncomfortable. It can then be fixed with a slight adjustment on a smartphone.

The wardens have a serious responsibility in the care of the roof, in its slates or tiles; the cleaning and repair of gutters, downspouts, and drains; in the pointing of joints; in the repairs of lead in windows; in the painting of ironwork, etc. Lack of concern for the roof and gutters has caused many a challenge to vestries who wish their predecessors had paid better attention to preventative maintenance and upkeep. The bell fittings and ropes need periodic examination, and the ironwork of the bell frames needs painting.

The parson and wardens must always remember that in all improvements to the church they will be but wasting their money—indeed, far worse than wasting it—unless they secure a real craftsman, whether architect or painter or worker in wood, metal, stone, or glass. Care should be given to prior work, particularly in the area of architecture, to ensure that there is solid understanding of the needs of a church that practices liturgical worship. Nothing should be put into the church that is not the best of its kind, though this does not at all necessarily mean the most expensive! Even the most barely utilitarian things must be sound and good, and everything that can in the least affect the appearance of the church must be real workmanship—that is to say, a real work of art, however simple and humble. One cannot insist too often upon this because it is still the exception for decent things to be bought for a church (and far too many churches are filled with gifts from parishioners who came across some item in a relative's estate after death and thought the church might have need of it). In nine cases out of ten, those responsible for buying such things fall victim to marketing and large corporations whose object is to make money out of the parson and wardens, not to improve their church or minister to the glory of God. As time goes on, these horrible articles are often recognized as valueless (as, indeed, those of twenty years ago are already), and they subsequently disappear. There are many churches to which an artist would, if that artist dared, recommend a big bonfire of ornaments to begin with. An untold sum of money spent on the ornamentation of churches has been altogether wasted, or, as I have said, worse than wasted. Finally, the wise parson will ignore advertisements. True artists do not advertise.

2

The Holy Table and Its Furniture

A FEW INTRODUCTORY WORDS on the Christian altar may be useful at the start. First, on the very word itself. The word "altar" is generally used in this book for convenience, though there are a variety of names by which it is known. (And new church staff—particularly administrative staff—will be grateful to be told that it is spelled with two *a*'s, and not "alter," which means to change something. This typo in bulletins and church websites is almost as painful as the lector who unknowingly pronounces the word "prophesy" as "prophecy" at the Great Vigil of Easter. As is so often the case, an ounce of teaching can avoid a pound of discomfort).

The word "altar" does not occur in the rubrics of the original 1662 Book of Common Prayer. However, in the revisions that produced the 1979 Book of Common Prayer, altar became the dominant word used in the book. It is the candles upon the altar that are lighted during the Lucenarium.[1] The very first instructions in the Holy Eucharist name the place where the ministers stand as "at the altar,"[2] this also being where the gifts are placed.[3] For a wedding, the couple approach the altar, either for the exchange of vows or blessing of the marriage.[4] The couple then returns to the altar after the birth of a child.[5] The suggested location for the sacra-

---

1. *1979 Book of Common Prayer*, 112, 143. A similar rubric is found in the way that the rite is adapted for the Great Vigil of Easter on 286 and 294.
2. *1979 Book of Common Prayer*, 322.
3. *1979 Book of Common Prayer*, 333.
4. *1979 Book of Common Prayer*, 437.
5. *1979 Book of Common Prayer*, 439.

ment of reconciliation is with the confessor sitting inside the altar rail and the penitent kneeling.[6] Much of the foci of ordination services occur at the altar[7] and it is service at God's altar that the priest acknowledges in the prayer at the celebration of a new ministry.[8]

Interestingly enough, despite the clear preference for this term, in the rite of consecration of a church, the 1979 prayer book is much more flexible in its terminology, using both "altar" and "table" somewhat interchangeably. On p. 573, the rubrics refer to it as a table, though the bishop prays for the setting apart of the altar. And on the following page, the bishop prays that God will "sanctify this Table dedicated to you," continuing,

> Let it be to us a sign of the heavenly Altar where your saints and angels praise you for ever. Accept here the continual recalling of the sacrifice of your Son. Grant that all who eat and drink at this holy Table may be fed and refreshed by his flesh and blood, be forgiven for their sins, united with one another, and strengthened for your service for your service.[9]

The point that both altar and table are appropriate words conveys the dual purpose of the altar in the church and this has been understood by various traditions through the centuries. As the prayer for the consecration of an altar reminds us, it is both the place from which we continually recall the sacrifice of God's Son (with sacrifices being offered at altars), while also being the place from which we are fed by Christ's flesh and blood (as one is at a table).

As Dearmer noted in his time, it is quite a mistake to attribute any doctrinal party sense to the word table. In the earliest York Pontifical we find the words *in hac mensa* used at the dedication of an altar, with *mensa* simply being the Latin word for table. Indeed, the fussiest Anglo-Catholics, who take great care to talk about the *mensa* when training altar guild members but who would react violently at being told it is a table, clearly would do well to learn at least a smidgen of Latin. Such phrases as "Godes table," "Goddes board," and "the holie bard," are common in medieval writings.[10] The word table is also used by the Eastern churches, and table

---

6. *1979 Book of Common Prayer*, 446.
7. See the instructions in *1979 Book of Common Prayer*, 553–555.
8. *1979 Book of Common Prayer*, 562.
9. *1979 Book of Common Prayer*, 563.
10. See, for example, the *Lay Folk's Mass Book*.

as well as altar occur in the writings of the fathers and mothers of the church. It is also a mistake also to think that table is devoid of sacrificial meaning—for while it is certainly true that *mensa* is the Latin word for table, that word is also used in classical Latin to speak of a sacrificial altar.

The primitive altar of the fourth and following centuries was a short table of nearly cubical shape, which stood under a canopy, supported by four columns. The canopy was called the ciborium or a baldachin and was placed in the middle of the sanctuary, usually at the west end of the building, perhaps in imitation of the sanctuary in the temple in Jerusalem. Around the sixth century, the entrance was moved to the west with the altar placed closer to the east end, and this approach began to prevail in churches. However, recent scholarship has demonstrated that even at an altar standing at a crossing on the east end of the church the priest still stood facing east (along with all the people, including any who were between the altar and the east wall of the church). The idea that ancient churches with the altar pulled away from the wall meant clergy would face the people across the altar is, quite simply, an error in liturgical scholarship of the last century.[11] What was key (as will be explored below) in this time was unified orientation in prayer, even if that point is often missed in contemporary conversations. In the Middle Ages, particularly in Western Europe, altars began to be permanently placed against the east wall of the chancel, this being the arrangement with which Dearmer was most familiar as it was the one most churches of his own time had inherited.

Much effort was made in the latter part of the twentieth century to restore the altar to the center of the worship space. When the Roman tradition began to pull altars away from walls and encourage clergy to celebrate facing the people (rather than all worshippers, priest and people, facing east), many Anglicans imported that practice due to the influence of the liturgical movement with its own goal of eliminating the liturgical distance between priest and people. However, it may be suggested that the importation of the Roman change of liturgical orientation has actually exacerbated the problem of the separation of priest from people in the liturgical act. Dearmer's primary biographer, Donald Gray, suggests that Dearmer would have approved of post-Vatican II developments like celebration *ad populum* (facing the people).[12] Increasingly, however, contemporary liturgical scholars and clergy have noticed that the actual

---

11. See Malloy, *Celebrating the Eucharist*, 40.
12. Gray, "British Museum Religion," 2.

change of focus has moved to the priest's hands and actions during Eucharist rather than the entire community—including the priest—all facing the same direction, towards an altar wherein God becomes present. As Malloy rightly notes, the slight pulling out of the altar to put the priest behind it can turn the congregation into an audience.

> In virtually every other instance in our culture where a room is arranged in this way a complex dichotomy is set up between the person facing one way and the group facing the other—think of a courtroom, a classroom, a theater. In each case, the person facing the group holds power, talent, or knowledge to which the rest of the group must listen, attend, and perhaps even submit.[13]

Dearmer himself believed strongly that eastward facing celebration helped emphasize the priesthood of all believers and, as noted earlier, even encouraged the clergy present at the celebration to sit facing east.[14] No less an advocate of twentieth-century liturgical renewal than Louis Weil has also argued recently that churches that are unable to redesign their space so that the community gathers around the altar are better off remaining with eastward celebration, rather than creating a situation where the focal point of the liturgical space is the priest at the head of a long nave where the activities of the clergy become the focus.[15]

Furthermore, the celebration of the liturgy facing the people has resulted in two distinct realities that in some ways seem to have heightened the clericalism of our liturgies, rather than diminished them. First, altars were often simply moved out from the wall instead of the entire liturgical space being redesigned. This turned the area behind the altar into a staging focal point, a place of performance, instead of the original goal of it being the table around which the community gathered, such as when it is placed at the crossing of the church, near or in front of the chancel steps. Second, celebration facing the people has resulted in several common liturgical tics that heighten clericalism and do the opposite of what Dearmer believed was essential for liturgical movement: "to hide the man and to exalt the common priesthood of the Christian congregation."[16] For example, there is the theologically questionable

---

13. Malloy, *Celebrating the Eucharist*, 40.
14. Dearmer, *Parson's Handbook*, 48.
15. Weil, "Anglican Liturgical Future." See also, Shaver, "O Oriens," 451–73. Shaver's work was supervised by Weil along with another noted liturgical scholar, Patrick Malloy. For a Roman Catholic analysis of this question, see Lang, *Turning Towards the Lord*.
16. Dearmer, *Parson's Handbook*, 216.

practice of priests holding up the two halves of the bread after the fraction in an oddly triumphal gesture, as though they have just sacrificed Christ again (as opposed to the reality that we have entered mystically into the presence of Christ's sacrifice made once for all time). Further, facing the people has only multiplied the fussiness of the manual actions of the presider in the eucharistic liturgy, as though their movements are now putting on a show, like Julia Child or a good bartender in Nashville, rather than making visible an ancient prayer.

Regardless of the decision that is made in constructing a new church, there is much on the side of the traditional east facing altar, and sometimes the people simply need to be taught current liturgical scholarship instead of treating the views of the previous generation as dogma. In particular, if a community prefers the more Gothic style of a long nave and chancel with the altar at the end (or, more likely, if one has inherited a space like this), it is often better to retain the practice of the altar in the east (pulled out to ease the work of the altar guild and ministers) but with the priest celebrating in the same direction as the people, facing the east from whence our Lord will return. If that approach is not deemed best for a particular context, then a handsome altar set at a chancel crossing around which the entire congregation gathers is a good and prudent liturgical choice.

Most of this book will assume an eastward facing orientation, as it is this author's contention that this remains a venerable practice. However, that should not discourage the parson who has—either through choice or inherited architecture—a space where the liturgy is celebrated *versus populum*. Almost everything, except for the most ornate use of the three sacred ministers (which are not generally advisable in most smaller parishes anyway), will still translate quite well.

Throughout history, the altar was sometimes of stone and sometimes of wood and generally shaped like a table. It was regarded as too holy to bear anything but the mystic oblation itself, and such objects as were necessary to the offering, including the altar coverings. In more ancient times, it was often veiled by four curtains, which hung from rods between the columns or from the architrave of the ciborium, and thus it stood in mystery and great dignity. In the East this veiling of the table was increased by the use of the solid screen, the iconostasis, which still shuts the people off completely from the altar except when its doors are open. In the West, however, the development was in the opposite direction. The curtain between the altar and the people disappeared altogether, and with the ciborium the necessity for a short altar went also. Thus, the altar lay open to the body of the church (except for the rood screen) in the Middle Ages, though the three remaining curtains continued to enshrine it on the other three sides.

A Bishop in Amice, Albe, Stole, Cope, and Mitre at an "English Altar."[17]

This understanding of an altar enshrined with three curtains came to be known as the "English altar" due to the influence of Dearmer on early twentieth-century Anglicanism. English altars were composed of the dorsal or upper frontal (often replaced by a reredos of stone, metal, or wood behind the altar) and the two riddels on either side. Thus, in this, the primitive idea of treating the altar as a holy object, marked off by enshrining curtains, was restored. Though it should be acknowledged that the use of an English altar was never nearly as widespread in history as Dearmer supposed. And, while it captured the imagination and approach of a small number of churches in the United States (even more in England), it never became the truly dominant way of marking off the altar as a holy space even after the publishing of his handbook.

At the same time, the English altar is still clearly connected with ancient ways of marking of an altar, and in new construction or renovation, it remains a splendid and beautiful choice for the parson to make, in consultation with artists and those leaders in the church who have knowledge, skill, and good taste in such matters. Those who have experienced the use of an English altar often find the beauty of the style overcomes any hesitancy in its adoption.

17. 1913. Photograph by V. K. Blaiklock. Vestments and altar by the Warham Guild.

ALTARS

Altars should be, as nearly as possible, three feet and three inches high and at least deep enough to take a corporal twenty inches square with a foot or so to spare. The length of the altar will depend upon the dimensions and character of the church, and, as the whole dignity of effect depends very much upon the length of the altar, the advice of a competent liturgical architect should be sought. As for the material of which the Holy Table should be made, it may suffice to state that wooden altars were sometimes used before the Reformation, while many stone ones were set up in the eighteenth and early part of the nineteenth centuries in this country. It is best for stone altars to be perfectly plain: no altars should ever be colored or gilt, for they have to be stripped bare in Holy Week. It is convenient for the top of the altar to project two or three inches, as this gives more room below for the feet of the priest.

Whether the altar stands clear of the wall and reredos or not, it is most important, both for the proper vesting of the altar and for its cleanliness, that the back of it should not be covered with gradines or suchlike encumbrances. When there is room, including in an eastward facing altar, it is often still convenient to have a clear passage between the upper frontal or reredos of the high altar and the east wall.

The Chapel, Jesus College, Cambridge, 1835[18]

18. 1835. Showing the retention of the old tradition at the time before the ceremonial revival. The altar is shorter than was customary in the century before the Reformation, and the dorsal is broader and higher; but otherwise there is little change. On the

The high altar generally stands upon three steps, but one or even two of these may well be dispensed within small chancels. The top step or platform on which the altar stands is called the foot pace. Thirty inches is a convenient width from the front of the altar to the edge of the footpace. To increase this width to thirty-six inches makes it more difficult for the priest to kneel down, but if it be much less, the priest is in danger of slipping off, and the proportions of the altar suffer. In an altar where the priest will celebrate facing the people, at least thirty inches, if not thirty-six inches of space, are needed both behind the altar and on either side if the ministers are going to be able to navigate the altar properly without seeming crowded or at risk of toppling over.

In the eastward facing altar, the next step is the deacon's step, and the step below is the eucharistic minister's step,[19] but where space is limited, the eucharistic minister can stand on the pavement below, and this step may be dispensed with. The deacon's and eucharistic minister's steps are generally made too narrow, and thus the ministers are huddled together to their discomfort and to the detriment of the general effect. I would suggest twenty-two inches as the minimum and twenty-five inches where the space admits it. These steps should not be high—six inches is the utmost, and five inches is better.

THE PAVEMENT

The pavement, that is, the level of the sanctuary between the eucharistic minister's step and the communicants' rail, should be of course unbroken and should extend six feet at the very least. The communicants' step may be dispensed with in smaller churches, and its place taken by a movable kneeling bench. Or, in churches where reception while standing is preferred, no kneeling bench may be needed at all.

While we are dealing with this subject, it is necessary to emphasize the fact that many steps, high reredoses, candles, etc., do not increase the

---

altar are two candles and two cushions. Two more candles stand on brackets at the corners of the dorsal.

19. In the original *Parson's Handbook*, Dearmer referred to this as the subdeacon's step. However, as mentioned in the introduction to this handbook, the office of subdeacon is no longer a part of the liturgical practices of the church (and was never truly a part of the prayer book). That said, given the liturgical reforms of the twentieth century, it seems rather clear that much of what was once seen as the role of the subdeacon can be ably fulfilled by what the current canons of the Episcopal Church refer to as the eucharistic minister.

dignity of the altar. Dignity is obtained by proportion, and proportion is the most subtle and difficult secret of the architect's craft; the plainest building may be beautiful if the architect has this sense and knows how to use it. The most elaborate may be (and too often is) ugly if the architect has it not. If the parson interferes with the proportions of the church even by adding to the altar a shelf a few inches high, this action may throw the whole building out of harmony. There are many churches whose east ends are spoiled even by so apparently slight a matter as a row of tall candles. There are others that once had fine and deep chancels, but they are now mean and shallow (for size is purely relative) because a reredos several sizes too large has been put into them. Altars and ornaments that are unduly high not only lessen the depth of the church but also destroy the very object the whole church aimed at—the height and dignity of the sanctuary and altar, because height is so entirely relative and the nice adjustment of measures, so delicate a matter.

But difficult as proportion is to practice, it is not difficult to appreciate. Anyone with a moderately good eye can find this out if the person simply takes away gradines, replaces high candles by low ones, and then goes to the end of the church and looks at the altar. This person will often be surprised to see how the altar has gained in prominence, dignity, and beauty. If one lowers the hangings behind the altar, then the improvement will be even greater. If one lowers the footpace, the effect is greater still. However difficult the parson may find it to rearrange the altar in proper proportion, the priest, the person who engages in this exercise, will at least have learned a lesson in proportion.

THE ALTAR CLOTHS

In the 1979 prayer book, the rubrics on p. 406 require that "the Holy Table is spread with a clean white cloth during the celebration." This is, at the least, a white corporal—though a fair linen that covers the entire altar is the more common interpretation, and judiciously so. But, before going into too much detail on that question, let's begin with the altar cloth most are familiar with: the frontal.

A proper frontal of silk or other decent fabric is most appropriate, extending all the way to the footpace itself. The canons of the Church of England at one time even required the use of a frontal.[20] And while this

---

20. Church of England, *Canons* (1604), no. 82.

requirement is not present in the Episcopal Church, the people will be grateful that the naked altar is not on display. Indeed, when the altar is properly vested, the stripping of the altar on Maundy Thursday becomes all the more powerful an experience. Furthermore, the Puritan fashion of a naked altar runs the risk of destroying that teaching power of the church's seasons, which needs so much to be enforced, and also because the element of color is sadly lacking in modern churches of the more contemporary or non-denominational variety. And no amount of lumber or flooring from the local hardware store nailed up behind a stage at the local megachurch can compete with the beauty of a properly arranged and traditional Christian worship space, complete with a handsome and well-vested altar.

The frontal, if accurately made with a backing of coarse linen, needs no frame. It can be hung by rings from hooks under the altar slab, without any rod or wooden lath; and it may be folded up when not in use and put on a shelf in a broad cupboard. However, the artist who created the frontal should be consulted, as many fabrics (silk, for instance) do not respond well to folding and there is danger of harm coming to the embroidery or metal work. Better is the use of a large chest where the frontals may lie flat without need for folding and from which the frontals can be changed in a moment. Frontals, if they are properly made, look the better for not hanging stiffly, unless they are heavily embroidered, in which case of course they cannot be folded and must be kept in a case. Plain fabrics should seldom be used, and figured silks or mixtures of silk and wool or other materials with bold designs are preferable.

It requires experience—as well as natural gifts—to know how a material will work out when it is taken out of a shop and set up in the peculiar light of a particular church. To avoid disaster (and many frontals are nothing less than ecclesiastical calamities), amateurs should only attempt frontals under the advice of those with significant experience.

The frontal should have a short fringe along the bottom and preferably at the sides as well. Fringes are nearly always made so vague and undecided that their effect is lost. If the pictures in the National Gallery and other collections are studied, it will be found that the old fringes on frontals look seemly because they are of bright and varied colors, boldly and distinctly spaced, and no attempt is made to work in the colors of the material to be fringed. For an average-sized altar, the fringe may be two inches deep at the bottom; but for the sides it should not be deeper than one or one-and-a-half inch. Sometimes one still sees two strips of other material and color sewn on to the end of a frontal. Many people came to look upon them as necessary, but they are mainly an expedient way to save money, and the frontal is generally better without them. On the other hand, very beautiful frontals can be made of alternate panels of different color and design.

The frontlet (often mistakenly called the superfrontal) is a practical necessity for hiding the suspension of the frontal when the traditional manner of hanging the frontal is used. For convenience in poor churches, it may generally be red in color, as that color will work well with the varied colors of the frontal throughout the seasons of the church year, but any color is admissible. It does not need to be changed with the frontal, although, of course, a particular frontal will often look best with a particular frontlet. It should never be of lace, nor have any lace upon it. Often it is made too deep. For an ordinary altar, a depth of seven and one half inches, including fringe, or even less, is sufficient. The fringe should be about one and one half of an inch (no deeper), and should be laid on the lower part of the frontlet, not hanging below it. The frontlet should not extend over the top or round the sides of the altar. It should be tacked to one of the under linen cloths, like an apparel. Sometimes it may be found convenient that the linen used for this purpose should be of a dark-blue color. In any case it should be stout, and the coarser it is, the more useful it will be in keeping the other cloths and the hangings from slipping. If the altar stands clear from the wall, the linen cloth can fall a few inches over the back, being held there by small brass hooks fitting into it or even by three to six leaden weights or an iron rod fixed in the hem. Velcro can be used, though the removal of the frontlet will thereby cause such a racket that anyone praying in the church will be jolted out of whatever spiritual state they thought they had found. If any shelves or steps rest on the back of the altar, which is a very objectionable practice, then the method of fixing the cloth with drawing pins or brass hooks seems to be unavoidable, unless weights are laid on the altar itself.

It is a very ancient custom that there should be three linen cloths on the top of the altar, the object no doubt being to provide against accidents with the chalice, as well as to secure a smooth and substantial surface. The custom of making, with the frontlet, a permanent velvet cover to the altar is not to be commended.

The outer cloth (the fair linen) should be of good firm linen, long enough to reach down to within a few inches of the ground at each end. It may have five crosses embroidered in linen thread on it, as a quincunx, or any other suitable device in white or color, and it may also have embroidery at the ends, or it may be altogether plain. The ends may be hemmed, but there is no English precedent for any lace on them. Furthermore, hemmed looks far better than fringed, as fringes often are simply inviting trouble. It should be exactly the depth of the altar (front to back) and none of it should hang over the frontlet.

The two undercloths should be exactly the size of the top of the altar, and quite plain. One of these is the cerecloth, which is customarily waxed to prevent liquids from seeping through. The other one of them may, as we have seen, also be tacked on to the frontlet. It is an ancient custom that no other material but linen shall cover the top of the altar. All the linen cloths may be of simple woven fabric, and undercloths especially should be neither thin nor smooth. The hem of the undercloths may be about one inch, that of the fair linen one-and-a-half inches at the sides and three inches at the ends.

It is cleaner and seemlier to follow the old custom of removing the linen after service, especially the outer cloth of an altar not in daily use. In churches that are at all subject to damp, this becomes absolutely necessary. The cloths can be taken on to a wooden roller and put away in a drawer. In any case the Lord's table should be protected by a coverlet. This coverlet should be exactly the same size as the top of the altar, unless the fair linen cloth is left on, in which case it may be twelve inches longer. It may be of silk (say a good yellow or green), lined with blue linen, or of a fabric like the older red American cloth[21] lined with blue linen and bound with blue silk ribbon, or simply of colored linen unlined. It should not be white but should be a decidedly different color, either in lining or fabric, so that it is not accidentally left on the altar for the celebration of mass.

While gradines have become common, they were an innovation of the sixteenth century. The general custom before then was for the two candlesticks to be placed on the altar itself and not on a gradine behind the altar. The true problem with a gradine is that they spoil the scale of the church and hide the reredos, or else disconnect it from the altar. If a gradine has to be tolerated at all, it should be a single low shelf only. The altar should not look like a sideboard, and it cannot be too often

---

21. This type of fabric was popular in the nineteenth and early twentieth centuries. It was a durable, waterproof, and washable material made by coating cotton cloth with linseed oil and other substances in order to create a smooth and shiny surface. It's durability and waterproof properties made it a popular choice for tablecloths and shelf linings. There are several fabrics and materials available today with the same properties that are well suited to this purpose.

remembered that the altar itself and not any of its adjuncts should be the central feature of a church. When a gradine is ugly or cold and difficult to remove, it might perhaps be temporarily covered with a piece of really good tapestry, which of course need not be changed except in Lent.

The other ornaments on the altar are a cross or crucifix, cushions or a small stand to hold the missal, and two candlesticks. Reliquaries, images, and plates were also formerly used in some cases for decking the altars. It was generally the custom to remove the cross and candlesticks from the altar after service, especially when they were small and of precious metal.

THE CROSS

A cross was sometimes set on the altar before the Reformation, but it was by no means the rule (even though nowadays many seem to consider a cross on the altar or the gradine above it to be a necessity). Remember that the best and most historic use of a cross in the church is the holy rood. In cases where a painting forms the altarpiece, the cross is often better dispensed with (even where there is room for a small cross below the picture), especially in the case of minor altars. Further, the appropriateness of using a cross where the crucifixion forms part of the altarpiece is more than questionable. Under no circumstances should a cross be placed on the altar when it would stand in front of a picture or the figures of a sculptured reredos. The idea that an altar is incomplete (or "Protestant") without a cross needs to be strenuously combated. Indeed, although altar crosses and crucifixes are certainly commonly in use, they are not the only image that may be well suited for use at an altar. For example, it may be urged that the resurrection or the ascension or our Lord in glory or as the good shepherd could be the prominent subject behind the altar.

THE CANDLESTICKS

The use of a row of six candlesticks on the altar, or on a shelf or gradine behind it, is a Roman Catholic practice, and one that has no basis in the traditions of Anglican Christianity. From the beginning of the thirteenth century on to our own time, every declaration on the subject has mentioned the two lights on the altar only, and to this ancient and universal use of two lights, at the most, every known representation bears witness. Indeed, though other lights are used around the altar, our Eastern Orthodox siblings still hold to the tradition of only two candles on the altar itself. Anyone who takes the time to consult historical portraits of altars online or in a library will see that there are many paintings that give fine typical examples of very rich altars that use this approach.

Now the instinct which led the church in the great ages of architecture and craftsmanship to use altar lights in this way was a true one; for an altar with two candlesticks upon it is more majestic and more beautiful than an altar with more than two. Furthermore, a row of candles hides the reredos or upper frontal, which ought to be one of the richest and most lovely things in the church. The miserable way in which priceless masterpieces are hidden in churches by tall candlesticks and tawdry sham flowers is a truly unfortunate practice.

Some people have been misled by the Sarum Consuetudinary, which orders eight candles for the great feasts. But these candles stood round about the altar,[22] and only two were upon it; and this represents the utmost to which even a gorgeous cathedral like Salisbury went in the matter of altar lights. Another cause of error has been the six lights which stood *in eminencia*; but these were for the rood, relics, and images, and were not altar lights at all, nor were they in any way connected with a shelf or gradine.

The Salisbury rules are useful as illustrating the very general custom of using additional lights round about the altar on the greater days; but they are not, of course, in the least binding upon us. For (1) they give the local use of Salisbury Cathedral, and we know that other places did not adopt all the ceremonial when they adopted the books of that church; and (2) they give a cathedral use, and we know that parish churches could not and did not adopt all the customs of their cathedral churches. Indeed, in the Sarum books themselves we find that in the customary, a book drawn up for parochial use, all directions as to lights are omitted.

At the same time, it is certain that parish churches, at the time to which we are referring, had lights around the altar in addition to the two on the altar (though sometimes there were none on the altar at all).

---

22. "Da uta e vesperas et ad missam ocot debet cereos administrare, unumquemque cereum unius libre ad minus, circa altare, et duos cereos coram ymagine beate virginis marie: ad matutinas totidem."—"In the evenings, he must lay eight candles, each candle of one pound at least, around the altar, and two candles before the image of the Blessed Virgin Mary: for the mornings as many." Dearmer, *Parson's Handbook*, 88.

There were very often two standards on the pavement (not placed on an altar step, as we sometimes see them), and sometimes four. And often there were additional lights, varying in number with the rank of the feast and the means of the church, placed on brackets or beams near the altar, especially in the larger churches. One very beautiful method was to have sconces for candles on the top of the four poles that sometimes stood at the four corners of the altar to carry the riddels. A church may therefore have (1) two lights on the altar; (2) two standards on the pavement or four if the sanctuary is large enough for their comely arrangement without overcrowding (as is seldom the case); (3) other lights near but not behind the altar (preferably two or four on the rods or pillars for the riddels) for use on the principal feasts; and (4) others hanging from the roof.

Tall candles are not at all necessary and often spoil the appearance of the altar. The height of candles and candlesticks should be settled by the architect. The best rule is that the candle should not be much longer than the candlestick and should be burnt down to within two inches of the socket. In our own time, churches regularly make use of plastic candles filled with oil. And while this convenience may be permitted, it is an increase in the use of things that simply are not true in worship, as the oil-filled plastic candle is playing pretend at being a true candle and those who attend the divine liturgy are being made to think there are candles on the altar when there plainly are not. Simple training on the proper care of pure wax candles may involve a bit more work, but the authenticity in worship that is gained will be well worth it. Nothing can be more beautiful and dignified on an altar than the simple white lines of two wax candles. And if oil-filled plastic candles must be used, there is certainly no reason for them to be several times larger than the candlestick, as their height will never diminish. Slightly more than the height of the candlestick (or, at most, one-and-a-half times the height) will give a much better sense of proportion to the space.

For many years after the Reformation candlesticks were made low and broad, even on the Continent, and unless they are so made there would often be a mess from the wax. The natural tendency of tasteless people is to make candles, and everything else they can lay their hands upon, as tall and obtrusive as possible. But let the parson once burn the candles till they are quite short and then replace them by a pair three feet high, and no one will fail to see that the altar has lost by the exchange.

It is always better to get a few good things than many bad ones. It is also better for poor churches to buy a good thing in simple material than a bad thing in more expensive material. For instance, if cheap standard candlesticks are wanted, they can be painted a good color for not too much cost. But if metal ones are wanted, a good price must be paid and a skilled craftsman employed. For altar use, also, wooden candlesticks can be turned and painted or gilt, where economy is an object. Standards should be weighty, and about five feet high; if there are two only, they should stand on the pavement in front of the steps and well beyond the line of the altar on either side.

CUSHIONS AND MISSAL STANDS

Cushions were generally used for supporting the missal, and they were common in Spain and Austria. Missal stands or desks, however, were also used sometimes; wood is perhaps better for this purpose than brass, which is cold to the hand, and in the cheap forms supplied by the shops, often scratches the book. A missal stand may be covered with a strip of silk brocade or tapestry of any good color, which should be long enough to cover the desk itself, and to hang nearly to the bottom behind. As cushions survived in the English Church through all the bad times, it seems a pity to drop them and a wonderful idea to recover them. As liturgical scholar Patrick Malloy pointed out not that long ago, in many congregations the most dominant item on the altar is the large and ornamented missal stand—when the most dominant item on the altar should be the bread and wine.[23] A cushion softens the view of the book and ensures the focus of the people goes in the right direction. They are also extremely convenient. And, if made of beautiful material, they add a pleasant touch of color and warmth to the general effect. The cushion can be left at the end of the altar out of service time. Very rich ones may be provided with an extra (but not ugly) cover to protect them from the dust—plain silk or linen of a rich color would be a good material for this. The size of the cushions might be eighteen inches square; they should be stuffed with down (not too lightly) and made up with cord in the usual way. They may have tassels.

---

23. Malloy, *Celebrating the Eucharist*, 23.

THE BOOKS

The books for the altar include the Book of Common Prayer (or, more commonly, the altar missal version of the prayer book) and a Gospel book, each richly bound. The Gospel book especially so since it is carried in procession and set on the altar. Five or six silk markers are a convenience in the altar missal, and so are tags marked to the pages at the beginning of the service, at the creed, at the *sursum corda*, at the proper preface, at the canon of mass, and then at the post-communion prayer at the end of the service.

The custom of using two embroidered markers, which are changed with the seasons, is a piece of fancy ceremonial that does not improve the condition of the book. On the whole, the most convenient plan is to have five or six rather narrow markers (e.g., half-inch ribbon), which may be separate from or sewed into the binding. These can be, if it is desired, of different colors (e.g., yellow, red, blue, and green). The ribbon for that portion of the service is then turned across the page before the book is set on the altar. If there are to be any extra collects, other markers are turned across the pages that contain them.

Flower vases are of late introduction, though flowers themselves (not on the altar) are a very ancient form of decoration. However, care should be taken that flowers are removed after a day or two. Anything like decaying vegetable matter, with its taint and slime, or wormy flowerpots, should of course not be tolerated near God's board or anywhere else in the church. Flowers should never be allowed to remain through the week. By far, the best plan is to remove them on the Monday if they have been set up on the Saturday and to give them to the sick and poor. The use of artificial flowers runs contrary to the gospel principle of authenticity and must be soundly rejected.

It must also be remembered that, in these days when many people are occupied about our altars, the tendency is always to lose simplicity; and the loss of simplicity is the destruction of dignity. A great deal of money that ought to be spent on necessary ornaments is usually wasted on flowers. Flowers are not necessary to worship, beautiful as they are, and they can easily be overdone. The idea that there must always be flowers on the altar except in Advent and Lent should be discouraged. Where they are used, it seems best to let them be the free offering of the people and not to buy them. Their only traditional use is for festivals and, then, not on the altar. The altar ought to be rich and beautiful in itself and ought not to need flowers to make it pleasant to the eye. If the altar is not beautiful and dignified before a single ornament is set on it, nothing will make it so.

A certain ugly shape of brass vase (decorated with sacred emblems at a slightly higher cost) has become almost an article of faith in some churches. The use of plain glass vases will help to remove the hard effect produced by these brazen jars and so will good earthenware, such as can be got by skilled artists. Tin shapes to hold flowers need only be mentioned to be condemned. Flowers should be arranged lightly, freely, and gracefully. Intelligent people hardly need reminding that, if flowers are used, there is no conceivable reason why they should follow the color of the frontal or be tortured into emblematic shapes. The parson should set one's face against the use, for instance, of white flowers only on a white day. Let the flowers be of red and yellow and blue and white with plenty of green leaves—even better, drawn from what is in bloom in the given season—and the white frontal will be all the more significant, while the church itself will look more beautiful.

THE REREDOS AND RIDDLES

Of the reredos little need be said here, as it is a concern of the architect. There is no part on which the richest color is more needed than over the altar, and really beautiful reredoses could be made for a quarter of the cost of the badly carved and uncolored stonework that defaces many of our churches and cathedrals. The simple upper frontal or dorsal of silk or other material forms the most inexpensive, and for many churches the most effective, backing to the altar. It should be about the same size as the lower frontal, and should not obscure the east window; it may be changed in a general way with the seasons—e.g., for Advent, Christmastide, Lent, Eastertide, and after Pentecost day. High dorsals and canopies should not be attempted without professional advice; and there is no space for high dorsals in most churches. In those modern churches that have a high wall space behind the altar, it is best to avoid the uncomfortable blankness, inseparable from a lofty dorsal, by still using a low upper frontal and treating the wall separately, either with hangings extending its whole breadth or with white distemper or with good painting. Canopies, when they are used, should be suspended over the whole width of the altar and not merely over the back of it.

The riddels, or curtains at the sides of the altar, should project at right angles to the wall and reach at least as far as the front of the altar. The rods should be strong so as not to bend in the slightest degree with the weight of the curtains; wrought iron is a better and stronger material than brass and cannot tarnish. The rods may have sconces for candles at their ends, and these may be of iron also, or of pewter, copper, or brass—in which case they may be lacquered since they are not easy to clean. Sometimes the riddels are hung between four colonnettes or posts that stand at the four corners of the altar—an excellent arrangement. The curtains should not be of a shabby material or washy in color, as they so often are, but should be of the richest tapestry or brocade. They should be replaced by hangings of unbleached linen in Lent, and they may be changed with the dorsal.

The riddels will hang all the better, and remain cleaner, if they are two or three inches off the ground. Their proper use is to enclose and enshrine the altar and its ornaments; and much of their beauty and dignity depends upon this use being maintained. They should never be spread open but should be parallel to the ends of the altar; the spreading of "wings" behind the altar is due mainly to our hankering after vulgar display. Nothing spoils an altar more than this pushing back of the riddels. Of course, if the riddels are set square in the proper way, they cannot be very high.

OTHER ITEMS OF NOTE

The credence table should be on the south side of the altar and, if there is room, against the south rather than the east wall. It is seemly to cover it with a linen cloth, but there is no need for placing a cross or candles upon it.

It has become quite common now for a tabernacle or aumbry to be in use in the church—the older fears and prejudices of the catholic traditions thankfully waning in our churches. One may be placed in the wall on the east end of the church, central to the altar. Or, alternatively, one may be placed in a side wall of the sanctuary or a nearby chapel.

Lamps can be hung before altars. One or three are generally enough. There is no requirement for the use of seven. Pure olive oil or specially prepared oil (which is cheaper and works just as fine) may be used. Floating wicks are the most convenient.

Altar rails were introduced in Archbishop Laud's time to protect the altars against irreverence and to prevent their removal into the nave. These rails were latticed "to prevent dogs from desecrating the holy table, as episcopal injunctions explain."[24] Oftentimes, they are very much in the way, because architects are apt to place them too near the holy table and to make the entrance too small. In some cases, they can be moved to a more convenient distance. The loss of chancel screens and gates has made the rails particularly important in our own time as they are one of the few remaining items that properly set off the altar and sanctuary from the rest of the liturgical space. A double step for the communicants is a source of perpetual discomfort. Where one exists, the rails must still be fixed on the pavement itself as if there were only one step, otherwise the communicants are forced to kneel on a lower level than that on which the ministers stand, which causes many an aching back to the clergy. The rails should not be more than two feet and three inches in height, and rails should be set back about twelve inches from the front edge of the step.

The piscina is necessary. It enables the water that has been used for rinsing the priest's hands after the ablutions, as well as that used for rinsing the purificators and altar vessels, to be conveniently disposed of. The ablutions themselves may also be poured into it. The drain should run on to the soil outside. The shelf, which is sometimes found above it, is for the cruets to stand on.

The alms basins are an essential part of the church, and the prayer book requires that the people's offerings of money or other gifts be carried forward with the bread and wine, so a seemly and handsome container is most appropriate. It should be noted that the alms basin is, of course, placed on the altar with the bread and wine and should be left there throughout the eucharistic prayer. There is no authority for removing the monetary offerings of the people as though they might contaminate the celebration of Communion. Quite the opposite, the rubric requires the placing of the alms on the altar[25] because they are a part of the people's offering and there they should remain, with holiness and reverence, throughout the duration of the service, until the altar is cleared. In churches or chapels where the altar is too small to hold the alms basin, eucharistic vessels, and altar missal, the basin should be set

---

24. Hatchett, *American Prayer Book*, 384.
25. *1979 Book of Common Prayer*, 333 and 361.

on a credence table near the altar. Though not ideal, this is preferable to removing it entirely.

The sedilia may be hung with some good material, and cushions may be placed on the seats. Chairs, stools, or benches will also be necessary for the servers. Where there are no structural sedilia, chairs must be placed for the ministers as well, but these should be of such a shape that the vestments can easily fall over their backs. In building a new church it is often convenient for the seats in the sedilia to be made movable, to be in fact wooden chairs with plain low backs, standing in a recess.

The carpets and rugs are far too important a factor in the color scheme of a church to be left to individual whims; they should be chosen under advice. Besides the rug in front of the altar, it is often advisable to spread other carpets or matting on the pavement to prevent the danger of the ministers slipping; in this way, too, glaring tiles can often be advantageously hidden. A long padded strip of good carpet may be laid along the place where the communicants kneel.

Flat cushions or mats for the servers are a convenience and may be provided for each server at every point where they will have to kneel. But nothing of the kind is required for the priest at the altar; the footpace where the priest stands should be covered only by the carpet. The mat one sometimes used to see in the midst of the footpace is a great nuisance and has come down only as a relic of the hassock used when the priest knelt at the north end.

3

Colors, Vestments, and Ornaments

LITURGICAL COLORS

When it comes to vestments and ornaments, it will clear the ground if we consider first the question of colors. Although there is still great confusion on this subject and almost universal misunderstanding, the question is a simple one. The use of liturgical colors for different seasons and different classes of saints' days, though very useful and beautiful, is of comparatively late development and is almost wholly Western. It arose by slow degrees early in the Middle Ages. But in the average pre-Reformation parish church there was no such hard and fast rule about colors as we are accustomed to now. People moved little from place to place in those days, and even the strangest local peculiarities caused no confusion.

Liturgical colors may be said to have reached their most elaborate development in France and then in Spain at a somewhat later date, where the color customs of the cathedral churches were developed and systematized for diocesan use with great elaboration only (alas!) to succumb to ultramontane uniformity, which imposed the Roman use upon unwilling people in comparatively recent times. Some of the English cathedrals, such as Wells, Exeter, and Salisbury, had more or less defined color sequences, which were perhaps followed by the richer parish churches, but there seems to have been great freedom of practice. The general rule seems rather clear: the best vestments are used on the highest feasts and older and faded ones on ordinary Sundays, simple feasts, and ferial days.

Taking England as a whole, we find that certain colors were generally used for certain purposes; people always used plain unbleached linen (it was a rough off-white or gray fabric), marked with crosses and other devices during the first four weeks of Lent and red during the last two weeks of Lent, thus marking in the most appealing and significant way, by the use of deep red frontals and vestments, the time when the church turns to contemplate the sorrow and the triumph of the cross. Hence, we find that the color on Good Friday was nearly always red. A bright white seems to have been very general during the paschal season, which included the Day of Pentecost (traditionally known as Whitsunday, as it would be the last use of white for some time), though red was prescribed in certain places, seemingly because it was the paschal color in those places. Indeed, the use of white on the Day of Pentecost can serve to make it clear that it is, at its core, the fiftieth day of Easter. On the other hand, the use of red on Pentecost also breaks up the season of Easter from Trinity Sunday. Either approach has merit, and so the question really is how the parson best communicates this seasonal change to the people. Red was used for apostles, martyrs, and evangelists. White was used for St. Mary and for virgins but not, as at Rome, for all saints who were not martyrs. In England, yellow, green, or blue, or sometimes a mixture, was used for confessors. Blue—the color of the sky—was used in some places for St. Michael. The general practice of the West rather inclined to the use of blue for saints of the old law and for holy women, such as St. Anne and St. Mary Magdalene, though rules varied. There is good English authority for using blue in Advent and Septuagesima[1] and even on the first four Sundays (not weekdays) in Lent. Before the Reformation, England was not particular about the Sunday or the ferial color; and, although

---

1. Septuagesima is so named because it falls seventy days before Easter Sunday. Its use can be noted as early as the sixth century Council of Orleans, which noted "many pious ecclesiastics and lay persons of the primitive Church used to fast seventy days before Easter, and their fast was called, therefore, Septuagesima, a name which was afterwards retained to distinguish this Sunday from others." Goffine, *Devout Instructions*, 75. This observance was removed in the liturgical reforms of Vatican II among our Roman Catholic siblings, and the Lutherans soon followed suit in their own revisions. See USCCB, "Requisites," VI.346; *Lutheran Book of Worship*, 9–12. Though it still exists in the 1662 Book of Common Prayer in England, it was removed in their revisions that led to the most recent edition of *Common Worship* and in our 1979 Book of Common Prayer. Its mention in the pages that follows is to explain why a change in color would have occurred before Ash Wednesday, but one should not take it as advice that Septuagesima be restored, as doing so would be contrary to the current authorized book in the Episcopal Church.

the Sarum Missal prescribed red for all Sundays out of Eastertide, this represented the more primitive use, which developed as time went on. It is a mistake to think that green was not used in England; it was very commonly used, on Sundays as well as weekdays. It is interesting to note that, even in the eighteenth and nineteenth centuries, there was still a color sequence—though a very poor one—in England.

To come to the practical question of what colors are to be used now, it is at once evident that very great liberty with regard to color is perfectly legitimate and the prayer book is wholly silent on this question. The old custom was fairly definite as to Lent: unbleached linen was used till Passion Sunday (the fifth Sunday in Lent), and then during the Passiontide, red. Feasts of confessors were kept in yellow, green, or blue, as has been said above. There is ample precedent for the present use of blue or violet in Advent; there is no need to make red the Sunday color; and if modern custom has tended to define the ferial color as green, instead of using a variety of faded old vestments, this is reasonable.

There used to be strenuous controversy about colors, but the points were really unimportant and are easily cleared up by a little common sense. In view of the undoubted diversity of usage throughout the Anglican tradition, no one can say that we are compelled to use the meaningless uniformity of red on all Sundays outside the paschal season required by the old rules of Salisbury Cathedral. No doubt had the word "Sarum" not been so stressed, the loyal Anglican clergy would have used the phrase "English use," and the hitherto untried plan of honestly obeying the prayer book would have become general, to the honor of the church and the confusion of her enemies. The misfortune was that many clergy in the twentieth century thought they must either be "Sarum" or "Roman" in approach, and the many difficulties of the former use drove them, as they thought, to the latter.

Putting on one side the fact that a rigid adherence to peculiar customs of modern Rome may not be required of those whose only oath is to the prayer book, let me point out why the so-called Sarum use is also undesirable. As noted in the introduction, even in the ornaments rubric of the 1662 prayer book, the one that stands as the bedrock of Anglican worship, we are not referred to the diocese of Salisbury of the thirteenth or fourteenth century, but to England of the sixteenth. And we know that, although the Sarum books were adopted very generally in other dioceses, all the details of the Sarum ceremonial were not. The Sarum books do not tell us about the colors for certain days. Consequently, the so-called Sarum uses of the previous centuries are partly made up from the fancy of nineteenth-century ritualists. Their idea was that only those four colors casually mentioned in the printed Sarum missals were used—white, red, yellow, and (in some manuscripts) black. But the inventories show that in Salisbury Cathedral itself there were, in 1222, vestments of *violette, purpurea,* and *de serico indico* (of blue silk), although the manuscript of the Consuetudinary (ca. 1210–46) mentions red and white only. In 1462 there were altar cloths of purple, blue and black, white, and blue; chasubles of purple and blue; and altar cloths and vestments of red and green. In 1536, three green copes and five green chasubles, with tunicles, etc. In the diocese also of Salisbury we have evidence that green was largely used in parish churches as well as in the cathedral.[2]

It is clear, then, that those colors, violet and green, which some have thought to be peculiarly Roman, were certainly used in Salisbury Cathedral in the fifteenth and sixteenth centuries, and violet and blue, at least in the thirteenth; and they were not only used there, but throughout the diocese of Sarum and throughout Great Britain.

The oldest English color sequence that has come down to us is that of Lichfield, which occurs in the statutes of Bishop Pateshull, ca. 1240, and is different in several ways than the supposed Sarum use outlined above. Briefly, it is as follows:

- Advent and Lent—black
- Passiontide—red
- Christmas Day—the most precious vestments
- Eastertide and Whitsun Week, St. John the Evangelist, Holy Name (then called Circumcision), Feasts of the Blessed Virgin Mary, Virgins, St. Michael—white
- Epiphany, Apostles, Martyrs, Holy Cross, Beheading of St. John the Baptist—red
- All Saints, Confessors, St. John Baptist—varied (i.e., mixed colors or shot silk)
- St. Mary Magdalene, Epiphany to Lent, Whitsuntide till Advent—*according to the will of the sacrist*, when the service is on Sunday

---

2. Dearmer, *Parson's Handbook*, 106–7.

COLORS, VESTMENTS, AND ORNAMENTS

Above all, there being no hard and fast rules, the principle that prevailed even then, though, was that "all things must be modified according to the means of the church."[3]

In this early sequence, it will at once be seen that the idea of a definite scheme of liturgical colors is not as yet fully developed. There is no dominical and ferial color, but the vestments for these days are left to the will of the sacristan. The black prescribed for Advent and Lent, according to the usage of the period, would have included violet or blue or gray—the latter likely being the Lenten "white" of the inventories. Indeed, the true reason for the difference between blue and violet is not the difference between English Christianity and that of Rome on the Continent but is the difference between the fading of the black dyes to either a dark blue or violet in each location. These prescriptions as to color were most liberally interpreted in practice, and outside the Cathedral, one may doubt whether any one attempted to follow them, especially at this early date.

Throughout the history of English Christianity, there was a good deal of liberty, particularly in the colors employed upon Sundays and weekdays in the ferial seasons. Indeed, there was in practice no ferial color because just before the Reformation the ferial mass was rarely said in parish churches, various votive masses and saint's day masses taking its place. Except in cathedrals, the service of the season after Epiphany and after Pentecost was of little importance, its place having been usurped by the cultus of the saints and by votive masses.

The Book of Common Prayer, however, has restored to us the service of the season—the dominical and ferial service, which is now, under the modern rite, a matter of vastly greater importance than it was on the eve of the Reformation. But what is its color? The importance of the ferial service under the prayer book scheme demands that it should have a distinctive color. The Sunday mass was red according to the rules of Salisbury and Wells Cathedrals; but those rules were not of authority elsewhere, and we are not told what the color was for an unoccupied weekday, even in those places. A more serviceable indication of a distinctively ferial color is to be found in the rules of Exeter, which order green, and in the color sequences in the fifteenth-century manuscript pontificals belonging to London and Canterbury, which also order green.[4] There is indeed no evidence that the sequences in the pontificals were

---

3. Statutes of Pateshull, cited by Dearmer, *Parson's Handbook*, 108.
4. Dearmer, *Parson's Handbook*, 112.

intended to be for more than the actual use of the bishops for whom they were written. But they are a good indication of what leading authorities felt was a suitable color for the seasons after the Epiphany and Pentecost, and this use of green is clear and intelligible, besides being very usual at the present day.

The Lenten Array[5]

A few words must now be said about the Lenten colors. The use of plain white unbleached linen marked with red or black crosses has already been alluded to and is known properly as Lenten array (since it refers not just to a color alone but also to the veiling of images, crosses, and crucifixes with unbleached linen). This use is akin to that of the Lenten

5. St. Mary-the-Virgin, Primrose Hill, 1904. Frontal, frontlet, dorsal, or upper frontal, and riddels of brown holland; frontal ornamented with roses and drops of red linen applique, and like the frontlet fringed with red flax. Cross veiled in fine linen of a toned white, tied with red ribbon and with a cross of the same. The unusually large triptych is closed, the outside of its leaves being painted the same toned white. Sanctuary walls hung with brown holland curtains. Other ornaments include two candles on the altar, four on the riddel-posts, two standards, and three sanctuary lamps.

veils for pictures, images, crosses, which in England are generally white. Those rules that prescribed black or violet are, at the utmost, fulfilled only by the use of colored vestments and altar frontal on Sundays, and even on Sundays the white is used by some churches. This use of unbleached linen for Lent was practically universal in the sixteenth century and earlier—it was in fact the one color use to which there was hardly any exception. Plain white stuff, fustian, linen, or canvas, with crosses, roses, or other devices of red or purple, was used to cover pictures and ornaments, as well as for vestments, for frontals, riddels, and other hangings.[6] The parson who tries it will find that it is as popular and as readily understood now as it was then.

In churches arranged and decorated well, this Lenten array looks extremely good if care is exercised in the choice of a good tone of white (such as unbleached linen is) and of the devices embroidered on or applied to the hangings. These devices should not be overdone; indeed, with the materials now available they may well be omitted and decoration confined, e.g., to narrow red linen stripes on the frontal. This practice has the great advantage of distinguishing Lent from Advent (a season to which it has little resemblance) and from the season between the Feast of the Epiphany and Ash Wednesday.

The use of violet for Advent does not of course mean the unpleasant color (so remote from the color of the violet flower) at present provided by so many vendors. There is no such restriction as to tints, and a rather dark blue, or even a bright blue, or purple, is equally suitable for Advent.

For the great feasts of the incarnation and paschal mystery, as well as other principal feasts of the church, the use of festal vestments has much to commend it. In many churches, this has been subsumed by the same white used for other feast days, which has the unfortunate effect of diminishing the key importance of Christmas and Easter (along with the other principal feasts of Ascension Day, Trinity Sunday, All Saints' Day, and the Epiphany). If festal vestments are procured, they should be the very best vestments a church owns and contain a good deal of bright and joyful color. In particular, cloth of gold may be used and is an excellent choice. White silk brocades hardly look rich enough, at least for the frontal. Then, the use of white on other lesser feast days give those days their own feel and experience apart from the principal feasts of the church.

---

6. Dearmer, *Parson's Handbook*, 113.

While allowing the optional use of violet for Passiontide red (which is an obvious convenience in the case of poorer churches, who might choose violet for Lent through Passiontide), I would plead for the use of a dark red (often crimson or what is known as oxblood red, with black or dark blue orphreys) at this season on these grounds. It is more in accordance with liturgical propriety to change the colors at Passiontide—all uses excepting that of Rome and a few others did so. It is more instructive to the people, and a most useful and beautiful enrichment of the color sequence. Even the pontificals of Canterbury and London left a place for this red. Violet was to be used "till Maundy Thursday, or, according to some churches, till Passion Sunday." The Exeter sequence, which is so close to those pontificals, also gives violet "to Maundy Thursday, or, according to some, until Passion Sunday." Later, in mentioning red it says, "according to some, within Passion week (and on Maundy Thursday if the bishop does not celebrate), red must be used," and again, "on Maundy Thursday, when the bishop consecrates the chrism, white, otherwise red." Salisbury, Lichfield, and Wells all order red only. The inventories prove that the Passiontide red was almost universally used in the sixteenth century.[7]

Little departure, then, is needed from the color sequences that have become general in the Anglican Communion during the twentieth century. But as the common sequence admits of enrichment for churches that can afford a larger number of colors, I give the following as a normal sequence of six colors (or seven, if a distinction be made between festal vestments and white) for use in such churches. That sequence would be as follows:

1. Blue
2. Festal (that is, the very best vestments that a church has—often white but can be an even more beautiful set, usually cloth of gold)
3. Pentecost red (a brighter red than what is used in Passiontide—for use on Pentecost and feasts of martyrs)
4. Green
5. Lenten array
6. Passiontide red
7. White

---

7. Dearmer, *Parson's Handbook*, 114.

COLORS, VESTMENTS, AND ORNAMENTS

Poorer churches would naturally at first keep within a narrower limit. In the sequence that follows, the preferred color is listed first, and the alternate is listed second, if there be one. A normal English sequence of colors would be as follows:

- Advent—blue or violet
- Christmas to Epiphany (including Holy Name)—festal or white, alternatively, festal on Christmas Day and Epiphany Day and white for the rest of the days of Christmastide
- After Epiphany—green
- Lent—Lenten array
- Passiontide (Palm Sunday–Maundy Thursday)—Passiontide red
- Good Friday—bare altar or purple
- The fifty days of Easter (including Ascension)—festal or white, alternatively, festal on Easter Day and Ascension and white for the rest of the days of Eastertide
- Rogation Days[8]—blue
- Day of Pentecost (Whitsuntide)—red or white, if the older tradition is preferred, unless festal is continued
- Trinity Sunday—festal or white
- Sundays after Pentecost—green
- All Saints' Day—festal or white
- Feasts of Apostles, Evangelists (with the exception of John), Martyrs (including St. James of Jerusalem, St. Stephen, and Holy Innocents)—Pentecost red
- Feast of St. John the Evangelist, Nativity of St. John the Baptist, Presentation, Annunciation, Visitation, Transfiguration, St. Joseph, St. Mary Magdalene, St. Mary the Virgin, St. Michael and All Angels, Independence Day, Thanksgiving Day—white

---

8. Rogation Days, noted in the 1979 prayer book as traditionally observed on Monday, Tuesday, and Wednesday before Ascension Day, have sadly fallen out of use. Given the increased awareness of the importance of climate change and stewardship of the earth, one hopes for their fuller restoration, along with the traditional color that should be used. See *1979 Book of Common Prayer*, 18.

- Dedication of a Church[9]—festal or white
- Patronal Feast—color of the saint
- Vigils (excluding, of course, the Great Vigil of Easter)—blue
- Baptisms and marriages—white
- Confirmations and ordinations—Pentecost red or white
- Funerals and Commemorations—festal, white, or black

VESTMENTS

With regard to all ornaments and vestments, one precaution is most necessary. The parson must make it clearly understood that the church will not accept a single thing for the church unless the advice has first been sought of a competent person who overlooks the decoration of the church. The final decision rests with the priest, but a priest will be grateful to cultivate a relationship with a true liturgical artist (meaning, one who is trained in the actual traditions of the church and not one who has learned to sew a stole online). If this precaution is not taken, the services of the church are certain, in time, to be vulgarized. Some kind friend will work an impossible stole. Another will compose a ruinous frontal, and, without warning anyone, present it as a pleasant surprise when it is finished. Another will be attracted by some brass work of the gilt-gingerbread type seen on eBay and with a smile of kindly triumph will deposit it one day in the vestry. It will be too late then for the parson to protest—all these good people will be hurt (and one cannot blame them) if their presents are rejected. But if it be publicly explained beforehand with some regularity that the attainment of beauty of effect is a most difficult task, for which at the present day much training is required—and that a church must suffer if left to the chance of a multitude of individual tastes—this catastrophe will be avoided.

---

9. See the rite, *1979 Book of Common Prayer*, 567; see also the rubric regarding the dedication, *1979 Book of Common Prayer*, 16.

COLORS, VESTMENTS, AND ORNAMENTS

Sir Adam de Bacon, Rector: Oulton, Suffolk.
Priest in a Vestment[10]

Sometimes one is tempted to think that folk consider anything good enough for a church. But the real reason for all this misplaced generosity is only that the elements of artistic knowledge have not yet entered the heads of many people—and will not unless the church educates them by its example. Simplicity, unity, proportion, restraint, richness of color, ecclesiastical propriety... these things are not understood by a vast number. It is not their fault. They have had no opportunity of learning. They want to help the church, and they will do so well if they are only taught.

---

10. In earlier times the chasuble was often simply referred to as the vestment. We would in modern times call the vestment pictured here a chasuble (which is a type of vestment in modern parlance). The image is brass, formerly at Oulton. Sir Adam de Bacon (ca. 1320) is pictured in apparelled amice and albe, stole, maniple, and chasuble without orphreys.

But, if not, it will not cross their minds that inharmonious decoration is just as excruciating as discordant music.

As a corollary, a wise priest generally has the wisdom to put the music under the charge of someone who has expertise in that field, no matter the experience they have (or think they have). Certainly, greater collegiality must still be found among clergy and musicians. As it becomes more difficult to find really well-trained church musicians, clergy should not be surprised, as they have often made it a rather undesirable vocation. When the clergy and church musicians function as a team, however, each with respect for the training of the other and a deep commitment to beauty and fidelity to the prayer book tradition of our church, the music that is offered will indeed perfect the praises of God's people.

This same seeking out of the wisdom of trained individuals should be practiced in regard to art, especially of the liturgical variety. The parson must remember that those with an eye for art will be driven from the church by faults that offend not only against the eye but against the intellect and the heart as well. If the vulgarities, both in music and other forms of art, with which nearly every church is at present soiled, do not soon pass away, the quiet alienation of those parts of our community who do understand art and beauty may go too far for recovery.

The principal habits and vestments are the cassock, gown, cap, surplice, hood, tippet or scarf, the albe and amice (with their apparels), girdle, stole, chasuble, cope, dalmatic and tunicle, the rochet, and the verger's gown. The maniple[11] or fanon fell out of liturgical use in the Roman Catholic Church during the revisions of Vatican II. It quickly fell out of use in the Anglican tradition as well. And while there are churches that retain its use, one does think that the sometimes less than elegant movements of the average cleric, combined with the risk of knocking over the

---

11. The maniple was first simply a piece of linen the clerics used to wipe their faces and hands as needed, similar to a handkerchief, and was used in the Western tradition since the sixth century. In that vein, it has often been connected to the towel with which Christ washed his disciples' feet and so, is a symbol of the cleric as the servant of the servants of God. It has also been described as an emblem of the tears of penance, the burden of sin, and the fatigue that comes with the vocation of the priesthood. The Roman Catholic redemptorist Alphonsus Liguori once claimed, "It is well known that the maniple was introduced for the purpose of wiping away the tears that flowed from the eyes of the priest; for in former times priests wept continually during the celebration of Mass." Liguori, *Dignities and Duties*, 218. Either this explanation, or the tears of penitence and the burden of vocation, can make meaningful the older prayer used when donning it, "May I deserve, O Lord, to bear the maniple of weeping and sorrow, in order that I may joyfully receive the reward of my work."

flagon of wine, suggests that this may be a time when we might follow the wisdom of our Roman Catholic siblings. At the same time, for those churches that maintain the maniple, it can be a potent symbol of the essentiality of servanthood to the vocation of anyone called to ministerial service. Whatever decision is made, let it be made thoughtfully and with competent instruction to the people with regard to the reasoning.

THE EPISCOPAL VESTMENTS

Bishop in a Vestment[12]

---

12. Effigy in Rochester Cathedral. John de Sheppy (ca. 1360), Bishop of Rochester, reproduced in Dearmer's handbook by permission of Mr. Murray and Bishop W. H. Frere, from vol. 2 of Rock's *The Church of Our Fathers*. The bishop is vested in full pontificals: apparelled amice and albe (stole hidden), maniple, tunicle (just visible at the side), dalmatic, chasuble, precious mitre, gloves (episcopal ring on left hand), and sandals. Under his left arm is the pastoral staff or crozier (the crook missing), swathed in the vexillum.

To the above clerical vestments must be added the bishop's mitre and chimere. But this does raise an opportune time to pause and explore the proper vestments of a bishop in more detail.

The first to be considered are a bishop's civil or choir habit. This is the habit that is worn on four occasions: when the bishop comes into the church (but not to celebrate a eucharistic liturgy); in choir; for preaching if not the celebrant; and at synods, diocesan conferences, and suchlike occasions. The choir habit consists of the cassock, rochet, chimere, and tippet. Some bishops prefer simply to wear the cassock at synods and conferences, presuming that they are not experiences of worship. While this is woefully true of most synods, synods simply cannot be faithful without the presence of the Holy Spirit and so the use of proper choir dress gives them the air of worship and prayer. If the bishop cannot be convinced of this, it is unfortunate. However, nothing forgives the wearing of a simple suit when presiding over the governance of the church. At least a cassock should be chosen. The bishop should not wear a hood, but should wear a black velvet square canterbury cap when in choir dress. The chimere may be black or colored. If two are owned, then black is good for ordinary use and scarlet for festival occasions. Bishops wisely keep to very simple attire as a rule and in particular wear the mitre only on special occasions and then not for long; but a few notes on the maximum use may be convenient here:

- When presiding at the daily office (especially at sung matins or evensong), the cope and mitre are optional, though allowed by tradition. If choir dress is chosen, then it should be done so clearly. In no case should the chimere be worn under the cope but the rochet only. If opting for true rochet and chimere, the bishop would wear the tippet over the chimere and rochet.

- At the litany, if sung in procession, the bishop may wear the cope and mitre. Indeed, this is true for all processions. Care should be taken, however, to be clear that the cope is not an exclusively episcopal garment but is one that is worn at solemn occasions by other clergy (and, at times, by lay people when serving in a particular role).

- At the Holy Communion, the bishop can choose between the cope or the eucharistic vestments (the full use being the stole, maniple, tunicle, dalmatic, and chasuble), along with the mitre. In practice, though, even this tradition of wearing the tunicle and dalmatic was

COLORS, VESTMENTS, AND ORNAMENTS

only utilized on great occasions. For ordinary use, a bishop's ordinary eucharistic vestment consisted of stole and chasuble with the mitre. The mitre is worn for much of the liturgy until the *sursum corda* (except during the confession), and is put back on when giving the blessing. The mitre should always be removed as well during any collects or prayers, the reading of the Gospel, and the censing of the altar.

- As for the crozier, the bishop carries it in the procession, or it may be borne by the chaplain. (It is better, though, if the bishop carries it, which is the more ancient custom.) If the bishop carries it, it is held in the left hand with the crook turned outward. It is turned inward if borne by a chaplain. The bishop holds it during the reading of the Gospel and while giving the absolution and the blessing. The bishop wears both cope and mitre and carries the staff during the procession back to the vestry. The crozier originally was simply part of the insignia of all bishops but later came to be a symbol of the pastoral authority of a bishop.[13] For that reason, the modern convention is for a bishop not to carry the crozier in areas where the bishop does not have ecclesiastical authority, unless that permission is given by the ecclesiastical authority of the diocese. However, there is no canonical rule in this regard and those who prefer the older convention of the crozier symbolizing the pastoral role of a bishop need not be corrected.

- The mitre may be of any color and often a simple white works best because then it can be worn with any liturgical color. The English tradition of the style and shape of the mitre has much to commend it compared to the Roman tradition. In the traditional English mitre, the peak at the top is less pronounced and more rounded. The mitre itself tends to be shorter and the lappets that hang down the back are also shorter. This more understated approach carries more dignity and beauty than the tall, pointy, mitres our Roman siblings wear, with lappets that sometimes hang down all the way to the middle of the back.[14]

---

13. See the development of this distinction in Armentrout and Slocum, *Episcopal Dictionary*, 131.

14 For more details, see Tribe, "History of the Mitre."

A Bishop Celebrating Holy Communion (Fifteenth Century)[15]

In all of these areas, the people are grateful particularly when the bishop takes time to learn the traditions of the church for the episcopal office and then inhabits that office humbly and faithfully, seeing the trappings and vestments not as signs of dignity but as the clothes of grace that must envelope any cleric who wishes to lead God's people by virtue of the Spirit's guidance and not one's own charm.

---

15. British Museum, MS. Add. 28962. Bishop, deacon, and subdeacon all in figured white and gold vestments; the bishop's dalmatic, like those of the other ministers, has gold apparels on the skirt; the orphreys of the deacon and subdeacon are also gold, and the bishop's chasuble has on it a gold cross of the Latin shape; all have gold amice apparels and black or very dark blue albe apparels. The bishop's mitre is white and gold lined with crimson; the deacon holds the crozier. On the altar one candle is clearly seen, a second is just visible at the other end; the bishop has his hand on the chalice and paten. The altar is covered with a long fair linen cloth, embroidered at the ends; a towel lies over the south end of the altar. Behind the altar is a painted and gilt reredos; and in the original the purple riddel at the north of the altar shows up in clear distinction from the scarlet and gold curtains that are hung behind the king. The frontal and frontlet are of red and gold, and the footpace and step are gay in white and fawn with red roses. Round the lectern are gathered chanters, and a figure in a red cassock edged with white fur, without a surplice; the chanters have surplices over blue or red cassocks.

COLORS, VESTMENTS, AND ORNAMENTS

THE CHOIR HABIT OF CLERGY AND LAITY

Priest in Official Habit[16]

The same principles for episcopal vestments noted above applies to the vestments of the other clergy. There were older people in the early twentieth century who could remember seeing old-fashioned clergy going to church in their cassock and gown in the early nineteenth century. Indeed, down to the last decade of the nineteenth century, some clergy continued to wear their canonical habit in their ordinary walks abroad. Yet so completely did they come to desert their cloth in the last century, that nowadays a priest in a cassock is taken for a Roman Catholic. One of the strangest blunders of the ceremonial revival in the nineteenth century was that its promoters missed the chance of restoring—one might say retaining—the customary dress of the clergy at a time when it was still to be seen more often than now and was everywhere well enough

---

16. 1913. Photograph by V. K. Blaiklock. Priest in cassock, cincture, gown, tippet, and square cap by the Warham Guild. The gown is of the earlier shape, the sleeves not being turned back.

remembered to make the restoration easy. There was at the time an odd and quite unreasonable idea that gowns were Genevan and Puritan—the truth being that the Puritans had opposed the gown almost as bitterly as eucharistic vestments. The next blunder was that of those ritualists who took to wearing cassocks, capes, and birettas of the Roman pattern—a practice that has helped to prejudice some Anglicans against the whole catholic movement, and has given that movement the appearance of a feeble imitation of Rome.

Dearmer's deep desire was for the revival of the cassock, academic gown, and canterbury cap as the proper attire of the cleric. That dream was never realized, though there was a renewed appreciation for the wearing of the cassock itself, which is a much more handsome garment than the black clothes clergy might order from the most convenient online retailer.

It was increasingly the case in the latter twentieth century that clergy resisted wearing clericals at all, wanting to dress like all other people. This rather strange idea forgets that uniforms (like clericals or a cassock) are precisely because you are not functioning as an individual person; you have been given a role by a larger body for a specific purpose. To refuse to wear the marker of that role is to highlight your own personality against who you are called and vowed to be: a cleric serving the community. And so, in daily life and work, wearing a black clergy shirt with similarly dark clothing seems fitting and marks one conveniently as a priest. This is particularly helpful because one never knows who is looking for God and, stumbling upon a properly attired priest, might open their spirit to some questions and searching.

For official occasions and for going to church, the cassock is the best choice. If one wishes to follow Dearmer's advice, then it may be paired with a university gown. Nongraduates cannot, of course, wear a university gown, but they have a perfect right to the full-sleeved priest's gown, the canterbury cap, and the tippet. The cassock (and gown) may be worn with or without the canterbury cap. A biretta is not the proper headgear for an Anglican cleric. All clerical headgear has its origin in the academy, with the biretta being the form of hat worn by those trained in Rome. For this reason, a proper Canterbury cap is more appropriate for the Anglican cleric. It is both fitting and convenient for the clergy to wear their proper clerical habit at clerical gatherings. And one hopes that the more this option is taken, the less an untrained cleric or layperson will mistake a properly attired cleric for a monk. Indeed, the sight of a priest so attired will, we may well hope, soon become everywhere so common as to excite no comment.

As for the cassock, it is a convenient walking dress (black for a cleric) if made in the proper way—in other words, some inches clear of the ground (just above the top of the shoes and not, God forbid, stopping in the middle of the shins) and without buttons down the skirt. Indeed, the clerical cassock has for many generations in the Anglican tradition been fastened on the shoulders instead of at the chest. Anyone who has tried to get dressed in a cassock with the multitude of buttons found in the Roman style quickly realizes the wisdom of the shoulder fashioning approach. It may be added that for convenience cassocks should be made with the pockets lying in front and not behind the legs, and with slits to give access to the pockets of the pants as well. They should also be girded with a short band of cloth lined with smooth material. Alternatively, they can be girded with a simple black leather belt (this tradition was far more popular in England than it ever became in the United States). It should be noted that in hotter countries there is nothing wrong with a white cassock—this is simply a choice of comfort and not an expression of a desire for the chair of St. Peter. Servers and choristers as well as priests should wear cassocks of the proper shape, ideally with cinctures.

As noted earlier, the canterbury cap has gone through several modifications: once of the comely shape that we see in the portraits of Cranmer, Fox, and others, it developed in the seventeenth century into the form familiar in portraits of Laud and his contemporaries (of limp material, with a tuft on the top), and then into the college cap in England, the mortarboard often seen in colleges and universities, and abroad, and finally into the less comely biretta. There is no conceivable reason for English churchmen to discard their own shape in favor of a foreign one. An English priest has no more right to adopt the distinctive headdress of the clergy of other countries than an English colonel has to wear the helmet of a French officer.

English tradition since the seventeenth century has been generally against the wearing of any other headdress except the skullcap (similar to the Roman zucchetto) in church. The original purpose of the skullcap was to keep a tonsured cleric's head warm. While some have perhaps thought that need was gone, in our own days of climate crisis (when it is often wise to keep thermostats lower in the winter months), its practical use has perhaps arisen once more. Regardless, almost every aspect of clerical clothing had a practical meaning that has since dissipated, and so this alone is not reason for insisting its use cannot be retained by the cleric who wishes to do so. The well-known painting *The Seven Sacraments* by Van der Weyden at Antwerp shows that in Flanders, at any rate, the skullcap was in general use at all kinds of services in the fifteenth century. A similar cap is found in English brasses and pictures. In my own life as a priest in the twenty-first century, I took to wearing a skullcap because of the way it made me more aware that I am here under the authority only of God. Furthermore, when taking the skullcap off at the *sursum corda* and then bowing at the altar towards the people, the bald spot on my middle-aged head that the skullcap had covered is made visible to all, an unexpected lesson in humility.

The choir habit may be summarized thusly according to the various roles one might hold in the church:

- Bishops—rochet, chimere, black silk tippet *or* rochet, cope, mitre; *either way*, crozier held
- Priests or deacons (holding degrees)—surplice, hood of their degree, black tippet
- Priests or deacons (nongraduate)—surplice, black tippet (in practice hoods may also are worn under the tippet by the licentiates of theological colleges)
- Laity—surplice, hood of their degree for organists, choirmasters, and leaders of the choir[17]

For laity in general, additional medals or ribbons are unnecessary with a few exceptions: choristers may be given medals as they advance in training and cantors may wear a cope over the surplice in a solemn service. Licensed readers are not a part of the Episcopal Church in the same way they are in the Church of England, and there is nothing extra worn by those serving in licensed ministries at offices of the church.

---

17. There has been significant debate on this question from time to time. When surpliced choirs began in the second part of the nineteenth century, very few of the choristers would likely have been graduates with academic hoods. Generally, Dearmer's view was that "readers, clerks, and choristers, who have a degree, wear also the hood of that degree." Dearmer, *Parson's Handbook*, 126. This approach will certainly still be allowed in collegiate or cathedral choirs, where choristers may be professionally trained musicians with degrees. However, in our time, a far greater percentage of the population hold degrees and a variety of them in the choir would likely look unseemly. Thus, it seems most appropriate to limit the use of the hood to those laity who have a position of leadership within the liturgy. For more details, see Groves, "Academic Hood in Quire."

Canon in Choir Habit[18]

The surplice worn before the Reformation, like that which has continued in use down to our own time, was very long and full. In the nineteenth century, however, a short garment known as a cotta—very undignified and ungraceful—came into fashion and still lingers in many churches. To wear a thing of this sort, though, comes from the tradition of the Roman Catholic Church and is not found within the heritage of Anglican Christianity. It lacks the beautiful falls of a full surplice and is best avoided by churches in our tradition.

The surplice should fall to within about six inches of the ground or else to the ankles; and at the very shortest nothing should be tolerated, even on the smallest chorister, that is not some inches below the knee. But even this half measure loses the graceful swing of a proper surplice, and surplices of insufficient length are apt to crease up when sat upon. It may be mentioned here that ministers are apt to think their surplices

---

18. Wells Cathedral. Carved panel from the tomb of Dean Russe (ca. 1305), showing cassock, surplice, almuce, and cappa nigra. This beautiful figure provides a good example of the pre-Reformation surplice.

longer than they really are, because, when one leans forward to look at the length of the garment, it drops several inches in front. A further cause that has led to the gradual cutting down of garments is the rage for cheapness and the desire of the tailor to save as much material as possible. Before vestments became a commercial article, they remained full, on the Continent as well as here. Now the worship of mammon has so far entrenched on the honor due to God that the factory shops have their own way with us, and it is considered seemly for a minister to appear in church in the garment that could better be called a "sausage-skin," a so-called surplice that is not only short but is entirely deprived of gathers, so that a few dollars may be saved from the cost of worship.

There is plenty of precedent for the smocking of surplices, and it adds to their beauty. But it is not in the least necessary, while shape is. As for fullness, the most beautiful surplice (that like those represented on medieval monuments) will have a circumference of about four-and-a-half yards. Surplices should never button in the front. The most graceful sleeves hang down within a few inches of the skirt hem and are turned back over the hands. For preaching it will generally be found more convenient to use a surplice with sleeves that, while hanging nearly as low, do not extend beyond the wrist at the top. Of all the many vestments used at different times in the church, a large and well-cut surplice is perhaps the most beautiful. It need perhaps hardly be said, yet again, that the use of lace is not an English custom. It simply destroys all beauty of drapery in any garment upon which it is placed. Every artist will realize how much this means.

The hood was well established in its academical form at the authorizing of the 1549 prayer book. Graduates in cathedral churches and colleges, it says, may use in the choir "such hood as pertaineth to their several degrees, which they have taken in any university within this realm."[19] We know, furthermore, the distinctive varieties of the academical hood were no new thing in 1549 and these distinctive varieties continue today. The hood should be worn, therefore, over the surplice at all choir offices and for preaching, unless the preacher is vested for the Eucharist. It should also be worn, in general, when assisting at a service. But it should not be worn by the ministers at the Eucharist and, as clergy who preach most often also will be distributing Communion, the hood is rarely appropriate for the preaching cleric the hood is rarely appropriate

---

19. *1549 Book of Common Prayer*, 126.

for the preaching cleric, as that person is usually also either the celebrant or distributing Communion at a service of Holy Communion. Even in those churches where the proper eucharistic vestments are not yet used, it is best that a hood should not be worn over the surplice, and ornaments of merely *personal* dignity are out of place on those engaged in offering the eucharistic sacrifice.

Priest Graduate in Choir Habit[20]

The almuce need only be mentioned here, as its place was taken by the hood and tippet. Originally a fur hood and cape combined, with long pendants in front, such as was much needed in the days when churches were very cold; it was replaced by the tippet or scarf, which was first of black material lined or edged with fur, then of black silk only. The furred scarf was reserved for dignitaries. The almuce, however, has now gone out of use.

"The tippet," says the Alcuin Club tract on the ornaments rubric, "was a scarf generally of black silk, sometimes lined with fur."[21] There is no known authority for confining the use of the tippet to dignitaries and chaplains—that custom grew up in the days when the direction of the canons as

---

20. 1913. Photograph by V. K. Blaiklock. Cassock, surplice, Oxford MA hood, and silk tippet or scarf, by the Warham Guild.
21. Micklethwaite, *Ornaments*, 46.

to copes also fell into abeyance and is paralleled by the general disuse of the hood among the parish clergy at the same time. There is plenty of evidence that the use of the tippet was enforced upon the clergy by the bishops from the time of Elizabeth to that of Charles II and was much opposed by the Puritans, who hated the cap and tippet as much as they hated the surplice.[22]

Surplice, Hood, and Tippet, in the Seventeenth Century[23]

The older distinctions in the fabric of tippet between clergy who hold advanced degrees and those who hold bachelor's degrees has fallen out of use. Indeed, as the tippet is a distinctly clerical garment, it should certainly still be worn by those clergy who have gone through local formation instead of the traditional process of seminary. Furthermore, deacons, being clergy, should wear the tippet, but of course they will wear it in the same way as a priest and not in the way a deacon wears a stole. This is, of course, because a tippet is not a stole. The tippet is in fact the vestment—and the only vestment—which distinguishes the clergy in choir from the lay choristers. The free use of black is so necessary to the beauty of all public services (a fact which artists well know, though it is generally forgotten by others) that the unlawful substitution of colored stoles for tippets is the more to be regretted. There is no authority, English or

22. Dearmer, *Parson's Handbook*, 133.
23. *Comber's Discourses*, 1684. Emblematic frontispiece, illustrating the hood before its elongation and its use with the tippet. Priest kneels before symbolic altar, wearing surplice, hood, and tippet. The left half of the picture, containing the congregation, is omitted.

Roman, for the use of the stole in choir, while the black scarf or tippet as part of the clerical habit has come down to us from before the Reformation, and the present authority for its use is unmistakable.

Both hood and tippet should be worn together for all choir services and also in the pulpit when the preacher does not retain the albe. Some dislike the tippet being worn in choir because it was originally an outdoor garment only. But, after all, so were the chasuble, pallium, and cope, which all occur as outdoor garments in the pictures in the catacombs at Rome.

The tippet should be worn over, not under, the hood; worn thus, it keeps the hood from riding up. The tippet should be made of a piece of silk or other black fabric long enough to fall within one or two inches of the bottom of the surplice, and from seventeen to twenty-two inches broad, so that, when it is folded double and joined up, it forms a flat band from eight to ten-and-a-half inches broad. If the material be thin and soft, it may be even broader. The ends may be peaked (in zigzags) in the nineteenth-century fashion, but it is better to have them simply hemmed. The tippet should be kept folded up flat, and a triple fold at the neck, in putting it on, will cause it to hang well, or—better still—it may be put on without any folding at all. The use of seals from seminaries and dioceses on a tippet is a modern innovation that spoils the beauty of the plain black silk. There is no need for demonstrating the particular club of clergy you come from when participating in the worship of the church.

The cappa nigra, or black choir cope, was more like a cloak or sleeveless gown than a silk cope. Old effigies and brasses show that it fell gracefully from the shoulders to the heels, almost covering the arms; it was worn over the surplice in cathedral and collegiate churches during the winter months for the sake of warmth. The use of such a black cloak over the surplice at funerals, where much of the service takes place outdoors, would save some washing and a few lives. It is heavy, often woolen, and is well worth the investment, for a proper cappa nigra will not only last throughout the life of the ordained cleric but may also usually be passed on to a succeeding generation.

THE EUCHARISTIC VESTMENTS OF CLERGY AND LAITY

Proper eucharistic vesture may be summarized thusly, according to the various roles one might hold in the church:

1. Bishops—If the bishop is the celebrant, the best choice is the eucharistic vestments of amice, alb, girdle, stole, and chasuble, with mitre worn at appropriate times as noted above, and the crozier held. The bishop may elect to wear cope and mitre for the first part of the liturgy, usually exchanging the cope for the chasuble before the *sursum corda*.
2. Priests (serving as the celebrant)—The eucharistic vestments of amice, alb, girdle, stole, and chasuble should be worn.
3. Priests (assisting but not celebrating)—Amice, alb, girdle, and stole should be worn, or, alternatively, choir habit with a stole.
4. Deacons—Amice, alb, girdle, diaconal stole, and dalmatic should be worn.
5. Laity—Amice, alb, girdle, with the option of a tunicle for the eucharistic minister should be worn, or choir habit of surplice only.

As noted in the introduction, the role of subdeacon was a minor order in the church that was abolished with the reforms of Vatican II. It has been custom for some time in our churches to have a lay person fill that role—though they are not ordained to the order of subdeacon in those instances. The eucharistic minister in the current canons of the Episcopal Church is actually very similar in role to the subdeacon. Incorporating the eucharistic minister into the fuller ritual of the role of subdeacon can be a lovely way of honoring that tradition in our own time and context.

The amice was always worn to hang outside the other vestments, and was appareled in older times, though many appareled amices have sadly disappeared among us. One longs for their return. Apparels are so beautiful a feature in the English ceremonial that it is the more regrettable that some clergy should have discarded them merely, it would seem, because they were supposed to be forbidden at Rome.

The size of the amice should be about twenty by thirty-six inches to allow for one double fold when putting it on. The tapes, if passed round the neck and waist to secure the amice in position, should be about seventy-five inches long. The apparel is tacked on to the side of the amice between the tapes. Loops are not needed.

COLORS, VESTMENTS, AND ORNAMENTS

Appareled Amice and Albe[24]

To put on an appareled amice, it should be laid on a table, and given a double fold under the apparel; it is then placed on the top of the head with the apparel outside, the unfolded part of the amice falling over the back of the head. The tapes, which have been hanging by either cheek, may then be crossed, taken round the neck rather tightly (completely hiding the clerical or shirt collar), and brought round to the front, where they are crossed again and brought round the back of the waist and then tied in front. A simpler and perhaps a better way is to omit the passing of the tapes round the neck, crossing them at once over the breast, then taking them, as above, round the back and tying them in front. Put on in this way, the apparel lies lower in front and has a rather less stiff appearance. Though care should still be taken to ensure that the clerical collar is covered up entirely. A collar showing in a eucharistic liturgy is an unneeded double marker of ordained ministry. The amice and albe, as the baptismal garment, should always be the base of every eucharistic vestment, with the stole and chasuble or dalmatic being the proper

24. 1913. From a photograph by V. K. Blaiklock. Rochet made by the Warham Guild.

eucharistic markers of one's order in the church. The amice is kept on the head till the other vestments are on, at which point the appareled edge is pulled back so that it forms a collar standing up well outside the albe and other vestments. No loops are needed on the amice, but the tapes must be about seventy-eight inches long.

The albe is that most basic and yet most essential of vestments.[25] It's original ancestor is the simple garment worn in the secular Roman world beneath the toga, as seen in early Christian catacombs. It later was associated with the baptismal gown of the early church. In both points of association, it is neither clerical nor special and in our church is worn as a symbol of one's baptism and a reminder that all those who serve in the liturgies of the church are, first and foremost, baptized Christians. When the albe is also worn by laity who are serving at the holy altar, this point is further underscored. As the baptismal garment, it is properly white. The use of oatmeal or flax-colored albes was an unfortunate invention of the twentieth century that one hopes will continue to wain as better tastes (and theological sensibility) prevail.

The albe was also appareled in the tradition of our church. But there is some precedent for wearing unappareled albes with appareled amices, nor do they look amiss. Therefore, those who prefer that albes should be without apparels might wear them thus. This will doubtless be found convenient in churches where there are few people to look after the vestments, or where there is little space for storing many sets of albes.

The albe, like the surplice, should be much fuller than it is usually made. It should not be of a semi-transparent material. It should be the same length as the cassock, and should never be made short. It loses all its gracefulness, indeed it ceases to be an albe, if it is cut short for servers with the object of showing a bit of the cassock, a particularly unfortunate choice when the cassock is red in cathedrals.

---

25. In Dearmer's time, the rochet (still used by the bishop) was sometimes substituted for the surplice or albe, all three being, at their foundation, variations on the white baptismal gown. The albe needs a girdle and amice, and requires some care in the putting on. The rochet can be slipped on in a moment; and therefore, it came to be very generally substituted for albes in the case of the clerk (but not in the case of the celebrant, deacon, or subdeacon) at ordinary parish churches. No doubt it was for the same reason of convenience that it came to be part of the bishop's everyday dress. The rochet may be described as something between the albe and the surplice. It has narrow sleeves like the albe, or else it is sleeveless, having a slit down each side. It only falls to within some six inches of the ground like the surplice, and it may button at the neck, but it has neither amice, girdle, nor apparels. See, for example, Dearmer, *Parson's Handbook*, 146–47, 298, 308.

Clerk in Appareled Amice and Albe[26]

Albes should be girded about the middle of the waist (this being, of course, at the belly button and not at the hips, despite the confusion of some clergy on this point). Anciently they were worn very long and pulled back over the girdle to reduce them to the required length, an arrangement that requires more care in the vestry than is likely to be given, and that is not easy to make graceful, perhaps because of the different texture of modern linen. It is therefore best for practical reasons that each server should have the albe fitted to the person exactly. But an exact fit means that the albe should be longer than the cassock—about two inches below the cassock hem and about one inch longer than the sleeve. If this is not secured, the albe will come to be a size too small after a little while. A well-trained tailor, if given the measurements of all servers, can help the parson determine if a certain set can be made that will have enough variation to fit anyone properly. The former remarks about lace apply to every kind of vestment and ornament, and lace on albes destroys their dignity and grace. It is convenient for the albe to be open a little way down the front; and to be buttoned at the neck or tied with two small tapes.

To summarize, albes should always be worn with amices and girdles, and should reach to the feet. Servers should not be allowed to wear them unless they are long enough. They may be ornamented in more

26. 1913. Photograph by V. K. Blaiklock. Apparelled amice and albe, and girdle, by the Warham Guild.

than one way, and each way is good; they may be fully appareled as well as the amice, or the amice only may be appareled and the albe quite plain.

A word is in order here about the so-called "cassock-albe." This garment was introduced to America by Almy, one of the largest ecclesiastical companies serving the Episcopal Church. Often made of an oxford cloth weave, it is an attempt to combine three garments—the cassock, amice, and alb—into one singular garment. It has largely taken over our church, given the increasing disuse of the cassock and the ease of donning the cassock albe compared to the traditional eucharistic vestments. While there is no authority for an outright condemnation of their use (and, indeed, I admit to owning one and using it in my own work from time to time), the primary goal of speeding the process of putting on one's vestments is one that is decidedly wrongheaded. As the learned Father Robert Hendrickson noted not too many years ago,

> The quickness and ease of the cassock-alb reinforces a desire to just "get on with it" and to get ready with haste.
>
> It also represents our desire to make the encounter with God an easier thing—we remove the more disciplined and difficult preparations to streamline the encounter and even domesticate it a bit. The cassock-alb represents a certain dumbing down—a lowest common denominator approach to preparation in which we substitute comfort and haste for careful adherence to older patterns of care and preparation. . . .
>
> The cassock-alb exists for one reason—haste. It takes longer to vest properly. It is inconvenient and the added layers are hot and uncomfortable. Yet, there is little in the Christian faith that is truly comfortable and there is virtue in taking our time tomake ourselves ready to offer our selves, and souls, and bodies in worship and adoration.
>
> The cassock-alb is the strip mall of vestments. Convenient, unattractive, and accessible—its impact is less one of commission than it is one of negligence. It, like a strip mall, reflects our lack of discipline and attentiveness rather than causing it. It is not a real thing—in the way that fast food is not real food. It is there as a sloppy habit that takes the place of investing the time and energy into a more focused and present experience.
>
> When preparing for the source and summit of Christian life—the encounter with Christ in the Eucharist—it is a good and holy thing to take some extra time. It's good to fumble with amice strings. It's good to add layer to layer in preparation.[27]

---

27. Hendrickson, "Cassock Albs," paras. 5–6, 8–10.

So, while the cassock albe is certainly not the worst liturgical choice the parson might make when preparing for Eucharist, it is certainly not the best and it runs the risk of ingratiating ease in exchange for discipline. At the same time, the traditional albe should never be worn without the amices. If the trouble of amices is too much for the servers, then the parson might allow for the use of cassock albes for servers, while retaining proper albes for the clergy.

The apparels, if used, are worn on the outside of the amice, like a collar, and on the sleeves and skirt (back and front) of the albe. They may be of any color and material that looks well with the vestments, and they need not follow the color of the day. For instance, red looks fitting with any vestments, bright blue sets off white very well, while plain black serge is effective and appropriate with the red Passiontide vestments. Some forms of Eastern work are excellent for the purpose and so are gold tissue and good old brocades and good embroidery; the color should be rich and distinct. A large pattern often looks well when cut up into apparels. They can easily be made and, if tacked lightly on to the linen, are not difficult to change when this goes to the wash. A capable volunteer should be found who will be responsible for changing the apparels. Those on the sleeves should be tacked to the outside of each sleeve, a third of their length reaching over the upper side. Those on the skirt should rest immediately above the hem in the middle of the front and of the back. That on the amice lies close up to the edge, at an equal distance between the tapes, and is, like the others, tacked all round—not on one side only.

They are simple to make. The apparels of both amice and albe need an interlining of canvas and a lining of white or blue linen; they generally also need an edging of cord or braid. The dimensions may vary. The following are suitable for adults, but children's apparels should be rather smaller: amice-apparel should be twenty inches by three inches; sleeve-apparels, eight or nine inches by about three or three-and-a-half inches; skirt-apparels, eight inches by ten or twelve inches (or they may be longer and rather narrower).

The girdle or cincture is generally of white linen rope, and may have a tassel at each end. About twelve feet and six inches long is a very convenient size if it is used double, one end being then turned into a noose, and the tasseled ends slipped through. The girdle, however, may be colored. It may also take the form of a flat band tied like a sash or fastened with a buckle, though this is not the most handsome approach.

The stole is still generally made too broad. The old ones were only about two inches across, slightly splaying at the ends. Crosses were never put on the ends and back of the stole, but ornamentation of various kinds placed the whole length of the stole (crosses being occasionally used in this way, continuously along the stole) was common, as were fringes. The length of the eucharistic stole should be about nine feet; it should be long enough for the ends to appear below the chasuble. The objectionable custom of sewing a piece of lace on the middle of the stole is unnecessary because our clergy are cleanly in their habits and because they may not preach in the stole except when vested as celebrant or deacon, in which case they almost always would have covered their neck with the amice (unless they were vested with a surplice because they were only functioning in choir and not assisting at the altar). This piece of lace seems to be a kind of antimacassar, invented in a period when hair oil and broad stoles were both in the ascendant. The amice is what properly protects the stole. The other stoles required for baptism, marriage, and ministering the chalice need not be much shorter if a proper surplice is worn, nor any broader. About eight feet should be the shortest length.

Chasuble in Gold Tissue[28]

28. 1913. Photograph by V. K. Blaiklock. Chasuble made by the Warham Guild.

COLORS, VESTMENTS, AND ORNAMENTS

There has been a great variety in the shape of the chasuble, not only at different periods but at one and the same time also. On the whole the tendency for the last six hundred years has been to cut down the material; this culminated in the strange and undignified stiff little vestment called the "fiddleback" chasuble, which was used by Roman Catholics in the early twentieth century. This type may fortunately be dismissed as beyond our province. But it must be acknowledged that a longer and more ample form of this square chasuble was in use in the Church of England in the early twentieth century. The chasuble should not be stiffened. It may have a Latin cross on the back, and it should be about as long as a Gothic vestment, i.e., about fifty inches from the neck behind. Indeed, the Gothic shapes, now commonly in use among us, are more beautiful and truer on the whole to our traditions. The shape most frequently seen reaches nearly to the wrists and very good vestments can be cut on these lines. The older shape is still fuller and the sides have to be turned back over the wrist. When one sits down in a chasuble, the back of the fabric ideally goes over the back of the chair and hangs freely. The bottom edge of the vestment should be folded up to lay upon the celebrant's lap so that, when hands are folded or placed on the lap, they lay upon the lining and keep the precious fabric on the front clean and free of oil and sweat.

Chasubles do not need any additional interlining, for stiffening only spoils their folds and makes them heavy. The best orphreys are undoubtedly the Y shaped, but these are generally made too broad—two inches is quite wide enough for ordinary orphreys, except where embroidered figures under canopy work are used. It should be stressed that if the Y shaped orphrey or any significant decoration is on only one side of the chasuble, the more decorated side goes on the priest's back. The medieval chasuble more often had no orphreys at all, the only ornament being a border round the edge. This large plain type, without any orphreys, is, I think, the most beautiful, and certainly arouses least prejudice. There is no need in a Gothic vestment for the pieces of ribbon without which it seems impossible to keep a "fiddleback" in position. A properly made chasuble hangs straight and well of itself, and to tie it on only spoils its folds. Once more, a good length for a chasuble is fifty inches behind, and the breadth at the widest part may be about forty-eight inches or wider. But they are not easy things to cut and make properly.

These vestments need not always be made of silk. It is a loss of effect to have the lining of the same color as the vestment, and at times it is better to have no lining—indeed in hot countries this is necessary. Silk or a silk mixture is more comfortable for linings than linen, though linen may be effective. Poor churches can make very beautiful chasubles out of inexpensive materials, unlined materials or even out of dyed linen. As a general rule, brocades or other materials bearing some designs are best, with orphreys (if they are used) of a different color and material such as will form a good contrast. Embroidery is always a difficult thing and should only be undertaken under an artist's direction.

The cope is nearly semicircular in shape, about ten feet and six inches by seventeen feet. It should have an orphrey from two to six inches in width and may have a small hood; the best kind for ordinary use is soft like a mantle, with very narrow orphreys (this is the earlier form), and with no hood. The cope is fastened by the morse, which may be of metal or, for economy, fabric. The hood may be detachable; it may hang either from above the top of the orphrey or from below it. The hood and the bottom edge of the cope may be fringed, but fringes add much to the cost of a cope, and for economy those on the cope itself may be dispensed with, and even that on the hood also. The cope, like the chasuble, may be of any comely material, silk or otherwise. The best kind of cope is not an exact semicircle, but is shaped round the neck.

The dalmatic for the deacon should have real sleeves and not the mere epaulettes that have rendered the dalmatic abroad almost indistinguishable from the chasuble. In some of the most beautiful examples, the sleeves reach to the wrist and the vestment itself almost touches the ground; in any case the sleeve should not fall far short of the elbow, and the vestment should be as long as the chasuble. If orphreys are used, they may be either two narrow strips at the sides, in which case they may have apparels between them, or they may take the form of single pillars. The deacon wears a stole over the left shoulder, crossed in the girdle on his right side. This point is particularly important when a "deacon's stole" has not been designed and procured. A proper stole with a flexible fabric will fall quite nicely when folded into a loop in the girdle on the right side and forgoes the needs of a specially designed stole for the deacon.

Clerk in Tunicle[29]

The tunicle, as noted above, can be an excellent choice for the eucharistic minister if one wishes that person to take the role previously given to the subdeacon. The tunicle only differs from the dalmatic in that it has a tendency to be somewhat less ornamental (usually just one horizontal orphrey compared to the two horizontal orphreys on the dalmatic). However, there is no precise difference in the ornament. For instance, both dalmatic and tunicle may have tassels on the shoulders. They are of the same color as the chasuble and may be interchangeable.

Servers and chorister cassocks may be black, blue, or green, or any other color, though black is often best. Scarlet cassocks certainly play havoc with the general color effect of the vestments and decorations if much of them is seen. Under a long surplice they may be tolerable, but it is best, if red is used here and there (as is so often the case in cathedrals), for it to be of a quieter tint.

The verger's gown is a very ancient garment, very similar to the bishop's chimere in style or, in more advanced approaches, with epaulettes and chevrons on the sleeves. The practice of putting the verger in

29. 1906. Photograph by the Rev. J. R. Fowler. Clerk holds processional cross. Apparelled amice and albe, with tunicle of blue velvet.

parish churches in a cassock only (so often an ill-fitting one of the wrong pattern) should be discontinued. It cannot be stressed enough that the cassock is not a vestment for worship but is an item of normal clothing, and for anyone, laity or clergy, to wear a cassock with no vestment in the worship of church is only mildly better than showing up in one's undergarments. The gown may be black, blue, or crimson; it is best with velvet down the front and on the collar and may be worn over a cassock of the English shape.

Where there is a surpliced choir, the adults should wear surplices over their cassocks that are nearly as full and long as those of the clergy—so also with the children, in proportion. The mean custom of putting them into cottas, things that are not really surplices at all, is not creditable to us. The cassock was by no means always worn under the surplice, even in Rome, for long after the sixteenth century. However, it has become necessary since the invention of trousers. Where there are *rectores chori*, or leaders/rulers of the choir, the copes of these chanters had best be of the mantle type. Such copes should match each other, and, if the church can afford it, may be of the color of the season. The rulers anciently held staves or wands, and these they carried also in processions. The staves were of wood, ivory, silver, and other materials and had sometimes elaborately ornamented heads. Wands or staves, besides adding to the beauty of the general effect, have the practical advantage of enabling the holders to attract the attention of any member of the choir without the use of disturbing sounds or gestures; if, for instance, a child (or adult!) is not attending, the ruler on that person's side has merely to point the wand in that direction.

ORNAMENTS

The ornaments now to be mentioned are those which are kept in the sacristy; those which stand in the church are dealt with more fully in other chapters.

The fair linen should be entirely without lace and not of a thin or flimsy material.

The corporal is a square piece of smooth linen of not less than twenty inches. It should be of a size to lie easily on the altar, for it should not hang at all over the front. It should always be folded in the same way. The most usual method is to fold it inwards, first in three parts, beginning at the front, then from the sides, again, in three. Thus, when spread out, it is divided by the folds into nine squares. On one of the squares, usually the front square, one small cross may be embroidered. It should not be unfolded and shaken out over the carpet. The whole point of the triple fold is to catch any remaining pieces of bread. When it is opened after a service to be cleaned, it should be done over the piscina so any remaining crumbs may go down the drain and into the earth.

The pall at the time of the 1549 prayer book was simply a second corporal. Originally one very large corporal was used, part of it being drawn up over the chalice from behind. Then for convenience it was divided in two, and thus we get the common phrase a pair of corporals. In the twentieth century, it was increasingly the case that a square pall, made of two or three pieces of linen stitched together and stiffened with starch mixed with wax, was used. Sometimes cardboard is used to stiffen this sort of pall, and as long as it is still wrapped with linen (or silk in the East), this is acceptable (only linen or silk having been allowed about the eucharistic elements from very ancient times). Dearmer resisted the firmer pall that is common in our own time because of the rubrical expectation in the Church of England at his time that the pall (being simply a larger corporal) was draped over the consecrated elements that were left after the distribution. That rubric no longer applying in the Episcopal Church, a firmer pall can indeed be used. Regardless, this covering of the chalice is an old tradition, the object being to prevent anything from dropping into it.

The purificator is basically a napkin of soft linen for cleansing the chalice. It might be marked with a very small cross in one corner for convenience. Sometimes purificators are made so small and of such thin linen that they do not properly serve their purpose. Thirteen inches square is a good size, and six purificators should be supplied with every set of altar linen. Thus, with a stock of two or three dozen, the clergy will not be in danger of running short and adopting the unpleasant custom of using the same purificators over and over again.

The burse is used to contain the corporal and a pall and is often helpful as a place to keep an extra purificator. There is no rule as to its ornamentation—it may have any appropriate device on the upper side and the lower side may be of the same material but without ornament or may be of a different color and material. It is not absolutely necessary for the burse to be of the same color as the vestments with which it is used. It should be covered with silk or other material, lined with white linen, and stiffened. It may have small tassels at the corners. A convenient size may be from eight to ten inches square. The spine of the burse should be kept flush with the chalice veil (if it is used) so that the burse does not hang out off the front (or sit open facing the people) and thus create an odd shadow down the front of the veil.

The use of a chalice veil to cover the vessels before the Great Thanksgiving is an innovation of modern times. Strangely enough, the chalice veil has been suggested on the ground of convenience. This argument could only be used by those who have never tried the experiment of celebrating without one. Some people seem also to imagine that there is something irreverent about the unveiled chalice, but (putting aside the fact that such was undoubtedly the general custom in the West) the opposite is surely the truth. For the veiling of the vessels is (by a special rubric in the historic prayer books of our communion) a sign that they contain the consecrated elements, and to veil them at the beginning of the service is to destroy the significance of a special act of eucharistic reverence. That said, their increasing use over the twentieth century has created a sense of affection for them among the laity and the parson will be judicious in whether or not to overturn this innovation. As the late sixth-century bishop of Rome, Gregory the Great, advised Abbot Mellitus during the ministry of Augustine of Canterbury in ancient Britain, "Whoever wishes to climb to a mountain top climbs gradually step by step, and not in one leap."[30] Similarly, in bringing the worship of a parish in line with the expectations of the prayer book and the tradition of Anglicanism, priority is always given to our vowed obedience to the rubrics, while points of attention to proper tradition that are not strictly rubrical, such as ending the practice of veiling the chalice before mass, are sometimes left to a more opportune time.

Towels for drying the hands are generally made much too small. They should be of linen cloth about three feet long by twelve or thirteen inches wide; then they will rest easily on the server's arm and be convenient to use. Like purificators, they are generally folded in three. While purificators and corporals are hemmed, these cloths may be pulled out at the ends, or all round, in a fringe. Two to a set will suffice.

The sacred vessels should be made by some genuine craftsperson who is familiar with the traditional forms. The chalice has varied much in size and shape. Gothic examples range from five to seven inches in

---

30. Gregory the Great to Melitus, in Bede, *Ecclesiastical Histroy*, 92.

height. A chalice six inches high may be large enough to communicate sixty people and is very convenient for ordinary use. Larger chalices will be needed when there are many communicants, but the largest for this purpose need not be more than about eight inches high and should not be too heavily decorated. The bowl should be quite plain within and without, or it will be difficult to cleanse. An ornamental knot is usually made on the stem for convenience in holding it.

The hospitable minister at Communion will be trained to keep a loose wrist at the distribution, so that the one communicating may grasp the base and tip it while sipping. Many a communicant has been refused a proper sip from the chalice by an overzealous minister who keeps too firm a grip and does not permit enough tipping for a sip of any meaning. Similarly, after communing someone, the minister should wipe the inside and outside rim of the chalice with the purificator and then rotate it a quarter turn. If these practices are followed, there is little scientific reason to fear infection at the common cup.

The paten is a circular plate, large enough to cover the chalice, with one or more depressions, circular or multifoil. Many post-Reformation patens have stems, like the patens used in the Eastern churches, but this may lessen their usefulness as a cover for the chalice. Nearly every extant medieval example has a sacred device engraved upon it. Whether or not a sacred device is engraved upon it, the surface should always be depressed and should not be polished so as to reflect the face like a mirror.

The standing pyx or ciborium is convenient for holding the bread when there are so many communicants that the paten is not sufficient. The standing pyx is generally taller and narrower, and the ciborium a bit shorter and wider, but both serve the same purpose. In smaller churches, an extra chalice (preferably the smallest) can be used for this purpose. A box for altar breads, which is made of silver or pewter, was anciently used and is even more needed nowadays when the preference for real bread in Communion is returning. It is particularly helpful if a parish does not have a standing pyx or ciborium with a cover.

The ordinary pyx was a small box (generally circular and of silver, with a base and stem and a cross on the top), which was often used when the Sacrament was carried to the sick. A bell and lantern were in medieval times carried before on these occasions. Very often there was a little detachable round box fitted inside the pyx that could be easily removed and put into a small bag or purse to carry to the sick. Those were the days when reservation had come to be in one kind only. Nowadays for carrying the Sacrament in both kinds, a plain glass cylinder with screw top should also be used to carry the consecrated wine. It should fit into a metal case, the upper part of which might contains a receptacle for the consecrated bread. The consecrated bread and wine can then be put into a small paten and chalice when at the home of the communicant for the distribution. Private Communion sets are often presented to the clergy. Such cases may contain a small (preferably not too small) chalice and paten, with cruets, canister, and a spoon. It may be well to add to their usefulness by ensuring that the chalice does not look like it came from a dollhouse but is large enough for the dignity of holding the Sacrament. Chalices are generally of silver or gold, or silver gilt. Nowadays silver is so affordable (comparatively and historically speaking, that is, among precious metals) that pewter has ceased to be a real economy for most churches who might struggle more with the cost.

The flagons for holding the wine and water were generally of silver or pewter, but they were sometimes of crystal. That for the wine was distinguished from the other by gilding or by a letter (such as *V* for the wine and *A* for the water) or by some other mark; and such a distinction is necessary for cruets of an opaque material. The rubric of our prayer book is clear: "During the Great Thanksgiving, it is appropriate that there be only one chalice on the Altar, and, if need be, a flagon of wine from which additional chalices may be filled after the Breaking of the Bread."[31] The use of multiple chalices on the altar during the Great Thanksgiving is a definite mark not only of a cleric who has not been attentive to the rubrics but one who has come to value speed and efficiency over the beauty and symbolism of the single chalice. When flagons have metal lids, these should be so hinged that they lie readily open without having to be held in that position. Such vessels generally have handles as well. There should always be one or two spare flagons in the sacristy in case of breakages.

The basin and ewer are required for washing the minister's hands at the Lord's Supper. Sometimes two metal basins were used, one of which often had a lion's head spout under the rim so that the water could be poured from it into the other. For economy a plain glass bowl can be bought and a glass ewer to stand in it. This ewer might be rather larger than the cruets.

The censer (or thurible) needs no special description here. Where silver is out of the question, it may be of white metal or of brass. The total

---

31. *1979 Book of Common Prayer*, 407.

length of censer and chains may be forty-three inches. An incense-boat (or ship) and the spoon are also needed. Censers nowadays are often made too large. Single chain or three chain may be used, but the minister will often find that a three-chain censer, though more difficult to get used to at the first, helps ensure that the censer bowl hangs much more evenly and level.

The processional crosses may be three in number, one for ordinary use, a second (which was in old times generally of wood and painted red and without a figure) being reserved for Lent (and in some churches Advent as well), and a third of precious materials and special design for use on great festivals. The principal cross may have a figure upon it—*facie crucifixi* in the Sarum Missal; sometimes there were figures also of St. Mary and St. John. Often the processional cross was so made that it could be taken off the staff at the end of the procession and placed on a base upon the altar. This was indeed the way in which altar crosses came to be used. Processional crosses are very ancient, but it was not till the medieval period that crosses began occasionally to be placed on the altar.

Crucifer with Processional Cross[32]

32. 1913. Photograph by V. K. Blaiklock.

Of the processional cross, as of most other things, it may be said that proportion comes first, workmanship second, and material third—the latter without the two former being worse than useless. A poor church can have a very beautiful cross of wood, which is much better than a badly designed and executed one of greater pretension. The cross should not be kept exposed out of service time but should be put away. A tall locker or stand in the vestry or sacristy will be convenient, and in new churches provision should be made for this. The smallest length for cross and staff together would be about six foot and eight inches. Care should be taken that a metal cross is not too heavy to be conveniently carried, especially when processions are long, as they ought generally to be.

The processional candlesticks or torches may vary much in size and material. Sometimes they were short and sometimes long, sometimes of metal and sometimes of wood, and sometimes tapers or torches were fixed on to a plain round staff or handle and sometimes the candlesticks were taken from the altar. Dearmer would suggest, as very convenient for ordinary use, candlesticks of wood painted red or green (unless original work in metal can be paid for), three feet and nine inches, with the bases separate and weighted so that the shafts of the candlesticks can be easily dropped into and lifted out of them when they are set down before the altar. In our time, something similar in brass or silver is not generally outside the realm of possibility for the average parish.

Font tapers and christening tapers were anciently used at holy baptism, the latter being lighted and placed in the child's hand (or, when the baptized is an infant, a sponsor's hand) after baptism, while the former was carried by the clerk to the font and held during the service. Perhaps the two were sometimes identical. While font tapers are not needed in our time, given the advent of modern light, they do still add to the dignity of the sacrament of baptism and could be restored by using the tapers carried in the normal entrance and exit processions for this purpose. And, of course, there is still a need for hand tapers for processions at liturgies like the Great Vigil of Easter and Candlemas. These handheld tapers were not usually borne in candlesticks but were held in the hand, sometimes with a napkin. In our time they can be found with a plastic or cardboard candle holder. When candles or tapers are used by acolytes for outdoor processions, it is almost a necessity to carry them in lanterns fixed to staves. Such lanterns should have glass panels all round and may conveniently be made to swing from a bracket shaped like a pitchfork and attached to the top of the staff.

Banners may vary considerably in size, shape, material, and device. It is possible to make them quite simply. Embroidered ones are doubtless the ideal, but they are expensive if they are worth having. If our churches had half as many banners and those banners had twice as much spent on them, it would be far better. A mere profusion of gold and silk is nothing in itself. A banner cannot be designed by amateurs who do not understand the craft (though they can often carry out the work under advice), nor can it be ordered from a shop like a pound of tea. The common idea is that the design is nothing and the materials, everything. But the truth is that the design is everything for it includes the selection of the right materials, and the design must be paid for apart from the materials—for artists have to live. Now, a serious sum thus spent is but a small proportion of the money usually wasted on pretentious and vain banners.

The virge or mace, which is carried by the officer to whom it gives a name, may be a wand of wood, either short (four or five feet) or long (six or seven feet), tipped with metal or with a device (such as a cross or the symbol or figure of the patron saint), or it may be altogether of metal, as in our cathedrals. The smaller wands, which are badges of office for the churchwardens, are of wood, according to a very constant tradition, either unpainted with plain metal heads or painted white with a few inches at the end blue or gilt. A revival of wands for the church wardens is sorely needed to demonstrate that worship and the administrative life of the parish cannot be cleanly separated.

Something may be said for the paschal candlestick, which may be, for economy, of painted wood but for which donations for a proper one made of brass or silver is hardly impossible. It should be not less than about six feet high. It is unfortunate that not all churches have followed the 1979 prayer book's revival of the Great Vigil of Easter, along with the corresponding importance it gives to the paschal candle—a reality that had not yet developed in Dearmer's time. The lighting of the paschal candle from the newly kindled fire at the Great Vigil carries profound significance that is almost entirely lost if a reusable oil candle is used. These reusable oil candles only communicate the value of saving a few dollars, and for the great paschal flame, we can surely do more.

The rubric indicates that "it is customary that the paschal candle burn at all services from Easter Day through the Day of Pentecost."[33] Here it is helpful to be reminded of how rubrics function. There are rubrics

---

33. *1979 Book of Common Prayer*, 287.

that are obligatory (those that say something is done in a certain way). There are also rubrics which are advisory and permissive. This particular rubric is of the latter kind. It does not say that the paschal candle shall burn at all services from Easter Day through the Day of Pentecost but only says that it is customary. The parson familiar with the tradition of the church (and the history of revision that led to the 1979 prayer book) will know that the paschal candle burning for the entirety of the Great Fifty Days is a custom in the Eastern Orthodox church that our prayer book sought to restore. In the west, the tradition of the Great Fifty Days had long since disappeared and the custom in Western Christianity was for the candle to be extinguished on Ascension Day. So, while the parson who wishes to follow the ideals of the prayer book framers is certainly encouraged to adopt the custom of the candle burning for the entirety of the restored Great Fifty Days, one should not cast aspersions at the cleric who seeks to hold to the more Western custom of extinguishing the candle on Ascension Day.

Regardless of when the candle burns, the rubric further elucidates that "from Easter Day through the Day of Pentecost, the paschal candle, if used, should be burning in its customary place before the people assemble."[34] This means that the candle should be lit before people arrive so that it gives a sense of an eternal flame; it should not be lit mere moments before the liturgy like the other candles. The rubrics of the prayer book clearly (and rightfully) assume the paschal candle will burn for all funerals as well. It is also traditional for it to be used at any baptismal liturgies that fall outside of the Great Fifty Days.

There are some who have developed the idea that it should be used in confirmation liturgies as well as anytime the bishop is visiting. This is a confusion, though, based on its use during the rite of baptism (which is wholly appropriate), the connection of baptism to confirmation, and the role of the bishop as the normative celebrant of baptism. The use of the paschal candle is not suggested in the rite of confirmation, which is a renewal and not a reenactment of baptism. Furthermore, the paschal candle is only used when the bishop is celebrating if the bishop is celebrating during the Great Fifty Days or if it is a baptismal liturgy. The person of the bishop is not determinative in the use of the paschal candle, but the liturgical moment and rite is what dictates its use.

---

34. *1979 Book of Common Prayer*, 143.

COLORS, VESTMENTS, AND ORNAMENTS

There remain to be mentioned the funeral accessories, which are further treated later in this book. The bier or hearse should not be more than about two feet high. It should have handles to avoid the necessity of shouldering the coffin in church. The hearse cloth or coffin pall may be crafted to communicate the truth of Easter joy that accompanies every funeral. There is at times an unnecessary hankering after gloom at funerals. Ancient palls in old miniatures are often of bright colors—the following examples being typical: cloth of gold; black velvet, with a wide cross all through of silver tissue; red with a gold cross; black with a gold cross; blue with a red cross.[35]

At the same time, one wonders if, in the nearly half century since the 1979 prayer book made it even more clear that the burial of the dead is an Easter liturgy, we have swung too far in that direction. After all, the prayer book is clear that the paschal truth does not make grief un-Christian, and the parson who refuses the use of black hangings or refuses to conduct a more somber funeral—particularly when the death was a true tragedy that has had a cataclysmic impact upon the family or community—can hardly be said to have a true pastoral sensibility. In most parishes, this can be resolved by having a hearse cloth or pall that matches the festal hangings used at Easter and a second one that matches the black hangings used at the Requiem Eucharist on All Souls' Day. Or, if a black requiem set is not possible, another perfectly acceptable approach is to have a second pall made to match the Advent hangings in a rich dark blue with Comper purple orphreys. This also allows for the vestments, including cope, tunicle, dalmatic, and chasuble, to match the pall. After all, blue was often the medieval substitute for black and the Advent symbolism redolent of hope and that curious "yes but not yet" feeling is also perfectly appropriate for a funeral liturgy. Whether black or dark blue is used for the second pall, the family and parson may choose whether white, gold, blue, or black better makes manifest the reality of the day and, in either case, the proclamation of the Easter Gospel can become more profound.

---

35. In Dearmer's handbook, he also noted of funeral palls, "they were also powdered with the badges and bore the scutcheons of the deceased sewn about the border. Several gorgeous medieval herse-cloths still remain, some of them in the possession of the London City Companies. At the funeral of George II a purple pall was used; the white pall used at Mr. Gladstone's funeral, and the white pall embroidered with the royal arms used at the Funeral of Queen Victoria, will be remembered." Dearmer, *Parson's Handbook*, 164.

The processional cross and funeral candlesticks may, as earlier noted, be different than those used at other times. These may be all made of wood and painted the same color, and that color is not bound to be black but should rather be chosen so as to harmonize with the hearse cloth; for instance, a blue or black hearse cloth with a red cross would suggest the use of red candlesticks. The candlesticks may be about four feet high. Seven candlesticks are perhaps the best number—three on each side and one at the east end of the bier—while four might be regarded as a convenient minimum. Sometimes there were only two, one at either end, while in other cases many more were used, and some old pictures show a rack standing on either side of the hearse into which the torches are dropped; the more elaborate use was to place the coffin within a frame which was covered with innumerable candles. Tapers in large numbers were also carried in the hands of those present at a funeral. A handbell was always rung before the funeral procession, as is still the custom in some places.

4

Vestries and Sacristies

THE TERM VESTRY COMES from the old French word *vestiarie*, which means a place where clothes are kept, and it was the word used in England to refer to the room where vestments and ceremonial items were kept, along with where clergy and lay leaders could gather for discussions and administrative tasks. This is why the Episcopal Church refers to the elected leadership of the parish as a vestry—that is the room in which they used to meet. The term sacristy, however, comes from the Latin word *sacrarium*, which means a place that is holy or sacred. It is a room used as well to store vestments and ceremonial items, in addition to often being where the ministers will vest before services.

If it is difficult to put up with the single vestry of an older church, it is still more inconvenient to find oneself in a parish church of earlier date where there is often no vestry at all. At the present day our architects are more liberal, and I shall in this chapter assume the existence of several different sorts of vestries that are almost indispensable. The exact makeup and number will vary from parish to parish but attention should be paid that there is a place for everything and everyone. In most cases, these will be the ministers' vestry and sacristy, the choir vestry, and the churchwardens' vestry (or the office, meeting room, and parson's study). In addition to these, a room where large articles can be stored will be found most useful.

THE MINISTERS' VESTRY AND THE SACRISTY

There is need of a place for the vestments of the priest and lay ministers to be stored, and it is convenient if the ministers may also vest in the same space. There is also need of a place to store the sacred items needed for the altar. In some churches, this is taken care of with a handsome ministers' vestry and sacristy in a single room. In other buildings, though, there may be need to divide up the two rooms, keeping the altar sacristy close to the altar itself and the ministers' vestry close to the nave, either at the rear of the church where the ministers will form the procession or at the front of the church.

For the ministers' vestry, when cupboards and chests are put in the church itself, it must be remembered that in the hands of an artist these may be beautiful articles of furniture. They should be seen as ornaments, not disfigurements to the church. It is far better to provide in this way for the vestments than to curtain off a transept or chapel for the purpose when there is no vestry. Vesting in church is a perfectly seemly proceeding if the parson arrives in a cassock, and a chapel may work well for that purpose, if the parson prefers. But the chapel should be left uncurtained, for chapels are very beautiful features of church architecture, and should not be turned into vestries or organ chambers for a solitary purpose.

In some churches with large chancels, a vestry can be made by building a wall or screen about eight feet high across the chancel, some seven or eight feet from the east end. The high altar stands against this screen, and the space between the wall and the east end of the church forms a vestry, to which doors on either side of the altar give admittance. This was a common arrangement in abbey churches, and existed also in some parish churches. It has been successfully adopted in more than one new church, but of course, it requires very careful planning in the hands of a good architect.

Regardless of whether a single vestry and sacristy is used, or some other approach, several items are essential. First, a table or shelf should be available upon which lies the service register. Where many vestments are kept, a press[1] or very large cupboard will be wanted. In modern churches, a combination of drawers and cupboards for hanging items can often be installed by a skilled cabinet maker who is provided the proper directions.

---

1. This is the more traditional British term for a wardrobe.

The parsons of small churches will not need more than two or three wooden or plated metal yokes or wide wooden hangers (such as can be procured from a vestment shop) hanging in an ordinary cupboard. These yokes hold chasubles and copes very well and are far superior to a normal hanger, which will invariably result in vestments sliding off or falling to the floor when the hanger breaks. Some people prefer to keep all their vestments hanging from yokes in a large cupboard, not shelves or drawers at all, and there is a great deal to be said for this arrangement—indeed, copes of the Gothic pattern need to be kept on metal yokes, bent to fit them.

The number of large drawers and cupboards will depend upon the size of the sacristy and the number of services. In churches where there are three ministers at the sung Eucharist, it is convenient to keep the vestments for this service in one large set of drawers about three feet and three inches high, nine feet long or more (so that all the ministers can vest at it). This may be divided by a partition into two sets of drawers, which may be used for vestments, altar linen, and other items. A smaller set of drawers can then be reserved for other celebrations, for which separate vestments will be needed.

A small set of drawers may be three-and-a-half feet high and four feet nine inches by two feet nine inches broad. The drawers should be shallow (two inches inside), so that only one set of vestments may be kept in each—this saves time and spares the vestments. If, in ordering a dresser or having a set of drawers constructed, the parson has twice as many drawers as might be wanted, there will be joy in this provision before very long. The burses may be kept in the drawers of the vestments with which they are generally used, or in a separate drawer. The top drawers will be found useful for appareled amices; and, if there is no cupboard for the priests' albes, they can be folded in the bottom drawer if it is made, say, six inches deep. A cupboard for the priests' albes and girdles is, however, more convenient. Vestments that are not of silk may need protection from moths, for which purpose a cedar-wood lining to the drawers is excellent. Cedar wood is most useful also as a corrective to the musty smell that besets vestries where incense is not used. A piece of white calico or stout linen laid over the vestments in each drawer will help to keep the dirt from them. Gold or silver embroidery may be protected by unbleached calico, and heavily embroidered vestments will need cotton wool under the folds if they are put in a drawer.

Sometimes drawers in a vestry have a folding lid on the top to keep the vestments clean if they are laid out some time before the service begins. A simpler plan is to cover the vestments with a piece of white linen. The top of the press where the vestments are laid out may also have a piece of white linen laid on it. The vestments should be put out in the following order (which is, of course, the opposite of the order in which they are put on so that that the first thing put on lies on top of the stack): chasuble (or dalmatic/tunicle), stole (for priest and deacon), maniple, girdle, albe, and on the top of all, the amice. If there is a procession, the cope will be laid above the chasuble, unless there is a cope stand.

A cope stand is extremely useful when the sacristy is large. It consists of a wooden upright, about five-and-a-half feet high, resting on a firm base, and having a well-rounded yoke on the top. After the procession the cope is slipped on to the stand in a moment and the morse fastened. The cope can then be properly put away at leisure after the service. If there is a very large cupboard, copes can always be kept thus on their stands with a linen cloth over them; and in shallower cupboards they can still be hung from yokes.

A picture may hang above the place where the vestments are kept and laid out. Under it might be placed the hymn "Come Holy Ghost" and the Forty-Third Psalm, "Give judgment for me, O God," both of which were formerly appointed to be said while vesting. A restoration of the habit of prayers while vesting can help quiet many an anxious parson's mind before the liturgy, and it is to be commended. A basin, if possible, fitted with a tap and drain, may be provided for the parson to wash hands before celebrating. Near it will hang a towel.

A special cupboard should be reserved for the servers' albes, cassocks, and surplices. If albes are worn, two hangers at least will be needed for each server, one for the albe and girdle and one for the surplice. A shelf above can be kept for a box to hold the appareled amices, if there is not a special drawer for them.

In the sacristy, the room should include two deep drawers, one for candle ends and one for dusters and polishing leathers, also two long drawers for candles of which a good stock should be laid in at a time, as wax improves by keeping. Supposing the cupboard to be a small one—four feet by five feet—the two bottom drawers might be nine inches deep (for dusters and candle ends); the next two, six inches deep by the whole breadth of the cupboard (for candles); the next two stages might contain six short drawers four inches deep; and above this might be two or three rows of shelves, the space between the two lower shelves being divided into wide pigeonholes by partitions.

Where incense is used a special cupboard is convenient. As for the incense itself, it is wisest to avoid compounds. Nothing is so good as simple *gum olibanum*, which is indeed "frank" or pure incense; it is this which is generally used in the East and also in the Roman basilicas. It can be bought at any large apothecary or from a reputable merchant online. However, care should be taken in choosing a merchant, as much of what is available online is far from the pure nard incense that burns cleanly and with a pleasant fragrance. Pure incense is cheaper as well as pleasanter and fresher than the compounds, which are for the most part rather sickly and stuffy.

If there are complaints about the incense, they should not be dismissed as mere prejudices. Instead, care should be taken that no benzoin or storax be mixed in the incense since these ingredients do affect certain people. When people do complain, it is usually not the incense that irritates but the chemicals in the popular quick-light charcoal. Instead, pure and sustainable coconut charcoal (taking care to ensure that there are no additives or chemicals added) will work well. This can be laid on an electric coil burner, turned once every two to three minutes until glowing and hot. It does require a bit more work, but it burns cleanly, and once the habit is learned, it is not too cumbersome in the least. The charcoal can also be heated in a minute if the lumps are held with tongs over a gas flame, but an electric coil burner is easier and a bit safer. Care should be taken that the burner is never left unattended when on and it should always be placed on a secure stand, lest someone trip over the cord and bring more excitement to the liturgy than was planned.

The incense should be kept in a canister holding not less than a pound. Many tea caddies form excellent boxes for this purpose. The incense boat or ship and the spoon should be kept near it. If the boat is broader than the usual shape, less incense will be wasted. The lid should lift up at both ends. The spoon will be less apt to spill if it is made more like an ordinary teaspoon than is usual and less like the small stick with a miniature depression that is more common and was likely used by primitive humanity.

Near these should stand a covered earthenware jar or steel bucket for the charcoal, filled partway with sand. The plain brown jars that are used for cooking purposes are very suitable and can be bought of a good shape. If a steel bucket is preferred, it can be found at most hardware stores. The packets of charcoal should be emptied into this and not kept loose near the vestries, as they make dust. If a pair of small tongs are kept near the jar, the thurifer can work without soiling the hands. The censer should always be emptied as soon as possible after use into this earthenware or steel bucket. It should never, under any circumstances (even if the thurifer thinks it has cooled sufficiently) be emptied into a regular trash receptacle. St. Paul's Second Epistle to the Thessalonians tells us our Lord will return with fire, but there is no need for carelessness on our part to hasten that return. Wrapping the removable pan at the bottom of the censer with foil and replacing that foil regularly makes the task of keeping the censer free from accumulated burnt coal and spent incense much easier. It will also keep the smoke cleaner and fresher.

A good plan, where there is room, is for there to be a narrow cupboard in which to keep all these articles. The cupboard may be divided by a partition from the top to within twelve inches of the bottom. One side will be for the censer, which will hang free from hooks screwed into the top of the cupboard; the spoon and tongs can hang near it on small pegs. The other side will be divided horizontally into shelves for the boat, canister, and jar. If there is no vertical partition, these articles may be kept on a shelf at the top of the cupboard. At the bottom of the cupboard will be a deep drawer in which extra packets of charcoal may be stored, for charcoal is cheaper if bought in large quantities. If there is no cupboard for the censer, it can be hung on an iron bracket about six inches long with a crook at the end, or it may hang from a hook in a small shelf, on which the canister and charcoal jar can stand. But a place should be chosen that is not accessible to children. In any case the censer should hang quite free, touching neither the wall nor the ground.

A little standing basin, under a filter, may also be provided for the purificators. After each service the purificator can be rinsed in this basin and then put by for the wash in a special basket or on a rail. The basin should be emptied in the piscina. The filter will also supply the pure water for the Eucharist. Another plan is to have on the table a glass basin into which the purificator is dropped; the server then empties the water cruet into the basin. In any case the purificator should be rinsed immediately after use, as stains are difficult to remove if they are allowed to dry. OxiClean does wonders for removing red wine stains and has lessened the complaints that might be given by those preferring white wine because it makes the cleanup simpler. As with all things, the easier approach, particularly when it removes beauty or obscures the rite, is rarely to be preferred.

A safe for the vessels is most necessary, and it is better to have it separate from that in which more or less musty registers are kept. A cupboard for the cruets, canister, basin and ewer will also be needed, and here too wine and breads might be kept, and perhaps the boxes containing the corporals and purificators. If real bread is used, a small refrigerator may enable the bread to be used a couple days later at a midweek service. Near the cupboards might stand a chest of drawers for altar linen. One of an ordinary shape would serve, but it would be better if it were made with shallower drawers. The lower drawers will be useful for storing such things as Lenten veils. One drawer will be needed for the spare linen cloths of the high altar (one extra fair linen and two under cloths at the least) and another for those that are in use. Another drawer for the linen belonging to other altars is needed along with another for keeping the sets of vestment apparels that are not in actual use. Bags of lavender or chipped sandalwood are useful against insects, and contribute to the general sweetness and cleanness.

The frontal cupboard, chest, or locker may be in some convenient spot near the altar. If the frontals are stretched on frames, the chest should open at the top and be large enough for twice as many frontals as are in use. A chest that is only just large enough will prove a nuisance when somebody presents a new frontal. If the frontals are folded up when not in use (which is much the better way, except in the case of some heavily embroidered frontals), a cupboard should be provided with shallow shelves large enough for each frontal to be folded in four, with a shelf or two for frontlets and some spare shelves, or the frontals may be put away in drawers. An inventory of all the linen belonging to the church should be carefully made and kept up to date.

It is obvious that many churches have no room for all the various cupboards I have suggested. But whatever arrangements are made, care should be taken that there is really a place for everything, even if cupboards and chests have to be put up in the church itself, which, indeed, was the usual ancient practice and helps to furnish the church if the cupboards are properly designed. Even the cheapest cupboard in the most out-of-the way vestry should be painted a pleasant color or the wood left in its natural state. Varnished pitch pine and imitation-wood stains are almost as destructive of beauty and warmth of effect as is the old-fashioned oak graining.

Even in a smaller parish, a dedicated sacristan is invaluable. The responsibility for everything must be laid upon the sacristan, who should not be a priest. The sacristan's position is a most important one, and the one who serves in it must be devout, sensible, and even-tempered. The sacristan will not have to *do everything alone*, but must see that *everything is done*, which means that the sacristan must be kind and pleasant in manner as well as careful and methodical. A competent one should have a general knowledge of the matters the sacristan has to deal with and ought to possess (or be lent from the parson's library) one or two sound books on ceremonial so that the sacristan may understand the principles and the practice of this work. The sacristan (or, in churches that have one, the verger) will see that everything is ready ten minutes before service begins on Sunday—the vestments laid out, the candles lit by a taperer, and the charcoal heated by the thurifer.

It used to be that the sacristan would see that a list of servers was posted on the wall for every service in the week, and when anyone is to be away, the sacristan would fill the open place. In our time, the advent of online scheduling programs has greatly lessened this burden. In particular, the system from Ministry Scheduler Pro is excellent and enables people to get reminders of when they are serving and to request a substitute, which then anyone on the system who is qualified can fill. It is still needed for a single person—sacristan or verger—who is not the priest to take responsibility for ensuring all are present and that substitutions are made at a liturgy, no matter the method used for scheduling.

The sacristan is well aided by an altar guild whose responsibility is to assist the sacristan in ensuring all is set properly for each worship service. Someone in the guild will be needed to care of the vestments, and another, of the washing and mending. Others may be needed to polish the brass work and to trim the candles, which may require two or three visits a week. Another may be needed to dust the high altar and see to the altar cloths, and another, to see to the chapel. The guild also should be charged with changing the frontals. If there are several helpers, each responsible for his or her own piece of work and all responsible to the sacristan and through that person to the parson, the most perfect cleanliness and order can be secured, a good deal of money will be saved, and those who work for the church will love the church better and use it more.

It is impossible to lay down rules as to the times for washing linen, as much depends upon the smokiness of the atmosphere; but the following general hints may be found useful:

- Wash the fair linen cloth of the altar once a month, and the undercloths, once a quarter.
- Strip the altar entirely twice a year on a fine day, from morning till evening, so that everything may be well aired; thoroughly clean everything connected with the altar.
- Wash such of the corporals as are in regular use once a month, and the towels, once a week.
- Let a responsible person wash the purificators every Monday.
- Let all the linen be clean on the greater festivals.
- Wash the chalice and paten after each service with soap and water.
- Empty the water cruet after use, and wash both cruets thoroughly once each week.
- Clean brass, pewter, copper, and silver, every week. Metal loses much of its beauty if it is lacquered, but unlacquered metal needs regular polishing. A good polish at least twice each year, often before Christmas and then before Easter, will help keep this up.

The church will often contract a sexton or a group of dutiful volunteers to be responsible for dusting the church, seeing that the font, pulpit, lamps (which have to be cleaned with hot water), pews, kneelers, and other items are kept clean and in good repair.

When it comes to the methods for cleaning, wash the linen in warm water, with white soap. Ink stains may be removed by lemon juice mixed with salt, or by salts of lemon. To take out wine stains, as mentioned earlier, OxiClean is an excellent product. The older practice was to hold the stained part in boiling milk, but boiled milk is now best left for adding to tea. To remove wax from fabric, cover with a piece of paper towel and iron with a hot iron, which pulls the wax up into the paper towel. To remove grease or dirt, clean with a flannel moistened with benzine. Wax can easily be removed from the tops of candlesticks if a little oil has been previously rubbed on them. To clean brass, rub with polishing paste, and polish afterwards with a leather. A very little oil of vitriol in the paste will remove tarnish. Brass is much less trouble if it is cleaned every week and polished regularly. Lacquered brass never looks nearly as satisfactory as polished brass; it is best, therefore, if someone can be found to see to the polishing to remove lacquer, which may be done with oxalic acid. To clean silver, use Tarni-Shield, Hagerty's Silver Polish (with gloves), or Wright's Silver Cream. Sweet oil is an ultrapure olive oil available from a pharmacy, and it removes burnt incense from silver censers if the disposable aluminum foil wrapping the basin has not sufficiently protected the censer. Painted woodwork, especially if it be covered with a coat of varnish, can be easily cleaned with soap and water and then Murphy's Oil Soap. Stone should be cleaned with brush, soap, and water. To clean wax candles, wipe them with a cloth damped with spirits of wine or turpentine. Stains may be removed from printed books by a solution of citric acid, the strength of which can be tested on a sheet of paper. Ancient silver should hardly ever be cleaned with whitening but should be washed with soap and water and wiped with a soft cloth. Paste should also be avoided on ancient brass work—a little oil and a weekly rub with a cloth ought to be sufficient.

THE CHOIR VESTRY

The room where the choir vestments are kept should be as large as possible and rather long for its breadth so that the choir can form up in a double row. If the chairs are arranged down the midst of the room in two rows with their backs to each other, the chorister can more easily be kept quiet while they are waiting. A card with the word "Silence" written may advantageously be hung on the wall. Large shallow cupboards will take up most of the walls. These will contain separate pegs or hangers for each cassock and for each surplice, with each pair bearing the wearer's name and number. Sometimes the cupboards have no doors but are protected instead by linen curtains hung from rods, the cupboard frame being retained—this has the advantage of cheapness. Every cassock and surplice should be numbered; and someone should be found who will take charge of all the surplices, send them to the wash, and keep them in repair.

Yet another cupboard will be needed for music, which may be divided into large pigeonholes and protected by a colored linen curtain. Music stored in lateral file cabinets, each set of given work in a hanging folder, often is more efficient spacewise and preserves the music better as well. If each set of music is kept strictly in its place by the librarian (who must be a responsible person) and duly inventoried, tidiness will be gained and much money saved.

VESTRIES AND SACRISTIES

THE CHURCHWARDENS' VESTRY (OR THE OFFICE, MEETING ROOM, AND PARSON'S STUDY)

The churchwardens' vestry has largely gone out of use, having been replaced by larger meeting rooms for the vestry to gather and modern offices in which most records are kept. So, it is of course the name that has gone out of use, not the need for dedicated space in the church for each of these various needs.

A well-organized church office will promote a decorous spirit, as well as save time and money, particularly if the little things this room should contain are kept in a fixed place and not in loose cardboard boxes or scattered about aimlessly. Provision should be made for the needed books, as well as for the minutes and papers of the vestry. Filing cabinets are a common choice, but a far superior choice in our time is to store documents on the cloud using a service like Google Drive. It will enable everything to be kept in a secure location, where moth and rust do not destroy, and where it is accessible to clergy and lay leaders whether or not they are in the building. As long as appropriate care is taken to ensure that sensitive data is secured in a robust church management solution (Realm from ACS Solutions is excellent for membership and financial data management), storing other records in a cloud service will be seen as a great help.

At the desk where people are greeted, whether it be one where a volunteer or a parish secretary or administrator sits, there should be kept a collection of decent pens and the church's kalendar. The Episcopal Church Revised Common Lectionary Lesson Calendar, published by Church Publishing, is currently the best option. Some of the others are not always up to date with the most recent revisions of *Lesser Feasts and Fasts*. An online resource that is often much more up to date and which follows both the Revised Common Lectionary and the current version of *Lesser Feasts and Fasts* is "The Lectionary Page."[2] In a nearby cabinet there should also be some notepaper, envelopes, and correspondence cards. A handwritten note from the parson can be one of the finest arts of the pastoral craft and is often much appreciated by the recipient.

In a safe, or at least in a securely locked drawer, will be kept the baptism register, marriage registers, burial register, and parish register. While much of this data can be maintained electronically through church membership systems like the aforementioned Realm, keeping the

---

2. "The Lectionary Page" can be found at lectionarypage.net.

traditional bound registers connects us to our past in a way that digital records never will. One only has to see a descendant pass their hand over the signature in the register of a bride from generations ago to see the value in such things.

On the walls may be hung a map of the parish and any portraits or other pictures of parochial interest. It is really a good work to keep in this way a memorial of the past history of the church and of the various officers who have served it. A shelf or two will certainly be useful, here as in the other rooms, and there should be a shelf also with some standard books on theology, church history, the management of church services and affairs. For church administration, the resources from the Episcopal Church Foundation are highly commended.

5

General Principles of Ceremonial

WHAT IS SOMETIMES LACKING in books on ceremonial and ritual are the overarching points of the principles behind good ritual and ceremonial. The result is that people are able to adhere strictly to an imagined standard but sometimes lack the ability to contextualize and adapt for different circumstances and contexts. This runs the risk of our Lord's warning about tithing mint, dill, and cumin but neglecting the weightier matters of the law (Matt 23:23). Attention to some general principles will enable the parson to weigh the advice and possibilities for public worship and make choices that are authentic to the Anglican tradition and edifying to the people.

THE INTEGRITY OF SERVICES

The practice in the last century of making one morning service out of two and a half has happily died out. I'm speaking of the nineteenth and mid-twentieth century practice of turning morning prayer, the Great Litany, and Ante-Communion (with or without Holy Communion) into one long service. With this elimination, the church has also lost the entirely disastrous custom of introducing a pause in the middle of the Communion service, in order that the bulk of the congregation may absent themselves from the Holy Mysteries. Neither practice was in any way sanctioned by the prayer book, which distinctly names the time of departure as after the dismissal. (I am aware that this may come as a surprise to some people).

The rubrics on the dismissal in a eucharistic liturgy are quite clear, though somewhat distinct in each rite. In Rite One, the blessing is required ("The Bishop when present, or the Priest, gives the blessing") and the dismissal is optional ("The Deacon, or the Celebrant, may dismiss the people with these words").[1] In the Rite Two form of the liturgy, this pattern is reversed with the blessing given as optional (using the "may bless" phraseology)[2] and the dismissal required. The prayer book's dismissal echoes the ancient form, *Ite, missa est*, translated as "Go, you are dismissed." The ideal of the current book was that, hearing the dismissal, the people would leave. This is seen in the allowance for a hymn before or after the post-communion prayer,[3] which clearly does not allow for the current innovation of inserting a hymn between the blessing and before the dismissal itself. Admittedly, after being dismissed the people may stay and sing a final song or listen to an inspiring postlude, but these practices function as the denouement of a liturgy that has been closed with a proper dismissal.

In Dearmer's time, the struggle was in the restoration of Holy Communion as the principal act of worship on the Lord's day (one of the very first rubrics for worship of the current prayer book).[4] People had become accustomed to the practice of attending Ante-Communion and then leaving after the prayer for the church militant. He notes that the provision for an Ante-Communion service, which is a very primitive practice, was not intended to result in the disuse of the liturgy, but to increase the number of communions. The Reformers had the admirable ideal before them of introducing frequent Communion, but they were defeated by the inertia of a people that had been for centuries accustomed to communicating at Easter only. The revisers in 1661 still hoped that the insistence, as a minimum, on the Ante-Communion service would remind people of the duty to receive the Holy Communion, "some at least, every Sunday."[5] At last, in our own day, this ideal of the regular reception of

---

1. *1979 Book of Common Prayer*, 339.
2. *1979 Book of Common Prayer*, 366.
3. *1979 Book of Common Prayer*, 409.
4. *1979 Book of Common Prayer*, 13.
5. The importance of this duty was one of the answers of the bishops at the Savoy Conference of 1661, where it was said, "The Priest standing at the Communion Table, seemeth to give us an invitation to the holy Sacrament, and minds us of our duty, viz. To receive the holy Communion, some at least every Sunday, and though we neglect our duty, it is fit the Church should keep her standing." Buchanan, *Savoy Conference*, 24.

Communion has come into general practice in our church and is enshrined in the principles of the 1979 prayer book.

That said, there is still at times a lack of sense for the integrity of a liturgy. This is seen in the allowance of the prayer book rubrics for morning or evening prayer to substitute for the liturgy of the word in Holy Eucharist.[6] This provision was not the ideal of the prayer book but, similar to Ante-Communion in Dearmer's time, was an allowance because of the widespread use of morning prayer as the principal act of worship in many Episcopal parishes by the time of the middle of the twentieth century. It was hoped the rubric would help move parishes towards Holy Communion in a time of transition. The intention was not to create the blending of two entirely distinctive rites as a permanent practice.

In the end, liturgies should be practiced in the form in which they were intended. One should not cobble together an office and Communion liturgy. Furthermore, one should not create a Communion service by drawing from various supplements of our church or prayer books of different provinces of the Anglican Communion. Without fail, these approaches result in liturgy that seems to be the haphazard creation of the parson and not an integrated whole. This principle also holds for the use of service music, which should ideally come from full settings rather than from a variety of mass settings that are actually musically disjointed from one another.

THE HOURS OF THE SERVICE

The intention of the prayer book undoubtedly is that the Communion service should be the principal service of the day, at which the Sunday sermon is preached, but that there should be no consecration unless there are communicants. This was carried out, with the result that England as a whole was a nation of communicants, though communions were infrequent (less infrequent than before the Reformation) until about the middle of the nineteenth century, when the pre-Reformation custom of fasting Communion was revived and pressed in many quarters. The prayer book had ignored fasting Communion, presumably because the standard of the English Church was that of Scripture, the early church,

---

6. *1979 Book of Common Prayer*, 322, 354.

and the godly and ancient Fathers.[7] The historical research of the liturgical renewal movement in the twentieth century, along with the discovery of important documents of the first four centuries, fully justified the position that the requirement of fasting before Communion is not in the tradition of the early church. The primitive Eucharist was the culmination of the agape meal, and followed it.

In Dearmer's time, the struggle was with churches that had Eucharist followed by morning prayer, an order that ignored good liturgical principle and sense. In our own time, the custom in many parishes is an early service of Holy Eucharist (often without music) followed by the principal service of Holy Eucharist. In smaller parishes, the work involved in doing two services well may very well commend the practice of simply having one service of Holy Eucharist at which the entire community gathers together. However, at Episcopal parishes where all cannot gather at the same time and in the same space (or in parishes where there are sufficient lay ministers and clerical energy to preserve multiple services), the practice of an earlier and a later service on Sunday mornings does have much to commend it. As Dearmer noted in his own time, the practice of having additional celebrations at early or late hours for

---

7. The patristic basis for a rejection of the requirement of fasting communion was important to Dearmer. As he explains, "The supposed instances of fasting Communion in the early Church have disappeared—they are a catena of missing links—the conjecture made from the famous letter of Pliny being a particular instance of mistranslation and wrong deduction. A foreshadowing of the custom appears at a Council at Hippo, A.D. 393, which prohibited feasting in church and forbade priests to celebrate after the prandium (which was the second meal of the day) except on Maundy Thursday. St. Augustine's letter to Januarius, A.D. 400, continuously misunderstood, which alludes to this new adjustment, is about the Maundy Eucharist, and freely allows the Maundy communion after the prandium, but recommends for preference communion after a light refection at 3 p.m. After this the Communion came gradually to be fixed not before the early breakfast but before the prandium, the midday meal which was so grossly heavy that men were not considered fit to give evidence in the law courts after it. In the ninth century we find Walafrid Strabo saying (as earlier authorities had said) that because a man may slip into 'excess of drunkenness' at the prandium, he should not have this meal before communion, and this is what Strabo means by fasting (*De Rebus Eccles.* cap. 19). It was not till Aquinas (Summa, P. II. Q. CXLVII, art. 7) that the custom was fixed: some said still in the thirteenth century that the fast began when digestion was accomplished (this is about three hours after a meal, or the time of a midday Communion at the present day), others at the beginning of the day; and since there were various theories as to when the day began, Aquinas chose that of the Roman Church which began the day at midnight. At the Reformation the custom of fasting before a sacrament was dropped, except in the case of adult baptism. Jeremy Taylor (1660), who believed the custom to be apostolic, represents a minority." Dearmer, *Parson's Handbook*, 181–82.

the convenience of different classes is sometimes further justified by the resulting increase in the number of communions. But it must be remembered that these are additional services, and they must not be allowed to supplant the principal Eucharist.

With vestries and faith formation hours, it is now easy for the parson to discuss the hours of service and to meet the wishes of the people. In the average church these have probably changed little in the last fifty years. In parishes where no one comes to the early service on Sunday morning, it would be good to drop this weekly celebration, since such a service in an almost empty church can have a discouraging effect. In towns where a few more people attend, the early service has its justification. However, at the same time, it must be noted that the parson who simply dumps the early service, summarily telling the people who are accustomed to it that they now must come to the later service, will be unlikely to find the pews at the later service any fuller. Any movement in that direction should only be made after significant teaching, conversation, and a sense of consensus in the community about approaching Sunday mornings differently.

In some of our churches, a trend has developed of adding an evening service on Sunday, at five or six o'clock. This service could be in a slightly different style than the Sunday morning liturgies. It could be a bit more contemporary, like the Breaking Bread at Six liturgy at Christ Church Cathedral in Nashville, Tennessee, which alternates between jazz, bluegrass, or other offerings using talented local musicians. It could also be more traditional (like the Sunday evening choral evensongs that have long been a part of our heritage). What matters is less the style and more the quality of the liturgy. In particular, youth and young adults often particularly appreciate a Sunday evening offering, particularly when they have work or school requirements on Sunday morning—a cultural reality that is impossible to deny at this point. I should note as well that the parson will often find that younger people are generally drawn to what is actually more traditional rather than what their parents think of as contemporary. The congregation that gathers for the Sunday evening mass at Christ Church, Georgetown, in Washington, DC, for instance, is attracted by a traditional service of Eucharist, which is preceded by a Rite One offering of choral evensong.

SAYING AND SINGING

The Village Choir[8]

Parsons cannot expect to render their part of the service properly unless they have first had lessons in voice production, elocution, and singing. It is difficult to see why a priest should take less trouble over the training of the voice than an actor, except that, in this, as in the other arts, there is a tendency to consider anything good enough for the worship of God. To give directions in this book would only tend to put off the one necessary thing—that the parson who is untrained should lose no time in finding a good teacher. When clergy do so, it is safe to prophesy that they will be surprised at the mistakes they have unwittingly made even in the simple matter of reading the prayers. These mistakes are generally doubled in those parts that are sung.

Of those who willfully gabble the service, it is impossible to speak too strongly. The way in which the lessons are read, and the psalms and prayers said, in some churches is a crying scandal and is doing infinite harm. One can only hope that incumbents will insist on the younger clergy having proper instruction and dropping this miserable affectation. In cases where the incumbent offends, it is surely the duty of the

---

8. From the picture by Thomas Webster in the Victoria and Albert Museum, which was exhibited in the Royal Academy in 1847. The parish clerk stands in the midst and is leading the choir, who are singing very earnestly, and the musicians who play the cello, clarionet, and hautboy. The Rev. P. H. Ditchfield, F.S.A., wrote in 1907 (*The Parish Clerk*), that this picture is a "very exact presentment of the old village choir of the better sort." See Dearmer, *Parson's Handbook*, vii; Ditchfield, *Parish Clerk*, 9.

GENERAL PRINCIPLES OF CEREMONIAL

laity to remonstrate with all gentleness. The strongest measures must be taken to suppress the profane practices of overlapping, interrupting, clipping, mangling, gabbling, and mumbling. It is hardly necessary to say that these offenses have been frequently forbidden in every part of the church, the Roman Church itself having made frequent pronouncements against them.

At the same time, all drawling or mouthing of the service is also to be avoided, though this fault is far less common than it was. The prayers, being better known by all and said with a different object (that is, spoken to God), should not be read with the same emphasis and deliberation as the lessons (which are not as familiar and are addressed to the people as the object). But the parson who omits a single syllable in the recitation of the prayers may be sure that bad habits are encroaching.

While some seminaries do some training in vocal production, more work could certainly be done. In those dioceses where there is an option for local formation, this sort of training remains just as essential. The majority get into so many bad habits during the first few years of their ministry that they are prevented from ever becoming good preachers and readers. Multitudes of people have gone elsewhere or nowhere because their clergy have not learned to stand up and speak out in an audible fashion with attention to proper diction and enough presence to hold a room. It is not that we are really affected; it is that many are never taught the art of speaking simply, naturally, audibly, and boldly. It is left to chance, or taught in a perfunctory and inadequate fashion. Yet those who can speak properly by the light of nature are very rare indeed. Parsons should remember that much of the liturgy is prayer to God and the person speaking should speak as though they are, in fact, praying and not as though they were an orator on the stage.

It is to be observed that the prayer book provides for the more deliberate recitation of those prayers and key parts of the liturgy the people say with the priest (such as the Lord's Prayer, creeds, and confessions) by dividing them into short clauses. It is important to make a slight pause before these phrases, as otherwise the people will not keep together. The people should also be encouraged to follow the monastic habit of attentiveness in speaking at the same pace as the worshippers around them. When all do this, the liturgy continues at a gentle and meaningful pace.

The rubrics of the prayer book for the Psalter are clear "an asterisk divides each verse into two parts for reading or chanting. In reading, a distinct pause should be made at the asterisk."[9] This rubric remains lamentably unknown and unfollowed. Getting a congregation to follow at a Sunday service—particularly when there are likely to be visitors who are already confused by liturgical worship—is rarely a successful project. However, in parishes where there is a daily recitation of the office, the practice can begin to be introduced at the office by saying something like: "The portion of the psalms appointed for today is _____, we will read together, with a slight pause at the asterisk during which you may breathe in and out." After some time making this practice regular, the second half of the instruction about using your breath to time the length of the pause may be omitted. Then, the practice having become appreciated, it may begin to be introduced during Sunday worship. Without the pause, the beautiful rhythm is lost in a miserable gabble.

It is clumsy and meaningless for the choir or people to repeat the opening words (known as the incipit) of the Lord's Prayer, creed, and other parts of the liturgy after the priest has said them. Common sense as well as the old rubrics would have them join in without this repetition, and so it is directed in the first prayer book. When bulletins are used, this can be explained by having the priest say the incipit with the people joining in after that first phrase. The modern innovation of announcing each moment in the liturgy is an intrusion in the liturgical action and would be like announcing each movement in a dance instead of being carried in the flow, which is how liturgical worship is meant to function.

As for morning prayer and evensong, the musical part does not begin till the priest says, "Lord, open our lips," and the people's mouths are opened for praise. That which precedes the versicle is a penitential introduction, and the service proper begins with the versicle, from which point the service should be sung as far as the anthem. It is far seemlier, and more helpful to the spirit of prayer, if the general confession is said in a humble voice, though audibly (*privatim ut audiatur*), the same with the Lord's Prayer. The exhortation and absolution are to be said in the natural voice in accordance with the sound tradition of our church.

In short, choir offices were never meant to be intoned throughout but to grow from the solemn quietness of the penitential introduction to the joyful song of the office proper and then (unless the litany is to follow) to drop back into the quiet intercessions at the close. All the prayers after the anthem should be said without note, and their amens, said quietly by

---

9. *1979 Book of Common Prayer*, 583.

the people, a practice that heightens their devotional effect and prevents the service from dragging.

A further distinction may be made in divine service by singing the creed and the Lord's Prayer a third or a fifth lower than the pitch at which the acclamations are sung, or else by using the natural voice. In the unreformed books they were said secretly up to the last clauses, which were treated as a versicle and response; and, though we of course now say them audibly, still, a distinction in the manner of their saying has a good effect.

In the Eucharist, also, a fashion came about of singing or monotoning the whole service from beginning to end. This is certainly without precedent. For in the first place, we have no tradition in its favor since the issue of the first English prayer book. In the second place we know that large portions of the Latin service were said in so low a voice as to be inaudible to the congregation. We are, of course, bound to say every part of the service quite clearly and audibly, but that is no reason why it should all be monotoned. The strongest tradition in Dearmer's time was that the Lord's Prayer and Collect for Purity should be said in a clear voice without note. If desired, though, the hymnal and altar book provide tones for the Lord's Prayer. The Collect for Purity may be sung on a monotone or using the same tone as the collect of the day. However, the exhortations, confession, absolution, comfortable words, and also the prayer of humble access should be spoken and not sung. We may take it as a safe rule that these (and of course the words of administration also) should not be monotoned. If clergy are attentive to those parts of the liturgy that have tones in the altar book for how they are sung, they will not go wrong.

To this it may be added that the following prayers may be said on a lower note or without note: the prayers of the people, the consecration prayer, and the post-communion prayer. With these it is perhaps a matter of taste, but many who monotone these prayers feel a certain inappropriateness in using a note for the consecration, and for this, of course, they have the precedent of the Latin rite.

MUSIC

A parson is not necessarily a musician, but is still responsible for securing certain broad principles, both musical and moral. In the first place the parson must insist on the fact being recognized that the normal musical parts of the service are the Psalms (and canticles in the office), along with the *Gloria in excelsis* (and/or *Kyrie* or *Trisagion*), creed, *Sanctus*, and *Agnus Dei*. These, with the hymns, must be sung properly before any time is given to special choral anthems. It will be acknowledged that the singing of the creed has fallen out of fashion but as one who sings prays twice, a double recitation of our faith through the practice of song may be needed in our own time. The average choir will not be able to sing anything properly if it is sung to elaborate music, and so attention must always be paid by the parson and those in charge of music to ensure that what is sung is actually singable by those who will make the attempt. This is frequently forgotten and in many churches the music is a hindrance, not a help, to devotion. One constantly hears a choir attempting elaborate musical compositions before it has learned to sing the Psalter.

Now the duty of the parson, whether musical or not, is to restrain those promptings of original sin that make people anxious to show off. This tendency is naturally most marked among those of small capacity, for the more modest our powers the less modest we are in their exercise, having no standard of perfection whereby to judge ourselves. The duty of the parson is to keep ever before everyone's eyes the simple but often forgotten truth that church music is for the glory of God and not for the glorification of choristers. And true art is at one with true religion. Unfortunately, there are some choirmasters who are not even artists enough to prefer a simple service well sung to a pretentious one sung badly.

Furthermore, it is of the utmost importance that the encouragement of congregational singing should be everywhere continued among us. For this end the parson must jealously guard the people's parts of the services. The choir has its opportunity in the choral anthem (though indeed there are some churches where it might be better for an anthem to be sung once in the month), just as in the old service it had (as it still can have) its grails, alleluias, offertories, and so forth. Except on special occasions, or in churches with excellent resources and highly trained choirs, it is to the people that belong the Psalms, canticles, responses, litany, *Kyrie*, creed, *Sanctus*, *Gloria in excelsis*, and *Agnus Dei*. In most churches, these are usually best sung to music suitable for congregational use. It is a usurpation for most choirs to monopolize the singing of any one of them on a regular basis. There are ways, in churches that have the musical resources, to balance this, and those churches with those resources exist in a special place in Christ's body. But they are the exception, and not the norm, and no matter what attention should always be paid to how the people may be involved. For instance, with the Psalter, if the choir will sing in full Anglican chant the people may respond with a singable antiphon or refrain.

On those principal feasts of the church at which the congregation is often smaller (for example, Epiphany, Ascension Day, and All Saints' Day) a fine choral setting from the Anglican tradition (provided the choir has the ability to sing it well or resources exist to bring in extra voices) can be a profound gift to those who attend and a connection to some of the best choral music in Western music that England has ever offered. But in most parishes these experiences should be a gifted exception and not the rule. Those congregations that have vigorous choral schools and programs which are accustomed to more choral settings of the liturgy may be allowed, provided they are not the only ways the congregation experiences Eucharist. For a worshiper to attend the divine service week after week and never sing the *Gloria in excelsis*, for instance, is an unfortunate experience out of keeping with the ideals of Anglican liturgy.

The best plan by far, and perhaps the only plan that will prove to be generally practicable, is to sing these parts always to the same music for a full season. There are indeed a small handful of good settings for the Eucharist in *The Hymnal 1982*. The trained musician will be aware of others that are available (though attention should be paid to ensure that proper copyright permission is attained). Done in this way, the congregational settings of the service music can give a sense of the feel of the season while at the same time teaching the people a piece of music that will eventually become familiar and beloved. For example, to move from the plainsong setting from David Hurd in Lent to the glorious Schubert or Mathias settings in Easter is a meaningful turn of the liturgy made manifest through music.

HYMNS

Hymns, it need hardly be said, rest upon a long-standing custom that has always been sanctioned by authority. They are therefore popular and authorized additions to the historical service and their arrangement rests in general upon the parson's discretion, guided by the rubrics of the prayer book. It must be remembered that this discretion in the choice of hymns carries with it a grave responsibility both as to words and music. The arts have far deeper teaching power than we realize and a bad tune (though it may be popular for a while) is demoralizing and irreligious in its effects, while a good one (though it will probably need to be used two or three times before it is appreciated) has a constant growing power over the minds of the congregation and helps to build up a real spiritual atmosphere in the worship of the church.

At morning and evening prayer, the proper place to sing the office hymn is after the office collects and before the authorized intercessions and thanksgivings, which then culminate in the General Thanksgiving. This is now clear in the rubrics for both Rites One and Two. There is not provision in the rubrics for supplanting the office canticles with hymns, though versions of the canticles set to a more singable metrical melody are quite appropriate.

A revival of the traditional office hymns sung to a plainsong melody is much needed, as these ancient office hymns contain some of the best poetry of our church, and few things are more beautiful and meditative than a hymn sung to a simple plainsong tone. I have attempted below to lay out a sequence based on *The Hymnal 1982*, according to the basic kalendar of the prayer book.[10] The exception to the prayer book's kalendar is that I suggest breaking the season after Pentecost up with the Labor Day holiday. While Labor Day is not a holiday in the church (though, perhaps, given the importance of the labor of all humanity, this is a question we should reconsider), Christians need not live oblivious to the cycles of seasons that surround them. Indeed, many churches begin their "program year" after the Labor Day holiday, so it makes sense that this is also an appropriate time to change the office hymn. For those who want a more diverse selections of hymns in ordinary time or who want to ascribe to a different order, the prayer book gives no instructions. That said, the following is one possible sequence to be followed:

---

10. I'm grateful to Derek Olsen for laying the groundwork of much of this. As Olsen has astutely noted, there are two common approaches one may take when choosing the office hymns. One is the list in the first edition of *Ritual Notes* (this is the more Anglo-Catholic approach) and the second is the list given in the tenth century English Benedictine customary of Ælfric. That said, the current kalendar of our church in the prayer book doesn't follow either of these sequences, which means neither can be fully adapted for worship in our prayer book's form. In the sequence I offer, preference is given to the hymns the in tenth century customary, with the second consideration being a plainsong English translation in *The Hymnal 1982*. In cases where either the hymns suggested by the Benedictine customary or *Ritual Notes* are not found in plainsong forms in *The Hymnal 1982*, I have offered my own suggestions so that this list may be usable to the average parson without having to scour the internet or libraries for the tunes to sing in worship. See Olsen, "Office Hymns."

GENERAL PRINCIPLES OF CEREMONIAL

Advent

- Morning—*Verbum supernum* (hymn 63)
- Evening—*Conditor alme siderum* (hymn 60)

Christmastide

- Morning—*Puer natus in Bethelehem* (hymn 103)
- Evening—*Salvator generis nostri lapsi* (hymn 85)

Epiphany through baptism of Christ

- Morning—*Venit sine peccato* (hymn 120)
- Evening—*O lux lucis* (hymn 134)

Season after the Epiphany

- Morning—*Alleluia piis edite laudibus* (hymn 619)
- Evening—*Alleluia, dulce carmen* (hymn 122)

Ash Wednesday and Lent

- Morning—*Ex more docti mystico* (hymn 146)
- Evening—*De profundis* (hymn 151)[11]

Holy Week

- Morning—*Pange lingua* (hymn 166)
- Evening—*Stabat Mater dolorosa* (hymn 159)

Eastertide

- Morning—*Quod dies paschae cum gaudio* (hymn 193)
- Evening—*Ad cenam Agni providi* (hymn 202)

Ascension Day and after

- Morning—*Gloriae hymnum canamus* (hymn 217)
- Evening—*Aeterme Rex altissime* (hymn 220)

---

11. Though if plainsong is not desired, hymn 152 is the text of the Roman vespers office hymn for Lent.

Pentecost and Octave

- Morning—*Beate nobis guadia* (hymn 223)
- Evening—*Veni Creator Spiritus* (hymn 502)

Trinity Sunday

- Morning—*Te Deum laudamus* (hymn S 282)[12]
- Evening—*O lux beata Trinitas* (hymn 30)

After Trinity through Labor Day

- Morning—*Pater te laudamus* (hymn 1)
- Evening—*Lucis creator optime* (hymn 27)

Labor Day until Advent

- Morning—*Iam dies caelos implet* (hymn 4)
- Evening—*Christe, Lux mundi* (hymn 34)

All Saints' Day (through following Sunday, if observed)

- Morning—*Gaudiaum pariter* (hymn 237)
- Evening—*Aeterna Christi dona* (hymn 233)

This list is, of course, far from perfect, being limited by the choices of the editors of *The Hymnal 1982*, along with the discrepancy between older kalendars and their classes of feasts and those found in the current prayer book. It should, however, be a helpful starting guide for those who wish to revive the tradition of an office hymn.

At the Eucharist hymns are often sung and are suggested by the rubrics in Rite Two, for the introit (p. 355), between the Epistle and Gospel (p. 357), during the offertory (p. 361), at Communion (p. 365), and at the ablutions (p. 409). As noted earlier, the rubric permits a hymn before the post-communion prayer (which would function as an ablutions hymn) or after it (p. 409). The rubrics do not permit a hymn to divide the blessing and dismissal as these are the two final words from the ordained sacred ministers (the priest and then the deacon) and they should be kept unified, both said from the altar. If, after being dismissed, the people wish to sing a further hymn, nothing prevents them, though a postlude

---

12. Though, on this day, one might relax the desire for plainsong and instead sing the glorious hymn rendering of the *Te Deum* found in hymn 366.

is often a better choice for the retiring procession. It is important that the hymns thus used should be appropriate to their position in the liturgy.

THE POSITION OF THE MINISTER

There are many directions as to the position of the minister in our rubrics. But in some cases, no positive orders are given, and the proper course for the minister to adopt has been disputed. It may, however, be safely assumed that, where no direction is given, the matter has (in accordance with the common habit of rubricians) been left to tradition. The sound principle therefore will be, when in doubt, follow church tradition, and do not invent a new "use." A further principle might be added: When in doubt as to the attitude for prayer, let the priest stand and the people kneel. Or, as has commonly been said as advice for people new to the Episcopal Church, "Stand to praise, sit to listen, kneel to pray."

In the offices, the rubrics are rather clear when it comes to the posture for the various parts of the liturgy. The first instruction given is that all kneel for the confession, if it is used. All stand for the invitatory. Though the rubric does not require it, custom dictates sitting for the Psalm (however, the lack of rubrical direction and the principle of standing for praise does call that custom into question). Custom then dictates sitting for the lessons and standing for the canticles that follow each lesson. Rubrical requirement returns for the creed, for which all should stand. At the prayers, the people are invited to stand or kneel, raising the question of the posture of the minister. The Lord's Prayer and suffrages are the liturgical introduction to the collects that follow, and they used to be prefaced by the rubric "then the Priest standing up shall say," while the people continued kneeling.[13] It is therefore reasonable to suppose that the officiant will maintain the same position for the collects as for their introductory suffrages. The matter is clinched when we remember that standing was always the position of the clergy when they said the collects and that the first prayer book has the rubric "the Priest standing up, and saying" immediately before the collects. If an office hymn is sung, all would stand for that, and it makes sense to remain standing for any of the optional closing prayers (General Thanksgiving, Chrysostom's Prayer, dismissal, and grace). If the office hymn is not sung, then the people remaining kneeling is the reasonable choice, but the

---

13. *1662 Book of Common Prayer*, 15.

officiant should remain standing because there is no hint in the prayer book that the officiant should say these prayers in a different posture from that which is adopted for the collects that precede them. In fact, the officiant should stand to speak, just as the people stand when they are saying or singing, and this position is always the best for the voice.

When it comes to the Great Litany, though, our rubrics are expansive depending on how the litany is said or sung, with the options given of kneeling, standing, or walking in procession. (Sitting during the litany would be such poor form that it hardly merits a mention.) An exception is found here, however, to the custom in the office of the officiant standing while the people kneel during prayer, and this exception is made by a well-established custom. The chanters may kneel as well as the people, unless the litany is sung in procession. But the litany proper ends with the last "Lord, have mercy upon us" and the Lord's Prayer, collects, antiphon, and versicles, which follow, ought not to be said in the same posture as the petitions. In the 1662 prayer book, the word priest occurs for the first time at the commencement of this new section; and even when the priest is taking the whole service alone, the priest should stand to say the Lord's Prayer and remain in the standing posture, which is usual for saying the versicles, collects, and the grace.

On all these occasions, the officiant will naturally hold the book in their hands. But during the Lord's Supper the book lies on the altar, and then the priest should follow the very ancient custom of saying the prayers with hands parted and raised, a custom so ancient that it is found in countless pictures of *orans* in the catacombs of Rome. Tradition also demands that the priest open the hands to say "let us pray" and join them at the last clause of any prayer. In saying the creed and *Gloria in excelsis*, the priest says the opening words with hands parted and then joins the hands and keeps them joined to the end. Now that the people say the Lord's Prayer with the priest, it is right that the priest should join hands after the opening words, as in the creed and *Gloria in excelsis*. This parting of the hands should not be done too obtrusively. The arms should never be swung about nor the hands moved with rapid gesture, but every action should be done with simplicity, solemnity, and restraint. It is also traditional that, when one says, "The Lord be with you," one should turn to the people and part hands.

GENERAL PRINCIPLES OF CEREMONIAL

TURNING TO THE PEOPLE

At the Savoy Conference, the Puritans desired that the minister should turn to the people throughout the whole ministration of the Communion service, as this was "most convenient." The bishops, in their reply, said, "The minister turning to the people is not most convenient throughout the whole ministration. When he speaks to them, as in Lessons, Absolution, and Benedictions, it is convenient that he turns to them. When he speaks for them to God, it is fit that they should all turn another way, as the ancient church ever did; the reasons of which you may see."[14] We have, then, a principle affirmed that settles in the most reasonable and catholic way a number of questions about which there has been much unnecessary division and dispute.

Regardless of whether one serves in an eastward facing parish where priest and people all face the same direction during prayer or one where all gather around the altar with the priest facing the people across from the altar, both the posture of the body and the custody of the eyes should make it clear when the minister leading worship is speaking to the people and when the minister is speaking to God with or on behalf of the people.

TURNING TO THE ALTAR

The ancient custom of turning to the east, or rather to the altar, for the *Gloria Patri* and *Gloria in excelsis* in offices and the Eucharist remains common. Furthermore, the practice of turning to the east for the creeds was introduced by the Caroline divines and has established itself firmly among us, though it was never embodied in a rubric, as were some of the other ceremonial additions of the Laudian school.[15] It thus rests upon a common English custom nearly four centuries old, and it is in every way an excellent practice. In chapter one I spoke to my own continued preference for eastward facing celebration of the Holy Mysteries (or, once more, for the sacred ministers and people to all be facing the same

---

14. Buchanan, *Savoy Conference*, 48–49.

15. Procter and Frere, *New History*, 391. As Dearmer further notes, "The custom at Salisbury (which concerned only the Nicene Creed) was for the choir to face the altar at the opening words, till they took up the singing, to turn to the altar again for the bowing at the Incarnatus, and again at the last clause to face the altar until the Offertory." Dearmer, *Parson's Handbook*, 199.

direction). But even in churches where the priest celebrates *ad populum*, the minister should take care with the posture of the body, the custody of the eyes, and the use of voice to make it clear when the prayer has turned from a conversation with the people (as in the *sursum corda*) to a prayer to God (as in the canon of mass).

KNEELING, STANDING, AND SITTING

In some churches it would be salutary if the parson reminded the people that one can indeed kneel in prayer and still believe in the grace of God to forgive and love us. It has been an unfortunate development of recent years that kneeling has been associated only with penitence and a feeling of being unworthy. This was never the case. Rather, kneeling is a posture of humility—but a humility that is conscious that, as it says in the comfortable words from Hebrews, we "come boldly unto the throne of grace, that we may obtain mercy, and find grace to help in time of need."[16] This tradition of kneeling when prayers are read remains a laudatory practice, and one that applies to the choir as well as the people.

The older canons of the Church of England only mention standing at the "saying of the Belief."[17] As mentioned earlier, our own prayer book contains clearer directions for the several points in the liturgy where one should stand. Further, in defense of the standing posture for the Psalms, it may be urged that it follows another reasonable principle, since as we kneel to pray so we stand to say and sing. Therefore, we stand also to sing hymns. On the other hand, when people listen to singing, as in the modern anthem, it is unreasonable for them to stand. It is likely for this reason that the custom arose of sitting during the psalmody—the people were used to sitting and listening to it sung by the choir. The sitting posture generally assists the people in quiet attention and devotion, besides giving them the best opportunity for rest and recollection at such times. Thus, when the psalm is being sung by a choir or cantor, then sitting certainly is a reasonable choice.

At the same time, sitting is one of those things that depends upon custom, there being not a single direction to sit in the prayer book. It is, however, a great mistake to imagine that there is anything irreverent in sitting—the practical value of this attitude in assisting devotion is, I

---

16. *1979 Book of Common Prayer*, 320.
17. Church of England, *Canons* (1604), no. 18.

repeat, great. The obvious occasions for sitting are during sermons, lectures, and homilies, and during elaborate musical performances. To sit during the earlier lessons is the ancient custom, as is to stand during the Gospel. The standing for the Gospel, then, is an exception—and a most reasonable one—to our third reasonable principle mentioned earlier, that, as we kneel to pray and stand to sing, so we sit to listen.

BOWING TO THE ALTAR

The custom of bowing to the altar never quite died out in England, even during the height of Puritan resistance to traditional ceremonial. It is thus commended by canon 7 of 1640: "We therefore (i.e. on account of the 'pious,' 'profitable,' and 'edifying' nature of outward acts) think it very meet and behoveful, and heartily commend it to all good and well-affected people, members of this church, that they be ready to tender unto the Lord the said acknowledgment, by doing reverence and obeisance, both at their coming in and going out of the said churches, chancels, or chapels, according to the most ancient custom of the primitive church in the purest times, and of this church also for many years of the reign of queen Elizabeth."[18]

But it is important to remember that bowing to the altar is quite a different thing from bowing to the cross on the altar when going from one part of it to the other. For this latter practice we have no authority, and it is very inconvenient, besides detracting from the significance of the reverence to the altar itself, which is the point insisted on both before and after the Reformation. The ministers may bow, as the Sarum rules direct, to the altar when crossing the chancel, but they should not bow to the cross when merely passing from one end of the altar to the other. And this is the maximum. Truth be told, simply bowing at the entry and the exit is the best practice.

BOWING TO THE HOLY NAME

With regard to bowing at the holy name, canon 18 of 1604 orders, "when in time of divine service, the Lord Jesus shall be mentioned, due and lowly reverence shall be done by all persons present, as it hath been

---

18. Church of England, *Canons* (1640), 38.

accustomed."[19] It should be noticed that there is no authority for singling out the creed as the only place at which "due and lowly reverence shall be done." The canon orders the reverence at all times when the name of Jesus is mentioned, and it makes manifest a custom that has long been true in Anglican worship and should be continued in our own time. This applies equally to those occasions when it is now generally omitted. But no English authority orders a reverence at the word "holy" in the *Magnificat* (though it is an acceptable—simply not required—choice and a nod to the holy name since that is what the word holy is referring to). Nor have we any authority for bowing towards any particular object when the name of Jesus is mentioned.

BOWING AT THE *GLORIA PATRI*

The ancient custom of bowing at the *Gloria Patri* is another one that never quite died out in England. It was enjoined by the statutes of St. Paul's Cathedral before 1305, by an Irish canon of 1351,[20] and by the Lincoln statutes, ca. 1440,[21] and references to it occur in both ancient and modern literature, as "ye incline at *Gloria Patri*" in the *Mirroure of Our Lady*.[22] In Dearmer's time there was significant debate as to whether the *Gloria Patri* should be treated as two verses of the Psalm or sung as a single full verse. The rubrics of our prayer book alleviate this anxiety. It is treated as a single verse throughout the prayer book, though there is a rubric that allows for it to be treated as two verses (which was Dearmer's preference) if so desired.[23] The rubrics of the 1979 book do suggest that the *Gloria Patri* is best said or sung in unison, including when the psalm is recited antiphonally.[24]

THE REVERENCE TO THE SACRAMENT

The 1662 prayer book and the canons of the Church of England from the same time order certain acts of reverence in connection with the Holy

19. Church of England, *Canons* (1604), no. 18.
20. Wilkins, *Britanniae et Hiberniae*, 20.
21. Bradshaw, *Lincoln Cathedral*, 333.
22. Blunt, *Myroure of Oure Ladye*, 82.
23. *1979 Book of Common Prayer*, 141.
24. *1979 Book of Common Prayer*, 582.

GENERAL PRINCIPLES OF CEREMONIAL

Sacrament. The 1662 rubric directing the people to receive the Holy Communion "all meekly kneeling"[25] was, as is well known, maintained in the face of strenuous Puritan opposition. The order to communicate "kneeling reverently and decently upon their knees" occurred also in canon 23.[26] Another rubric from the 1662 prayer book said that the minister shall "reverently place upon it what remaineth of the consecrated Elements."[27] Here there is no word about kneeling, but the rubric does seem to imply some quiet bending of the head by the word "reverently." Otherwise, there would be no distinction between this direction and that at the offertory, which is simply "shall then place upon the Table so much Bread and Wine."[28]

With regard to the people, canon 7 of 1640 orders that they "with all humble reverence shall draw near and approach to the holy table, there to receive the divine mysteries."[29] Now it is certain that "reverence" in the canons of both 1604 and 1640 meant to bow the head. All bowing is a slight inclination of the head only. Many people have thought that this act was insufficient, and have adopted the Roman practice of genuflecting (dropping on one knee). But this practice does not hold bearing in antiquity nor in the English tradition. In the first place, all the old books mention bowing in connection with the Holy Sacrament, and no other action, with the exception that the people knelt during the canon of the prayer and at reception. Some have imagined that the word used for bowing, *inclinare*, meant some sort of semi-genuflection, but this is not so. For in many rubrics the action at the consecration itself is carefully restricted to a very moderate bow. The word *inclinare* is the same as that used for bowing to the altar and for bowing in the earlier part of the service before the canon. When we find the reverence to the Sacrament mentioned in English, it is the word "bow" that is used. Where we do find a semi-genuflection in the Carthusian rite of the last three centuries, it is a survival of the ancient practice of bowing, maintained in spite of the later Roman order to "genuflect."

In the second place, people have been misled by assuming that the word *genuflexio* means what Roman Catholics now mean by genuflection, i.e., a dropping on one knee. Now the word *genuflexio* does occur

25. *1662 Book of Common Prayer*, 156.
26. Church of England, *Canons* (1604), no. 23.
27. *1662 Book of Common Prayer*, 156.
28. *1662 Book of Common Prayer*, 156.
29. Church of England, *Canons* (1640), 38.

in our old books, but it does not occur in connection with the Blessed Sacrament, and it does not mean dropping on one knee but has the same sense as the "kneeling" of our rubrics. The word *genuflexio* is found in one missal, that of Hereford, where it occurs in the creed, and is followed after the *Crucifixus etiam pro nobis* by the direction *et tunc fiet levatio*.[30] The word occurs also in the Sarum Consuetudinary, Customary, and Processional as follows: At evensong the priest knelt before the altar prior to censing it. As the priest also kissed the ground in so doing, that means the priest must have knelt on both knees.[31] Again, the choir knelt at the beginning of the divine hours in Lent, and the word *genuflexio* is shown by the context to have had the same meaning here as *prostracio*.[32] Again, on Palm Sunday the choir knelt while they sang the *Salve* before the relics,[33] making at the same time a prostration and kissing the ground.[34] Again, on Palm Sunday the word *genuflexio* is used at the unveiling of the rood, when the choir sang on their knees and kissed the ground.[35] Again, on Maundy Thursday, at the consecration of the oils, the bishop knelt at the horn of the altar to begin the hymn *Veni Creator*.[36] Lastly, the choir knelt at the beginning of *Gloria in excelsis* on Easter Eve, and while in this attitude they took off their black choir copes.[37]

So much for the meaning of *genuflexio*, which clearly meant fully kneeling and not a short drop to one knee. We may conclude that we have no precedent in our tradition for ministers or people dropping on one knee when passing the Holy Sacrament, but that both natural reverence and our Anglican canons, rubrics, and tradition do suggest that they should bow when approaching for Communion. I have given rather

---

30. Maskell, *Ancient Liturgy*, 75.

31. "Facta genuflexione ante altare terram deosculando." Frere, *Use of Sarum*, 183; see also 44, 144.

32. "Fiat genuflexio in incepcione matutinarum laudum," "prostratus eciam debet esse chorus," and "de prostracione." Frere, *Use of Sarum*, 32.

33. "Incipiat Salve, conversus ad reqliquias, quam prosequatur chorus cum genufleccione." Frere, *Use of Sarum*, 60.

34. "Cum genuflexione osculando terram" and "in prostracione deosculando terram." Henderson, *Processionale*, 50.

35. Frere, *Use of Sarum*, 61. See also Henderson, *Processionale*, 53.

36. "Incipient alta voce ymnum Veni Creator cum genuflexione." Frere, *Use of Sarum*, 204.

37. "Facta genuflexione clerici deponant capas nigras." Frere, *Use of Sarum*, 24. "Omnes genuflectent exuentes capas nigras deponant et in super-pelliceis appareant." Frere, *Use of Sarum*, 151.

full references to this matter because it is one in which so many directories have gone astray by recommending a particular form of reverence that is without justification either from those primitive customs to which the prayer book makes so strong an appeal, from the formal directions of the late medieval books, or even from still later custom. Many have been misled in the matter and have now to correct their errors. It is full consolation to find that the prayer book and canons were in the right and that their restraint as to acts of reverence had been, as a matter of fact, the universal tradition of the catholic church. Here is a point in which the advanced school of Ritualists had been in the wrong while the moderate school and the Tractarians and Anglicans for generations before them—and indeed the average devout lay person of today—have been in the right. When we come to the acts of reverence during the consecration prayer itself, the point is brought out with even greater distinctness.

BOWING AT THE CONSECRATION

The 1662 prayer book ordered the priest to kneel for the Prayer of Humble Access but to stand for the prayer of consecration, and said nothing as to the priest kneeling during that prayer. The prayer book did, however, order the priest to lay one hand first upon the bread, then upon the chalice, and these acts may imply a slight bow if they are to be done, as the rubric directs, with both "readiness" and "decency."[38] In the 1979 prayer book, the instruction to kneel is, almost without fail, given when there is a confession (or during the Decalogue, which prepares the people for confession), or as an option during the prayers of the office, the Great Litany, or the prayers of the people. Kneeling is also enjoined during the nuptial blessing and during ordination rites and celebration of a new ministry, signifying the humility of both moments and perhaps the deep meaning of entering into a new state of being. (People would do well to be attentive to this point, for if couples saw marriage as a vowed state like ordination instead of a romantic and sentimental enterprise, much could be gained.) For our purposes at this time, the most important rubrics for kneeling occur when the people are invited to "kneel or stand" (Rite One) or to "stand or kneel" (Rite Two) during the canon of the eucharistic prayer.

---

38. *1662 Book of Common Prayer*, 155.

It is reasonable that we should furthermore turn to those books from which our liturgy was taken to see what the tradition is there as to decency and reverence. When we do so, we find them little different from our own. The various editions of the Sarum Missal only agree in directing the priest to bow twice—each time before the words when the priest gave thanks, which preceded the consecration both of the bread and of the chalice—and it is clear from the context that the bow was a momentary one. A third bow is given in some editions after the words "this is my Body" (in one case this is specified as a bow of the head), but, interestingly enough, in no edition is a bow mentioned after the consecration of the chalice. This third bow, which does not occur in all editions of the missal, came into practice as a result of the elevation, which was introduced in the twelfth and thirteenth centuries, and lasted in England till it was abolished by the rubric of the first prayer book.[39]

A word may be helpful here about the question of bowing or other acts of reverence during the words of institution themselves. In Dearmer's time, actions of reverence, such as a solemn bow or genuflection, after the words of institution were a question of strong debate. There was a desire of some to avoid the perception many had that Roman Catholics believe the words of institution are when the bread and wine is transubstantiated into Christ's body and blood. While the words of administration are indeed at the core of a valid Eucharist in Roman Catholic teaching, they are not always and clearly understood to be consecratory in precisely that way. After all, in 2001, the Pontifical Council for Promoting Christian Unity, with the approval of Pope John Paul II, determined that the Holy Qurbana of Addai and Mari (a version of the anaphora that is likely from the second century) can be considered valid even though the words of institution are not spoken.[40] Central to that decision was the idea that it is the entire eucharistic prayer that is consecratory because of the way it evokes those words of institution, whether or not they are literally repeated in the prayer. All that said, the debates on this question have significantly cooled in our more ecumenical age and if the custom of a congregation is a slight bow or other act of reverence for the sacred words of institution, that can hardly be argued against. After all, whether or not the words are consecratory, they are certainly some of the most sacred words of Christ revered by Christians over millennia and they

---

39. Dearmer, *Parson's Handbook*, 208.
40. PCPCU, "Admission to the Eucharist," sec. 3.

remain one of the most important moments in the canon of the mass. What is essential and key is that the reverence at the Great Amen remains the most profound and key conclusion to the eucharistic prayer.

When it comes to bowing as an act of reverence, we must stress that bowing is not a Sarum peculiarity. It is the same, not only with all the English uses, but with those of most other places. Dr. Ebner examined a very large number of missals in Italian libraries without finding any instance, among those of earlier date, of a genuflection at or after the consecration: in some crucial cases no bow at all is mentioned till the priest says the *Supplices te rogamus*. In the Roman ordinals and missals the bow is defined as being of a moderate nature and of the head only—a fact which might well be remembered by some modern priests who have been known to put their heads, when bowing, below the level of the altar slab. It was not till the post-Tridentine Roman Missal of 1570 that the present Roman customs were formally sanctioned; previous to that date there had been dozens of editions of the Missale Romanum printed without any mention of a genuflection but with an *inclinato paululum capite* ("bowing his head a little"), which practically excludes it.[41] That kneeling had been for some time spreading, in spite of the rubric, is not denied, although it appears from old pictures that the priest did not drop on one knee before and after the elevation, as in the present Roman rite, but knelt down on both knees (much as in our prayer of access) while he made the elevation.

The Roman Missal of 1570 sanctioned these new practices. The English prayer book did not but carried on the tradition of all the previous missals by maintaining a great reserve as to acts of reverence, and by abolishing the elevation, it struck at the root from which these popular practices had sprung. In so doing it was but reverting to the sober traditions of what the eminent nineteenth-century Roman Catholic liturgist Edmund Bishop called the true and unadulterated Roman ceremonial of the mass.[42]

Doubtless some people have adopted the practice of genuflection in order to render some special reverence to the Sacrament, under the impression that it is confined to this purpose in the Roman Church. But such is not the case: Roman Catholics genuflect to the altar cross and to the bishop, as well as to the Sacrament. Thus, every part of the church,

---

41. Dearmer, *Parson's Handbook*, 210.
42. Bishop, *Genius of the Roman Rite*, 10.

East and West, in every age, is against reserving one particular form of reverence for this purpose.

What has already been said about kneeling at other times applies also to the congregation during the prayer of consecration. The tradition of our church has historically been that the people will kneel. The framers of the 1979 prayer book, by reversing the rubric in Rite Two, clearly preferred the option of standing with the priest, in line with what they understood to have been the practice of the early church. Regardless of the posture of the people, the deacon and eucharistic minister, along with the servers, should follow the very ancient custom of standing quite upright, like the celebrant. Standing was their position in early times, though in the later Middle Ages they did, in practice, very often kneel at the consecration or elevation.

With regard to this, as to other things, it may be stated once for all that the notion is false that supposes a certain position or action to be fixed for everybody at every point. There has always been a great diversity in small matters, the rule of common sense having been followed until recent times. Some people have put their necks under the yoke of a tyrant of their own imagining, fearing, lest they do so, they should not be "correct." They need have no such fear. The only incorrectness is to break rubrics of our church that, it has been demonstrated, are generous in their options. For the rest, if they do things in the simplest and most natural way, they need have no fear of being ridiculous—that danger lies all in the other direction. The pre-Reformation consuetudinaries are indeed useful in supplementing the prayer book, just as they were useful in supplementing its progenitor, the Sarum Missal, and a knowledge of earlier customs helps us to avoid the innovations of the fancy ritualist, but the consuetudinaries themselves leave ample freedom as to the positions and actions of the ministers.

THE SIGN OF THE CROSS

The ancient and venerable sign of the cross was retained by the Church of England at holy baptism in the face of a long and determined opposition. Thus the principle of signing the baptized with the cross was maintained, although the ceremony was only ordered to be made at this one solemn occasion.[43] It was out of the question in that hard period to order it at

---

43. *1662 Book of Common Prayer*, 162.

GENERAL PRINCIPLES OF CEREMONIAL

other times, but our church did manage to secure that no one should belong to her on whom the sign had not been made, and at the same period it was, in practice, used during Holy Communion and at other times. Canon 30 defended at great length the use of the sign at the baptismal service and, while admitting that it had come to be abused, mentioned the "continual and general use of the sign of the Cross," which the early Christians "used in all their actions" as a profession "that they were not ashamed to acknowledge him for their Lord and Savior, who died for them upon the Cross."[44] Since the sign, then, is declared to be good in itself, and its continual use a primitive custom, we do right in using it, and we may well remind folk of the wise words of the first prayer book, "As touching kneeling, crossing, holding up of hands, knocking upon the breast, and other gestures, they may be used or left, as every man's devotion serveth, without blame."[45]

The sign is only ordered to be made publicly in the old books at the end of *Gloria in excelsis*, at the *Gloria tibi* before the Gospel, and at the *Benedictus qui venit*. But it was customary also to make it at the end of the Gospel, and in the thirteenth century, the sign was made at the end of the Nicene Creed, the Lord's Prayer, and mass, when the priest gave the blessing. It was also often used at the beginning of the Hours and at other times. It may be thus safely left to every person's own individual devotion.

The manner of making the sign of the cross has varied. In the earliest times it was the custom to use one finger, but in the seventh or eighth century it had become usual to employ three "for the Holy Trinity," i.e., the thumb and the two next fingers (as is still done in the East), the two remaining fingers being curved inwards. This method changed afterwards in the West to that of using the open hand, though in the eighteenth century there were still some who used the three fingers only. The custom of signing from left to right (instead of from right to left, which is still the Eastern practice) was not unknown in the twelfth century. Before the Gospel the thumb only was used, and the forehead and the breast were signed separately, according to some rites.[46]

---

44. Church of England, *Canons* (1604), no. 30.
45. *1549 Book of Common Prayer*, 126.
46. Dearmer, *Parson's Handbook*, 213–14.

PRIESTS AND SERVERS

It may be worthwhile to add some general remarks on deportment that apply to most of the services in which the priest and assistants may be engaged.

The crucifer and taperers should move together with something like a military precision. They should avoid all ostentatious reverence but, still more, all carelessness or irreverence. The taperers should carry their tapers in both hands, upright, and at an equal height, and as far as possible, depending on the heights of the taperers themselves, the hands of one taperer should correspond in position with the hands of the other. When not employed they should kneel, stand, or sit in their appointed places. When they have to do anything, they should do it in the simplest and most straightforward manner, avoiding all fuss and needless running about. Their proper place is by and just below their tapers, which are set down on the first step above the pavement (if there is room there), beyond the ends of the altar. They must stand still, with their hands together, but there is no direction for them to stick their fingers out. They may bow when passing the altar, but none should bow when merely passing from one part of the altar to the other, nor should anyone bow to the altar when passing it in a procession. For the rest, that service is most impressive where there is least bowing.

The thurifer, when the censer has been put away, will stand in some convenient place near the end of the choir stalls till the end of the service. When in procession, the thurifer should not swing the censer with its lid open, since the excess of smoke thus generated may inconvenience members of the congregation and bits of charcoal or burning incense have been known to escape from an overly zealous thurifer who has kept the lid open. Indeed, the lid should always be kept carefully down, except perhaps in the choir of some vast cathedral where the thurifer also has sufficient training to know how to use centrifugal force to keep the incense and coals well in place in the censer.

The verger, when not otherwise engaged, will stand facing the altar in the appointed place, which may be near the credence. The verger may sit in the westernmost place of the sedilia, if there is room, or near the sedilia, or in any other convenient place. The task of this minister is to look after the priest and deacon, along with the other ministers, providing any music or prayer books to the sacred ministers that are needed. If anything goes wrong, the verger is responsible and will go very quietly

GENERAL PRINCIPLES OF CEREMONIAL

and naturally to put it right. No one should ever whisper during service. If anything has to be said, it should be spoken quietly in the natural voice, which is much less likely to attract attention than a whisper. The verger should also bend as little as possible towards the person being addressed. A mistake matters little, particularly if no one makes a fuss about it.

As for the priest, this minister in particular should be quiet and dignified, as well as reverent, in all movements. The priest should not poke out hands in front, nor let the eyes wander over the congregation. The priest must avoid at once a jaunty and a mincing gait and must never sidle along the altar nor stand at an undecided angle. When moving, the priest should turn and walk straight. When standing, the priest should face squarely in the required direction. If anything goes wrong in the singing, or among the congregation, the priest must not look round unless it is absolutely necessary. If it is likely a handkerchief will be desired, it is wise to put a clean one in the sleeve, or tuck it in the girdle, so that the priest will not have to pull the albe up and search for a pocket. The same attention should be paid to where the microphone pack is clipped or held, if one is used, so that the priest may turn it on or off with minimal movement. When the priest bows, she or he should do so by moderately bending the head, and not imagine that the congregation will be moved to greater devotion by the contemplation of well-meant exaggerations.

If the priest is reverent with thoughts intent on worship and, at the same time, is also naturally graceful and has been taught deportment at some point, all of these things will be done instinctively. But, as many parsons do not have these qualifications, some directions are needed. The priest occupies a prominent position in church, and faults that may be tolerable in a roomful of persons are seriously distracting and sometimes painful to worshippers in a church. In preaching, a marked individuality may be an advantage, but in saying the services the priest's individuality should be as unnoticeable, and all actions as normal, as possible. For the priest does not stand—in the stall or at the altar—as an individual person but as the minister of the people and the representative of the church, saying in the name of the congregation the common prayers of them all and administering the sacraments and other rites and ceremonies of the church. Clericalism is a constant danger in all forms of religion, certainly. The Anglican tradition of Christianity is essentially not clericalist, and therefore she does not unduly exalt the minister by putting the people at the mercy of the priest's own ideas of prayer or by enthroning the priest in a pulpit at the east end of the church to overshadow the congregation. The set forms of prayer, the eastward position, the ministerial vestments, the cooperative service, the appointed gestures—these are all to hide the person and to exalt the common priesthood of the Christian congregation.

LIGHTS AND THE CLASSIFICATION OF FEASTS

In view of the still prevalent confusion on the subject of lights, it seems worthwhile to repeat that the universal pre-Reformation custom is at one with post-Reformation English custom in using two lights on the altar, and no more, although additional lights were both before and after the Reformation often placed round about the altar.

The only distinction is that in post-Reformation England churches very often fell below the ideal, owing to Puritan influences. Before the Reformation one candle only (sometimes placed on the altar, sometimes held by the clerk) was regarded as sufficient,[47] and the candlesticks were generally removed out of service time. The ancient use of two altar candles survived—even in the churches of the Roman Communion—in many places well into the middle of the eighteenth century, only gradually succumbing to the tastes of the latter times, which preferred a plethora of lights.[48]

The same candles will, as stated earlier, be used for the office and for Holy Eucharist, with the same number of lights used for the morning office as for the evening. At the same time there is good precedent for lighting two candles only for the offices, but four for mass on ordinary Sundays (the two upon the altar and the two standards). There is, possibly, something to be said for using the two standards for morning prayer on Sundays and then the two on the altar being only lit when the Eucharist begins. There certainly is no harm in this tradition. On ferial days, of course, there are no lights at all for the offices, but always two (or one at least) for mass. It is, however, important to remember that the Sarum rules, which supply this precedent, though useful as giving a general principle for the number of lights, cannot be taken as in any way binding. The parson has the general old English custom in one's favor if the choice is made to burn additional lights around (but not on) the altar

---

47. This practice of a single candle only was especially prevalent during the last half of the eighteenth century, as can be seen by the list of instances in the appendix to the Lincoln Judgment. It was in the early nineteenth century that the norm began to return towards an insistence upon two lights.

48. Dearmer, *Parson's Handbook*, 216–17.

according to the rank of the day, and reason also supports this manner of increasing the intelligibility of the Christian year. But neither old custom nor reason binds the parson to an exact reproduction of the cathedral use of Salisbury, valuable though that use is for general guidance.

Taking, then, the Sarum use for guide, one should burn no lights at all at ferial offices but should always burn two at Communion. One will also find that the custom of lighting the two standards only at Sunday offices and of lighting the two altar candles as well at the principal Sunday Eucharist is intelligible and convenient. But when one comes to consider the classification of feasts, the parson may well doubt whether there is any right to give up the simple method of the prayer book and revert to the elaborate classification of the consuetudinaries. In the old prayer book, we find a broad distinction between what are conveniently called red and black letter days—red letter days being the feasts that are to be observed of the kalendar that have special collects, Epistles, and Gospels, while black letter days are those other days that (as the bishops said in 1661) "are useful for the preservation of their memories."[49]

These distinctions have been made definite and enlarged in the 1979 prayer book, whose kalendar lays out a new and clear classification of feasts:[50]

1. Principal feasts (of which there are seven) take precedence of any other day or observance.

2. The higher classed Feasts of our Lord include all Sundays, along with the Holy Name, the Presentation, and the Transfiguration (the latter three supplant the regular Sunday observance when they fall on a Sunday). The prayer book allows for the feast of a dedication of a church, or of its patron or title, to take this class as well (except in the seasons of Advent, Lent, and Easter).

3. Holy days include other feasts of our Lord (including the three listed above when they do not fall on a Sunday), other major feasts, and the fasts of Ash Wednesday and Good Friday. The feasts in this category are all supplanted by Holy Week and Easter Week, however, and when they fall in these weeks, they are moved to the week following the second Sunday of Easter, in the order of their occurrence.

---

49. Buchanan, *Savoy Conference*, 21.
50. *1979 Book of Common Prayer*, 15–18.

4. Days of special devotion include the above-mentioned fast days on Ash Wednesday and Good Friday, along with the weekdays of Lent and Holy Week (excluding the Feast of the Annunciation, if it falls during this time), and all Fridays in the year (excluding the Fridays in Christmastide and Eastertide and any feasts of our Lord that fall on a Friday).

5. Days of optional observance include those listed in the prayer book along with those listed in whatever sanctorale is currently in force (right now that is the current edition of *Lesser Feasts and Fasts*).

For feasts of our Lord, which includes all Sundays according to our current kalendar, the Sarum customs suggest some additional lights, the same number being lit at the offices and at mass. At Salisbury there were four around (*circa*) the altar, and two before the image of Blessed Mary (who was the patron saint of the church), besides some extra lights for use at night. In a modern parish church two on sconces or on top of the posts of the riddels will suffice in addition to the two altar lights and the two standards.

For the principal feasts, the Sarum customs suggest a double use of additional lights at the offices and at mass. In a modern parish church four (on the four riddel posts or elsewhere around the altar) would suffice in addition to the two altar lights and the two standards. The arrangement of any such additional lights is a matter for the artist who designs the altar to settle. For instance, in very large churches there may be room for one or more pairs of extra standards. In any case, additional lights should never be set on, behind, or immediately above the altar.

Naturally, the rules as to additional lights apply to the principal Eucharist only on those days; other celebrations should have just the two lights upon the altar. It will be noticed that the offices had their lights according to the rank of the day, and as they were always sung, the question of music did not come in at all. Therefore, if we follow the old customs, we should have no lights at all for sung offices on ferial days.

It is hardly necessary nowadays to repeat that there is no authority for branch candlesticks on or above the altar. Reverence for the altar and good taste alike forbid them, nor can they find any place within the ornaments rubric or the traditions of Anglican Christianity.

GENERAL PRINCIPLES OF CEREMONIAL

INCENSE AND PROCESSIONAL LIGHTS

In Dearmer's time, he noted that the Lambeth Opinion of 1899[51] on the subject of the liturgical use of incense and of processional lights did not have the authority of the Lincoln Judgment of 1890.[52] Its only claim to obedience was in those dioceses where the ordinary should enforce it. There was much variety and confusion at the beginning, when the opinion was enforced. Since then, it seems to have been long forgotten. Such sporadic energy developing into oblivion is an example of the ineptitude of past liturgical action.

It must be said, though, that the opinion led to the most extraordinary misconceptions in the early twentieth century, the strangest of all being the idea that the Lord's Supper could no longer be celebrated with gospeler and epistoler, who assisted when incense was in use, because forsooth in the modern Roman Church the use of incense is usually (though by no means always) confined to such a service. The odd subservience of a few English priests to papal ideas could not have been more strikingly illustrated. One's only consolation was in the thought that this adoption of the peculiar Roman Catholic service known as *missa cantata* may have been due to sheer ignorance of the fact that such a limitation of the use of incense has never been known in any other part of the church.

The general public, on the other hand, jumped to the conclusion that the opinion forbade the use of incense. As a matter of fact, the opinion authorized it, and the clergy then had a stronger argument for the introduction of incense than they had before. They had indeed two primates on their side. The opinion allowed incense to "sweeten" (in George Herbert's language) the church. The judgment furthermore refused to condemn incense in itself, and asserted that even the "liturgical use" is not by law permanently excluded.[53]

---

51. During the controversies between Ritualists and lower-church Anglicans in late-nineteenth-century England, the Public Worship Regulation Act of 1874 moved the regulation of worship practices from the Judicial Committee of the Privy Council to a new secular court—a move that created much consternation among high-church Anglicans who strongly resisted secular judgments on affairs of the church. The act having failed to resolve the controversy, the archbishops met at Lambeth in 1899 to render a final judgment on these questions, looking particularly at the issues of the liturgical use of incense and the use of processional lights. For more details on this particular controversy, see Stielau, "Censer in and After the Reformation," 234–39.

52. Dearmer, *Parson's Handbook*, 221–22.

53. Temple and Maclagan, *Archbishops*, 9–14.

Now this "nonliturgical" use the archbishops allowed was so far from being uncatholic, as some have hastily imagined. It was actually the original liturgical use of the church and still the use in Rome in the ninth century. Indeed, in the tenth century, or later, incense was still only used to accompany the entry of the ministers and the carrying of the Gospel book to the place where the Gospel was read. Dearmer relied upon Cuthbert Atchley's book on the subject,[54] finding it useful to classify the two methods that seemed to emerge, troublesome though such details are.

1. The medieval use, as it is preserved in the Salisbury books, is retained in the text of this handbook through the instructions that will be found in the next chapters. Even this use, though, might well be simplified, if desired, by not censing the choir or people.

2. The use of the primitive church, as noted above, but with the exclusion of all censing both persons and things, is also sound in principle and perfectly easy to understand. Some parsons might regret the simplification at first, but others might discern that a simplification in approach increases the beauty of the action.

Under this second and simpler approach, the use of incense would be as follows: At the introit the thurifer carrying the censer (with incense in it) leads the crucifer and taperers in the usual manner and stands in the midst of the pavement, swinging the censer until the last verse of the hymn (if a hymn is sung for the introit), during which the thurifer exits. During the sequence, the thurifer prepares the censer and precedes the crucifer and taperers to the lectern (or to the middle of the people, if the Gospel is read from there) and gently swings the censer during the reading of the Gospel. At the offertory, the thurifer fetches the censer and stands in the midst of the pavement, gently swinging the censer while the hymn is being sung. Dearmer would then have the censer put away after that hymn. Thankfully, in our own time a good deal of the prejudice against incense has gone away and it seems fine and in keeping with the tradition of the church that the thurifer remains on the pavement, gently swinging the censer, for the entirety of the eucharistic prayer. The censer is then put away after the Great Amen.

The principles of this simpler approach might also be used at festal evensong. If the simpler use is desired, when the *Magnificat* begins, then the thurifer brings in the censer, as above, and gently swings it in the

---

54. Atchley, *Use of Incense*.

GENERAL PRINCIPLES OF CEREMONIAL

midst of the pavement till the end of the canticle. At processions, the thurifer brings in the censer as above, and swings it during the procession in the usual way.

I would suggest therefore that the introduction of incense, with the goodwill of the people expressed through the vestry, is desirable at the present day in some places—at least on festivals—if it is used with moderation. It is hardly necessary to add that festal evensong (with the cope) is perfectly right, whether incense is used or not, just as the celebration of the Holy Communion with the full complement of sacred ministers is perfectly right without incense.

With regard to processional lights, we are also not, of course, bound by the Lincoln Judgment. However, some sound advice in the use of lights is needed, as it is needed in the case of incense. Experience has shown that it is not possible to trust the wisdom of every individual incumbent, or sacristan. To carry lights in connection with the reading of the Gospel is, for instance, as old as the pilgrimage of Etheria (ca. 385), and the carrying of lights in other processions is almost as ancient. However, to bring them in especially for the prayer of consecration is a late medieval development without sanction from the pre-Reformation service books and without modern Anglican sanction either.

To attempt then to regulate the use of lights beyond the excellent rules of the old rubrics is not really possible, nor would it be desirable. I have therefore no modification to suggest in the methods described elsewhere in this handbook.

In the case of incense, the position, as we have suggested, is different, because some modification is desirable in the interests of sound ceremonial. The evil in all religious customs, throughout history, has been the piling up of trivial details. Both wisdom and learning are constantly needed to prevent the perpetuation of individual follies.

6

The Daily Office

IN THE CHURCH OF England, all priests and deacons are ordered by the prayer book to say morning and evening prayer every day. The parish priest is also ordered to "say the same in the Parish-church or Chapel where he ministereth," having a bell tolled beforehand, if the priest is at home and not otherwise reasonably hindered.[1] This ideal was rarely realized in the average parish church, and that this is not required in the Episcopal Church makes it even more unlikely. Truly, we may admit that there are many churches where it is not practicable every day. Yet the very titles of the services in the 1662 prayer book contain the words "daily throughout the year,"[2] and in the 1979 prayer book the word "daily"[3] was included at the beginning of the title also to affirm this as the daily office of the church (instead of the principal service on Sunday, as had become the custom in so many places). There are generally some hours in the week at which a small congregation will be able to assemble, and the parson can find out the best times by consulting the people. When it is known that a service cannot be said on a certain day, notice should be given on the Sunday before or online.

Everything should be done, when it is possible, to restore the cooperative nature of the office and to avoid the "duet" of parson and congregation, which is a survival of that of parson and clerk. The officiant and the readers of the two lessons should, if possible, be different persons.

---

1. *1662 Book of Common Prayer*, 6.
2. *1662 Book of Common Prayer*, 9, 18.
3. *1979 Book of Common Prayer*, 35, 37, 61, 75, 115, 136.

In many places laity will be glad to attend on certain days to read the lessons. Similarly with the Psalms and their *Gloria Patri*, it is common to say them alternately with the people. Properly however, even at the daily service without music, the ministers and congregation should recite the verses from side to side: all those on the south side of the middle alley joining with the minister on that side for the first verse, and all on the north side joining together for the second verse, and so on. But this is not, of course, possible in a chapel where there is no middle alley.

In the 1979 revision of the prayer book, the person leading the liturgy is termed "Officiant," whereas previous versions had labeled the person leading as "Minister."[4] This change was intended to make it explicit that a lay person without any special license from the bishop is permitted to lead the public offices of the church. It also more clearly situated the offices where they belong for many of our people, in their own daily prayers at home as lay persons. This change also meant that the salutation ("the Lord be with you," responded to by "and with thy spirit" or "and also with you") was no longer reserved to the clergy as it had been in previous versions. In times past, this exchange was a hierarchical one, with the phrase "and with thy spirit" meaning the spirit conferred upon the minister at ordination.[5] In our current book, the exchange is flattened and is a mutual exchange of blessing as opposed to a hierarchical recognition of the special spirit present in those who are ordained.

The current prayer book also made a few other revisions. It permitted silence after each reading (an excellent practice much to be commended), the preaching of a sermon, and the receiving of an offering. The latter two had grown up in custom and were now explicitly allowed by the rubrics. It also allowed for a reading from non-biblical Christian literature after the biblical readings. Here the work of J. Robert Wright in *Readings for the Daily Office from the Early Church* is an invaluable

4. See, for example, the use of the word "Officiant" on p. 37 of the 1979 book compared with the use of "Minister" on p. 9 of the 1662 book.

5. For example, the late fourth-century author, Theodore of Mopsuestia, wrote, "In this sense that the phrase: 'And to your spirit' is addressed to the priest by the congregation, according to the regulations found in the Church from the beginning." Theodore of Mopsuestia, *Commentary on the Lord's Prayer*, i–xxv. Similarly, the fifth century theologian, Narsai of Nisibis, wrote, "They call 'spirit' not that soul which is in the priest, but the spirit which the priest has received by the laying on of hands. By the laying on of hands the priest receives the power of the Spirit so that he may be able to perform the divine mysteries. That grace the people call the spirit of the priest and they pray that he may attain peace with it and it with him." Narsai of Nisibis, *Liturgical Homilies*, 8.

addition to the church—not nearly well enough known in our own time—as it provides a reading from the early church for all of the liturgical days of the prayer book kalendar. Parsons, laity, and congregations would all benefit from its use.

MORNING PRAYER

When an office is immediately followed by another service (before which it is advisable to ring the bells), it may begin at "Lord, open our lips" and then may end with the collects (the rubrics only require one but, as noted below, three are traditional). The General Thanksgiving, Prayer of St. Chrysostom, dismissal, and grace are all optional ways of concluding the office and it makes sense to omit some, if not all, of those concluding pieces when the office is moving to another liturgy. This includes when the parson has made the unadvisable choice to substitute the office for the liturgy of the word in Holy Eucharist.

The fore-office contains optional pieces that can lead into the traditional "Lord, open our lips" beginning. This includes the opening sentences of Scripture and the confession. In parishes where both offices are said, it is wise perhaps only to include the confession at one of them. Though, if there is a different community gathered regularly at morning compared to evening prayer, then having the confession at both might be preferable. There are two invitations to confession, one longer and one shorter. The longer is best used in Advent and Lent and the shorter during the remainder of the year.

The optional nature of the various fore-office items is a point to be attentive to. On feast days, it might make sense to eliminate some of these items. In particular, the confession may well be omitted from time to time, either due to a feast day, the parish schedule, or the season in which the church finds itself. However, in the seasons of Advent and Lent, maintaining the confession seems important.

As noted, the office begins in earnest when the officiant says, "Lord, open our lips" at the start of the invitatory and Psalter. One of the invitatory psalms comes next, generally either the *Venite* or *Jubilate* (which may well be alternated). The entirety of Ps 95 is a good choice in Lent for a broader expression of the *Venite*. The rubrics instruct the use of the *Pascha nostrum* during Easter Week and allow it also to be said daily during Eastertide. In practice, daily use during the entirety of Eastertide might be a bit much, but including it in the rotation of invitatory psalms would be a good choice. If the seasonal antiphon is used, the officiant says the first half and the people respond with the second half (almost always "come, let us adore him" or a variation thereof). If it is sung, then it is best sung in full, with the congregation repeating. After the antiphon, the invitatory psalm is said or sung, and then the antiphon is repeated at the end of the invitatory or it may be sung at various points during the invitatory.

The Psalter has long been one of the richest parts of the prayer book tradition, particularly because it was translated with an ear for poetry, song, and recitation. The rubrics wisely encourage the parson to avoid a single method of recitation, which is "needlessly monotonous."[6] The same rubrics suggest direct recitation for when the gradual Psalm that is in between the lessons at Holy Eucharist is said. Antiphonal recitation, as noted above, is a particularly venerable tradition, alternating between one side of the congregation and another. Responsorial recitation, when a cantor sings the verses and the choir and congregation respond with a refrain, is greatly favored in modern times. The restoration of the invitatory antiphons noted above encourages the restoration of the responsorial practice. Finally, responsive recitation (with the minister and congregation alternating verse by verse) is the most common method used in our churches. However, its commonality should encourage the parson to take advantage of the other methods suggested as well. And as the psalms are, at their core, songs, finding a sung method of recitation that works with a congregation on a somewhat regular basis is greatly to be encouraged. Also, as mentioned before, the asterisk does not give a place to break for responsive reading but, rather, indicates where a distinct pause in the recitation should be made.

The lessons and canticles then follow, with two lessons being the tradition of the church, one from the Old Testament and one from the New Testament. A table of suggested canticles is found on p. 144 and helps one determine which canticles to use on which day. There is an option to include a third lesson after the second canticle (which would then be the lesson from the Gospel), but to do this entirely overweighs the Scripture reading in the office. It is the recitation of the Psalter that forms the bedrock for the use of Scripture in the office, and two lessons

---

6. *1979 Book of Common Prayer*, 582.

are certainly sufficient for morning prayers, particularly when the Gospel may thus be kept for the evening office.

After the lessons and canticles, one finds the Apostles' Creed followed by the prayers. The prayers begin with a salutation, a shared recitation of the Lord's Prayer, and then the suffrages, which lead into the collects. The rubrics in the current prayer book are unfortunately vague about the collects. The tradition of the church, of course, is that there are three. Following the rubrics of the 1979 prayer book, this would indicate that first the collect of the day is said (either of the preceding Sunday or the feast being observed), then the collect for the day of the week (though only Sunday, Friday, and Saturday are listed, the remaining four collects can easily be assigned to each of the remaining days), and then one of the three prayers for mission.

The rubric on p. 14 is clear that the only hymns to be used in public worship are those that have been authorized by this church. Anthems (musical pieces sung by a vocalist or group) are only required to be from Scripture, the words of the prayer book, or "texts congruent with them." Instrumental music may substitute for a hymn or anthem, but this is allowed only on occasion at the office and should not be the norm. The only allowance of a hymn during morning prayer is a hymn (or anthem) after the collects and, as noted earlier, the office hymns are often the best choices and well worth learning.

All of the offices permit "authorized intercessions and thanksgivings" after the collects and office hymns.[7] Common practice and prudence indicate that inviting those of the congregation is a quite hospitable choice. The intention, however, was that the prayers and thanksgivings beginning on p. 801 would be used. A system for rotating through those will open the worshipper to the breadth of concerns and gratitude the prayer book offers. Thus, such a rotation should be followed in addition to any prayers or thanksgivings from the gathered congregation.

The closing pieces of the General Thanksgiving, Prayer of St. Chrysostom, dismissal, and grace are all optional and care should be taken to choose an ending that is fitting, clear, and does not give the impression that the officiant is constantly circling the runway looking for a place to land. It must be stressed that the General Thanksgiving and the Prayer of St. Chrysostom are not unvarying parts of the service but are for occasional use. When the Prayer of St. Chrysostom is used, the wise parson

---

7. *1979 Book of Common Prayer*, 58, 71, 101, 125.

will notice the italicized "amen" at the end, which indicates that it is a prayer said by the officiant and answered by the people's amen, not one said altogether. Regardless, variance in closing of the office according to the context of the service and the liturgical season will be appreciated by the congregation.

EVENING PRAYER

The rite of evening prayer is similar to that of morning prayer in structure, yet there are a few points of note to be made. Whereas morning prayer, either said privately or publicly on Sunday morning, naturally leads into the Communion liturgy later on in the parish, evening prayer much more rarely precedes an observance of Communion. An exception would be if there is a special feast day necessitating an evening celebration of Holy Eucharist or if one is in a parish with a tradition of a Saturday or Sunday evening mass. In these cases, those serving in the liturgy of Holy Communion might be invited first to join for the public offering of evening prayer, after which final preparations for the Eucharist might be made.

There are two options for the fore-office when it comes to evening prayer. The first is similar to morning prayer: opening sentences of Scripture, and the confession. The advice given above about omitting the confession from time to time remains important. Similarly, there is a longer and shorter introduction to the prayer of confession, and using the longer form in Advent and Lent is a good approach. As an alternative to the fore-office structure of morning prayer, the traditional Lucenarium was restored in this prayer book as the "Service of Light."[8] Thus, when it is used it replaces the fore-office along with the opening versicle, response, and invitatory.

After the fore-office items, as with morning prayer, the rite then begins in earnest when the officiant says, "O God, make speed to save us" at the start of the evening's invitatory and Psalter.[9] There is more generosity in the rubric for the invitatory, with the allowance of either the *Phos hilaron* or "some other suitable hymn, or an Invitatory psalm."[10] However, the *Phos hilaron* has the distinction of being one of the earliest

---

8. *1979 Book of Common Prayer*, 109–112.
9. *1979 Book of Common Prayer*, 63.
10. *1979 Book of Common Prayer*, 64.

known hymns that is not found in Scripture but is still used in modern worship. It was known as the "lamp-lighting hymn" and is still used that way in the service of light from the order of worship for the evening.[11] It is a good practice to follow as well in evening prayer, as there are no other rubrics in that office for the lighting of candles. If it is sung (which well it should be) there is a plainsong setting of the text to the tune *Conditor alme siderum* as hymn 26, along with a more metrical setting to "The Eighth Tune" by Thomas Tallis in hymn 25. While plainsong is the traditional form of song in the office, none can deny that the setting to *Le Cantique de Siméon* in hymn 36 has a lovely alternative translation along with an absolutely lovely hymn tune. When supported by a small schola of singers who can sing all the parts, this may be the most beautiful of all settings.

There are no antiphons given with the invitatory for evening prayer, so unless an alternative hymn or invitatory psalm is chosen that includes antiphons, they are, quite naturally, absent. The instructions for the psalmody in the above section for morning prayer apply as well in the evening.

As with morning prayer, the lessons and canticles then follow. While the table of canticles gives suggestions for an alternating use of canticles during evening prayer, a superior choice is to stick with the ones appointed in the rite itself: the *Magnificat* and the *Nunc dimittis*. If the Old Testament was read in morning prayer, then the lesson from the alternating year may be used in the evening. However, a superior choice once more, as noted above, is to use the Old Testament and Epistle at morning prayer and the Gospel reading alone at evening prayer, followed by the *Magnificat*. In this way, the *Nunc dimittis* is kept to its most traditional place in the prayers for compline.

Then, once more, one returns to the Apostles' Creed and the prayers. The instructions above about the prayers, including the suffrages and collects, should be heeded. A custom has arisen where the people join the officiant in the prayer for mission that begins "Keep watch, dear Lord." While one appreciates the enthusiasm for this prayer, which is indeed beautiful and lovely, the intention of the prayer book (as with all collects) is that it is read by the officiant alone. This is underscored and made evident by the italicized "amen" at the end of the prayer.

---

11. For more details, see Hatchett, *American Prayer Book*, 138, 140.

After the collects, there is the same invitation for a hymn or anthem, with the evening office hymn being the best choice. Then, as with the morning office, the officiant should choose an appropriate conclusion from the optional ones offered: the General Thanksgiving, Prayer of St. Chrysostom, dismissal, and grace. Once more, all four are unnecessary and a rotation of the options is a wise choice. As with Dearmer, we shall doubtless all continue to make some use, especially at evensong, of the Prayer of St. Chrysostom, which is one of the most beautiful passages in the English language.

NOONDAY PRAYER, COMPLINE, AND HOUSEHOLD DEVOTIONS

In an attempt to restore some of the daily rhythm of Benedictine prayer from which the Anglican office was developed, the current prayer book restores a short service of prayers to be used at noonday and another short service to be used when going to bed, known as compline.

Noonday prayer begins with the versicle and response (there are no optional fore-office pieces). A hymn may be sung and then a few psalms are suggested, followed by the *Gloria patri*. Three short chapters are offered. These are not, of course, full chapters of Scripture but instead come from the offices of terce, sext, and none where, in lieu of a full reading (*lectio*) from Scripture, there would be a little chapter (*capitulum*), a short verse or two from Scripture. There is then provision for a silent or spoken meditation, with the liturgy then moving directly to the *Kyrie* and the Lord's Prayer (without doxology). Then, instead of a normal salutation we have the *Domine, exaudi orationem meam* from Ps 102. Given the penitential nature of this psalm, this cry to God gives a more penitential nature to the collect that follows (in keeping with the theme of noonday prayer being on the Lord's crucifixion). There then may be free intercessions, which are concluded by a dismissal, which is not optional.

The liturgy of compline has an altogether gentler tone and mood, as is fitting for prayers at bedtime. After a brief opening prayer and versicle and response, there is an optional abbreviated form of the confession. Instead of an absolution, the declaration of forgiveness indicates that the framers of the prayer book envisioned this liturgy as one that would be said in homes more often than in churches. (The fully sung plainsong version of compline in the accompaniment edition of the hymnal, though, is a marvelous offering in the church). The opening prayer and versicle and response are not optional, as in the fore-office matter for morning and evening prayer. That said, given the above noted structure for offices, they are best still understood liturgically as preparatory fore-office material before the use of the same versicle and response of evening prayer, "O God, make speed to save us." A variety of psalms are suggested (with an allowance for different ones to be used, if desired, though this would hardly be necessary in most cases). As with noonday prayer, there are several optional chapters of Scripture, followed by an invitation for an evening hymn. The office hymns suggested above all would be fine choices, especially if they are not being used at evening prayer. The verses from Ps 31 that our Lord spoke at his own death are then the entry into the prayers, which continue in the same way as noonday prayer with the *Kyrie*, the Lord's Prayer (without doxology), and the *Domine, exaudi orationem meam*. Several collects are then offered, with the clear instruction that only one is to be used, followed by an optional additional prayer that brings to our attention the reality that whenever we lie down to sleep, others rise up to work. After an optional silence and offering of free intercessions, the service concludes with a version of the *Nunc dimittis* to which a special antiphon is appended. The liturgy then ends with a required dismissal and grace.

In an attempt gently to invite households into a practice of daily prayer, knowing that the full offices might be intimidating to some, the framers of the current book created a set of four "Daily Devotions for Individuals and Families." The structure for each is the same: a psalm or canticle, followed by a short chapter of Scripture, options for silence, hymns, and prayers, and then a conclusion with the Lord's Prayer and a collect appropriate to that time of the day. It cannot be stressed enough that these were intended to be devotions for individuals and families in households. They were not intended to supplant the offices of the prayer book in the public worship of the church or to be creative ways of saying the prayers of the church differently at diocesan or parochial gatherings. To use these pastorally sensitive exceptional liturgies that were crafted for households in this way entirely misses the nature of the public offices of the church universal.

THE LITURGICAL OBSERVANCE OF THE OFFICES

The average church that observes the offices will probably continue in the old ways, having a hymn after the third collect and then the prayers and thanksgivings, followed by (as is the more popular custom in the Episcopal Church) the General Thanksgiving, dismissal, and the grace. In those few churches where most people come to morning prayer as a preparation for the Holy Eucharist, care should be taken for the office to close properly, followed by a brief break in worship for those who are coming only for Holy Communion to arrive and prepare for that divine liturgy.

Anciently, before the office began, each minister went to their place in the choir separately and then said their own preparatory prayer privately. At the present day it is more usual for the choir to enter in order, after a prayer in the vestry or other gathering space, but there is no reason why this prayer should be intoned. However, the ancient practice has much to commend to it and is to be preferred. The candles will be lit for morning prayer. The minister will wear surplice, hood, and tippet, or if the office is festal, surplice and cope. The notion that, if a priest, one should wear a stole for pronouncing the absolution is absolutely without foundation.

Assuming the more ancient practice is followed, with no procession before the service, the ministers will thus enter without cross or hymn-singing and take their places. The fore-office will be said in the natural voice until the opening versicle and response, which begins the liturgy proper, and which should thus be sung. The current prayer book gives instruction for how to vary the opening sentences of Scripture in the fore-office according to the season of the church. When multiple options exist, it would seem best generally to select those sentences that are short and of the nature of a prayer. As noted earlier, the longer invitation for confession should be reserved for Advent and Lent. On other Sundays, the parson should use the shorter form. After the invitation, the silence (which should be brief) is still clearly required. If a deacon or lay person is leading the office, they remain kneeling and change the pronouns to convert the priestly absolution into a declaration of forgiveness.

The officiant should always turn to the people when saying the invitation to confession, also (if a priest) for the whole of the absolution. The officiant should return to facing the normal direction (whether that is east or north, depending on the architecture of the church), for the opening versicle and response that begins the invitatory.

Though there is no rubrical requirement, common sense indicates the reader of Scripture shall stand and turn in order to "best be heard of all such as are present" (as encouraged by the rubrics of the older books). The lessons therefore should be read as audibly and as naturally as possible, "distinctly with an audible voice."[12] This rubric, also from the older books, implies that the prayers need not be said in the best acoustic position, but of course they must be pronounced clearly, reverently, and audibly.

The lessons should be read by the laity in attendance. Up to 1662 the rubric had "the minister that readeth,"[13] and often the clerk read at least the first lesson. In 1662, the rubric was altered to "he that readeth,"[14] which put the matter beyond dispute. The ideal indeed is that each lesson should be read by a different person, just as is done at the Eucharist. Liturgical worship should be cooperative—priest, chanters, readers, choir, and congregation each taking their appointed part.

The reader must begin and end the lessons according to the rubric, "a reading (or Lesson) from" and then saying the title of the book of Scripture.[15] The chapter and verse may be added, and while this seems unnecessary in celebrations of Holy Eucharist where there is often a leaflet of some type with that information, it is a good practice at the office because it helps the people to situate the reading within Scripture. It may be noticed that a plethora of opinions and ideas exist on how to name the books of Scripture. Thankfully, the Daily Office Lectionary gives a helpful guide to the minister. For those who will use a Bible instead of the lectionary book, the following titles of books should be given:

The Old Testament

- Book of Genesis
- Book of Exodus
- Book of Leviticus

---

12. *1662 Book of Common Prayer*, 12.
13. *1549 Book of Common Prayer*, 7.
14. *1662 Book of Common Prayer*, 12.
15. *1979 Book of Common Prayer*, 47, 64, 84, 118.

- Book of Numbers
- Book of Joshua
- Book of Judges
- Book of Ruth
- First Book of Samuel
- Second Book of Samuel
- First Book of the Kings
- Second Book of the Kings
- First Book of Chronicles
- Second Book of Chronicles
- Book of Ezra
- Book of Nehemiah
- Book of Job
- Proverbs
- Ecclesiastes
- Song of Songs or Song of Solomon (not appointed in the *Daily Office Lectionary*, but appointed in the *Revised Common Lectionary* and in the eucharistic propers, using both titles)
- Book of Isaiah
- Book of Jeremiah
- Book of Lamentations
- Book of Ezekiel
- Book of Daniel
- Book of Hosea
- Book of Joel
- Book of Amos
- Book of Obadiah
- Book of Jonah
- Book of Micah
- Book of Nahum

- Book of Habakkuk
- Book of Zephaniah
- Book of Haggai
- Book of Zechariah
- Book of Malachi

Deuterocanonical Books

- Book of Tobit (not appointed in the Daily Office Lectionary, but appointed in the rite of marriage)
- Book of Judith
- (The rest of the Book of Esther, not appointed in our lectionaries)
- Book of Wisdom
- Book of Ecclesiasticus (referred to as the Book of Sirach when appointed in the *Revised Common Lectionary*)
- Book of Baruch
- (Letter of Jeremiah, not appointed in our lectionaries)
- (None of the additions to the Book of Daniel—the Prayer of Azariah and the Song of the Three Jews, Susanna, or Bel and the Dragon—are appointed in our lectionaries, but the prayer and song are canticles of morning prayer)
- First Book of the Maccabees
- (Second Book of the Maccabees, not appointed in our lectionaries)
- (First Book of Esdras, not appointed in our lectionaries)
- (Prayer of Manasseh—not appointed in our lectionaries, though used as canticle 14, *Kyrie Pantokrator*).
- (Psalm 151, not appointed in our lectionaries)
- (Third Book of the Maccabees, not appointed in our lectionaries)
- Second Book of Esdras
- (Fourth Book of the Maccabees, not appointed in our lectionaries)

New Testament

- Gospel according to Matthew
- Gospel according to Mark
- Gospel according to Luke
- Gospel according to John
- Acts of the Apostles
- Letter of Paul to the Romans
- First Letter of Paul to the Corinthians
- Second Letter of Paul to the Corinthians
- Letter of Paul to the Galatians
- Letter of Paul to the Ephesians[16]
- Letter of Paul to the Philippians
- Letter of Paul to the Colossians
- First Letter of Paul to the Thessalonians
- Second Letter of Paul to the Thessalonians
- First Letter of Paul to Timothy
- Second Letter of Paul to Timothy
- Letter of Paul to Titus
- Letter of Paul to Philemon
- Letter to the Hebrews
- Letter of James
- First Letter of Peter
- Second Letter of Peter
- First Letter of John

16. The epistles to the Ephesians, Colossians, Second Thessalonians, First and Second Timothy, and Titus are all disputed by some scholars when it comes to Pauline authorship. The anxious parson may, of course, omit Paul's name from them—but if the *Revised Common Lectionary* book is used, they would need to strike it there so as not to confuse readers. Leaving Paul's name in the title due to the tradition of the church (and the reality they come from the Pauline school, much like we call the book of Isaiah by that name though at least the second half of it comes from the Isaianic school) is also an appropriate choice.

- Second Letter of John
- Third Letter of John
- Letter of Jude
- Revelation to John

The words "Holy Gospel" are used only for the liturgical Gospel at the Eucharist, when the formula is "the Holy Gospel of our Lord Jesus Christ according to." The word "Saint" or the abbreviation "St." is not included in naming the author of the Gospel (see the example in the burial rite on p. 495). Since this title is not used for the four evangelists in the liturgical proclamation of the Gospel at mass, it would certainly not be used when naming any persons that are mentioned in the titles of the Epistles.

When anthems are sung by a choir, the congregation should sit and not stand. They are, like the sermon, an offering to God for the edification of the people, who should therefore adopt the position best suited for hearing them. No outward action of the body should be without meaning if it is to be pious in itself, profitable to us, and edifying to others. Standing has always been a solemn act of reverence in church, as solemn as kneeling, and there can be no place less appropriate for such an act and no place where its adoption is more likely to destroy its meaning than at the listening to the anthem. The parson, therefore, should ask the people to sit and should also set the example.

The minister may, before the appropriate prayer or bidding, announce the names of any who desire to be prayed for or to return thanks.

FESTAL EVENSONG

Festal morning prayer is as lawful as festal evensong but very rare. Incense might be used at the *Benedictus* and on principal feasts at the *Te Deum* also. Much more common is the celebration of festal evensong.

For convenience, I shall treat here the more elaborate form of evensong, which should be called festal, since for the plain service the directions above will suffice. As for the canticles, the *Magnificat* and *Nunc Dimittis* should always be used. They are (with *Benedictus*) the evangelical canticles and have from time immemorial formed part of the daily services of the church.

THE DAILY OFFICE

The candles will be lit, as for the morning office, no difference being made whether the service is festal or not. But for festal evensong the taperers' candles will be lighted and placed in readiness within the altar rails (or on the choir step, i.e., the step between choir and sanctuary), unless the officiant is to begin the service vested in cope. A special seat will be prepared for the priest—this seat will be set apart in some conspicuous and convenient place in the northern part of the chancel or, as is often more convenient, in the southern part. It had best be a straight-backed chair and not too high, so that the priest can easily swing the cope over the back when sitting down. On either side may be placed a seat and hassock for the taperers, and in front of the priest's seat will be a desk to hold the books and to allow for kneeling.

The servers should vest in cassock and surplice. It may be convenient to state here that when there are rulers of the choir, these officials should have a lectern and stools in the midst of the choir, whether the service be mattins, mass, or evensong. They may wear copes of the color of the day. They may hold staves, and they will follow the same rules for standing, kneeling, and sitting as the choir. There is very little precedent for a boat boy to accompany the thurifer, and we have none for the subtleties of "double swings" incensing. With the clergy (the officiant in surplice and cope and the rest in surplice, hood, and tippet); the rulers (in surplice and cope); the taperers, thurifer, and choristers (in surplice); and the choristers (in surplice) being in their places, one of the clergy will commence the service as usual from their own stall. The highest in rank should invite the confession and pronounce the absolution.

Shortly before the *Magnificat*, if the officiant has not begun the service in a cope, they should now put a cope over the surplice, either in the vestry or at the altar (as was the general custom in parish churches). In the latter case the taperers and thurifer will come up and assist, but if the officiant comes from the vestry, then they will enter the chancel the short way (preceded by the thurifer), and the taperers will come and meet the officiant at the communion rails (i.e., the step between choir and sanctuary). The priest puts incense into the censer, after which the priest goes up to the altar with the taperers and thurifer and kneels down for a moment. If the censing of persons and things during service time is the custom (as well it should be, as much of the prejudice against this has thankfully departed), the priest then censes the altar—first in the midst, then at the south and north parts. The priest then walks round the altar on the pavement, censing throughout. Returning to the front of the altar, the priest bows to it. The taperers and thurifer (who have been standing before the altar on the pavement during the censing) then precede the officiant to the appointed seat. Here the officiant is censed by the thurifer, after which the thurifer censes the rulers, then the taperers, and the choir, and finally the congregation, in order, bowing to those who are censed, who then bow in return. The thurifer then takes the censer back to the sacristy and returns to the appointed seat in a convenient place.

The priest then sits in a convenient place while the second lesson is being read, the taperers being seated on either side. The priest takes the rest of the service as usual (kneeling and standing as the rubrics direct) until the conclusion of the Lord's Prayer. The taperers or verger must always see that the priest is provided with the necessary books, opened at the right places. The suffrages and collects are then said solemnly, as follows: the priest in cope, preceded by the taperers, goes to the midst of the choir and stands within the altar rails or on the choir step. There, the priest meets a server (either an acolyte or the verger) carrying a prayer book with a marker at the suffrages and another at the collect for the day (after which the priest can then flip back to the marker for the suffrages for the remaining two collects). The taperers take up their candles and stand on either side of the priest, turned towards the priest. The person holding the book stands facing the priest and holds the prayer book at a convenient height for the priest to read. The priest chants the suffrages and collects and then goes out, preceded by the servers, and takes off the cope (or leaves the cope on for the entirety of the service, if it has been on since the beginning).

The essential ceremonial is now over, and anything that follows the third collect may be said by one of the clergy from their stall, the officiant and servers being now in their usual places. There is, however, no reason at all for the altar lights being put out before the end of the service. As has already been pointed out, the minister should stand for these prayers and say them without note.

Certain rites and ceremonies that have been added to evensong need a few words of comment. It has been noted that the rubrics permit two hymns: the *Phos hilaron* (or an appropriate substitute) and the hymn after the collects (normally the office hymn). The rubrics are clear that "a sermon may be preached after the Office; or, within the Office, after the Readings or at the time of the hymn or anthem after the Collects."[17]

---

17. *1979 Book of Common Prayer*, 142.

The rubrics of the 1662 prayer book used to provide for baptism and catechizing as inserted between the second lesson and *Nunc Dimittis*. One wonders if our religion would have been in a far better condition than it is now if the clergy had obeyed the very important rubric that "the Curate of every Parish shall diligently upon Sundays and Holy days, after the second Lesson at Evening Prayer, openly in the Church instruct and examine."[18] If the clergy had taught sound theology every Sunday and holy day during the last three centuries, how different would the position of the people be at the present day! The rubric being absent in the current prayer book does not diminish the need, and such catechizing must still be done at other times. Before or after evensong on Sundays is, indeed, still a good time to offer it. Even if none is offered, if there is a sermon in the liturgy, it would be an advantage if the Sunday evening discourse were of the nature of an instruction. The gain to us would be very great in thus escaping from the conventions of the sermon, and learning instead to instruct our people, who stand in much need of sensible and systematic teaching.

After the sermon a collection is often made. To this there can be no objection, and the rubrics on p. 142 permit that "an offering may be received and presented at the Office." In some churches, however, the alms are ceremonially presented at the altar, and the ceremonies are often of a rather idolatrous nature—the dish being solemnly elevated, signed with the cross, and afterwards carried out with the utmost reverence by the priest at the tail of a procession. A simple presentation at the altar is all that is truly needed. Furthermore, it does not look good for the priest to carry out the alms basin as if it were the priest's own private booty. Moreover, it is a serious abuse to introduce a peculiar eucharistic ceremony related to the offertory into evensong. Few things are stranger than the spectacle of a priest at evening prayer vested in a sacramental stole, presenting the alms at the altar, then giving the eucharistic blessing, and actually speaking of this ceremony (and sometimes even of the offering themselves) as "the offertory."

The collection, therefore, having been made, the clerk will receive it in a bason at the chancel steps, and will carry it direct to the altar, the credence, or some other safe and convenient place.

There is no reason why the clergy and choir should not go out at the conclusion of whatever concluding rites are chosen. Though the

---

18. *1662 Book of Common Prayer*, 173.

rubrics do not envision a hymn at the exit, the custom has become far too beloved of the people to ignore it entirely and if, after being properly dismissed, the people desire to stay and sing one more song of praise, it is hard to imagine how a devout parson would refuse them. It seems best in this case for the priest to go to the pavement in front of the altar at the conclusion of the office hymn and, standing there, to lead any of the "authorized intercessions and thanksgivings," followed by the General Thanksgiving, Prayer of St. Chrysostom, dismissal, and grace (the parson remembering that all four are not needed). The people having been thus given time to kneel down quietly and to pray, the priest kneels for a short private prayer, goes down from the altar, bows, and goes the short way to the sacristy while the people sing a final hymn, if desired, or the musicians play a postlude. But if there is no other priest to go out with the choir, the priest may find it more convenient to remain, standing at one side on the pavement while the choir bow and go out, and then follow them to the choir vestry.

Whether evensong is festal every Sunday (which will be the case only in a few rather exceptionally placed churches), or whether it be not, it will be convenient to mark festivals and other important liturgical events by a procession, for which chapter 8 of this book may be consulted.

It is of some importance, both as a question of principle and as a practical matter of parochial activity, to make much of the Saturday evening service—the first evensong of Sunday—if it is observed in a parish. Therefore, if in any way it can be managed, this evensong should be sung, and it may well be festal even in churches where the second evensong on the Sunday itself is not. People should also be taught to regard this service as a preparation for their Sunday Communion.

There is no need for us to follow the cathedral use of Salisbury as to the occasions for processions in a parish church where, for instance, Saturday evensong processions are generally difficult to provide for. The matter rests with the discretion of the parson, who may safely follow the reasonable and common practice here suggested.

CONCERNING BENEDICTION OF THE BLESSED SACRAMENT

Practices of eucharistic adoration are an ancient part of the church, and the liturgy known as Benediction of the Blessed Sacrament dates from the thirteenth century, the same time at which the Feast of Corpus Christi was first proposed. It was abolished during the English Reformation and is thought to be spoken against by article twenty-five of the Thirty-Nine Articles, where we find it written, "The Sacraments were not ordained of Christ to be gazed upon, or to be carried about, but that we should duly use them."[19] It seems even more clearly spoken against in article twenty-eight: "The Sacrament of the Lord's Supper was not by Christ's ordinance reserved, carried about, lifted up, or worshiped."[20]

Now, the loyal parson is certainly aware that the Thirty-Nine Articles were moved to the "Historical Documents" section of our prayer book and are no longer authoritative in our church. They represent an important moment in the development of Anglican understandings of theology, but they are also clearly reactions (and many seem to be over-reactions) to the theological debates of their own time. The practice of eucharistic reservation, for example, is now a common practice in all Episcopal churches as the old prejudices have faded away.

I would suggest the time is ripe for a similar putting aside the prejudices and fears related to the practices of eucharistic adoration, particularly as found in the liturgy of Benediction of the Blessed Sacrament. And in favor of that reappraisal is none other than John Macquarrie. In the *Handbook of Anglican Theologians*, Bradshaw writes that Macquarrie was "unquestionably Anglicanism's most distinguished systematic theologian in the second half of the 20th century."[21] In 1965, Macquarrie wrote an article for the monthly newsletter of the Church of St. Mary the Virgin in New York City where he spoke favorably about the practice of benediction.[22] The article went on to have a life of its own and is often printed in service bulletins of congregations who practice this devotion.

In the article, Macquarrie notes that eucharistic reservation arose in primitive times as a common practice during times of persecution when the faithful could not safely attend corporate worship with any real regularity and so would reserve the Sacrament in their homes so that they could communicate themselves. He reminds us as well that the development of the rite of benediction drew much from the writings of Thomas Aquinas, who reminds us that "when we look on creaturely beings within the world and consider them 'in depth' . . . our mind is carried beyond

---

19. *1979 Book of Common Prayer*, 872.
20. *1979 Book of Common Prayer*, 873.
21. Bradshaw, "Macquarrie," 167–68.
22. Macquarrie, "In Memoriam."

them to that divine Being by whom every creature exists."[23] He also points to Archbishop William Temple's point that Christianity is "the most materialistic of religions" because of the way the incarnation has changed how we experience matter.[24] Furthermore, though Anglicans have generally declined to define a theory of the method of real presence, we do still believe in the real presence of Christ in the Eucharist.

With this foundation, he argues that benediction is a perfectly appropriate form of contemplative prayer, one in which we are guided by focusing our attention on the Blessed Sacrament. He pushes aside rejections or anxiety over this devotion.

> Let us assure any who may be perturbed over such matters that we are not being so stupid as to worship a wafer, nor do we have such an archaic and myth-laden mentality that we believe the object before us to be charged with magical power. Rather, it is in and through the Sacrament that we adore Christ, because we, being men and not angels, have need of an earthly manifestation of the divine presence, and because he, in his grace and mercy, has promised to grant us his presence in this particular manifestation.[25]

As the article continues, Macquarrie provides a theological commentary on the whole of the devotional practice and, in one of the most profoundly important theological points in the whole article, he reminds us of the wisdom of Father Hugh Blenkin, who said, "God can never be the object of a man's worship, he is always the subject."[26] This is the reason why our time of adoration results in the reception of the blessing of God as the sign of the cross is made with the eucharistic host.

Macquarrie also points out that though the church has, from time to time, expressed some discomfort with the service, it remains one deeply important to the people of God. He writes,

> Benediction is a popular service, that is to say, a people's service. The clever and sophisticated do not come much to Benediction, but the simple, the poor, those who acknowledge an emptiness in their lives that only God can fill. Even those who might not come to Holy Communion will sometimes come to Benediction where God reaches out to them though they think they

---

23. Macquarrie, "In Memoriam," para. 13.
24. Macquarrie, "In Memoriam," para. 14.
25. Macquarrie, "In Memoriam," para. 16.
26. Macquarrie, "In Memoriam," para. 17.

are only on the fringes. I think of some of those with whom I have knelt at Benediction: harassed city-dwellers in New York, working-class people from the back streets of Dublin, soldiers serving in the deserts of North Africa, Indian Christians living as a tiny minority in a great Hindu city.... They have all had the grace of humility—a quality which, alas, is not greatly encouraged in our new liturgies.[27]

This all resonates with my own experience of this rite, where a focused attention on the presence of Christ has created a more profound sense of that presence than I have ever experienced in Eucharist alone. And, in our own time, when people suggest unlawful practices such as communing the unbaptized, perhaps a wiser approach would be to open up more services of benediction where anyone, baptized or not, can come and experience the presence of Christ.

Furthermore, I would argue that the offering of benediction as a devotional practice is lawful in our prayer book on three distinct points. First, the rubric on p. 457, at the end of the Ministration to the sick, maintains the historic teaching of the church known as "spiritual Communion." That is, even if one is unable to consume the bread and the wine, the benefits of the Sacrament can still be received by the worshipper.

Second, the idea that the theology of benediction is foreign to our church cannot be maintained for the additional reason that our duly authorized hymnals include the traditional hymns for benediction, including those written by Thomas Aquinas, which have been used in the church for centuries with regard to this rite. If our hymnal includes the phrase "therefore we before him bending, this great sacrament revere"[28] how can one reject the reverence for the Sacrament found in the liturgy of Benediction?

Third, and finally, silence is enjoined at various points in our liturgy throughout the prayer book but is very rarely mandated. Usually, there is an invitation that silence "may be kept." The exception is the silence in the Ash Wednesday liturgy, when we reflect upon the start of Lent, and after the fraction in the eucharistic prayer. Though far too many clergy violate the rubric by moving directly into the fraction anthem, the framers of the prayer book clearly intended a time of very real silence. I would suggest that the service of benediction is taking that often far-too-short

---

27. These reflections are included in the Scottish Episcopal Church's "Order for Solemn Evensong," 7.

28. This line is from hymn 330 of *The Hymnal 1982*.

time of silence and stretching it out like taffy, giving us room to truly be in the presence of Christ in the Blessed Sacrament.

As to the possible final objection that sacraments are, in Anglican teaching, to be used, I would not disagree in the least. But allowing time for devotional and contemplative prayer *before using them* is certainly meet and right so to do. That is why in the form of benediction I suggest below, there is an offering of Communion wherein all those present consume the bread after the time of adoration and benediction.

One final note: When benediction was suppressed during the Reformation, it was during a time when regular reception of the Sacrament no longer existed among the people. Indeed, in some quarters eucharistic adoration and benediction may have become a substitute for reception of the Blessed Sacrament. In our own time, however, we are faced with the opposite problem, the people have become so accustomed to regular reception of the Sacrament that all sense of preparation to receive seems to have been lost. One only has to read the exhortation beginning on p. 316 of the prayer book to discover that the venerable wisdom in that exhortation is unknown among many of the laity. Thus, restoring eucharistic adoration and benediction might help reconnect the people with the ideals of our prayer book in exhortation and heighten the power of when they do receive the Sacrament.

A PRAYER BOOK CATHOLIC LITURGY OF EVENSONG AND BENEDICTION

For the parson who wishes to obey the prayer book while also offering this devotional rite to the people, the practice is very simple and rubrically sound, particularly when a liturgy of the following form is presented to the bishop with a request for permission to offer it.

First, there is traditionally an offering of solemn evensong, following the instructions already found in this book. In some churches, they have offered benediction after a service of sung compline, a particularly fine approach at retreats or other times when an even more restful and quiet experience is desired.

After the liturgy of evening prayer concludes according to the rubric, those who wish to stay for the devotional practice of benediction may do so. At this point, in some Anglican parishes, the ministers exit to prepare for the rite—the priest and deacon, if there is one, change from office vestments to eucharistic vestments while the people sing a hymn such as *Adoro devote*, hymn 314. Most, however, retain the cope and do not change vestments, which is certainly an appropriate choice and helps to eliminate some of the fussiness that can arise with popular devotions like this and keep the focus where it needs to be—that is, on the Blessed Sacrament and not on the clothing of the clergy. Additional candles may also be lit around the altar. The censer should be refreshed at this time.

At the conclusion of the hymn, the Blessed Sacrament is taken from the tabernacle and placed on the altar by the deacon, if there is one, or by the priest, if there is no deacon. The Sacrament is often placed in a monstrance (a special vessel whose name simply means "showing" and whose purpose is to display the consecrated bread). However, a monstrance is not required, and the bread may instead simply be placed on the altar in a ciborium or even laying upon a paten (or even slightly propped up on the paten), which is set on top of a chalice for easier viewing.

Once the Sacrament is placed on the altar, a bell sounds and all kneel. The cleric who placed the Sacrament on the altar carefully walks backwards and then kneels on the footpace with the other ministers. There is a time of silent devotion and adoration, generally at least one if not two or three minutes or more. If desired, the priest may speak a brief meditation, often addressed to Christ as a prayer that the people overhear, beginning with "Lord Jesus Christ" and then speaking of the concerns of the time and the grace of the Sacrament. This meditation can often help guide the people in their own time of silent prayer and adoration.

The officiant then bows, which is a signal for all the ministers to bow profoundly, directly on the floor, and for the organist to begin the first hymn, *O Salutaris Hostia*, found in the hymnal as hymn 311 (though the words can be set to many tunes of the same meter). After bowing during the first phrase, the thurifer hands the censer to the officiant who censes the Sacrament. The censer is then handed back to the thurifer who swings it gently while the hymn continues. All bow profoundly once more at the conclusion of the hymn.

After the hymn, there is a second time of silent devotion and adoration, which may end by the priest saying, "May the Divine Assistance remain with us always" and the people responding, "And with our absent brothers, sisters, and siblings. Amen." Before that concluding invocation, a litany or short meditation may be spoken, if it has not already been offered, helping to guide and center the people's devotion.

The officiant bows once more, along with all the ministers, and the organist begins the hymn *Tantum ergo Sacramentum*, found in the hymnal as hymn 330. After bowing during the first phrase, the thurifer hands the censer to the officiant who censes the Sacrament again. The censer is then handed back to the thurifer who swings it gently while the hymn continues. All bow profoundly once more at the conclusion of the hymn, during the invocation of the Trinity.

The priest then sings the versicle, "You gave them bread from heaven," with the people responding, "Containing within itself all sweetness." The priest sings "let us pray" and then says the collect given for the proper "Of the Holy Eucharist" in the prayer book:

> God our Father, whose Son our Lord Jesus Christ in a wonderful Sacrament has left us a memorial of his passion: Grant us so to venerate the sacred mysteries of his Body and Blood, that we may ever perceive within ourselves the fruit of his redemption; who lives and reigns with you and the Holy Spirit, one God, for ever and ever. Amen.[29]

Customarily, the verger will then place the humeral veil (which is always white or gold, no matter the color of the cope or chasuble being worn) over the shoulders of the priest. The humeral veil is a sign that the blessing about to be offered truly comes from Christ himself in the Sacrament and not the priest. The priest approaches the altar, takes the monstrance or other vessel holding the bread into hands that are wrapped with the humeral veil, and then turns towards the people, moving clockwise, very slowly. Once facing the people, the Sacrament is lifted high vertically, then lowered, and then the priest slowly turns to the left, rotating almost the entire way, nearly perpendicular to the people, and then to the right, at the same perpendicular angle. The priest then returns to the center for a moment and then slowly turns to the right back to the altar to place the Sacrament back where it was, on the altar. The organist might play during the benediction itself or silence may be kept.

The priest walks slowly backwards once more and joins the other ministers kneeling on the footpace. Another time of generous silence for devotion is kept and then the priest begins the divine praises, the people repeating after each phrase:

Blessed be God.
Blessed be the holy and undivided Trinity.

---

29. *1979 Book of Common Prayer*, 252.

Blessed be God the Father, maker of heaven and earth.
Blessed be Jesus Christ, true God and true Man.
Blessed be Jesus Christ in his death and resurrection.
Blessed be Jesus Christ on his throne of glory.
Blessed be Jesus Christ in the Sacrament of his body and blood.
Blessed be God the Holy Spirit, the Lord and giver of life.
Blessed be God in the Virgin Mary, Mother of God.
Blessed be God in Joseph, guardian of the Incarnate Word.
Blessed be God in all the angels and saints.
Blessed be God.[30]

There is a final period of silence and then the priest (or deacon if there is one) goes to the altar and returns the Blessed Sacrament to the tabernacle. When the tabernacle doors close, a bell rings and all rise. The minister turns and then walks down the steps of the altar, as is normal (instead of walking backwards when the Sacrament is exposed), to return to her or his place with the other ministers. Psalm 117 is then sung, traditionally, with the following antiphon preceding and following: "Let us forever adore the Most Holy Sacrament." The *Gloria Patri* should be included in the recitation. An alleluia may be added to the antiphon in Eastertide.

The devotion of adoration and benediction being concluded, the priest may then begin the rite for communion under special circumstances.[31] One of the opening sentences is said by the officiant, all recite the Lord's Prayer, and the officiant then prays the collect. The Sacrament is then retrieved from the tabernacle one more time. All should be invited to receive, and the bread may be broken into smaller pieces to enable this. If one finds there are more present than can reasonably consume the bread used in the benediction, then more should be retrieved from the tabernacle. Ablutions are done reverently and simply. The priest then says the appointed post-communion prayer and dismissal. A postlude may be played as the ministers exit.

---

30. This particular version of the divine praises comes from *Saint Augustine's Prayer Book*. Cobb and Olsen, *Saint Augustine's Prayer Book*, 198.

31. *1979 Book of Common Prayer*, 396.

7

The Great Litany

The Great Litany (known in the Church of England simply as "The Litany") is a liturgical treasure that is increasingly unknown among the average Episcopalian. However, it was the first piece of liturgy translated into English during the Reformation—before any of the offices or even Holy Communion itself—and it remains a rich experience of prayer to God. Originally developed in the fifth century as a processional set of prayers for divine protection, this liturgy finds its home in the traditional Rogation Days of Monday, Tuesday, and Wednesday before Ascension Day. The prayer book invites the use of the Great Litany before Eucharist, after the collects of morning or evening prayer, or as a separate devotion, commending it especially in Lent and on Rogation Days.

There has been a widespread idea that the litany, so beautiful a part of the prayer book, is wearisome, and in consequence there persists a most regrettable tendency to omit it from the liturgies of the church. Admittedly, it may be wearisome when sung in the usual dragging and monotonous way, but not when its beauty is brought out by proper rendering. On Wednesdays and Fridays, and at other simpler times, the priest may well kneel and read it without note, which takes but little time and is most devotional. Then on Sundays, particularly in Advent and Lent, it can be sung to the beautiful plainsong setting in our hymnal as S-67. For parishes with established choirs, it may also be sung with the choir responding on behalf of the congregation. Peter Hallock (published by the Peter R. Hallock Institute) and Robbe Delcamp (published by St. James Music Press) have each written settings for the current prayer book responses. Furthermore, settings written for older prayer book versions of the litany by Thomas Tallis and Henry Loosemore have been adapted for the current responses by Robert McCormick and others. This sung version, of course, should be sung after the manner of good reading and not in that style of chanting, which Dearmer believed was like an "elephant waltzing."[1] The points of the service are fully brought out when it is sung well and properly divided up between chanters, priest, and people—still more, when it is sung in procession. In churches where it is usually said or sung at the litany desk, it might be sung in procession on Rogation Sunday.

As to the manner of praying the Great Litany, attention to history will help here. The Great Litany was instructed to be said on Wednesdays and Fridays as well as Sundays, according to the 1662 prayer book.[2] There was no direction as to where or how it is to be "sung or said," but, from the first year of Edward VI to the time of Bishop Cosin in the late seventeenth century, it was several times appointed to be said in a special place in the midst of the church, and a "faldstool" was mentioned.[3] A rubric in the liturgy for a commination in the 1662 prayer book also speaks of the place "where they are accustomed to say the Litany," and directs the "Clerks" (i.e., the cantors) to kneel with the priest at the same place to sing the *Miserere*.[4] In some churches it may be found more convenient for the litany desk, if one is used, to be in the choir itself, as was sometimes the custom and still is in many cathedrals.

When we consider how carefully the priest's and other ministers' parts are defined for them in morning prayer, evening prayer, and the other offices of the prayer book, it is clear that the omission of all mention of the priest in the first part of the litany in the 1662 prayer book was done with the definite intention of allowing for reserving this part to lay chanters. The marked change in the character of the service at the *Pater noster* is also in favor of its being sung in procession. Even when the litany is said in the simplest way by the priest alone, in choir habit,

1. Dearmer, *Parson's Handbook*, 250.
2. 1662 *Book of Common Prayer*, 26.
3. This particular faldstool is not the folding chair properly used by a bishop when visiting churches outside the cathedral (see page 296 of this book), which is the more common meaning. See Armentrout and Slocum, *Episcopal Dictionary*, 199. It was, rather, a term used in the Church of England to describe the litany desk. As a close corollary, it also is the word for the prie-dieu at which the sovereign kneels for coronations and weddings. See "Authorised Liturgy," 17.
4. 1662 *Book of Common Prayer*, 194.

kneeling in the midst of the church, the priest may well stand at the *Pater noster* and so remain till the end.

No doubt the best way of singing the litany is to do so in procession. This was the old custom and there is nothing against it in the prayer book. It brings out the meaning of the litany in a way that nothing else can do and helps the people to keep up their attention. The procession should be arranged with stations as follows: The opening invocations are sung standing in the midst of the choir before the altar. At "Remember not," all turn, and the procession starts in the same order and in the same vestments as in other processions before mass, and the verger may hold a book like all the rest. The cantors walk in front of the priest, at the head of the choir, and sing the deprecations, obsecrations, and intercessions as they go, with the clergy, choir, and people answering. The procession should be timed to reach the rood (or chancel steps) for "Son of God, we beseech thee to hear us" and the *Kyries*. Then a station is made before the rood, and the Lord's Prayer, versicle, and collect are said by the priest, during which all in the procession remain standing.

If the supplication is used instead of the normal versicle and collect after the Lord's Prayer, then at the *Exsurge* ("O Lord, arise") all go slowly up into the choir, where the suffrages (beginning with "From our enemies, defend us, O Christ") are sung by the cantors and choir alternately. The priest then says the concluding prayer, standing before the altar (in a cathedral at the "choir step"), after which all go to their usual places. Care must be taken by the verger who times the procession that it shall arrive at the rood at the end of the intercessions. This can be easily done if his book is marked to show when the various points in the church should be reached. In practice it seems most convenient, when the litany is sung in procession, for the people to stand until the station is made for "Son of God" and then to kneel until the end of the litany.

Even when it is sung kneeling, there is no reason why the first part of the litany should be sung by the priest, though of course the priest may do so when necessary. It has always been the custom in some cathedrals for lay clerks or cantors thus to sing it, and it is always best to make the service as cooperative as possible and to avoid the appearance of sacerdotalism.

The litany may therefore be sung by two chanters up to the last *Kyrie*, the people answering and all kneeling, after which the priest stands in the priest's stall to say the Our Father on a note and the clerks and people join in. The priest then says the versicle and the collect, as the rubric directs. But, once more, if the supplication is used instead then the antiphon and preces that follow ("O Lord, arise" to the last response of the suffrages "Graciously hear us") should be sung by the cantors and choir alternately, the priest not being mentioned again till the final collect. All kneel throughout except the priest, who stands up to say the appointed parts.

The litany is the historical prelude to the Eucharist and ought not to be treated as a mere appendage to the offices, as was sometimes the case in times past. The practice of so regarding it was a gradual result of the neglect to celebrate the Sunday Eucharist, thankfully overcome by the 1979 prayer book. At the same time, the parson would be wise to be attentive to ensuring that the offices of the church and the Great Litany do not become unknown to those who only ever experience Holy Communion. The liturgical heritage of the Anglican tradition is much broader than that and the people will be grateful to be invited into that breadth.

When used in its fullest way as the prelude to Holy Eucharist, the litany ends with the *Kyrie*[5] and moves directly into the liturgy of Eucharist with salutation and collect of the day.

---

5. *1979 Book of Common Prayer*, 153.

8

Processions

THE PROCESSION IS A distinct, significant act of worship. It is not an aimless walk round the church, but it has a definite objective, such as the rood, the Lord's Table, or the font. Whenever a procession takes place, the first question the parson should ask is what the object of the procession is, and second, has the procession thus been structured clearly towards that object in order to make clear the liturgical purpose of the movement.

A Procession Before the Eucharist[1]

1. 1906. From a painting by Simon H. Vedder. The verger is leading the procession down the south alley. The chanters are coming through the chancel gates, and the rest

PROCESSIONS

A procession is not the triumphant entry and exit of the choir, nor is any such thing known to the church as a "recessional." In Dearmer's view, the best approach was for the choir to go quietly to their places when they arrive and occupy the time before the service with prayer and recollectedness in the stalls, instead of with chatting in the vestry. This was, of course, because of the structure of the rite in the 1662 prayer book, which had no provision for an introit. In the 1979 prayer book, the rubric permits (though, interestingly enough, does not require) the use of a hymn, psalm, or anthem as an introit at the start of the liturgy. The people are, by this time, well accustomed to an entrance hymn during which the ministers enter, with acolytes leading and the choir and ministers following. There seems little reason to discard that practice, so long as it can be clear that the point of the procession is to move to the altar and not the solemn display of the choir and ministers.

In attempting to ground this principle, the common forgetfulness of the real meaning of the procession is much to be regretted. A study of the Bible and of Christian usages would correct it. For in the Bible there are three great processions mentioned, as well as other lesser ones: the encircling of Jericho (Josh 6), the bringing of the ark into Jerusalem by David to the accompaniment of Psalms and instrumental music (2 Sam 6 and 1 Chr 16), and the procession of palms (Matt 21).

In the Christian church, the earliest form of procession was the singing of the litanies, with stations or stopping places for special prayers. This feature is preserved in our Great Litany, the meaning of which can only be fully brought out if it is sung in procession and stations made for the prayers, as was described in the last chapter. There were anciently several distinct processions in connection with the Eucharist in the English Church. The three principal processions were (1) the solemn procession before the service, not from the vestry but from the choir, round the church to the rood and altar; (2) the procession to the lectern for the Gospel; and (3) the offertory procession. The last of the three, the offertory procession, is a very ancient ceremony when the sacred vessels were carried in. It is still seen in the Great Entrance of the Orthodox Churches, where the elements are carried in, and is a particularly striking feature of

---

of the choir are leaving their stalls to fall into the procession behind. In a great church there may be two (or three) crosses carried on great festivals (and by tradition there might be two thurifers). On the other hand, the cope-bearers are not an essential feature even of the most elaborate ceremonial.

their liturgy. There were also many special processions, such as that to the font at Easter.

THE PROCESSIONS OF THE PRAYER BOOK

The prayer book orders six special processions (in addition to the wise approach of the Great Litany being said in procession), and the tradition of the prayer book suggests a seventh (which will be noted below). There are two during the sacred time of Holy Week and then allowances for processionals, given the circumstances, in three of the liturgies of the church. During Holy Week, the prayer book encourages the use of the traditional procession on Palm Sunday (p. 270) and the traditional procession with the newly lit paschal candle at the Great Vigil of Easter (p. 285). Both of these are meet and right and are processions that should be planned and executed with great care and solemnity.

Additionally, the rubrics allow for a procession at holy baptism. They state that if the movement to the font (before the blessing of water) "is a formal procession, a suitable psalm, such as Psalm 42, or a hymn or anthem, may be sung."[2] The rubrics also indicate that if it is desirable to return to the front of the church for the prayer ("Heavenly Father, we thank you . . ."), then "a suitable psalm, such as Psalm 23, or a hymn or anthem, may be sung during the procession."[3] Even in the simplest form, these processions should involve the verger. For any procession to or from the font, the question will be what the architecture of the church dictates. If the architecture does necessitate moving to another part of the nave, then a procession highlights the solemnity of the service.

The prayer book also has a note for the procession at a funeral (which is often missed, since it occurs in the rubrics on p. 467 at the end of the rite for "At Time of Death," in the section with the prayers for the reception of the body at the doors of the church). Though the rubric is permissive, saying, "A member of the congregation bearing the lighted paschal candle may lead the procession into the church," one cannot imagine a good reason not to have a fellow member of the church bear the lighted paschal candle to lead the body into the church for Christian burial.

Finally, in the liturgy for the consecration of the church, the prayer book assumes a procession to the door of the church where "singing and

---

2. *1979 Book of Common Prayer*, 312.
3. *1979 Book of Common Prayer*, 313.

instrumental music are appropriate."[4] On p. 575, the prayer book encourages that a procession goes around the building(s) that are to be consecrated and then goes to the principal door of the church. The same page indicates that it is also desirable that the sacred vessels, ornaments, and decorations be carried into the building (along with the deed, blueprint, keys, or construction tools—though one doubts that the carrying of a hammer has as much power as the carrying of the sacred vessels for Eucharist). That procession concludes with the bishop standing at the door of the church, which is then opened and blessed by the bishop with the pastoral staff.[5] The procession then moves into the church to the singing of Ps 122 or other hymns or anthems.

The rubrics of the current prayer book also assume the restoration of the traditional offertory procession in Holy Eucharist, when the people, as "representatives of the congregation[,] bring the people's offerings of bread and wine, and money or other gifts, to the deacon or celebrant."[6] While it is unlikely that this will reach the height of the tradition in the Orthodox liturgy, it should still be a key procession with the alms, bread, and wine all carried together and placed on the altar *together*. The monetary offerings of the people should not be carried off to a sacristy as though they are contaminated but should remain on the altar as the rubrics clearly indicate.[7] This procession highlights that the body and blood of Christ in Eucharist come from the offerings of the people gathered.

Interestingly, contrary to the rubrics of the 1662 prayer book, the 1979 prayer book does not include an explicit rubric for a procession to the altar in the marriage liturgy. However, the parson who knows the rich traditions of the marriage service will certainly invite the couple to join a small procession to the altar after the homily and before the marriage proper.[8]

All of these are all true processions, full of significance and solemnity. The first two are processions that come from the ancient rites of the church; the first marks the climax of the paschal cycle, as Jesus enters into Jerusalem to be crucified and the church gathers in watchful prayer for the celebration of the paschal mystery in the Great Vigil. The next, the going forth of the priest and assistants with the candidate for baptism

---

4. *1979 Book of Common Prayer*, 567.
5. *1979 Book of Common Prayer*, 567.
6. *1979 Book of Common Prayer*, 333, 361.
7. *1979 Book of Common Prayer*, 333, 361.
8. *1979 Book of Common Prayer*, 427.

and their sponsors to the font, highlights this profound moment of entrance into the church. That procession is then reflected in solemn form when a member of the congregation bears the lighted paschal flame (the same that is carried into procession each year at the Great Vigil) ahead of the body as it enters the church to receive the last offices of the church, thereby connecting the entrance of the body in a funeral both to the mystery of the Great Vigil and the eternal significance of baptism. As noted, the offertory procession connects the people's gifts to the Sacrament they are about to receive. Finally, the solemn conducting of the married pair to the altar, there to be blessed, is a rich part of the Anglican tradition.

At the present day, processions before the Eucharist and after evensong have again become customary among us. While at most liturgies, the proper procession is the simplest route in for the acolytes, choir, ministers, and clergy, when a longer procession is desired for a more fulsome liturgy of prayer or a longer hymn (for example, St. Patrick's Breastplate at an ordination), then the longer route may be chosen. The longer route in churches of average size may be the same as for the litany: to the altar, then down to the chancel gate, down the south alley (and, if time is needed, also up the middle alley and down the north alley), up the middle alley to rood (with a station at the rood, if needed), and then up to the altar for the final station.

But in churches that have two choir aisles or an ambulatory, the procession before the Eucharist on great feasts should go out by the western gate of the choir, thence round by the north choir aisle, behind the high altar (or in front of it, without bowing, if there is no way behind), down the south choir aisle and the south aisle of the nave, and up the middle alley to the rood. On other days in such churches the procession should leave the choir by the north door, go round by the north choir aisle behind the altar to the south choir aisle, and thence forward as usual. At evensong, however, in all churches, the procession may go through the western gate of the choir.

The longer procession then is that of a cathedral church with choir aisles—though, some modification is necessary in parish churches that very seldom have these aisles. In an exceptionally large church, there may be a long enough route without them. But the average church will need to lengthen the nave route by taking in the north aisle of the nave, as suggested above. There remains another type of church, which has only one alley. In such a church a procession can be arranged down this alley, round the font, and back the same way.

The best plan is to sing the litany in procession before the Eucharist in Advent and Lent (or, at the least, on the first Sundays of each of these seasons) and to sing a longer processional hymn (such as *Salve festa Dies* or some other longer festal hymn) on the great principal feasts of the church, if one wants a longer procession on those solemn festival days.

It should be noted that the traditional Anglican order for processions before the Eucharist and after divine service was for the ministers to walk before and not after the choir. This is actually a matter of great convenience when the prayers are said at the proper stations. Evidence for this older tradition is affirmed by J. Neil Alexander, who encourages the more traditional order in the procession for Palm Sunday, noting it is not only the more traditional approach but also has the above noted practical implications.[9]

It should be noted that the rubrics expressly forbid a procession in one instance: the order of worship for evening. They make clear that any musical prelude or processional is not an appropriate part of this liturgy.[10]

BEFORE THE HOLY COMMUNION

There was anciently a procession before high mass every Sunday and on many other days. Here is the order of that traditional procession (with all of the possible ministers given, along with the repeated acknowledgment that, though the full complement is given, it is very rarely needed, especially in a parish church):

1. Verger, in gown, holding the mace or verge, from whence comes this minister's name

2. Thurifer in albe (if incense is used)[11]

3. Crucifer in albe (or the eucharistic minister in albe and tunicle), carrying the cross

4. Two taperers, in albes, carrying their candles and walking side by side

---

9. Alexander, *Celebrating Liturgical Time*, 103–4.

10. *1979 Book of Common Prayer*, 142.

11. Dearmer's preference was for the thurifer to enter after the trio of acolytes (crucifer and taperers), but the more common tradition in our time is for the thurifer to precede the acolytes. This is the approach suggested most recently by Malloy in *Celebrating the Eucharist*, 141. It is also the approach suggested by Michno, *Priest's Handbook*, 86; Stuhlman, *Rubrics Expanded*, 60; and Galley, *Ceremonies*, 75.

5. Rules of the choir, in surplices and copes
6. Child choristers in surplice
7. The rest of the choir in surplice
8. Banners, if being carried in procession
9. The rest of the clergy in surplice, hood, and tippet, those of higher rank walking behind those of lower
10. Banners again, if needed
11. Eucharistic minister in albe and tunicle (if not leading the procession)
12. Deacon in albe and dalmatic
13. Acolyte in albe, for holding the book for the priest (if desired)
14. Bishop, if present, or Priest in albe, stole, and cope (for the procession, changes to chasuble at the start of the eucharistic liturgy)

If the liturgy is not a pontifical mass (that is, one celebrated by the bishop), then the priest who is celebrating take the final places in the procession instead of the bishop.

In cathedral churches a station was made before the rood at the great screen, and the bidding prayer (also called the station collect) was then said. But in parish churches that do not have a proper rood, this prayer can also be said at the chancel step. The current authorized rites suggest stational collects that are said at the rood or chancel steps on two specific occasions. On Palm Sunday, the stational collect is noted vaguely in the rubric of the prayer book on p. 271, with the stational collect itself listed at the top of p. 272. This was clearly the intention, because the actual collect of the day is given farther down on p. 272. For the blessing of a crèche on Christmas, the *2022 Book of Occasional Services* gives an anthem, versicle, response, and station collect on pp. 35–36. Following the station, a short hymn may then be sung as the procession enters the chancel and the ministers go to the altar.

In any case, the tradition of the church was that a station was then made before the high altar (for this is the object of the procession). The priest, after a versicle and response, would say "let us pray" and a collect. This is the older root of the current prayer book's opening acclamation and Collect for Purity. In our time, the arrangement may be as follows: When the verger reaches the altar rail, the verger turns and goes off to one side, and the thurifer goes off to the other. The crucifer turns to allow the three sacred ministers to pass and then stands facing east behind the priest. The taperers go to their usual places and stand facing east on either side of the three ministers. The choir may stand in the chancel facing east. The acolyte (or the verger, if an acolyte is not used for this role) holds the book at the place arranged and brings it to the priest, standing in front of the priest with his or her back to the altar. The acolyte holds the book while the priest reads the opening acclamation and Collect for Purity. After this the ministers and servers bow to the altar and go to their respective places; this takes place during the *Gloria* (and/or *Kyrie*, *Trisagion*, or other hymn of praise). The priest goes to the stall or sedilia, from which is said the salutation and collect of the day.

AFTER EVENSONG

In times past, it was also a custom to have processions to the altar after evensong on festivals. If there is a desire for that tradition to be revived, then the following is the order:

1. Verger in gown with the mace
2. Thurifer in albe or surplice, if incense is to be used
3. Crucifer in albe or surplice, with cross
4. Taperers in albe or surplice, with tapers
5. Rulers in surplices and copes
6. Children of the choir in surplices
7. The rest of the choir in surplices
8. Banners, if used
9. Other clergy in order as before the Eucharist
10. Banners, if more are desired at this point
11. Acolyte in albe, for holding the book for the officiant (if desired)
12. Bishop in rochet and cope, if present, or if no bishop, then the Priest surplice and cope

A few further practical directions may be useful. During the hymn at the conclusion of evensong, the priest and servers go into the sacristy, where the priest puts on the cope, the censer is prepared (if needed), candles are lighted, and the cross is taken from its cupboard. At the last verse, they go to the sanctuary the short way and form up before the altar, the crucifer standing behind the thurifer. If using incense, the priest turns, puts incense in the censer, and then turns back to the altar. After the first verse of the processional hymn has been sung, all turn, and the verger leads the procession through the chancel gates in the usual way.

Having gone round the church by the south and middle (and north and middle) alleys, the procession reaches the rood. Here a collect may be said and a second hymn of two or three verses may be sung while the ministers go up to the altar and the choristers follow to their place in the choir. In any case a station is made before the altar; the priest stands on the pavement and says "let us pray" and a suitable collect. The priest then goes up to the altar, turns, and gives the blessing, while all are kneeling.

FINAL NOTES ON PROCESSIONS

Parts of an English Coronation Procession[12]

12. F. Sandford, *The History of the Coronation of James II*, 1687. This procession

The ancient use of banners was much more restrained, and consequently more significant, than the modern. "Banners," says the editor of the Salisbury Processional, "were carried on Palm Sunday after the first station, and on Corpus Christi, and with the special banners of the lion and dragon on Rogation Days and Ascension; on Ash Wednesday and Maundy Thursday a hair-cloth banner was carried at the ejection and reconciliation of penitents."[13] That was all at Salisbury, though banners were more freely used elsewhere, and most parish churches also possessed a small banner, called a cross cloth, which was hung on the processional cross. There may, then, be a banner of the patron saint in ordinary parish churches, and one or two other banners.

The use of wind instruments in outdoor processions is almost a necessity. Processions should be rehearsed from time to time, since much care is required, especially with choristers, to prevent huddling and rolling. Singing ministers often sway about in an ungainly fashion, which would not be tolerated for an instant at a military parade or indeed anywhere else except in church. The way to avoid this is to teach everyone to take steps no longer than the length of the feet. Those who walk in procession (including sometimes the clergy) will also need drilling before

---

has been chosen because of the excellence of the engraving: it is typical of others. We read, for instance, of "the Sergeant of the Vestry in a scarlet mantle," and of "the Children of the King's Chapel in scarlet mantles" in Ashmole and Sandford's description of the coronation of Charles II. The coronation service for James II was drawn up by Archbishop Sancroft. Three parts only are given of the procession, which is too long for reproduction in full:

1. The sergeant porter in a scarlet robe (overlay dress), with his black ebony staff; the sergeant of the vestry in a scarlet robe (over his cassock with his gilt virge); the children of his majesty's Chapel Royal in their surplices, with mantles over them of scarlet cloth, i.e., cloth choir-copes, apparently without hoods; there were twelve of these boys, followed by the choir of Westminster in surplices only.
2. Then came the groom of the vestry in a scarlet robe (over his cassock), with a perfuming-pan in his hand (a censer of curious shape), burning perfumes all the way; the organ blower in lay dress, i.e., a short red coat, with a badge on his left breast; three musicians, each in a scarlet mantle over lay dress, two playing on a sackbut, and one on a double curtal; gentlemen of his majesty's Chapel Royal, in surplices, with mantles over them, four abreast; there were thirty-two of these. After them came the confessor to the king's household and the sub-dean of the Chapel Royal, each in a scarlet mantle and surplice.
3. Then came the canons of Westminster in their surplices and rich copes, carrying their caps. They were twelve in number, though only eight are shown. Behind them, the dean of Westminster, his rich cope of purple velvet, embroidered with gold and silver being worn over a bishop's rochet, for Dr. Spratt was also bishop of Rochester. He rightly does not wear a chimere under the cope.

13. Henderson, *Processionale*, xiii.

they learn to keep their proper distances. Each person should walk as far from one's neighbor as the width of the alley will allow, and each pair should rigidly keep a distance of three or four feet between themselves and the pair in front—a good measure is that from one pew or row of chairs to the other. Thus, the choristers may be taught (1) to keep as near to the pews as possible, and (2) to remember that they must always be a row behind those immediately in front of them. Whenever two persons have to turn round together, they should turn inwards so as to face one another as they turn. All must remember, though, that the procession is not a march and does not have to be in time with the music. Those who make that mistake sometimes create the unintentional result of ministers moving at the pace of a gallop, which entirely destroys the dignity of the procession.

No one will walk well while swinging the arms. If anyone is not holding a book, then that person should join hands, but this may be quite simply done without feigning stained-glass attitudes. The priest should not stick the hands out but should hold a prayer book or hymnbook when the litany or any hymns are being sung. The thurifer should swing the censer (with the lid shut) in a simple manner backwards and forwards with short swings—and not attempt any gymnastics—with the free hand held against the chest. The censer will not need replenishing during the procession if natural incense is used. The verger should be careful to time the procession (carrying a small prayer book or hymnbook in one hand for this purpose), so that the procession reaches the chancel steps at the proper time, whether it be a hymn or the litany that is sung. No one should bow when passing the altar, or when passing the reserved Sacrament, in any procession.

9

Introduction to Communion

THE ORIGINAL *PARSON'S HANDBOOK*, and its subsequent editions, were published during the time in which the Anglican tradition was recovering the centrality of Holy Eucharist to Sunday worship. As the 1979 prayer book restored Holy Eucharist to its place as the principal act of worship on the Lord's Day, greater attention to the celebration of this rite makes sense. That the emphasis on the centrality of Eucharist was present in the original *Parson's Handbook*, before this change was made in the authorized rites of the church, is one of the many ways in which Dearmer's work is reflective of the liturgical movement of the twentieth century. Many of the fruits of that movement were realized in the second half of the twentieth century.[1]

OCCASIONS FOR CELEBRATING

The Lord's Supper, or, as it is sometimes called, the mass, should be celebrated at least on every Sunday and holy day. First, though, a few words about the choice of words when it comes to this divine liturgy. When words have assumed a party significance the wisest and most charitable course seems to be that we should so use them as to restore their real meaning. The word mass still excites a considerable amount of prejudice among some, and it would be wrong to cause needless offence by hurling it at those who do not like it and perhaps do not understand it. Helpfully, the 1979 prayer book has sought to alleviate party anxiety by focusing

---

1. For more on this, see ch. 1 of my earlier book, *Percy Dearmer Revisited*.

on Holy Eucharist as the fundamental term for this liturgy but noting in the prayer book that this service is also called "the Lord's Supper, and Holy Communion; it is also known as the Divine Liturgy, the mass, and the Great Offering."[2] In the end, the word mass, in particular, has its usefulness as a technical term in ceremonial, just as it has in music. It is as convenient to speak of mattins, mass, and evensong as it is to speak of music for mass or a mass by Mozart. The word in itself is innocent and indeed meaningless. The word occurs in the Reformation period as a link with the past, which is not without value. In the first prayer book the old popular title is preserved, "The Supper of the Lord, and the Holy Communion, commonly called the Mass."[3] In 1549 Cranmer, in the king's name, solemnly assured the Devonshire rebels that "as to the Mass, the king assures them the learned clergy have taken a great deal of pains to settle that point, to strike off innovations, and bring it back to our Savior's institution."[4] This is in fact an accurate description of what did happen.

Holy Communion (Fifteenth Century)[5]

2. *1979 Book of Common Prayer*, 859.
3. *1549 Book of Common Prayer*, 20.
4. Collier, *Ecclesiastical History*, 271.
5. British Museum. MS. Add. 35313, f. 40. Priest, deacon, and subdeacon in golden vestments and apparels. Deacon swings a golden censer; subdeacon holds a torch; on

But we must be careful not to hand over the title "Lord's Supper" (*Coena Domini*) to one section of Christians. It is an official title of the service and may therefore be used as well as Holy Eucharist, Communion, and Holy Communion in official announcements. Dearmer urged against the use of the word mass or even Eucharist, suggesting that Eucharist, despite being a beautiful word, does not have the same Reformation authority as mass. In my mind, much depends on local context and goal. If the goal is to be the most intelligible to those around you, then Holy Communion is a good generic choice. If the goal is to set the Episcopal Church off as a distinct tradition, then Holy Eucharist has the benefit of being the prayer book's current preferred term. If one's goal is to lean into the catholicity of the church, then mass is certainly an appropriate and acceptable choice.

The essentiality of the celebration of mass on every Sunday and holy day is made evident in the very first rubric of the 1979 prayer book where it is made clear (even if it is apparently lamentably invisible to far too many clergy) that "the Holy Eucharist, the principal act of Christian worship on the Lord's Day and other major Feasts, and Daily Morning and Evening Prayer, as set forth in this Book, are the regular services appointed for public worship in this Church."[6] This means that every Sunday and every principle feast of the church should have a service of Holy Eucharist offered—even if the gathered congregation will be quite small.

There is not a requirement for an offering of Holy Eucharist on all of the feasts of our Lord and other major feasts, provided that the parson is utilizing the rubric that allows that "Feasts of Our Lord and other Major Feasts appointed on fixed days, which fall upon or are transferred to a weekday, may be observed on any open day within the week."[7] However, it must be stressed that the rubric is also quite clear that "this provision does not apply to Christmas Day, the Epiphany, and All Saints' Day."[8] An additional Sunday observance of All Saints' Day is allowed by the rubric, but that is "in addition to its observance on the fixed date."[9] This means that the parson who observes All Saints' Sunday instead of All Saints'

---

the right of the subdeacon lies a handbell. Open triptych, gilt; riddel posts and images gilt, with iron curtain rods. Two candles on the altar. Frontal and frontlet of rose color; green carpet.

6. *1979 Book of Common Prayer*, 13.
7. *1979 Book of Common Prayer*, 17. Other major feasts are listed on pp. 16–17.
8. *1979 Book of Common Prayer*, 17.
9. *1979 Book of Common Prayer*, 15.

Day is violating the clear standard of the church. Though the rubric does not also explicitly exclude Ascension Day from transference, that is likely because the framers could not imagine someone moving the fortieth day of Easter to another day within the week to observe it. Sadly, many clergy simply do not observe Ascension. Some even ignore the Feast of the Epiphany, even though it is the more ancient of the incarnational feasts; the other, Christmas, was first observed after the church had begun celebrating Epiphany. A return to the standards expressed in the first rubric of the prayer book is sorely needed in our time. As long as there is someone there to communicate with the priest, the feast is kept, and the tradition of the church maintained.

Many parsons will not be content with Sunday and one weekday observance, especially in churches where congregations can be secured more frequently. Even the 1662 prayer book allowed for daily Communion by the rubric "that the Collect, Epistle, and Gospel appointed for the Sunday shall serve all the week after, where it is not in this Book otherwise ordered."[10] The church in our own time has authorized *Lesser Feasts and Fasts* as the guide for these daily celebrations (along with weekday eucharistic lectionaries for Lent and Eastertide to use when a feast is not being observed). Much current hand wringing in the church today regarding the kalendar could be avoided if people simply remembered that the commemorations in *Lesser Feasts and Fasts* fall under the rubric of rank five feasts, "Days of Optional Observance."[11] No one is required to observe them all (and it is likely unwise for most to try). Furthermore, the general propers given in the prayer book for other saints and martyrs encourage the local observance of great heroes of the faith regardless of their place on the official sanctorale. This local observance is the truly historical and authentic way (albeit infrequent in our own time) sanctity has been recognized in the church—that is, from the local parish on up to the higher authorities.

Every effort must be made, both at sung and said Eucharists, to obey the tradition manifest in the 1662 rubric, which orders that there shall be three to communicate with the priest.[12] While this rubric is not a requirement in the 1979 prayer book, it remains a good principle. And never, of course, should a priest celebrate when there is not at least one person to say the responses, pronounce the Great Amen, and share in

10. *1662 Book of Common Prayer*, 9.
11. *Lesser Feasts and Fasts*, 17.
12. *1662 Book of Common Prayer*, 159.

Communion. The only appropriate time to cancel a celebration of Holy Eucharist is when the parson is alone in the church. In such cases, a short recitation of prayers, and perhaps some time meditating on the appointed Scripture lessons, ensures that the feast has been honored as far as it is in the power of the parson.

We should also be clear that, in the Anglican tradition, solitary masses have always been strictly forbidden. Even the medieval rule, as late as 1528, was that two or three should be present. The prayer book rubrics, as to communicants, attacked the very grave evil by which, before the Reformation, attendance at the Lord's Supper had taken the place of reception, and Communion only once a year had become the rule. This evil was indeed reprobated also by the Council of Trent, which expressed a hope that some of the faithful would communicate at every mass.

In country parishes the difficulty of getting a congregation will often prevent very frequent celebrations. Thankfully, the idea that a priest must celebrate every day is without foundation, and so there is no need for worrisome fuss. At the same time, the daily Eucharist, where it can be had, is a great privilege and blessing. What days then should be chosen for weekday services? First, of course, principal feasts should be chosen—if the goal is to follow the prayer book ideal, which requires all principal feasts. After that, attention should be paid to Sundays, feasts of our Lord, and other major feasts. Additionally, Wednesdays and Fridays have great tradition in antiquity, as they were the old station days for which special masses were provided in the old missals in Sarum, York, and Hereford. If feasts of our Lord and other major feasts are not celebrated on the day on which they fall, then transferring them to the nearest weekday observance, be that a Wednesday or Friday, is both allowed and an appropriate option.

In the end, thus, if there can be only one additional celebration in the week, the day chosen should be Wednesday (which is the midpoint between Sundays). The next step would be to add Friday and, after that, the feasts of our Lord, and then the other major feasts. In some central town churches, a daily Eucharist is most desirable, particularly if there are two or three priests and sufficient communicants to make it possible.

THE FIRST RUBRICS OF THE PRAYER BOOK

It is often lightly assumed that many of the prayer book rubrics are impracticable. When that is indeed the case, permission should be sought from the ordinary before they are put aside, for parsons should always be in a position to account for everything that is done within their cure. But as a matter of fact, the impracticability of a rubric generally vanishes when an attempt is made to practice it.

In Dearmer's time, the first rubrics of the 1662 prayer book focused on the importance of announcing services of Holy Eucharist and inviting people to let the parson know if they intended to communicate.[13] That requirement is absent in the church in our own time, but attention to the first rubrics of Holy Communion in the 1979 prayer book still gives important markers and guidelines that the parson should follow.

Bishop, Deacon, Subdeacon, and Chanters (Fourteenth Century)[14]

13. "So many as intend to be partakers of the holy Communion shall signify their names to the Curate, at least some time the day before." *1662 Book of Common Prayer*, 144.

14. British Museum. MS. Add. 20787, f.117. Bishop in red chasuble powdered with gold, blue dalmatic, and white mitre with gold orphreys; the three sacred ministers all have amice apparels of similar gold ornament. Deacon in greyish dalmatic powdered with gold crescents. Subdeacon in red tunicle differently ornamented holds golden

First, it is always the bishop's prerogative, when present, to be the principal celebrant and to preach the Gospel. This is in keeping with the bishop's role as the chief shepherd and priest of the diocese. Regardless of who the principal celebrant is, the next rubric makes it clear that it is fitting for the celebrant to be assisted by other priests, deacons, and lay persons. The rubrics next invite other priests who are present to stand with the celebrant at the altar, joining in the consecration, the fraction, and the distribution. In the next rubric, the duties of the deacon are made clear: reading the Gospel, leading the prayers of the people (which may either involve saying the bidding to those prayers or reading them in full), preparing the altar, and assisting in the distribution. These duties may be delegated to an assisting priest but only in the absence of a deacon. Finally, the laity should read the lessons and are invited to lead the prayers of the people. There is then the allowance (unadvisable as it may be) to substitute one of the offices for the word of God.[15]

What one notices in these first rubrics is the profound concern the framers of the 1979 prayer book had for the rights and privileges of all four orders of ministry in the celebration of Holy Eucharist. This also indicates that the fullest celebration of Holy Eucharist is one celebrated by the bishop, assisted by priests, deacons, and laity, each exercising their own order well. Thankfully, many parsons are familiar with the ideal of these rubrics and could scarcely imagine a celebration of Holy Eucharist where they would read the lessons properly appointed to the laity.

However, an unfortunate development in recent years has been confusion over the role of a eucharistic minister. The canons of our church permit the laity to be trained and then licensed by the bishop to serve as eucharistic ministers. However, the prayer book provides the ideal form of our worship and, thus, the allowance of laity to serve as eucharistic ministers is an allowance of expedience in the cause of practicality. As it is, few parishes will have sufficient priests and deacons to distribute Communion. Thus, it is fine and good to train and license laity for this

---

paten. Chanters wearing copes over their surplices hold staves, each of which is surmounted with a small gilt ball; one of these copes is blue, but all the colors in this miniature are somewhat faint. The end of the altar is covered by a long white cloth (perhaps part of the frontal), fringed and ornamented, over which is a short linen cloth of plain material. The bishop holds a gold chalice in his left hand, signing with his right. In the original the small gold altar cross is more clearly visible. The crozier rests against the north end of the altar. Two lamps hang from the arches.

15. *1979 Book of Common Prayer*, 142. This allowance is followed by a note stating additional directions can be found on p. 406.

role. However, it is quite clear that laity are only to administer the Sacrament "in the absence of sufficient deacons and priests."[16] Thus, to have laity serve as eucharistic ministers when there are sufficient priests and deacons (especially, for example, at diocesan gatherings or gatherings of the larger church) is a usurpation of the rightful responsibility of the deacons and priests and a misunderstanding of the fundamental vocation of the laity.

That this is so often done under the guise of "affirming the ministry of the baptized" demonstrates the profound confusion in our church. The catechism is clear that the ministry of the laity is to "represent Christ and his Church; to bear witness to him wherever they may be and, according to the gifts given them, to carry on Christ's work of reconciliation in the world; and to take their place in the life, worship, and governance of the Church."[17] That is, the ministry of the laity is first and foremost their work and witness in the world and, after that, to take their place in the life, worship, and governance of the church.

Thus, if there are sufficient clergy present at Communion, the rightful place of the laity is to read the first lessons of Scripture and, after the deacon has introduced the prayers, to lead the prayers of the people. It cannot be stressed enough that to treat the laity as mini clergy is destructive to their true mission and calling in the world as agents of Christ's reconciliation. One hopes bishops will soon come to their senses and find more ways to empower the laity for service in the world, instead of ensuring they are administering the chalice while vested clergy sit in the pews with nothing to do at mass.

SUGGESTIONS FOR COMMUNICANTS

A note on the following lines might be inserted in the parish newsletter from time to time, with a view to preventing the indecent crowding up of communicants:

As every effort should be made to avoid the undue lengthening of the services, the following suggestions are offered to communicants. To prevent the awkward pause that sometimes occurs, the verger will go to the chancel step *immediately after* the priest says the words of invitation ("the Gifts of God for the People of God"). While priest receives

---

16. *1979 Book of Common Prayer*, 408.
17. *1979 Book of Common Prayer*, 855.

INTRODUCTION TO COMMUNION

Communion, the people immediately begin coming forward so that when the priest comes down to the rails the people are ready to receive. The ushers should ensure that no more than two dozen come up at a time in most churches (as the standard altar rail can fit about a dozen). The rest of the communicants are then ready to come to the altar when a space is opened. Thus, the chancel will never be empty, while at the same time there will rarely be any standing idle in the alleys. This enables the rest of the communicants to go on quietly with their prayers without anxiety as to their turn and without the distraction that is caused by a crowd of persons standing about the church.

Every effort should be made to avoid the practice of the people watching solemnly while the clergy and eucharistic ministers are communed at the altar. Once the invitation is made, all are equal, simple recipients of the Sacrament, and so there is no need to wait for the minister to receive before coming forward to take one's place at the altar rail.

Furthermore, it must be stressed that the modern innovation of the clergy receiving last as a "symbol of humility" is deeply misguided. Any guest at dinner knows that you do not touch your utensils and begin eating until the host has done so. The priest receiving the Sacrament is the customary indication at dinner—for the Eucharist is the supper of the Lamb—that all may now come and eat. Furthermore, the rubrics make it abundantly clear that "the ministers receive the Sacrament in both kinds, and then immediately deliver it to the people."[18] Violation of this rubric is not only misguided on basic etiquette, it also inevitably creates the situation where the people, having received, watch reverently while the ministers then receive in their own special ceremony at the end of the distribution. This, of course, is precisely what the rubric requiring the people to come forward at the invitation sought to avoid.

The rubrics of the 1662 prayer book also state that communicants were to receive the Sacrament of the Lord's body "into their hands."[19] They were not to receive it with their fingers, nor with one hand only. This is conveniently done, according to the direction of St. Cyril of Jerusalem, by "making the left hand a throne for the right, and hollowing the palm of the right to receive the Body of Christ," that is, by placing the left hand under the right, both hands being held open.[20] The above-noted rubric in the 1662 prayer book made it obligatory for the communicants also to

18. *1979 Book of Common Prayer*, 338, 365.
19. *1662 Book of Common Prayer*, 156.
20. Cyril of Jerusalem, *Catechetical Lectures*, XXIII.21.

use their hands in the reception of the chalice: "Then shall the Minister first receive the Communion in both kinds himself, and then proceed to deliver the same to the . . . people also in order, into their hands."[21] The 1979 prayer book eliminated that phrase (along with a posture for those receiving). It also became the first prayer book to legalize the use of intinction, with the restriction that the exact manner must be approved by the bishop.[22] When it comes to the chalice, the Communion will be made safer and quicker if all communicants take the chalice in the same way, grasping it firmly with both hands, the right hand holding the foot of the chalice, and the left hand the stem. It is also convenient if each communicant leaves the rail after the next person has been communicated.

THE EUCHARISTIC SPECIES

The eucharistic species are, at their basic, bread and wine. Wafers had become the common replacement for bread in the Middle Ages and the first prayer book did not forbid their use. Rather, it affirmed the continued use of unleavened bread, but also required that this bread be larger, thicker, and able to be broken into at least two pieces.[23] In the 1552 prayer book, a new rubric specified that "the bread be such as is usual to be eaten at the table with other meats, but the best and purest wheat bread that conveniently may be gotten."[24] In the nineteenth century, wafers once more began to replace bread in the service.

The current prayer book does not require only bread or only wafers. However, good liturgical sense dictates that the use of bread that is recognizable to the people is much to be preferred to wafers. (As the saying goes, "It is easier to believe a wafer is the Body of Christ than it is to believe that it is bread.") Indeed, there is very great precedent in antiquity for leavened bread, and the Eastern Orthodox churches continue to use it, though their loaves are very carefully made in a special shape and stamped with a sacred device. In the West, till after the eighth century, breads like small rolls were used.

At the same time, if wafers are used, the small individual wafers should be avoided. Rather, it is better to use large round wafers that can be broken

---

21. *1662 Book of Common Prayer*, 156.
22. *1979 Book of Common Prayer*, 407–8.
23. *1549 Book of Common Prayer*, 45–46.
24. *1552 Book of Common Prayer*, 159.

INTRODUCTION TO COMMUNION

for the people. The scriptural symbolism of the "one bread, one body" is thus kept and the traditional method of the early church, from which the East has never departed. These large round wafers may then be broken into either five or six parts for Communion and several can be broken together at the fraction; the communicants can then be easily reckoned in either tens or dozens. The use of smaller breads for the people, though it is convenient when there are very many communicants, is difficult to justify and the very existence of something known as the "priest's host" is far from the tradition of the early church and carries an air of clericalism. A canister or box should be provided for the wafers consecrated and not used. This must be cleaned out every week with the remaining wafers reverently consumed before new ones are added at the Sunday mass.

If the parson takes the better choice of using real bread ("such as is usual to be eaten at the table"), it is not at all too difficult a custom to establish—though a few points of advice are needed. First, though no longer rubrically required, the Anglican tradition of using the best and finest wheat has much to commend itself. Regular bread can be purchased at the store, but this is not recommended because most bread that is purchased at stores has much foreign matter and ingredients. A better approach is for members of the parish who have the gift of baking, and enjoy the work, to make the bread using a singular recipe chosen by the parish. Indeed, if the parson takes this approach, often a small group of parishioners will rather quickly be found who will approach this task with enthusiasm and reverence. The recipe should be kept simple, with nothing but the basic ingredients. Honey should not be used to sweeten the bread, as this might create an allergic reaction in some people. An excellent recipe is the one used by the monks at St. Gregory's Abbey in Three Rivers, Michigan:

Ingredients
1½ cup whole wheat flour
1½ cup all-purpose flour
2 tsp. sugar
¼ tsp. salt
1 tsp. highly active "Rapid Rise" yeast
1 cup warm water (100°F)

Directions

Mix dry ingredients. Slowly add water. Knead into smooth ball. Cover and let rise 30 mins. Preheat oven to 300°F. Roll out with rolling pin to ¼" thickness. (Your first few times, you might want to measure. This is thinner than you might expect. As you roll it out, you should not need to add flour as the dough should be smooth enough.) Cover baking sheet with kitchen parchment. Cut out with 3½" diameter cookie cutter or glass. Pierce with toothpick or fork. Score deeply with a knife (almost cut through) to form a cross. Mist with water, then bake 12 mins. at 300°F.

This recipe will yield sixteen pieces of bread, which can then, at the fraction, be broken into quarter pieces, and each quarter piece, broken into thirds. Thus, up to 192 people may be communicated with a single recipe. The recipe can be modified to make smaller or larger batches. However, the parson must strenuously reject the suggestion of freezing what is not used for a later date. Freezing bread removes the moisture and, once thawed, produces a crumbly mess that does not befit the Sacrament of Christ's body and blood.

The most significant drawback to real bread is that it cannot easily be reserved for more than a day or two (because, of course, it contains no foreign preservatives). If the parson desires to reserve some of the Sacrament for taking to those who are ill, then the parson who has daily mass will be doubly grateful as the bread can be refreshed each day. However, in most parishes, the better option is to consecrate a single round wafer, broken into pieces, and reserve it for Communion to the sick. Or, if gluten-free wafers are consecrated as well, then these can well be reserved without the added fuss of an extra type of bread.

Speaking of gluten, in our time there is an increased awareness of the issue of gluten intolerance. Thus, it has become common (and is indeed hospitable) to ensure that a gluten-free bread is provided. Either an alternative gluten-free recipe can be used for all who commune or gluten-free wafers may be purchased. We have no requirement, as those in the Roman tradition do, that a percentage of gluten remain, so anxiety about that question may easily be put away. If separate gluten-free wafers are used, then every effort must be made to create an unobtrusive way to signal to the minister when a communicant desires it. Whispering "gluten-free" is disruptive to the service and gives the impression one is placing an order at the rail. A better approach is to have those who are content with regular bread to have their palms open at the rail and those who require gluten-free bread to clasp their palms together when the minister approaches. Seeing clasped palms, the minister may then offer the gluten-free wafer, at which point the palms may be held open in the normal manner to receive.

For the wine, red wine is more in accordance with the ancient customs of the church than white wine. The wine should be the pure fermented juice of the grape, not adulterated with extra alcohol nor heavily sweetened, as are many so-called eucharistic wines, which are sticky and strong-smelling and altogether unfit for sacred purposes. The use of a fortified wine like port is preferred in many parishes, but it must be admitted that it is not the ideal. After all, if the best practice is to use bread "such as is usual to be eaten at the table," then a natural corollary would be to use wine "such as is usual to be drunk at the table." To wit, the eucharistic wine should taste like the wine one might drink at home. A slightly sweeter red wine (like a Beaujolais, Merlot, red Zinfandel, or a Malbec) will be appreciated in the morning, as a dry wine can be a bit bracing when one has only woken up an hour or two earlier. In our time, there are excellent box wines of red Zinfandel or sweet Merlot that carry the added benefit of being able to be measured out so that the wine does not go bad like wine in a bottle might.

THE PREPARATION OF THE ELEMENTS

The prayer book affirms the tradition of adding a little water to the wine[25] and the judgment of the archbishop of Canterbury's court in the bishop of Lincoln's case affirmed that the ancient rule as to the mixed chalice has never been changed.[26] Therefore, it is not in the tradition of the church to use unmixed wine for the Holy Communion. The parson might wonder, though, when to mix it—whether before the service, as was the general medieval custom, or between the Epistle and Gospel, as was done at high mass at Salisbury and Lincoln, or at the offertory, as in the Hereford Missal, the first prayer book, and at Rome.

The aforementioned archbishop's judgment was to mix the water into the wine before the service. This decision was based on several reasons. First, the direction for the chalice to be mixed at the offertory in the first prayer book was omitted in all subsequent revisions, and Dearmer believed that this omission was made "in accordance with the highest

---

25. *1979 Book of Common Prayer*, 407.
26. For more details and context, see Reed, *Glorious Battle*, 254–55.

and widest liturgical precedents."[27] Indeed, this was the custom at Westminster, it was the custom all over England for low mass, and it is still practiced in the Mozarabic rite. It is as old as the Celtic Stowe Missal.

However, the rubrics in our current book require an alternative approach. As Dearmer noted in the original handbook, Seabury introduced to the American church the tradition of doing the preparation of the elements at the offertory. Furthermore, the intention of the 1979 prayer book when it came to the offertory was twofold. First, there was an intention to draw a distinction between the word of God in the first part of the liturgy of Holy Eucharist and the Holy Communion in the second part. Second, there was an intention to restore the proper role of the deacon in the preparation of the altar.[28] For that reason, there are more specific rubrics about the preparation of the gifts in the section "Additional Directions." On p. 407 of the prayer book, the order of the rubrics is clearly intended to be read chronologically in the liturgy. Thus, the rubric—"It is the function of a deacon to make ready the Table for the celebration, preparing and placing upon it the bread and cup of wine. It is customary to add a little water to the wine"—is meant to be understood to take place after the peace and before the Great Thanksgiving. At the same time, this mixture of water into wine should be done simply and unobtrusively, without the need for any kind of extensive ceremony.[29]

OMISSIONS

The prayer book of 1549 allowed the omission of the creed and the *Gloria in excelsis* on certain occasions. In the 1979 prayer book, the rubrical allowances for omissions are more fulsome and must be carefully considered by the parson to ensure the liturgy celebrated matches the solemnity of the day.

Both Rites One and Two allow for the older penitential order to be used when desired. The placement of the *Gloria in excelsis* as the third option in the continuation indicates the ideal of the prayer book was that the order would not normally be used on those Sundays when the *Gloria in excelsis* was said (though it can, of course, be used if there is a reasonable purpose for a more penitential beginning). Rather, this order

---

27. Dearmer, *Parson's Handbook*, 277–78.
28. Hatchett, *American Prayer Book*, 348.
29. Hatchett, *New Prayer Book*, 47.

is best used in Lent, perhaps in Advent, and in other times when the need for penitence becomes acute (for example, in times of war or national distress).

In Rite One, when the penitential order is not used, the summary of the law is allowed before the *Kyrie*, *Trisagion*, and/or *Gloria in excelsis*. It should be noted that Rite One also preserves the use of the *Kyrie* followed by the *Gloria in excelsis*, if so desired, and when a choral setting of mass is used on a special occasion, there is good reason to keep to this practice. In Rite Two, the summary of the law has been removed and only now exists in an altered form within one of the sentences of the penitential order. In 2024, the Eighty-First General Convention approved resolution A11, directing "the Standing Commission on Liturgy and Music to prepare a contemporary-language version of Rite I prayers not currently available in the contemporary idiom."[30] This would include, of course, the summary of the law, along with other prayers from that rite. One hopes this resolution will result in an increased flexibility for use of the historic prayers of the Anglican tradition in Rite Two offerings of Holy Eucharist. After all, the use of the summary of the law at the start so clearly grounds the rule of love of God and love of neighbor as the bedrock of Christian faith upon which hang all the law and the prophets.

The *Gloria in excelsis* was restored to its ancient place at the start of the service by the 1979 prayer book, but the prayer book instructs to use it "when appointed"—that is, from Christmastide through Epiphany, on the Sundays of Eastertide through Pentecost, on all the days of Easter Week, at the Feast of the Ascension, and at other times when desired.[31] It is not used on Sundays or (ordinary) weekdays in Advent and Lent. Using it on all Sundays outside of Advent and Lent is still the common practice in our church and one finds it difficult to disagree with this approach. When the *Gloria in excelsis* is omitted, the rubrics require the use either of the *Kyrie* (in English or Greek) or the *Trisagion*. It should be noted that in Advent and in Lent, when the *Gloria in excelsis* is not used, the rubrics do not permit the use of a substitute hymn or anthem in place of the *Kyrie* or *Trisagion*.

The 1979 prayer book further indicates that the creed is only said on Sundays and other major feasts. The inability of clergy to pay attention to this rubric and to, thus, include the Nicene Creed in all manner

---

30. Episcopal Church, *81st General Convention*, 201.
31. *1979 Book of Common Prayer*, 406.

of services has much to do with the feeling of the laity that our liturgies at weekday services can at times move at the pace of a sloth. The truth is that if the clergy are attentive to the rubrics, they will discover that following them aids in a well-run and efficient liturgical service that edifies the people without spending undue time on what is not essential.

THE SERMON

The time ordered for the sermon in both rites of the prayer book is after the Gospel. The sermon has been required at the Eucharist from the time of the 1549 prayer book[32] and an explanation of the lessons has been a regular part of the eucharistic rite from the earliest centuries of the church. The infrequent nature of the sermon grew in the Middle Ages to the point that it was sometimes ordered only to be offered four times a year. All the reformers, however, sought to restore the sermon to every offering of Holy Communion. The first prayer book allowed the sermon to be omitted on weekdays, but this allowance was removed in the 1552 prayer book. The importance of the sermon was underscored in the current prayer book, as Hatchett noted, with the reality that "the permission in many of the previous Prayer Books to allow announcements, hymns, or prayers to be inserted between the Gospel and the sermon has been totally deleted in this present revision."[33]

Thus, in the current book, the sermon may never be omitted. This does not, of course, require that every celebration of mass must include a twenty-minute exposition on the readings. Indeed, at weekday services one might read the biography of the saint in *Lesser Feasts and Fasts* or offer a brief meditation. However, it is incumbent upon the parson to say something after the Gospel that illuminates God's good news for the people. It must be stressed that this includes the liturgy for Palm Sunday. In recent times, some clergy have taken to the bizarre idea that the passion narrative stands on its own and does not require a sermon to say more. Given the gravity and weight of the passion narrative, one certainly questions that logic. One also finds it unfortunate that clergy would find it difficult to say something important after having heard the story of our Lord's suffering and death. However, even if one believed the

---

32. *1549 Book of Common Prayer*, 24.
33. Hatchett, *American Prayer Book*, 332.

passion narrative did not require a sermon, the prayer book still does, and so even a brief meditation on the passion is absolutely required.

Dearmer encouraged the preacher to remove the chasuble or tunicle and maniple for convenience when preaching and encouraged the use of the gown for lectures and mission addresses. In our own time, when the chasuble is not as stiff and heavy as it once was, changing clothes before the sermon seems unnecessary. If the preacher is not one of the ministers at the table, then the preacher may wear either gown or surplice. The preacher should on no account wear a stole over the surplice simply because they are called upon to preach. This practice takes away all sacramental meaning from the use of the stole and has been ignorantly copied from Rome.

It is convenient and seemly that the verger, in accordance with ancient custom, should conduct the preacher to the pulpit, whenever there is a sermon. The verger may go, mace in hand, up the chancel steps to the preacher's stall and stand before the preacher until that minister follows. The verger then leads the way to the pulpit, stands aside for the preacher to mount the stairs, and if there is a door the verger closes it behind the preacher.

There is no requirement in our book for beginning the sermon with an invitation or a bidding prayer (though the use of a bidding prayer was required in England in older times by the fifty-fifth canon).[34] Some short prayer or invocation of the Trinity, however, seems a devout and pious custom. It is customary (dating from the days at least of St. Chrysostom) to conclude the sermon with an ascription, such as, "And now to God the Father, God the Son, and God the Holy Spirit, be all honor and glory, both now and for ever. Amen." The preacher should say the ascription in a natural voice, with the custom being to turn east to say it.[35] A painful impression of unreality is sometimes produced by the preacher suddenly wheeling round, taking a note, and singing at the end of an earnest discourse. The preacher should avoid this, turning slightly and saying the ascription in a quiet, impressive way. The amen also should be said by the people in the natural voice. The introduction of semi-musical habits into the pulpit is altogether to be deprecated. Some preachers let a trace of intonation run through their sermons and the effect was something Dearmer described as that of a "dismal howl."[36] When words are sung,

34. Church of England, *Canons* (1604), no. 55.
35. See *Ritual Conformity*, 31.
36. The point about the requirement of the custom comes from *Ritual Conformity*,

they should be sung in tune, but when they are said, they should be said with a proper and natural elocution.

THE MINISTERS

Holy Communion, with Deacon and Subdeacon[37]

It is a great mistake to suppose that a hard and fast distinction should be drawn between a celebration of the Eucharist with three ministers and a celebration with one. A service in which the priest is assisted by a deacon and eucharistic minister (the latter taking the older place of the subdeacon) is the norm of the eucharistic action. Celebrations without these assistant ministers are makeshifts allowed by the church as a concession to circumstances, but the eucharistic rite remains perfectly valid. Some people imagine that the deacon and eucharistic minister are a sort of enrichment suitable for a "ritualistic" church and that they ought only to

---

31. The suggested version, quoted here, comes from Dearmer, *Parson's Handbook*, 284.

37. Exposition de la Messe, late fifteenth century. Priest, holding paten (at the end of the Lord's Prayer), in chasuble with Y cross; the long maniple of the priest is shown, but those of the deacon and subdeacon are omitted. Deacon and subdeacon in dalmatic and tunicle behind the priest; behind the subdeacon a figure (apparently the clerk or verger in his cassock) is kneeling. Altar of the usual type; chalice stands on corporal. Reredos with carved figures; one riddel shown; footpace without deacon's or subdeacon's steps. Piscina with cruets on shelf and basin below.

be present when an elaborate ceremonial can be carried out. There could hardly be a greater error. The sharp distinction made by our Roman siblings between high and low mass is a modern innovation contrary to the general practice of the whole church and therefore should be more particularly eschewed by those who appeal most strongly to the practice of the historic catholic church. This innovation has produced the peculiar service known in the Roman Church as a *Missa cantata*, which is a low mass sung by a single priest who is assisted only by a pair or two pairs of servers, and which is often in practice replaced by a low mass pure and simple. It would surely be difficult to imagine a greater degradation of the central Christian service.

This then should be the rule at the principal Eucharist: if there are two other ministers in holy orders, the celebrant should be assisted by both clergy, without need for a lay eucharistic minister, with one cleric serving as deacon and one as subdeacon, if desired. If one of those ministers is a deacon that person should, of course, take the role of the deacon in the liturgy. At no point should a priest take the role of a deacon when a deacon is vested and serving. If there is only one other minister in holy orders, whether deacon or priest, that person should assist as deacon, and the lay person should serve as a eucharistic minister, taking the duties often prescribed to the subdeacon. If there is no other minister in holy orders, the priest should be assisted by one or two eucharistic ministers (but never, of course, should a lay person take the roles that would have gone to the deacon—they are, instead, subsumed by the presiding priest).

The ceremonial used in cathedral churches is generally very simple. A good form of it is outlined below. The deacon and eucharistic minister stand on either side of the priest at a lower step, the deacon being on the right, the eucharistic minister on the left. The deacon reads the Gospel and either the eucharistic minister or a lay person from the congregation reads the lessons. The deacon and eucharistic minister serve together at the offertory, and they assist in administering the Communion to the people. There are excellent practical reasons for this simple ceremonial. On the other hand, there is undoubtedly a danger of overlaying it with too elaborate ceremonies, nor can it be denied that in some churches a point has been reached when the service ceases to be either lawful or dignified.

The persons, then, needed for the full service are these—the priest, with the deacon and eucharistic minister (unless there are other priests or deacons). To these may very well be added the thurifer, two taperers, and a crucifer. In many churches, a simple ceremonial is necessary, and the taperers and the thurifer may be dispensed with but not the crucifer.

OUTLINE OF THE SERVICE

It may be useful before proceeding to further detail that the reader should have a general outline of the ceremonial. This will be a sufficient practical guide for a stranger, unused to anything but a single-handed service, who is called upon to assist as deacon or eucharistic minister. It may also prove sufficient for a service of the simple "cathedral" type—the best type of all, which has been alluded to above.

The Preparation and Approach. All gather in the vestry to put on their vestments and pray. All then go to the altar, the crucifer first (carrying the cross), then the eucharistic minister, then the deacon (carrying the Gospel book), then the priest. When the three ministers arrive at the altar rail, the eucharistic minister goes to the left of the celebrant, the deacon to the right, and then all bow towards the altar together. The celebrant may osculate the altar.

Opening Acclamation. The ministers stand facing east at the north or left part of the front of the altar where the book lies open on its cushion. As to position, a few words may be helpful. The old normal position of the deacon was immediately behind the priest and that of the eucharistic minister, immediately behind the deacon; the eucharistic minister knelt whenever the priest turned westward. More commonly now, however, when the priest faces westward the other ministers divide and go to each side (eucharistic minister to the left and deacon to the right). This ordering and approach is known as "alignment." Post-Reformation custom, in contrast, often avoided this alignment, with the deacon remaining throughout all the prayers at the right of the priest and the subdeacon at the left (each on the pavement or each on their respective step). In my opinion, this latter approach is the better custom, particularly if simplification is desired. The directions that follow would then be much reduced because there is no need to move in and out of alignment. Given the prevalence of the tradition of remaining in alignment, however, it is the approach of alignment that will be explained in what follows.

Collect for Purity and Gloria. The priest then says or sings the Collect for Purity, still facing the altar. All remain facing east for the *Gloria* (or, on more penitential occasions and seasons, the *Kyrie* or *Trisagion*),

INTRODUCTION TO COMMUNION

with the eucharistic minister and deacon exiting alignment to stand up at the altar on either side of the celebrant. If the penitential order is used instead of the Collect for Purity and *Gloria*, then during the Decalogue the deacon turns to face the people with the priest, and the eucharistic minister remains standing or kneels. Near the end of the *Gloria* (or after the song that concludes the penitential order), the clergy then return to their aligned position, now in the center of the altar.

Collect of the Day. The celebrant faces the people, with the other ministers dividing once more to either side but staying on their respective sides. The celebrant sings the salutation and, after the people respond, the ministers take the aligned position once more but now at the south end of the altar for the collect of the day. At the "amen," the ministers then go to their stalls or seats for the lessons and psalmody.

Lessons and Psalmody. The appointed laity come forward to read the lessons and psalmody from the lectern or ambo. The celebrant and the others sit in their stalls or seats while it is being read. At the sequence hymn, they stand and sing until the time for the (procession and) reading of the Gospel.

Gospel and Sermon. The current custom in the church is for a short procession to be made to the midst of the people during the sequence hymn for the reading of the Gospel. This has become much beloved of the people, with the people turning towards the deacon who reads the Gospel facing west while the eucharistic minister holds the Gospel book. If a Gospel procession is not the custom in the parish, then the Gospel is properly read from the same lectern or ambo from which the rest of the lessons are read. The sermon should flow directly from the Gospel, with no second half of the hymn or other strange innovation inserted between the two. The sermon should, of course, be offered from the pulpit or ambo.

Creed. At the creed the sacred ministers form up once more, facing the altar at the bottom of the steps. If the celebrant is also the preacher, then they wait for the celebrant to take position in the middle. Once in place, all then bow and ascend to stand at the altar, facing east for the creed, with the deacon and eucharistic minister standing at the altar on the right and left of the priest, respectively. The celebrant begins the creed with the incipit, the people joining thereafter. It is customary to kneel or bow at the mention of the incarnation, in reverence for that great mystery.

Prayers of the People. The ministers divide once more, each going down to their step. The priest remains facing the altar along with the eucharistic minister who has moved down and to the left. The deacon, who has moved down and to the right, introduces the prayers of the people and then either leads the prayers from the deacon's step on the altar or turns back to face east while a lay person moves to the lectern or ambo to read the prayers. They may stand or kneel, according to the custom of the people (though if the deacon is leading the prayers, that person remains standing).

If the Gospel is read in the midst of the people, with the deacon facing west, it is also a fine tradition for the prayers to be read in the midst of the people, with the deacon facing east. If that is done, then the deacon should move to the center of the people during the end of the creed so as to be in place for the prayers. The other ministers take the positions noted above.

Confession and Peace. The confession is then introduced by the deacon or celebrant. The ministers then kneel, with the priest kneeling in the middle, the deacon kneeling slightly to the right, and the eucharistic minister to the left, so as to make room for the celebrant. After a moment of silent prayer, the deacon or celebrant says the incipit to the prayer, after which the people join in the confession. At the words "Lord, Jesus Christ" the celebrant rises to stand in the middle of the altar and faces the people, while all others remain kneeling. The celebrant pronounces the absolution. The deacon and eucharistic minister rise, as a signal to all others that they should rise, and the celebrant invites the exchange of the peace. Every effort should be made for the peace to be what it is intended to be—a liturgical symbol of our unity with one another, having confessed our sins, before coming to the eucharistic meal. It is not an early coffee hour or an extended meet and greet. There is also no reason for an elaborate passing from one minister to the other. All may simply greet those near them. After the peace is also the most common point at which to offer any necessary announcements.[38] If announcements are made, they should be kept short and concise. When the announcements take the same amount of time as the sermon, one begins to wonder if the parson has lost all sense of proportion in liturgy.

Offertory. After the peace, the celebrant may say an offertory sentence and the deacon and other ministers go to the Lord's table and begin the offertory. If it is desired for the sacrament of unction to be offered during the liturgy, this is also a fine time for that (particularly when there

---

38. However, the rubric also suggests before the service, after the creed, and at the end of the service. *1979 Book of Common Prayer*, 407.

INTRODUCTION TO COMMUNION

is a deacon who is at work setting the table). Those who desire prayer for healing may then be invited to come to the rail (often at the side works best) or a side chapel near the altar. So long as this takes roughly as long as the rest of the offertory, balance is kept. At no point, however, should unction be offered in a side chapel after the people have received communion. The rubrics are clear in all places that unction precedes Eucharist, which is the great Sacrament of healing, and never follows it.

While the alms are being collected the altar is prepared. An acolyte brings first the burse, and then the chalice and paten, from the side credence table to the deacon who prepares the table as far as possible until the bread and wine are brought forward. While it is not an uncommon approach to bring forward the bread and wine and then to collect the people's offerings,[39] it must be stressed that the rubrics clearly intend a single offertory procession of the bread, wine, and alms: "Representatives of the congregation bring the people's offerings of bread and wine, and money or other gifts, to the deacon or celebrant."[40] After the people's offerings are collected, all the offerings are brought forward in a procession led by the verger. When the alms basin is placed on the altar, it should remain there, on the other side of the altar missal. There is no rubrical permission for removing it and thereby separating the people's gifts of money from the bread and wine, all of which are meant together to symbolize the self-oblation of those gathered. After the alms, the bread and wine are presented to the deacon who concludes the preparation by placing a single piece of bread on the paten and pouring some wine (and bit of water) into the chalice. There is no reason, of course, for this to be tedious and a well-trained deacon (or, in the absence of a deacon, a priest) should be able to prepare the table in a few moments. Then, the priest washes her or his hands, being ministered to by the acolyte or eucharistic minister (which can be done while the deacon concludes the preparation of the preparation of the table). Once all is ready, the priest, deacon, and eucharistic minister then return to their aligned position in the center to be ready for the Great Thanksgiving, which follows.

Sursum Corda. When the priest turns to the people to sing the salutation and then sings, "Lift up your hearts," the deacon turns with the celebrant, standing to the right, and the eucharistic ministers remain facing east or turn as well, standing to the left. After the people's response

---

39. This was suggested as an allowable approach by Hatchett, *New Prayer Book*, 46–47.
40. *1979 Book of Common Prayer*, 333.

at the end of the opening dialogue, the priest should bow slightly to the people, an expression of gratitude for their consent, as they have said that they do agree that "it is right to give him thanks and praise."[41] Then the priest faces the altar, with the deacon and eucharistic minister standing behind the priest as usual for the preface. Near the end of the preface, the deacon and eucharistic minister ascend to stand on either side of the priest, so that they are ready to bow with the priest at the song of the angels that follows.

Sanctus and Benedictus. At the beginning of the *Sanctus* all bow and may cross themselves at the *Benedictus qui venit*. The eucharistic minister at this point can often be helpful to the celebrant by pointing to the proper line on the altar missal for the prayer that follows.

Consecration. During the consecration all remain standing at the altar. The priest continues without any pause, saying the whole in the same clear and distinct voice, not too slowly, without any noticeable and solemn pause until after the prayer is fully concluded. At the words "our Lord Jesus Christ took bread," the priest lays a hand upon any other bread that is to be consecrated and then takes the paten into her or his hands. If it is desired, a slight pause and inclination of the head may be made at the conclusion of the sacred words. Again, at the words "he took the cup of wine," the priest touches any vessels containing wine to be consecrated and then takes the chalice into his or her hands and then replaces it after saying "do this for the remembrance of me." Once more, if it is desired, a slight pause and inclination of the head may be made for these sacred words. At the words "we offer you these gifts,"[42] the pre-Reformation rites told the priest to stretch out the arms in *modum crucis*. Another option is simply to gesture to the gifts or to follow the old non-juring tradition and make a considerable elevation of both chalice and paten simultaneously, with the paten in the right hand and the chalice in the left—not raising them, however, above the shoulders. This is what is done at the corresponding place in the Liturgies of St. Basil and St. John Chrysostom.[43] At the *epiclesis*, the priest bows the head and may make the sign of the cross over the bread and wine. At the Great Amen, all make a solemn bow as the Great Amen signifies the final consent of the people and is the fullest and most complete moment of consecration in the Anglican tradition.

---

41. *1979 Book of Common Prayer*, 361.
42. *1979 Book of Common Prayer*, 363.
43. Dearmer, *Parson's Handbook*, 295.

INTRODUCTION TO COMMUNION

The priest turns to the people to invite the Lord's Prayer. The priest then turns back, as all face the altar, standing, while saying the Lord's Prayer.

Fraction. The celebrant then breaks the bread, but it must be underscored that this should be done as simply and unobtrusively as possible. The moment of silence after the fraction is not optional and must be kept. If there is a sung fraction anthem, it is often wise for the priest first to speak (or sing) the "Christ our Passover," as this ensures silence is kept and an anxious musician does not begin the sung fraction too early. After this, the bread is further broken, as needed, and additional chalices made ready. To give time for this is the reason why the rubrics permit the use of an additional anthem,[44] and the most traditional approach is to use the setting of the *Agnus Dei* that goes with the rest of the service music while the additional bread is broken and chalices are filled. Once that concludes, the priest then issues the invitation to Communion: "The gifts of God for the people of God."[45] The rubrics do not permit parsons to create their own invitation to Communion and the one in the prayer book is the only one that can lawfully be used in our church. In Rite One, the invitation to Communion is optional, but the rubrics do not permit an alternate invitation to be used. The priest is a servant of Christ and the church at this table. Christ is the true host, and clergy have no right to create their own invitation as though the altar was theirs.

Communion. After the invitation to Communion, the people should be instructed immediately to begin coming forward while the priest first eats of the bread and drinks of the wine, the key point of etiquette being that now is the time for the meal to begin. The celebrant then communicates the deacon and eucharistic minister. After the ministers have received, a slight bow to the altar is appropriate before all take the elements from the altar to begin communicating the people, who will now be in place, usually beginning at the south end of the rail.

Ablutions. After all who desire have received, the older tradition in our church is that the remaining elements are simply covered with the chalice veil and placed on the credence to be reverently cleaned later. However, ablutions, where the ministers consume what remains of the Holy Sacrament, have become common in many parishes and may be performed if that is the local tradition. For ablutions, the acolyte or eucharistic minister gives the deacon the water, with which the vessels

---

44. *1979 Book of Common Prayer*, 337, 364.
45. *1979 Book of Common Prayer*, 364.

may be quickly rinsed and wiped. Once more, elaborate ceremonial here can obscure the rite, and a well-trained deacon (or priest in absence of the deacon) can rinse the vessels and clear the altar in a short moment's time. What is important is to demonstrate care for the Sacrament that remains—not to add several minutes of fussy messing about with the eucharistic vessels. The deacon moves the book and its cushion to the north part of the altar. While the celebrant washes hands once more, the deacon folds up the corporal and puts them in the burse. The acolyte receives from the deacon the chalice, paten, and burse, which are then carried to the credence or vestry.

Post-Communion. After the altar is cleared, the deacon and eucharistic minister may stand in a line behind the celebrant at the center of the altar during the post-communion prayer, dividing once more as before when the priest faces the people to pronounce the blessing. The deacon then pronounces the dismissal, at which point all the ministers face the altar and reverence once more at the signal of the verger; they then immediately turn to go out in the same order they came in.

In the following chapters directions are given for all possible forms of service, in accordance with the number of ministers that are available:

Chapter 10 contains a simple form for the priest and eucharistic minister alone, such as is suitable for most churches, especially in the country, and for plain celebrations everywhere.

Chapter 11 gives the priest's part in full, with authorities and a discussion of all difficult points. This chapter is so arranged as to include the full complement of servers either with or without deacon and eucharistic minister.

I have endeavored to use proper authorities and custom for these directions. I have assumed throughout that we have the right to supplement (though not contradict or avoid) the brief directions of the prayer book by English tradition—not necessarily because it is better than that of the rest of the church in the West or the East, but because it is that tradition upon which the prayer book is based. It may be added that a rigid uniformity and exactitude was neither secured nor desired by the framers of the prayer book in any generation.

The directions given in the chapters that follow have been worked out with extreme care, but a reasoned simplification of them would not therefore be incorrect. Fancy ceremonial is incorrect; any attempt to patch together fragments of the Roman ceremonial often seems rather ludicrous in a tradition like our own, but things done for the sake of convenience and simplicity will be perfectly correct. At the same time, it may be added that the method of sticking closely to precedent and principle, which has been adopted in these chapters, does work out extremely well in practice and results in a service that is exceedingly beautiful, convenient, dignified, and reverent.

10

Holy Communion, the Simple Form

IN MANY CHURCHES WHERE the congregation is not prepared for any very rich ceremonial, there is a danger lest essential things should be omitted while many unnecessary and unauthorized things are added. It used to be common to see an elaborate altar with unauthorized ornaments in churches where the vestments ordered by the prayer book were not worn. But if parsons let it be felt that they make a point of obeying the prayer book and conducting their work in a "sober, peaceable, and truly conscientious"[1] manner, they will not find it difficult to obey the prayer book in this also.

The celebration of Holy Eucharist with only a priest and eucharistic minister is, of course, the most common form in many of our churches these days when it comes to Sunday worship. One hopes the bishops will take seriously the restoration of the diaconate (a restoration which is decades in the making and never seems to come to its fruition) so that this ancient and venerable order will exist in every parish—not only to lead the people out in service but also to symbolize that essential aspect of Christian ministry in the liturgy of the church. However, absent a deacon, even in somewhat more moderately sized churches, the only increase in ministers is likely an additional eucharistic minister.

In no way should the simpler form indicate that the solemnity, reverence, and beauty of the liturgy is compromised. Reverence and beauty, after all, are not found in a multiplication of personnel and ceremony but in ritual that is clear, direct, and done with care and a sort of quiet joy.

---

1. *1662 Book of Common Prayer*, 5.

The directions in this chapter will serve also for plain celebrations if the references to the choir are omitted.

The eucharistic minister (or assistants in the altar guild, if they exist in a parish) removes the altar coverlet, places the book on the altar, lights the candles, puts the cruets and other items on the credence, lays out the vestments, and helps the priest to vest. Before vesting, the priest ensures there is a purificator on the chalice, the paten is on the purificator, and on the paten, the burse, containing the corporal and an extra purificator.

The choir being in their places, the priest enters the chancel preceded by the eucharistic minister. Each bow at the altar before going to their respective places. At simpler celebrations, the priest may say the first parts of the liturgy (opening acclamation, the Collect for Purity, *Gloria*, and the collect of the day) either at the altar or at the priest's stall. If said at the altar, the eucharistic minister should kneel at the altar step whenever the people kneel and otherwise face east. Regardless of position, one of the principal jobs of the eucharistic minister is to know the responses of the people and to lead them, for in smaller congregations there is often some timidity of response, which can hamper the entire liturgy.

For the word of God, the eucharistic minister may also serve as a reader, but a better choice is to select from those in attendance to read the first lessons. These readers, not serving at the altar, do not, of course, vest but come forward in the clothes they wore to church. The Gospel at simpler celebrations may very well be read from the lectern or ambo rather than in procession among a small crowd of people. If the chasuble is heavy, the eucharistic minister may assist with removing it for the homily, though this is rarely needed with modern vestments. After the sermon, the creed, prayers, and confession may also be led from the stall rather than the altar, so long as the absolution and peace are pronounced from a place well in sight of the people; often the altar is best. When leading the confession, this should be done in a humble voice but quite loud enough to be clearly heard by the people and matching their pace. This is important, as one often hears the congregation entirely at a loss through the ministers being inaudible. The priest and eucharistic minister must also be careful to make a very slight pause at the end of each clause so that the congregation may keep together. The prayer book has line breaks to assist in knowing where these clauses are.

After the offertory sentence, the priest and eucharistic minister go to the altar, and the eucharistic minister takes the burse up to the priest, who spreads the corporal on the altar without letting any part of it hang over the front. Representatives of the congregation should still bring forward the bread and wine, along with any offerings collected. With a little practice, this is easily established and demonstrates how keeping the rubrics often just needs a little intentionality. The priest then receives the offerings of bread, wine, and money, placing them on the altar. The eucharistic minister comes to stand at the priest's left hand (not hanging behind the priest and thus causing the priest to look nervously round). The priest, having taken the alms basin, shall humbly present it and place it upon the holy table, but there is no need for further elaboration, ceremonial, or recitation of Scripture verses. It must further be stressed that the alms basin should not be handed back to the eucharistic minister or some other minister who might take it away elsewhere. The people's offering of money goes upon the altar along with the offerings of bread and wine. The priest will naturally place the alms basin on the right of the corporal. The alms will remain on the altar during eucharistic prayer for they are an offering along with the bread and wine. There is no direction as to when they are to be removed. The simplest and most theologically sound choice is that they may be left on the altar till the end of the service.

With the alms being presented, the priest finishes preparing the gifts at the altar. When there are many communicants at a service, it is usual for the usher (or, in smaller liturgies, the eucharistic minister) to count the people while the alms are being collected and to tell the number to the priest, who can then ensure that bread and wine is placed upon the table so much as she or he shall think sufficient. If the lavabo is desired, this is then offered by the eucharistic minister, at which point the liturgy continues with the *sursum corda*.

The eucharistic minister stands with the priest for the *sursum corda* and then bows with the priest for the *Sanctus* and *Benedictus qui venit*. The eucharistic minister then kneels when the priest continues with the prayer of consecration and until the time comes for the eucharistic minister to stand and receive Communion. At the Communion of the people, the eucharistic minister will receive after the priest and then, with the chalice, will go to a convenient place from which she or he can follow the priest, who will have the bread.

After all who desire have received, the eucharistic minister will take the cruets to the south side of the altar and pour a little wine into the chalice when the priest holds it out. Next the eucharistic minister will pour a larger amount of water over the priest's fingers into the chalice and a little into the paten. The eucharistic minister will then fetch the basin, ewer, and towel (placing the towel on the left arm) and pour water over the priest's hands. The eucharistic minister then kneels with the people for the post-communion prayer and blessing and stands with the people for the dismissal.

The eucharistic minister bows with the priest to the altar and precedes the priest to the sacristy, assisting the priest with removing the vestments. The eucharistic minister then extinguishes the candles, brings in the alms, puts everything away (emptying the water cruet and dish into the piscina), and places the coverlet upon the Lord's table.

If a priest or a deacon is the only assistant, then that clergyperson will vest in albe and stole and take the duties of the eucharistic minister as described in this chapter, except, of course, any which are properly reserved to the laity. In those instances, it is desirable for the deacon or assisting priest to stand with the celebrant at the altar instead of kneeling with the people. If the one assisting is a deacon, then those duties reserved to the deacon should of course be followed. If the one assisting is a priest, then the assisting priest may or may not take on the duties of the deacon, depending on what is customary in the parish and desired of the ministers. The assisting clergyperson will also, of course, administer the chalice. Whether deacon or priest, the stole is worn properly according to one's actual order. If, however, the assisting clergyperson comes in only to administer the chalice at an extra service, it seems reasonable to follow the general custom of wearing a surplice and stole, which is certainly convenient. A priest wearing a surplice may thus just put on a stole for when administering Communion.

11

Holy Communion in Detail

IN ORDER TO MAKE this book equally useful for all parishes, the names of the deacon are in this chapter placed in square brackets. This does not mean that the deacon is to be dispensed with in churches where there are sufficient clergy. But, as the revival of the diaconate remains woefully slow in coming, it is important to acknowledge that in many parishes there will not be a deacon and therefore the brackets will be needed. When there is only one clergyperson, the words in brackets can simply be omitted; the deacon's duties will then be found to be absorbed by the priest.

At no point, however, should a lay person (including a seminarian or one preparing for holy orders) take on the role of the deacon. One is reminded of the story Marion Hatchett often told of a priest who invited a visiting seminarian to read the Gospel, set the table, and pronounce the dismissal, saying, "One only needs to be a deacon to do that." The astute (and well-trained!) seminarian responded smartly, "What if I just took the whole canon of the mass, since it only takes a priest to do that?" The diaconate is a full and equal order to the priesthood and while a priest may indeed do the duties prescribed to the deacon (having been first ordained a deacon), it is inappropriate for a lay person to assume them.

When it is desired to simplify the ceremonial, this should be done by dispensing with the thurifer and taperers—not by having a service without a eucharistic minister. The priest's duties are described with special fullness in this chapter. The maximum is necessarily given but simplicity is best.

THE PREPARATION

Preparation for Holy Communion[1]

The verger and eucharistic minister should be in church at minimum a quarter of an hour before the service begins in order to do their work and for the verger to look after the other servers. Often it will be found that a half hour before is much better. The coverlet must be taken off the altar and the fair linen cloth laid on it (if it is not there already); the candles lit; and the canister of breads, along with the vessels, corporals in the burse, purificator, and cruets with the basin, ewer, and towel must be placed ready in the sacristy or on the credence table. The cushion or desk

---

1. Exposition de la Messe, late fifteenth century. Priest in pointed chasuble with Latin cross says the confession with the clerk (in girded cassock) and people, who join in the confession and strike their breasts. Altar with figured frontal and frontlet of the same material and fringed fair linen; behind the altar a reredos with the Crucifixion, surmounted by an image of the Virgin and Child. On the altar are the missal (on a desk), one candle, and the vessels; the paten lies on the chalice covered only by the folded corporal; one riddel is shown. Beyond is a chapel with a similar altar.

will be placed on the altar, as well as the altar missal. The charcoal will be heated, incense will be placed in the boat, and the processional cross will be taken out of its locker. In the sacristy, the vestments will be laid out and placed on a table. The verger will see that the albes and amices of the eucharistic minister, taperers, crucifer, and thurifer are properly adjusted, and she or he will wear the chimere over the cassock.

The verger, or a eucharistic minister, may assist the priest in vesting. The priest will put on, over the cassock, (1) an (appareled) amice, (2) an albe, (3) a girdle (which is most easily tied double in a running noose), (4) the maniple, if used (on the left arm near the wrist), (5) a stole (crossed at the breast, the left part being crossed over first, and the whole held in position by tucking the ends of the girdle round it at the left and right), and (6) the chasuble. If the priest desires to kiss the cross on the neck of the stole, one can hardly judge the act of piety as unbecoming, but it should be noted this is nowhere required in our rubrics or traditions. If there is to be a procession, the priest wears a cope and does not put on the chasuble till after the procession. Saying the traditional prayers while vesting will often help to calm the mind of the priest and center all those in the sacristy on preparation for worship:

> *With the amice*: Place upon me, O Lord, the helmet of salvation, that I may overcome the assaults of the devil.
>
> *With the alb*: Purify me, O Lord, and cleanse my heart; that, being made white in the blood of the Lamb, I may come to eternal joy.
>
> *With the cincture*: Gird me, O Lord, with the girdle of purity, and extinguish in me all evil desires, that the virtue of chastity may abide in me.
>
> *With the maniple*: May I deserve, O Lord, to bear the maniple of weeping and sorrow in order that I may joyfully reap the reward of my labors.
>
> *With the stole*: Restore unto me, O Lord, the stole of immortality, which was lost through the guilt of our first parents: and, although I am unworthy to approach your sacred mysteries, nevertheless grant unto me eternal joy.
>
> *With the chasuble*: O Lord, who said: My yoke is easy and my burden light: grant that I may bear it well and follow after you with thanksgiving.[2]

2. These vesting prayers have their roots in the ninth century in both the East and West. See, for example, in the East, Glibetic, "Byzantine Vesting Rituals," 265–76. For

One finds that ministers often have a hard time avoiding small talk in the sacristy when vesting and that this often makes it difficult to prepare one's heart and mind for worship. The use of prayers such as these by the priest can help set a tone of reverence and quiet preparation, which, once experienced, will be appreciated by almost all ministers.

[The deacon will vest in the same way, except that the deacon will substitute a stole worn deacon-wise, i.e., resting on the left shoulder, the ends being crossed under the right arm and held in position by the ends of the girdle. Instead of the chasuble, the deacon will wear a dalmatic. If the maniple is worn by the priest, it is rightfully worn by the deacon as well.]

The eucharistic minister will vest as well in amice, albe (which is, once more, the ancient garment of the baptized), and girdle and may wear a tunicle. Whether or not the eucharistic minister should wear a maniple is a difficult question since this is a licensed ministry and not one of the older minor orders to which one was ordained (and it was at one's ordination to the minor order of subdeacon that the bishop would place the maniple on the left arm of the ordinand). However, as the eucharistic minister is licensed by the bishop, if this minister wears a tunicle according to the custom of the parish, the use of the maniple seems an appropriate choice.

THE ENTRANCE

If there is to be a procession, the ministers and servers enter the chancel the short way, the choir and assisting clergy being already in the stalls. The servers form up on the pavement in front of the altar and all

---

the West, see, Thomas, "Amice and Papal Fanon." The ones given above are the form that developed in the West and were eventually formalized into the form given above that are widespread in the catholic tradition of the church. If the parson is, instead, desirous though of a more historically Anglican prayer of preparation, this one from the Sarum Missal has much to commend to it:

"O God, Who makes of the unworthy worthy, and of sinners people who are just and holy, and pure of the impure, cleanse my heart and body from all taint and defilement of sin, and make me a worthy and earnest minister at your holy altar, and mercifully grant that on this Altar to which I, so unworthy, now draw near, I may offer a sacrifice acceptable and pleasing to your loving-kindness for my sins and offenses, and for my numberless daily transgressions, for all here present, and for everyone united with me by friendship or kindred, or who persecute or oppose me with any manner of hatred, and likewise for wiping away of the sins of all Christian people, and for all faithful Christians quick and dead, and let my prayer and sacrifice be acceptable to you, through him Who offered himself unto you, God the Father, a sacrifice for us, Jesus Christ your Son our Lord. Amen." (Pearson, *Sarum Missal*, 276)

reverence together. The priest turns, [the deacon] puts incense into the censer, which is held out for the priest [deacon] by the thurifer, and the choir begins to sing the procession, which goes in the usual order as described in the chapter on processions. After the station has been made before the altar at the conclusion of the procession, the priest goes with the [deacon and the] servers to the sacristy, where the priest changes the cope for a chasuble. Or the chasuble may be set somewhere convenient, and an acolyte can return the cope to the sacristy.

After the procession, the choir may now begin the introit. Of course, if there is no formal procession, it is with the introit itself that the liturgy begins, as the ministers then go to the altar in this order: verger with mace, thurifer, crucifer, taperers, eucharistic minister, [deacon,] and priest. If desired, the choir can enter with the ministers (after the acolytes and before the altar ministers), rather than being at their stalls—though having them begin at their place can greatly help the singing. When the priest has arrived at the altar step, all bow at the signal of the verger. The taperers set down their candles at the altar step, and the crucifer sets the processional cross in its usual place. Meanwhile the priest [with the deacon] and eucharistic minister go up to the altar. The thurifer comes up to the priest when the priest turns. The thurifer holds out the censer; the [deacon or] eucharistic minister, taking the boat and spoon, puts incense into the censer;[3] the priest receives the censer at the hands of the [deacon or] eucharistic minister, and proceeds to cense the altar. This the priest does by taking the ring in the left hand, grasping the chains near the lid with the right, and swinging the censer at the south and north sides of the altar and in the midst. Going back to the south of the altar, the priest hands the censer to the [deacon or] eucharistic minister and remains standing while the [deacon or] eucharistic minister censes the priest. The priest bows before and after being censed, and then the [deacon or] eucharistic minister gives the censer to the thurifer.

The priest stands at the north side (i.e., at the north part of the front of the Lord's table) and, facing the people, says the opening acclamation, and returns to face the altar for the Collect for Purity, with [the deacon and] eucharistic minister standing behind the priest in alignment. The

---

3. In the Sarum rite, the deacon said, "Bless." The priest made the sign of the cross over the incense, saying, "Lord, may this be blessed in honor of him for whom it is burned." There is no blessing in the York and Hereford Missals, though, and so this is clearly not required but is an option that may vary according to local custom and desire. Frere, *Use of Sarum*, 66.

priest shall then intone the *Gloria*, still facing east, with the ministers coming up to stand with the priest, who now moves to the center of the altar, and the choir and people joining in the song of praise. Near the end of the *Gloria*, the deacon and minister return to their aligned position, now at the south side of the altar, as the priest also crosses to the south side. The celebrant then faces the people to sing the salutation (the ministers divide, as normal, but remain facing east) and hear the response of the people. Then, once more facing the altar, with the other ministers moving back into alignment, the priest sings the collect of the day, to which all respond, singing the amen. All then move to their seats for the lessons.

If it is desired to simplify these opening portions, the priest can lead both the acclamation and the Collect for Purity, along with the salutation and collect of the day, from the center of the altar instead of moving from the north to the south end.

THE WORD OF GOD

According to old custom, the liturgy would proceed immediately with the Epistle, which would be read at the south part of the altar. In the current book, the expectation is that the laity take the fore at this part of the service. Thus, as the ministers move to their stalls or seats, the reader for the first lesson should approach the lectern, guided by the verger if so desired, and read the lesson in a clear voice.

Though it has sadly become the custom in our time to print the entirety of the liturgy, including all the lessons, in the service leaflet, this custom must be strenuously avoided. Scripture in liturgy is intended to be an aural experience and to give the people a script of the whole of Mass would be like handing someone a script when they walk into a play—true, they may catch more of each specific word of Shakespeare, but they will very likely miss the actual drama of the story. If readers are properly trained (and informed that the only way the people will hear the lessons is through their skill), then there is no need for the crutch of printed lessons to which the people's attention will otherwise inevitably be drawn. The use of modern audio technology and hearing loops can ensure that those with hearing impairment are still able to participate by hearing fully.

If desired, the Epistle and Gospel may both be chanted, and tones are given in the altar book for this purpose. The Episcopal Chant database is a particularly helpful resource. At this website, Arlie Croles and Richard Pryor host fully pointed Epistles and Gospels for all the readings of the *Revised Common Lectionary* and the major feasts of our prayer book, drawing from the admirable work done by Bill Gartig before his passing.[4] Reciting the first lesson from the Hebrew Scriptures, chanting the Epistle to the plain tone, and then chanting the Gospel to the Gospel tone, provides a meaningful growth of impact upon the people and is to be commended.

Before the Gospel, the sequence, or another appropriate anthem may be sung, with all standing (even if it is an anthem, the people should stand for the procession of the Gospel). During the sequence the [deacon or] priest goes to the midst of the altar to retrieve the Gospel book. The thurifer approaches the priest to refresh the thurible and then goes to stand with the acolytes. At the same time, the crucifer, preceded by taperers carrying their candles, go to the pavement in front of the midst of the altar where the three stand, leaving room in front of them for the [deacon or] priest. If a Gospel procession is formed, it then goes to the midst of the people. Otherwise, all may go to the lectern, the [deacon or] priest walking last. The tapers stand on either side of the [deacon or] priest and the crucifer stands facing the [deacon or] priest in the aisle if there is a procession (or near the lectern if that is where the Gospel is read). The [deacon or] priest announces the Gospel, first signing the initial letter in the book with the thumb and saying the proper introduction to the Gospel and afterwards signing the brow, lips, and breast as well. Then, resting the book on a lectern or holding the book, and facing west, the [deacon or] priest reads or sings the Gospel for the day, with all turning towards the Gospeller while she or he reads or sings. When the Gospel is complete, and the people respond with the concluding acclamation, a small procession is made to return the Gospel to the altar while the preacher takes her or his place at the pulpit or ambo. Some light organ music may be played, but the Gospel is meant to flow directly into the sermon in the current book, and so the practice of singing the second half of a hymn is to be discouraged as unrubrical and out of good liturgical taste.

The sermon itself should be an exposition of the good news of God in Jesus Christ as explored in the appointed texts for the day, along with

---

4. The database can be found at https://episcopalchant.com/about.html.

the festal observance and/or contemporary experience of the congregation. The requirement in the 1604 canons was that the sermon be given from the pulpit.[5] While this requirement is not in our own prayer book, good sense indicates that the pulpit or ambo connects the sermon symbolically to Scripture and avoids the preacher giving the impression that the people are about to hear a clever Ted Talk from someone who speaks from their own opinion and not God's word. There is no reason to preach only on the Gospel appointed and, indeed, such an approach has led to the people no longer knowing the riches of the Hebrew Scriptures and the rest of the New Testament. At the same time, the attempt to string all the appointed texts together into the homily often results in at least a bit (and sometimes a good deal) of exegetical violence being done to the appointed readings. A better choice is to pick a text, exegete it fully, and then lead the people, through the sermon, to a deeper understanding of the good news as that text articulates it and as the people might apply in their own time.

THE RESPONSE TO GOD'S WORD

After the sermon, the sacred ministers form up once more at the pavement, facing the altar at the bottom of the steps. If the celebrant is also the preacher, then they wait for the celebrant to take position in the middle. Once in place, all then bow and ascend to stand at the altar. Facing east, the priest begins the creed, standing in the middle of the altar, with [the deacon on the right and] the eucharistic minister on the left, singing "We believe in one God." The priest opens the hands at these words and joins them as the people and choir respond with the rest of the creed. It is more in accordance with the spirit of English worship that the ministers should remain standing with the priest at the altar while the creed is being sung, and this seems to have been the old custom. All may bow at the mention of the incarnation and make the sign of the cross at the end.

The ministers divide once more, each going down to their respective step, and the [deacon or] reader then introduces the prayers of the people, which may be led either from the lectern or, if the Gospel is read from the midst of the people, the prayers may also be read from the midst of the people, with the reader facing east. The ministers remain at the altar, facing east and either standing or kneeling, according to the posture

---

5. Church of England, *Canons* (1604), no. 83.

of the rest of the people. They remain facing east in divided positions with the [deacon to the right and the] eucharistic minister to the left.

Once more, attention in the service leaflet should be given to the responses of the people and not to a full reprinting of the prayers. This is another place where a sense of proportion must be maintained. It is far too easy to accumulate a variety of concerns and cycles of prayers in the intercessions to the point that one gets the sense that the church's goal is to pray for "the entire state of Christ's church and the world,"[6] quite literally and with great detail. While we do pray for the church and the world, we do not have to mention each part of the entire whole. The prayers should follow the requirements of the rubric and have a good rotation of concerns without giving the impression that, unless the person leading the prayers mentions something specifically, it was ignored by the congregation. The people must be taught that their own individual concerns are best brought in the times of silence through their own prayers rather than everyone's list of concerns being read from the lectern. In this way, the ability of the people to affirm that their own prayers truly do matter is highlighted and a form of the prayers approaching the length of a homily can be avoided.

After the prayers, the [deacon or] priest stands, turns to the people, and invites the confession of sin. The confession of sin may be omitted from time to time. This may be done perhaps only on principal feasts, but never on Christmas or Easter, as those who only attend those days still have need of confessing and hearing God's absolution. Indeed, omission of the confession is rarely needed. Furthermore, the curious custom of omitting it for the entirety of the Great Fifty Days of Easter seems to confuse the joy of the resurrection with the reality that we all continue sinning during those days and still stand in need of the grace of our resurrected Lord. All kneel for the confession and near the end, at the mention of our Lord's name, the priest rises, goes to the middle of the altar, and turns and faces the people to pronounce the absolution. All then rise and the priest offers the peace of Christ, which is then exchanged. The rubrics do allow for the peace after the fraction, though most eschew this as unworkable and not the best liturgical flow. This does work in particularly small celebrations of Eucharist but not in most normal parish celebrations.

---

6. *1979 Book of Common Prayer*, 328.

As noted earlier, it is customary to share announcements at this point when notices and banns of marriage would have been said in former times. Of all the items that could be announced (and certainly not everything should be!), one of the most essential in the tradition of our prayer book are what holy days or fasting days will occur in the week to come. In large modern parishes there are many things which need announcing, and they ought certainly to be announced at this point, but if the people can be taught to read an insert with the appropriate announcements, all in attendance will be grateful.

THE OFFERTORY AND PREPARATION

In the 1662 prayer book, the rubric instructs, "Then shall the Priest return to the Lord's Table, and begin the Offertory."[7] The current prayer book gives several possible offertory sentences[8] and a rotation among them is wise. Even better is to choose a short text of Scripture that might resonate with the sermon for the day and thus draw the people from the sermon to the altar.

After the offertory sentence, the ushers or other fit persons receive the alms of the people while the eucharistic minister or crucifer fetches the burse and lays it on the altar and the [deacon or] priest takes out the corporal and spreads it. This is also a good time to ensure the altar missal is properly marked and that no ribbons have gone askew. In large churches, additional ushers or servers may often assist in the collection. If the church is properly mapped out (e.g., one collector to each quarter of the nave and one to each aisle, transept, and gallery), much time is thus saved.

The collectors then assemble at the west end of the church and go in a body up the middle alley, carrying the people's offerings of bread and wine as well as the alms and any other gifts. If desired, the crucifer or eucharistic minister may stand at the chancel steps to receive the gifts, but in most cases, this creates more confusion and, so, does not help. The taperers may meet the ushers with their candles (or without them, if it be so ordered) at the chancel gate and precede them as far as the altar steps. Once the alms are placed on the altar, the priest takes the basin, slightly raises it at the middle of the altar, and places it on the right of the corporal. The priest

---

7. *1662 Book of Common Prayer*, 147.
8. *1979 Book of Common Prayer*, 343–44 (for Rite One); 376 (for Rite Two).

should not use any audible special prayer or versicle and response (such as "all things come from thee, O Lord"), as the alms are formally presented along with the bread and wine in the eucharistic prayer itself.

If an anthem is sung by the choir while the alms are collected, a hymn is a fine choice for the people to stand and sing while their gifts are brought forward and the final preparations with the bread, wine, and water are made. As has been said several times at this point, the alms are to remain on the altar with the bread and wine. They are just as holy and symbolic of the people's oblation and do not need to be carried away out of sight of the people for the Great Thanksgiving.

The use of a hymn here also gives sufficient time to complete the preparation of the altar. The deacon or priest places a piece of bread on the paten, with any further bread remaining on its container on the corporal. Then the wine and a small bit of water is poured into the chalice. The deacon (or eucharistic minister or crucifer) then lays a towel over the left arm and offers a small basin and pitcher of water for the lavabo, if desired and incense is not being used (if incense is used, the bread and wine are censed before the lavabo). It must be stressed that the rubrics are clear that multiple chalices are not permitted upon the altar during the Great Thanksgiving and that, instead, a large flagon should be used from which additional chalices may be filled after the fraction.[9]

In some churches, the priest then takes the censer from the [deacon or] thurifer and censes the oblations—first making three signs of the cross over them, then swinging the censer round them, and then giving one swing on each side and one in front of them. The priest does not need to cense the altar, as that has already been done and the censing of the elements is what has the strongest place in the tradition of our church. The [deacon or] thurifer then receives the censer, and while the priest washes hands for the lavabo, the [deacon or] thurifer goes to the pavement on the south side, bows to the priest, and censes the priest. The thurifer then censes the [deacon,] eucharistic minister, the choir (beginning with the rulers, then the clergy in order of rank, and then the choir in their rows), and then the gathered congregation. Whoever holds the censer always bows to those being censed, who should bow in return both before and after the censing.

Once all is prepared, the taperers should be at their positions below the first steps to the altar, with [the deacon on the right of the priest on

---

9. *1979 Book of Common Prayer*, 407.

the next step and] the eucharistic minister on the left of the priest on the next step. Finally, the priest should be standing in the center of the altar, ready to begin the Great Thanksgiving.

THE CANON

The canon of the mass properly begins with the salutation and *sursum corda*. The priest, facing the people, first sings the salutation with hands extended to the people and then slightly raises the hands for the *sursum corda*. When the people have responded, "It is right to give him thanks and praise," the priest shall join hands, bow to the people in gratitude for their consent for the prayer to begin, and then "facing the Holy Table," the celebrant shall proceed with the preface with hands held apart.[10] The other ministers stand behind the priest in alignment as the priest sings the preface.

Near the end of the preface, the other ministers go and stand on either side of the priest so that they are ready to bow for the *Sanctus* and *Benedictus qui venit*. The priest's hands should be joined again and a bow made at the *Sanctus*; the old Sarum rite instructs this is to be done with the arms raised (so that the joined fingers are just beneath the priest's chin). The choir and people sing the *Sanctus* and *Benedictus qui venit*, all bowing.

After the *Sanctus* and *Benedictus qui venit*, the ministers remain standing at the altar. At this point, all manual actions done should be unobtrusive and in line with what is happening in the rite, without drawing any attention to the priest and keeping the focus of all on the holy table itself.

The priest says the consecration prayer in a clear and audible voice, humbly, solemnly, and without note. At the phrase "on the night he was handed over," the priest may rub the thumb and forefinger of either hand on the edge of the corporal. At the words "our Lord Jesus Christ took bread," the priest should lay a hand upon any bread that is to be consecrated. At the words "when he had given thanks," the priest should raise hands briefly once more in the outstretched position of prayer before taking the paten into her or his hands and speaking the words of institution in a clear, strong, and yet profoundly reverent voice. The paten is

---

10 *1979 Book of Common Prayer*, 333, 341, 361, 367, 370, 373.

then replaced on the altar, and all may then bow slightly (though not as fully as they will for the Great Amen).

Again, at the words "he took the cup of wine," the priest touches any vessels that contain wine. Then, at the words "when he had given thanks," the priest stretches out her or his hands to signify that moment of prayer. The priest then grasps the chalice and raises it up, saying once more in a clear, strong, and yet profoundly reverent voice, "This is my Blood of the new Covenant." If all bowed slightly after the words of institution for the bread, all bow once more after the words of institution for the wine.

The priest then continues with the memorial acclamation without any pause or gesture of reverence. At the epiclesis, the priest bows the head and may make the sign of the cross over the bread and wine.

At the Great Amen, all make a solemn bow, as the Great Amen signifies the final consent of the people and is the fullest and most complete moment of consecration in the Anglican tradition. The priest turns to the people to invite the Lord's Prayer, and the [deacon and] eucharistic minister move[s] once more as at the *sursum corda* before returning to position behind the priest. All stand and face the altar while saying or singing the Lord's Prayer.

The celebrant then breaks the bread, but it must be underscored that this should be done as simply and unobtrusively as possible. During this sacred moment Christ's sacrifice is made present once more, and for the priest to hold the two pieces aloft like a triumphant gladiator is far from the appropriate choice. The moment of silence after the fraction is not optional and must be kept. To keep an anxious musician from beginning the fraction anthem too soon, a good choice is for the priest to keep the silence and, after a moment, to say or sing the "Christ our Passover," after which the people can say or sing the *Agnus Dei* while additional chalices are filled and the bread is broken. This is absolutely essential if the rubric that requires the people to come forward upon the invitation "the gifts of God for the people of God" is to be fulfilled. If the priest proceeds with the invitation before having made the gifts ready, then the people will be coming forward while all is being made ready instead of while the ministers are receiving (which is the clear requirement of the rubric[11] and is meant to underscore that we all receive together—no one is more or less important).

---

11. *1979 Book of Common Prayer*, 407.

If all is not prepared by the end of the fraction anthem, the priest should continue the preparations (assisted by other ministers) quietly and without seeming hurried or rushed. Indeed, for there to be a dead silence for one minute or so while the clergy finish preparing for Communion is not to be feared. Nothing is so impressive or so helpful to recollectedness as this complete silence. Once all is ready, the priest says the invitation.

THE COMMUNION

Communion of the People[12]

Immediately following the invitation to Communion, the priest proceeds to make her or his own Communion—this act of course includes the usual brief interval for private devotion. But this interval must not be lengthened by the insertion of anything but genuinely private prayers. If the priest wishes to prepare for Communion in a set form, there are three prayers in the Sarum Missal for the priest's Communion, and there are

12. Liber Cathecuminorum, Venice, 1555. Priest, in chasuble cut away at the arms but very long, carries paten and large host to the communicants; clerk in chasuble-shaped surplice holds a candle. Altar entirely covered by ample linen cloth with two broad and low candle sticks; chalice of Renaissance pattern; reredos with picture. Bench covered with houseling cloth for Communion.

other prayers in more ancient liturgies, which are better. But the use of set private communion prayers such as these is best done on one's own, before the liturgy has begun and out of sight of the people. It is as true of the priest as of the people that one will do best to pray in one's own words or thoughts and, that, very briefly, for the whole service is the priest's preparation, as it is that of the people. The Anglican prayer books have fortunately never given the priest a burden of additional words at this solemn moment.

It is essential for the integrity of the rite that the priest and ministers communicate. "The ministers receive the Sacrament in both kinds."[13] No form of words is given the priest for this purpose, but the older Scottish Liturgy, from which our American rite is derived, directed the priest to use the same words of administration that are used for the people.

The rubrics require that the people come forward while the minsters are receiving Communion.[14] This way it is not only clear that all are equal when it comes to reception of the Sacrament, but that the people will also be ready at the altar rails when the priest and other ministers turn to communicate them. The people, of course, will be instructed to observe this signal so as to avoid the bad habit of keeping the priest waiting while the communicants approach. A hymn or anthem may be sung while the Communion begins.

When the ministers have made their Communion, the priest takes the paten to the south end of the altar rails and proceeds to deliver the Sacrament to the people, saying in a low voice (and yet still audibly) to each communicant the words of administration. Some ministers have taken to saying the names of those coming forward, but this practice is to be discouraged. First, it is lawless, as the prayer book otherwise instructs when we call people by name, and it does not indicate we should do so when distributing Communion. Second, it can create an inadvertent sense of exclusion when someone at the rail is unknown to the minister. Finally, it is an intrusion of the personal relationship at a moment when the minister truly should blend into the action. What matters is the Sacrament, not the gregarious nature of the cleric or minister. The reverent parson will seek to blend into the liturgy and not intrude upon the communicant's time with God, during which the minister is only a humble servant. Some of

---

13. *1979 Book of Common Prayer*, 338, 365.
14. *1979 Book of Common Prayer*, 407.

those who receive will want to make eye contact for a moment of pastoral connection, and a kind smile for those persons is all that is needed.

During the distribution, [the deacon and] the eucharistic minister follow the priest with the chalice, administering to the first communicant while the priest is administering to the third, and keeps this distance so far as possible.

The rubric is clear that "opportunity is always to be given to every communicant to receive the consecrated Bread and Wine separately," and that intinction is permitted but only in a manner approved by the bishop.[15] Those who think that intinction carries less risk of infection should be gently informed of science. Hands are one of the dirtiest things on a person and germs are like glitter. For multiple people to hold their hands over the wine or to press the bread into their hands (which means the bread now has the germ of the hands) and then to dip that bread into the common cup causes an increase of the spread of germs, and not a decrease.

Furthermore, the strong tradition of our church has been that the Sacrament in "both kinds" is to be delivered "into their hands." It is hard to see why some priests should have taken upon themselves to break this tradition, instructing ministers to hold the chalice with a vice-like grip, which makes it impossible for the communicant to guide the chalice to their lips. One imagines they must believe that the cup is too sacred to be touched by the people, which could only mean that it is more sacred than that which it contains. As for safety or risk of spilling, it seems clear that the traditional way of administering the chalice is much more secure. It is very difficult for the minister to guide the chalice unless the communicant takes it firmly with both hands, and the innovation or refusing control of the chalice to people has produced an element of uncertainty in the action of the different communicants. This has not made things better but, instead, has made Communion in some churches a matter of risk and anxiety. Besides this, many excellent people resent the apparent want of confidence of the minister who refuses to deliver the cup into their hands. The minister should leave hold of the chalice entirely, unless the communicant be infirm. If anxiety will not permit this, then it is essential that the person administering the chalice maintain a firm grip on the center of the stem of the chalice but a loose wrist so that the person receiving can drink from the chalice freely.

---

15. *1979 Book of Common Prayer*, 407.

Some authorities think that in case of a second consecration both kinds should be consecrated and not one only. But great care should always be taken to avoid the necessity of any second consecration. Sometimes a miscalculation does make it a necessity, but this should very rarely happen if the priest always allows for slightly more communicants than expected. When there are many communicants, two chalices should be used, or even more, while another chalice or a standing pyx might be used for the breads. When there are many communicants and the church has more than two clergy and there is a chapel, much time is saved if a priest (better still, a priest and a deacon) take a chalice and paten to the chapel and there communicate people at the chapel rails while the Communion at the high altar is proceeding.

CONCLUDING RITES

In the older books, the clergy were directed that "when all have communicated, the Minister shall return to the Lord's Table, and reverently place upon it [bowing therefore, presumably] what remaineth of the consecrated Elements, covering the same with a fair linen cloth."[16] This fair linen cloth is a corporal; the priest has hitherto kept it folded square, now [the deacon or] the priest must unfold it and spread it as a veil over the consecrated elements. It is difficult to understand why some have discarded this act of reverence, which is so valuable an illustration of the English Church's adherence to church tradition.

If, however, the parson prefers to perform traditional ablutions, then this should be done as simply and unobtrusively as possible. Immediately after the last person is communicated, the ministers reverently eat and drink what remains. Traditionally, the priest first consumes what remains of the consecrated bread, and then, holding the paten over the chalice, the priest rubs any crumbs that may remain into the chalice. Then, without bowing again, the priest drinks what remains in the chalice.

What follows now is the later medieval way of consuming what remains of the consecrated elements and if it can be done quickly, reverently, and unobtrusively while the last communicants are making their way back to their seats, there is nothing wrong with it. The priest takes the chalice to the south end of the altar and holds it out to the eucharistic

---

16. *1662 Book of Common Prayer*, 156 (Dearmer's brackets). See also Dearmer, *Parson's Handbook*, 348.

minister or crucifer, who pours a little water therein. The priest then drinks this first ablution (not holding the chalice higher than necessary) while still facing the altar. The priest then holds the bowl of the chalice with the three last fingers of both hands, so that the thumbs and forefingers can be joined over the bowl. The eucharistic minister or crucifer then pours a little wine or water over his thumbs and forefingers and then pours more water into the chalice. The priest then holds the paten in the left hand for a little water to be poured thereon, and this the priest empties into the chalice, which is held in her or his right hand. The priest then turns and drinks this second ablution, being careful to see that the chalice is properly rinsed.

In all circumstances, whether a simple practice is used or the more ornate tradition, the priest will consume the ablutions quietly, without ostentation and without delay. The priest then lays the chalice sideways on the altar so that the bowl rests on the paten, placing the purificator also thereon as a matter of convenience. Leaving the vessels thus, the priest turns and washes hands at the south horn of the altar, with the eucharistic minister or crucifer ministering thusly. All this may be simplified, of course, according to the custom of the parish and desire of the parson. A hymn may be sung during the ablutions. The use of the *Nunc Dimittis* is not to be recommended—it had better be kept to its proper place at evensong.

Once all is consumed, and the altar is cleared, the priest then stands one final time in the center of the altar, with the [deacon and] eucharistic minister standing to the side. The servers and choir all stand facing the altar. The priest invites the post-communion prayer, turning to face the altar as the other ministers move into alignment and the prayer is said by all. All kneel immediately at the conclusion of this prayer, with the ministers dividing one final time. The priest turns to the people (standing a little to the north of the corporal) and says the whole blessing facing the people. There is no authority for the priest to say part of the blessing away from the people nor to make other than the accustomed reverence at the name of Jesus. The priest should lift the right hand to about the level of the face in giving the blessing, making the sign of the cross. The [deacon or] priest then pronounces the dismissal, with the people responding as appropriate.

The priest comes down the steps with the [deacon and] eucharistic minister and all bow to the altar, along with the taperers and crucifer. All then return to the sacristy in the same order as they came from it, the verger meeting them at the chancel gate and leading the way to the sacristy or vestry.

Having arrived in the sacristy, the priest begins to take off the vestments, first putting the amice over the head. The priest then goes to a quiet place to say his or her thanksgiving while removing the vestments. All the vestments should be carefully laid down and not thrown about in disorder. The verger will see that everything is put away and that the lights are extinguished. There are no directions in our books as to the order in which this is to be done—it is left to convenience and common sense.

The warning "avoid elaboration" needs constant repetition because all through history the harm done to public worship has been due to the accretion of small ceremonies. In a book like this much detail has to be given, but it is given in order to prevent mistakes and not to prevent simplification.

12

Holy Baptism

THE PARSON IS ORDERED by the rubrics of holy baptism to remember

> Holy Baptism is especially appropriate at the Easter Vigil, on the Day of Pentecost, on All Saints' Day or the Sunday after All Saints' Day, and on the Feast of the Baptism of our Lord (the First Sunday after the Epiphany). It is recommended that, as far as possible, Baptisms be reserved for these occasions or when a bishop is present.[1]

The intention of this rubric draws from the rubric of the 1662 prayer book, which admonished the people that "it is most convenient that Baptism should not be administered but upon Sundays, and other Holy days."[2] These principles exist for the excellent reasons that a congregation should be present to testify to the receiving of the newly baptized into the number of Christ's church and that those present should be reminded of their own profession. To maintain the baptismal foundation of those feasts, the current prayer book also instructs that if baptism will not occur, the Renewal of Baptismal Vows may take the place of the Nicene Creed on these appointed days.

But the rubric is not absolute, and the ideal of baptism being reserved to these days is ordered to be preserved "as far as possible." Thus, baptism is allowed upon any other day, provided the parson uses good liturgical and pastoral sense; that is, the parson should encourage the ideal while also being pastorally sensitive to those times when baptism

---

1. *1979 Book of Common Prayer*, 312.
2. *1662 Book of Common Prayer*, 160.

should occur outside of the suggested times. In particular, when there is a need to schedule it along with the availability of a sponsor who may not be available on those four days, then having the baptism on a different day so that the best possible sponsor may stand for the candidate is a wise and judicious choice.

In all this, the desire of the prayer book has long been to make much of this holy sacrament and is against the former custom of making the service, practically, one for the private baptism of children. Furthermore, the rite in the current prayer book sought to restore the centrality of baptism to the worshipping life of the congregation especially by anchoring it in the restored Great Vigil of Easter and, on all occasions, making it clear that the bishop is the normative celebrant (not the most regular but the one from whose celebration of the rite flow all others). The current prayer book also restored the rite to its connection to Holy Eucharist. The prior practice often had been that it was linked to an office. In the new restoration, the baptism is performed first and Holy Eucharist follows as the climax and completion of the ritual action.

INSTRUCTION BEFORE BAPTISM

Of course, sponsors must be arranged and must be present for the liturgy, as no one comes to faith alone. It is important that the parson meet with the sponsors and baptismal candidate. The current prayer book restored adult baptism as the normative rite (once again, normative does not mean most regularly done but, rather, the ideal form and base of the rite). When the baptism is of an adult, careful consideration should be given to opting for the longer catechetical preparation outlined in the *Book of Occasional Services* or for a briefer form of preparation with the priest. While a longer form of preparation is ideal, when such a practice becomes a barrier to the baptism of an adult seeker, the practice must be set aside. The canons and prayer book expect that a time of catechetical instruction will take place at some point, and it could be that the newcomer to the Christian faith might prefer to go through that catechetical instruction afterwards (and, thus, be in the same boat, so to speak, as those who were baptized as children and undergo catechetical instruction later in life). To paraphrase our Lord, baptism was made for people, not people for baptism.

In the more common practice of the baptism of infants and small children, an hour with the parson, parents, and sponsors can often suffice. During this time, the parson has three goals: First, to inquire after the understanding of baptism the parents and sponsors bring to the rite. Once that is ascertained, then the teaching of the church with regard to baptism can be more easily elucidated. What the priest will often find is that the parents and sponsors come with an entirely reasonable but partial understanding of baptism (for example, it makes the child a part of the church or saves the child from sins), and they are quite open to hearing the broader and fuller teaching of the church. The catechism can be quite helpful on this point; it teaches baptism "is the sacrament by which God adopts us as his children and makes us members of Christ's Body, the Church, and inheritors of the kingdom of God," and, further, that the grace of baptism is "union with Christ in his death and resurrection, birth into God's family the Church, forgiveness of sins, and new life in the Holy Spirit."[3] As with so many points of theology, it is often not that people believe wrongly, it is that they only know a portion of the church's teaching and must be taught the remainder.

Therefore, on these points, the parson might acknowledge that though our first instinct as parents is to protect children (and this is surely one of the reasons parents bring their children to be baptized), the promises of this rite are not to protect the child but to identify the child with Christ's death and resurrection and, so, to raise the child to be aware of the hurt, pain, and suffering of this world and know that it is the job of every Christian to be present with and seek to be a healing force with regard to that pain.

The second goal of the parson is to get to know the family a bit more fully. Young families in our time are quite busy, and unfortunately, church sometimes feels like yet another responsibility where they feel they are not doing as much as they should. Rather than encourage this guilt, if the parson can build an authentic relationship and rapport, making it clear that the priest and people of the community are making promises for this child as well and that they want to be a resource to the family as they raise the child . . . well, then the family will hopefully begin to see the church as a strength and help instead of simply a task or burden.

Third, the parson should prepare the family and sponsors for the rite itself, letting them know where to stand, what to say (if they are reminded to bring their leaflet or prayer book with them to the font, they will fumble less with the words), and what to expect.

---

3. *1979 Book of Common Prayer*, 858.

THE NORMAL BAPTISMAL RITE

We will, therefore, first consider a really public service, with full ceremonial, as this will be the most common experience and practice of the baptismal liturgy. The second rubric is clear that "Holy Baptism is appropriately administered within the Eucharist as the chief service on a Sunday or other feast."[4] Thus, though "as far as possible" baptism should be kept to the five occasions noted at the beginning of this chapter and though it is "appropriately administered" within the Eucharist at the principal service on a Sunday, there are still pastoral reasons that another approach might be taken. For example, if the family is most active at a smaller early service of Holy Eucharist, the baptism should be administered in that liturgy so that the community who makes the promises is the one who actually knows the family and child the best. Furthermore, when dealing with a person who has significant anxiety issues as a true mental health concern or previous trauma of some sort, to force them to be baptized at a large service on Sunday is an unkind act and not likely to create an experience of grace. In those circumstances, ministration at a smaller eucharistic liturgy (such as a weekday Mass, for example) might be pastorally appropriate and is still within the rubrics of our church. It is only private baptisms with no one present that must be studiously avoided. The prayer book's indication of ideals is not meant to supplant the priest's common sense and pastoral sensitivity.

Regardless, those exceptions to the normative practice will be just that—exceptions. Most baptisms will quite easily take place at the principal liturgy on Sunday. If the parson announces the opportunity for baptism on the five ideal occasions, many will have their minds triggered by the announcement to apply, and baptism is thus conveniently kept on these days. Baptism on Sundays throughout the Great Fifty Days of Easter is also quite appropriate and is an excellent way of allowing for latitude in scheduling, when needed, while still keeping baptism's connection to the church's paschal feast.

All should vest as they would for the eucharistic liturgy. However, if there is a procession (either as a part of the liturgy for the day or one to and from the font), then a cope may be substituted for the chasuble throughout the first part of the liturgy. The priest would then change from cope to chasuble after the peace, during the offertory.

---

4. *1979 Book of Common Prayer*, 298.

Much of the liturgy is done as is normal for Holy Eucharist, with a few changes for the baptismal rite. After the opening acclamation, the liturgy does not continue with the Collect for Purity and *Gloria*, but instead it continues with the baptismal versicles and responses, which are drawn from Eph 4 and make it clear that baptism is not a partisan or denominational rite but one in which we join with the whole church catholic. There is a rubrical permission for the *Gloria* to be sung after the baptismal versicles and before the salutation, but this is a rubrical permission best declined in favor of the rite flowing in a meaningful and sensible way.[5]

The lessons, psalm, Gospel, and sermon all continue in the normal way (with the allowance that one of the lessons for baptism given on pp. 203, 254, or 928 may substitute for the appointed propers). It is appropriate that the lessons (and the prayers for the candidate) be led by at least some of the sponsors. The sermon should draw the attention of those gathered to the meaning of baptism, in light of the readings and the current festal observance. Ideally, the sermon leads quite naturally into the baptism itself and motivates the congregation to respond with conviction when they renew their own baptismal promises in just a few short moments.

Then, the priest stands at the chancel steps and the candidates for baptism come forward with their sponsors. The people may be instructed to remain seated until their part of the baptismal rite arrives. Those who come forward will be grateful for the reminder to bring their prayer books or service bulletins with them so they know the responses for what will follow. Once all are in place, the priest says, "The Candidate(s) for Holy Baptism will now be presented," and the presentation begins. Adults and older children are presented first, always by name, to make it clear that this is the normative baptismal practice in the prayer book. Adults and older children are asked if they desire to be baptized, as the rite is never forced; an older child who is hesitant and whose parents are insistent will not be baptized.

Infants and younger children who cannot yet answer for themselves are then likewise presented by name. Instead of the question of desiring baptism, which is asked of adults and older children, sponsors are given two different questions. Indeed, the current question for the sponsors of infants and younger children, "Will you be responsible for seeing that

---

5. *1979 Book of Common Prayer*, 312.

the child you present is brought up in the Christian faith and life?"[6] is much richer than the question in the prior books, which only required affirmation that the child would be taught the creed, the Lord's Prayer, the Ten Commandments, "and all other things which a Christian ought to know and believe to his soul's health."[7] The ability to answer the new question honestly and with commitment is helped by the proper preparation beforehand with regard to the shape of the Christian faith and life. Sponsors can also be reminded in the preparation that the shape of the Christian faith and life is helpfully articulated within the rite through the Apostles' Creed and baptismal covenant (which they will affirm for the child as evidence of their commitment to their promise). The rite also includes asking for the "prayers and witness" of the sponsors, a helpful reminder that their own regular prayer and daily pattern of living is what will most influence the newly baptized as they grow up.

The priest then asks the adults, older children, and the sponsors of infants and younger children the three renunciations and three affirmations. The three renunciations aptly describe evil and sin in three different forms. First there is a renunciation of "Satan and all spiritual forces of wickedness that rebel against God." This is a renunciation of cosmic evil—all those forces that are beyond our understanding and comprehension but that are at work to thwart the purposes of God's healing and saving love. The second renunciation is of "the evil powers of this world which corrupt and destroy the creatures of God." This is a renunciation of social evil—all those systems and prejudices that turn people and creation from God's intent, and that cause them harm. Finally, there is a renunciation of "all sinful desires that draw you from the love of God." This is personal evil, and even that is helpfully clarified to be not a violation of a list of rules but instead anything that draws us from love of God (or, implicitly, the way that God's love calls us to love our neighbor).[8]

These renunciations are followed by three affirmations, drawn from the act of adherence first found as early as the fourth century. As Hatchett notes, "In some rites the renunciation of Satan was said facing West as a sign of rejection, of detestation of Satan. The candidate then turned to the east, which signified light and life and the eschaton, for the act of adherence."[9] The rubrics do not forbid this practice and, with instruc-

---

6. *1979 Book of Common Prayer*, 302.
7. *1662 Book of Common Prayer*, 163.
8. *1979 Book of Common Prayer*, 302.
9. Hatchett, *American Prayer Book*, 270–71.

tion as to why it is used, it can perhaps be a helpful symbol in the liturgy. Whereas the renunciations involve a turning from three types of evil, the affirmations are focused instead on the desire to be a disciple of Christ. In the first question, the candidate affirms the turn to Jesus and acceptance of Christ as Savior. In the second, the candidate affirms trust in the grace and love of Jesus. In the third, the candidate promises to follow Jesus as Lord. The weight, clearly, is not on the perfection of discipleship but on the willingness to receive God's grace, love, and forgiveness.[10]

The people are then invited to join the priest, candidates, and sponsors standing as they are asked if all those present who are witnesses to these vows will "do all in your power to support these persons in their life in Christ?" The response of "we will"[11] should be a thunderous affirmation that those who are baptized and those sponsors of children will not walk the path of discipleship alone but that the entire gathered community commits *not just to be nice and friendly* but to do all in their power to support these persons in the Christian life. This is a place where preparation of the congregation in advance is helpful, and if they are reminded of this (especially, perhaps, by a line in the sermon that day), they can fill their role quite well.

The priest then bids the renewal of the baptismal covenant. The rubrics allow for this bidding to occur in the words given or in "similar words."[12] The liturgy for the Great Vigil of Easter gives an example of a more fulsome invitation to the renewal.[13] Helpfully, in recent years, J. Neil Alexander has also offered proper invitations that he has collected for the other great three baptismal days.

> *For Pentecost*: "Dear People of God: Our Lord Jesus Christ sealed the Paschal mystery of his death and resurrection in his ascension and gift of the Holy Spirit on the Day of Pentecost. That same Spirit continues to give birth to God's people by the waters of baptism. I call upon you, therefore, to renew your own baptismal covenant."[14]
>
> *For All Saint's Day*: "Dear People of God: In Holy Baptism we have been made part of that great fellowship of believers in all

---

10. *1979 Book of Common Prayer*, 302–3.
11. *1979 Book of Common Prayer*, 303.
12. *1979 Book of Common Prayer*, 303.
13. *1979 Book of Common Prayer*, 292.
14. Alexander, *Celebrating Liturgical Time*, 23.

times and places, the Communion of Saints. In baptism God adopted us as children and made us members of Christ's Body and inheritors of God's kingdom with the saints in light. Let us, therefore, renew the vows of our baptism by which God has made us a holy people."[15]

For the Feast of our Lord's Baptism: "Dear People of God: In Holy Baptism we follow the pattern of our Lord Jesus Christ. As he came up from the water he was anointed by the Spirit of God and designated as God's Son. So we also are anointed by that same Spirit in baptism; we are reborn and adopted as sons and daughters with whom God is well pleased. Let us now, therefore, renew our own baptismal covenant."[16]

After the whole congregation joins the candidates and sponsors in the baptismal covenant, the priest invites the prayers for the candidates (which, of course, take the place of the prayers of the people in a baptismal Mass).

If the font is near the chancel steps, the ministers now go there for the Thanksgiving over the Water. However, if it is not near the chancel steps then a formal procession to the font is most appropriate and the rubrics suggests that "a suitable psalm, such as Psalm 42, or a hymn or anthem, may be sung."[17] The hymn "Come, Holy Ghost," a paraphrase of the *Veni Creator Spiritus*, is provided as hymn 503 and was especially written for this purpose. Marion Hatchett, who edited *The Hymnal 1982*, once told me that this version was offered with the full knowledge that many clergy (especially bishops) lack significant skill in chanting, and so the hope was that the simple chant offered here could enable it to be led by the cleric celebrating the baptism. Even with this hymn, confidence in a cleric's ability to sing such a simple chant may still be less than realistic, and it is better that a cantor sings it well, if needed, than a cleric sings it poorly.

For the procession to the font, the cross, taperers, and incense may be omitted, but it seems better to have this procession led in the way others are led. If the priest desires to cense the water, the inclusion of the thurifer in the procession to the font is essential. The rubrics on p. 313 instruct that "where practicable, the font is to be filled with clean water immediately before the Thanksgiving over the Water." Herein is wisdom.

---

15. Alexander, *Celebrating Liturgical Time*, 30.
16. Alexander, *Celebrating Liturgical Time*, 38.
17. *1979 Book of Common Prayer*, 312.

Let us attend. "The font is to be filled"—not a tenth-part filled, nor some small vessel only standing in the font, but the font itself is to have an ample measure of water now poured into it. The rubric also indicates that the font is filled "immediately before the Thanksgiving over the Water," and not during the prayer. Furthermore, the custom that has arisen in some places of having the children fill the font with innumerable bottles of water, though adorable, is an excellent demonstration of missing the point liturgically. The focus of baptism is not the filling of the font but the baptism itself, and the ceremony should focus the people in that direction. Here one of Patrick Malloy's principles is instructive: "The essential elements should always be highlighted, not hidden or dwarfed."[18] Baptism does not need further high drama. It is the height of liturgical drama on its own. Using Malloy's principle and division, the primary action is the washing itself; the filling of the font is not even secondary (the secondary act would be the Thanksgiving Over the Water). Filling the font is purely utilitarian, and it should not be turned into a primary part of the rite by introducing a practice that takes more time and draws more attention than the blessing of the water and the baptizing of a new child of God.

In the older forms, the priest would stand at the font facing east. However, the current prayer book has a clear rubric that "the celebrant, whenever possible, should face the people across the font, and the sponsors should be so grouped that the people may have a clear view of the action."[19] A server, ideally the deacon, should assist on the right, and somewhat in front, holding the baptismal candle, which may be lighted from the paschal flame at the proper time, if that custom is followed (see the rubric on p. 313). Another server should assist on the left, holding the book for the priest. A eucharistic minister and verger, respectively, can also quite ably fill these duties. In front of the font should stand the thurifer and crucifer, facing the font, with taperers on either side of the font, giving light to where the focus of the liturgical actions should be. If the architecture of the church and font, though, mean that the crucifer would thereby entirely obscure the view of the people, then the crucifer should instead stand directly behind the priest. The candidates and sponsors should be close to the font and prepared for the baptism itself.

---

18. Malloy, *Celebrating the Eucharist*, 23.
19. *1979 Book of Common Prayer*, 313.

During the prayer of Thanksgiving over the Water, the ritual act is for the priest to touch the water at the words "now sanctify this water, we pray you." If the baptism is at the Great Vigil of Easter, the tradition is that the paschal candle is carefully removed from the stand and plunged three times into the water, with that same phrase of sanctification each time being sung on a successively higher note. (When this is done, it is better to modulate lower for the first one and then work back up on the next two to a normal pitch than it is to send one's voice into the stratosphere through anxiety. If needed, a note from the organist can help.) In all other circumstances, the parson might divide the water with the right hand in the form of a cross, afterwards wiping the fingers with the cloth the server holds out.

Holy Baptism[20]

Each candidate is then presented by name to the priest, who can assist the action with the request to the sponsors to "name this child," after which the sponsors respond with the Christian name (that is, the first and middle names) of the candidate. The naming of the child was required in the baptismal rite of the 1662 prayer book.[21] The current

---

20. Liber Cathecuminorum, Venice, 1555. Priest in the usual ample surplice with full sleeves and stole with continuous decoration, pours the water from a vessel; clerk in chasuble-shaped surplice holds the candle.

21. *1662 Book of Common Prayer*, 162.

rubric, where the candidate is presented by name, gives room either for maintaining the older tradition or for the family simply to present the candidate by name. Either way, the claiming of a baptismal name is what matters. For those who come to the church having been given one name at birth and then having claimed a new name based on a different gender than the one assigned at birth, the naming at baptism can be an excellent and powerful way to claim one's own baptismal name and true identity.

The priest then takes the candidates (the caps on any children or infants having been removed) and baptizes them one by one. The rubric, which instructs that the priest "then immerses, or pours water upon, the candidate,"[22] once more makes a normative statement that immersion is the preferred form of baptism (in keeping with the practice of the ancient church articulated as early as the Didache in the late first century and still maintained by our Orthodox siblings).[23] Dearmer preferred immersion in his own time, recognizing it as the best form of the rite, and further encouraged that if immersion is practiced, it would be best for the water to be warmed.[24] The candidate will be grateful for this thoughtful touch.

If the candidate is an adult or child being immersed, the candidate enters the font at this time. For immersion there should be provided a very loose woolen garment for the baptism itself—something that can get wet. The priest may enter as well, wearing only the albe and a stole that can get wet or, depending on the architecture, the priest might stand or kneel outside the pool. The candidate may then be gently laid down backward into the water or may kneel down until the water comes over the head. Alternatively, if the font is too shallow for full submersion, then the candidate may stand in the baptismal pool while water is poured liberally over the head, saturating whatever is being worn. (This was, as noted earlier in the section on fonts found in ch. 1 on church architecture, the traditional method). It should be poured three times, once for each person of the Trinity. Then, immediately after the immersion, children should be dried and wrapped in a warm towel or else dressed in their clothes. For adults, they may change into dry clothes after the exchange of the peace.

If the candidates are not being immersed but are old enough to reach the font on their own, they then bow their heads over the font for the thrice pouring—but, even then, it should be an actual pouring of

---

22. *1979 Book of Common Prayer*, 307.
23. Milavec, *Didache*, 19.
24. Dearmer, *Parson's Handbook*, 384–85.

water, not a mere trickle or sprinkle. To get baptized one ought to get at least somewhat wet. A small towel should be nearby to dry the head afterwards.

If the candidate is an infant and the priest is inexperienced, it is wise to ask for some instruction in the proper manner of holding babies. It is really important, both for the sake of the parents and for that of quietness, that the parson should be handy with children. The priest takes the child so that the child's head lies on the left arm and then uses the right hand to pour water over the head, gently drying it with a towel afterwards. A shell or other vessel may be used to pour the water and, once more, it is rightfully poured three times, at the name of each person of the Holy Trinity.

Our present prayer book gives no direction as to when the child is to be returned to the sponsors, leaving the clergy to the tradition of the first book and of the manuals. In accordance with these the child should be given back immediately after she or he has been baptized and therefore should properly be held in the arms of a sponsor while she or he is signed with chrism oil. Our prayer book requires the prayer of being sealed with the Spirit and allows for chrism as an option, not a requirement. It further allows for the prayer after baptism to be said after the baptism of all candidates, with the chrismation then following.

The most natural flow (particularly when there was a procession to the font) is for the baptism to occur, with a child then being given back to sponsors. Next, the candidate is signed with chrism oil using the prayer provided. If desired, a baptismal candle may be presented to the candidate, using the traditional words "*N*. receive the light of Christ that you may be a light to the world." Then, the priest moves on to the next candidate.

Once all have been baptized and chrismated, there is a procession back to the chancel steps (during which the congregation may be aspersed with water from the font) so that the rubric that requires the candidates to be "at a place in full sight of the congregation" for the final prayer over the candidates is followed. The priest then invites the congregation to welcome the newly baptized, who respond in a strong voice with the priest (note the rubric requiring the celebrant join in the welcome), saying the words of welcome in the prayer book. The peace is then exchanged, and it is fitting that the peace be especially exchanged among the newly baptized, the sponsors, the ministers, and those standing near them.

Care must be taken that the filling in of the register be not forgotten on these occasions. The verger must see that one of the parents or sponsors either fill in the register on the spot, while the procession is returning, or else go to the vestry for this purpose when the liturgy is over. The liturgy continues with the rest of the eucharistic rite, as is normal. The parson will find it helpful to let parents (particularly those without a strong church background) know that they should indeed stay for the entirety of the service. (Yes, I have been witness to parents who thought they should leave after the baptism itself.)

As baptism is full admission to the church, it is rightfully completed by the reception of Holy Communion. This point should be made to the parents of infants and children, along with an explanation of how it takes place. If the newly baptized are children, they simply receive the bread and wine like adult communicants. If the candidate is a very small child, but one who can chew, then simply receiving the bread (or the bread dipped by the priest into the wine) shall suffice. If the newly baptized is an infant, then when the family comes to the rail, the priest dips a pinky into the chalice, allowing the child to suck a few drops of wine, after which the priest wipes the pinky with the purificator.

SMALLER SERVICES OF BAPTISM

At the less public ministrations of holy baptism, which may be pastorally needed from time to time, as noted above, care should be taken that there is at least one server to assist, often the eucharistic minister of the smaller service of Holy Eucharist. This person may also hold the book during the Thanksgiving over the Water and baptism. The priest will wear a white stole but not a cope. Either the prayer book or a simple service leaflet can be used. If those being baptized, or their sponsors, are quite new to the church, then a simple service leaflet with responses and instructions is a kind gesture. After the service one of the parents or sponsors should go to the vestry, that the register may be carefully filled in.

An emergency baptism can be administered by a priest or lay person. If one is a priest, a surplice and stole should be taken. A special vessel ought to be used; this should not be a toy font but a basin employed for washing the altar linen or that used for washing the priest's hands at Mass can often serve quite well. If a priest is celebrating, the Thanksgiving over the Water may rightfully be used. If a lay person, it is not needed. (Indeed, the early church fathers and mothers insisted that all water has been sanctified for the sacrament of baptism by the baptism of our Lord in the Jordan River.[25] The retention of special prayers is an ancient tradition but is not an essentiality to the rite.) After the baptism, all say the Lord's Prayer and then other prayers may be added (any from the baptismal rite are appropriate), and a thanksgiving over the newly baptized in an emergency baptism is given on p. 314. If the officiant was a lay person, the priest should be promptly informed so that the baptism can be registered. The rubrics also indicate that if the newly baptized recovers, a special public celebration may be offered that contains all of the normal rite (without, of course, administering the water a second time). In these celebrations, a joyful sprinkling of all gathered with newly blessed baptismal water can be an appropriate method of celebration.

OTHER NOTES

There is no authority with us for the use of a second stole of another color. Some sort of vessel was anciently used for pouring the water at baptism, and though not in the least necessary, it is convenient. Nowadays shells are sold that are sometimes too shallow for the purpose. A silver or pewter vessel about the size of a saucer is more convenient than these, or else a deeper shell of some capacity. Rather than a small stock filled with cotton ball saturated by chrism oil, the oil should be kept in a small glass flagon. After the washing with water, the oil can then be poured into the same shell, or some other vessel, and the thumb dipped into it so that the chrismation is fulsome.

The font should remain full after the baptism so that the people may piously "take water" as a reminder of their own baptism when passing by. Normally, the water blessed at a baptism (or at any of the baptismal feasts) will last until the next baptismal feast day, especially if the font is covered after each service of Holy Eucharist. The ability of the people to touch the water as a reminder of their baptism before coming to Communion is an excellent connection of these two great rites of the church. If the font does seem to be running dry or if it has lost the look of clean and pure water, any remaining water should be poured into the piscina or the ground. New water may then be blessed using the Thanksgiving of the Water in the baptismal rite.

25. Hatchett, *American Prayer Book*, 274.

13

Catechism and Confirmation

CATECHISM

The rubrics of the 1662 prayer book direct that the curate shall "diligently upon Sundays and Holy days, after the second Lesson at Evening Prayer, openly in the Church instruct and examine" some children "in some part of this Catechism."[1] It seems unlikely that this rubric was ever observed with great care, even though the canons of the Church of England in Dearmer's time ordered parents and masters to send those in their charge and also ordered the bishop to inflict excommunication for a third offense on any minister that neglected one's duty therein. Dearmer noted regularly in the various versions of his original handbook that it is a pity that this rubric should have fallen into such abeyance.

At the same time, in Dearmer's consideration of this rubric, he believed that certain principles clearly emerged:

1. Young people should be both instructed and examined. (After trying many ways, his own opinion was that they are best examined by the spontaneous questions of a good catechist.)
2. There should be such instruction every Sunday.
3. On holy days there should also be such instruction.

---

1. *1662 Book of Common Prayer*, 173.

4. The church catechism is to be the text of all instruction. (His own experience was that this admirable summary cannot be explained in less time than a five-year course. Every opportunity is therefore useful. The parson might deduce that this amount of time is not needed, but care should still be taken to find the amount of time required for a fulsome teaching of the church's catechism.)[2]

When this handbook was first written, children's services were just starting and Dearmer believed they were generally carried out in a haphazard and unscientific way. He also believed that Sunday schools were often deplorably inadequate. During the twentieth century, there was great development; the science of pedagogics was applied to religious instruction, methods were reorganized, and much was done to improve Sunday schools.

In our own time, though, we face similar problems even after nearly a century of growth, adaptation, new methodology, and now even newer challenges. It is true that catechetical instruction at evensong is such a minuscule curiosity of the 1662 prayer book that few of our clergy likely even know the principle ever existed. At the same time, there does remain the need for the solid catechetical instruction of children.

This ever-present need has faced new challenges in recent years, many of which were exacerbated by the COVID-19 pandemic. Leading up to the pandemic, the robust participation of families (indeed, almost all demographic groups) in church was waning. For families, whereas Sundays were once set aside for worship and family, Sundays are now filled with travel, sports, and other extra-curricular offerings so that a family scarcely has room to breathe on any day of the week, much less the one that has historically been a day of rest and worship. During the pandemic, as in-person participation in worship and formation was halted, those families which had hitherto kept to this discipline found it suddenly absent. And, as the world gradually reopened, other family activities worked more quickly to adapt and churches often fell behind, being some of the last to reopen. The end result was that, by the time most activities in the church were once more normalized and possible, many of our families had lost that prior connection to weekly worship and formation. Those families are slowly coming back, but the emphasis is on the word "slowly," and the church must demonstrate to tremendously busy

---

2. Dearmer, *Parson's Handbook*, 392.

households that time spent in worship and formation remains deeply important to the spiritual development of children.

Dearmer wrote before the Sunday school movement transitioned from providing education to working families (as was the case when it began in eighteenth-century England) to providing specifically religious education on Sunday mornings (as it developed in the first decades of the twentieth century, particularly in the United States). Indeed, much hand-wringing over the state of children's faith formation could be set aside if one remembered that the model of Sunday morning catechesis for children before or after the service is one that is less than one hundred years old—which means that for 95 percent of the church's existence, this has not been the dominant method of forming the faith of children. So, while Sunday school still has much to commend it, it is far from the only way of inculcating faith in children as they grow up.

For those churches in our time who seek to continue the tradition of Sunday morning catechesis of children, several options exist. First, I would commend the Catechesis of the Good Shepherd. Developed in the mid-1950s, the approach of Catechesis of the Good Shepherd is centered in the Montessori method of instruction. That is to say, it is inductive (learning through curiosity instead of deductive instruction), centered on children, and focused on tactile learning. It was originally developed in a Roman Catholic context but since then has been adopted by many Episcopal churches as well with a positive result.[3]

Later in the twentieth century, a priest of our church, the late Jerome Berryman, went through training in the Montessori method in Italy and then training in Catechesis of the Good Shepherd. Working with a professor of Christian education, Sonja Stewart, at Western Theological Seminary (an institution of the Reformed Church in America), they developed a similar curriculum known as Godly Play. Their goal was to adapt the approach of Catechesis of the Good Shepherd to a more Protestant audience and also to incorporate the existentialist theological concerns that were on the forefront of mainline theology in the latter part of the twentieth century. The Godly Play method is more easily introduced and, for that reason, is also a very popular approach in the Episcopal Church.

---

3. Schwartz, "Theological Differences."

In the end, though, Victoria Schwartz has aptly characterized the difference between the two curricula.[4] Father Berryman was influenced by the work of Samuel Terrien at Union Theological Seminary, particularly his book *The Elusive Presence: Toward a New Biblical Theology*. Rather than setting God's covenant at the heart of the Christian faith (as is normally done in the Protestant tradition), Terrien set God's presence at the heart and argued that this presence is elusive and often experienced as a sense of God's absence. Thus, the focus of Godly Play is pursuing the presence of God, centering that pursuit in the individual experience. As Berryman believed God's presence is often experienced as hidden, Scripture and the church then become mechanisms, or ways into, that pursuit. That is to say, Berryman paired Terrien's understanding of the elusive presence of God with late twentieth-century existentialist approaches to psychotherapy, with the goal of helping children to "play at the edges of one's knowing and being, so as to discern creatively meaning and purpose in life," from whence comes the name "Godly Play."[5]

By contrast, the methodology of Catechesis of the Good Shepherd focuses on the revelatory nature of God and God's covenant in Scripture and history, emphasizing both God's gifts and our response. Berryman himself has noted that this is one of the basic theological differences between Godly Play and Catechesis of the Good Shepherd. Given the entirely open-ended and individual-centered approach of Godly Play, the point of the lesson is whatever the children, in their discussion, make it to be. Catechesis of the Good Shepherd, by contrast, has doctrinal teaching objectives that are clear and laid out. As Schwartz notes (though, admittedly, with a clear bias), "While Godly Play seeks to help children make meaning of their lives, CGS seeks to help children fall in love with Jesus and seek to follow him."[6]

Having experienced both curricula as a priest, and also observed the impact of each curriculum in practice in various churches, my own personal preference is for Catechesis of the Good Shepherd. However, having spent most of my own priestly ministry in a parish that is larger than the average Episcopal Church and which, even then, still struggled to build programming and train teachers for children's catechesis, I have

---

4. Much of what follows comes from Schwartz's excellent essay "The Theological Differences Between Godly Play and Catechesis of the Good Shepherd," published by the Center for Children and Theology.

5. Berryman, quoted in Schwartz, "Theological Differences," para. 12.

6. Schwartz, "Theological Differences," para. 43.

turned to Godly Play because of its ease of implementation. However, if this is the format chosen, the parson would do well to encourage two things: First, a strong connection must be made between the lessons and the Scripture and sacraments a child will experience in the church. This is where Catechesis of the Good Shepherd shines and Godly Play falters. Second, much of the existential angst in Godly Play has more to do with the concerns of late twentieth-century mainline theology than with the actual needs of children. Thus, I would suggest downplaying those concerns and instead seeking to connect the children's wondering questions to our Lord, who is indeed their good shepherd.

Lastly, while these two approaches are indeed helpful for Sunday school curricula, given the sociocultural changes of the past several years, one wonders whether they will remain dominant or if some other form of catechetical instruction might come to the fore. Remembering that the mission of the church, as defined in our catechism, "is to restore all people to unity with God and each other in Christ,"[7] this same goal should be the focus of catechesis—namely, to help children grow to love God and their neighbor with faithfulness, according to the teachings of Christ.

Now, the aforementioned catechetical instruction has been focused on children, but as those children grow up the question of catechetical formation in preparation for the rite of confirmation comes to the fore of the parson's mind. Here, two points must be stressed. First, as already noted in this book, baptism is full membership in the church. Thus, there was even movement to remove confirmation entirely in the revisions that led to the current book. For this reason, when it comes to the formation of children and teenagers, their full membership in the body of Christ must remain quite clear.

Older practices of First Communion or mandatory confirmation classes at a young age are simply not in keeping with the theology of our prayer book. In the area of First Communion, though, the sensitive parson will also acknowledge that every person comes to the church with sociocultural expectations and hope. These must be gently engaged with the teaching of our church. So, for instance, those who do come with a strong desire for "First Communion" instruction might be taught that none of us ever fully understand Communion and, thus, are welcome by virtue of our baptism. At the same time, a practice of sustained teaching on the nature of Holy Communion when a child is older may be

---

7. *1979 Book of Common Prayer*, 855.

combined with a "Solemn Reception of Communion,"[8] ideally preceded by the renewal of the baptismal covenant. In the area of the proper age for confirmation, our canons require one to be at least sixteen years of age before they may be considered adult members,[9] and this is likely a more appropriate age for the catechetical instruction that might lead to confirmation.

As to content, the focus of catechetical instruction is rightly "an Outline of the Faith, or Catechism."[10] Much of the content of this catechism would be affirmed by most Christians. The rest would be specific understandings of Christian teaching as our church has received and understood them.

Here, a three-fold understanding of Christian teaching is often helpful. Dogma is the basic and clear teaching of the Christian church. In our tradition, dogma is kept to the Apostles' and Nicene Creeds. This point is articulated in item *b* of the Chicago-Lambeth Quadrilateral, where these creeds were said to be "the sufficient statement of the Christian faith."[11] While we, as individual Christians, might struggle with doubt on the dogmatic truths expressed in the creeds, they remain for us the sufficient statements of the Christian faith and we are grateful that the plural pronoun "we believe" (in Rite Two) allows for the rest of the church to believe for us when our own faith might falter. If the quadrilateral remains the base of what we believe constitutes Christianity, then belief in both testaments as the word of God, the sacraments of baptism and Eucharist, and the historic episcopate locally adapted may further be articulated as Anglican understandings of dogmatic beliefs.

Second, there is the area of doctrine. These are the teachings of Christ as our own tradition has received them (and which may very well have been received differently by other traditions); that is, these are beliefs that are beyond the basic sufficient statements of the Christian faith that

---

8. The "Solemn Reception of Communion" is the name several clergy I know in ministry have given to a pastoral adaptation of the First Communion rites of the catholic church, especially those of us who have worked in Latinx ministry. Since first communion in our prayer book always takes place immediately after baptism, when a parent is new to the church and inquires, this rite is suggested instead. It gives the communion instruction that is needed, ties it to a renewal of the baptismal covenant, but also doesn't create the idea that this sort of preparation and liturgical experience is required in our theological tradition.

9. Episcopal Church, *Canons* (2022), §I.17.1.b.

10. *1979 Book of Common Prayer*, 845–62.

11. *1979 Book of Common Prayer*, 877.

comprise the dogmatic beliefs of the creeds. They are further concepts and understandings of God and the church as received in the Anglican tradition and as expressed in the Episcopal Church. On this matter, the canons give instruction: it is the duty of all rectors or priests in charge to ensure that all members "receive Instruction in the Holy Scriptures; in the subjects contained in An Outline of the Faith, commonly called the Catechism; in the doctrine, discipline, and worship of this Church; and in the exercise of their ministry as baptized persons."[12] Doctrine is further explained as "the basic and essential teachings of the Church and is to be found in the Canon of Holy Scripture as understood in the Apostles and Nicene Creeds and in the sacramental rites, the Ordinal and Catechism of the Book of Common Prayer."[13] Thus, points of Episcopal doctrine are those elucidated in the prayer book and especially in our catechism.

Finally, there is a third category of what our communion calls "pious belief." These are beliefs that cannot be contradicted by Scripture or the creeds but that also cannot be expressly proven thereby. Thus, one may hold them piously as one's own belief and opinion, but one cannot raise them to the level of doctrine (this is what all Episcopalians believe) or the level of dogma (this, what all Christians believe).

Take, for example, the Sacrament of Holy Eucharist. There is no *dogmatic* statement on the presence of Christ in the Eucharist found in the creeds. The aforementioned quadrilateral does affirm, though, its essentiality "ministered with unfailing use of Christ's words of institution and of the elements ordained by Him."[14] Thus, it may be taken as dogma that Communion is a dogmatic part of the faith. On the level of *doctrine*, the Episcopal Church in her catechism further articulates that the grace of Communion "is the Body and Blood of Christ given to his people, and received by faith."[15] However, how the body and blood of Christ is present is not articulated in our doctrinal formulas, which means the method of Christ's presence is a pious belief, whether that opinion is the method of transubstantiation based upon Aristotelian metaphysics as taught by Thomas Aquinas,[16] the receptionist understanding (Christ is only present when received in faith by the communicant) as taught by

---

12 Episcopal Church, *Canons* (2022), §III.9.6.b.1.

13 Episcopal Church, *Canons* (2022), §IV.2.

14. *1979 Book of Common Prayer*, 877.

15 *1979 Book of Common Prayer*, 859.

16. See Armentrout and Slocum, *Episcopal Dictionary*, 525; Attwater, *Catholic Dictionary*, 401, 499.

Richard Hooker,[17] or some other method of understanding. Pious beliefs are also often found in questions related to the Blessed Virgin Mary,[18] the charismatic bestowal of spiritual gifts, Christian socialism, and a variety of other possible Christian beliefs that may indeed be edifying and help the Christian to love God and neighbor more faithfully but cannot be required of others.

Thus, for instructing those preparing to make a mature affirmation of their Christian faith in the presence of a bishop, one can hardly do better than a careful examination of the catechism itself. If further resources are desired, then I would commend one published by the Forward Movement titled *Walk in Love: Episcopal Beliefs and Practices*. As with all resources from the Forward Movement, this book is steeped in the ethos of our church and the prayer book model of the Christian life and has much to commend it to the parson.

CONFIRMATION

The first rubric in the directions for the rite of confirmation indicates the purpose of this rite: "In the course of their Christian development, those baptized at an early age are expected, when they are ready and have been duly prepared, to make a mature public affirmation of their faith and commitment to the responsibilities of their Baptism and to receive the laying on of hands by the bishop."[19] One may wonder, however, why it is situated as the first of the pastoral offices of the prayer book when it may not be led by the priest in the local community (as is the case with the rest of the pastoral offices). It may seem that it would have been better placed under the section for episcopal services, since a bishop is the one who presides at this liturgy. Indeed, as Hatchett notes, the requirement of the presence of a bishop as the chief celebrant is what made the other liturgies fall under that heading of episcopal services.[20]

---

17. See Littlejohn, "Word Made Flesh." As Littlejohn notes, Hooker himself says, "the real presence of Christ's most blessed body and blood should not be looked for in the sacrament, but in the worthy receiver of the sacrament." Hooker, *Laws*, cxii. It might be noted that Thomas Cranmer himself also likely held a receptionist understanding of the presence of Christ. See Armentrout and Slocum, *Episcopal Dictionary*, 432.

18. On this, a collection was published in 1963 that aptly explored the dogmatic, doctrinal, and pious beliefs related to the mother of our Lord. See, Mascall and Box, *Blessed Virgin Mary*.

19. *1979 Book of Common Prayer*, 412.

20. Hatchett, *American Prayer Book*, 501.

CATECHISM AND CONFIRMATION

The reason for its placement is twofold, the first of which is noted by Hatchett in his commentary and the second of which is theologically essential. As Hatchett notes, the intention of the rite of confirmation in the prayer book was for that rite to be offered when there might not be anyone to be baptized at the bishop's parochial visit but there are candidates who wish to be confirmed, received, or to renew their baptismal vows.[21] This would indicate that the intention of the framers of the prayer book was that this would be a parochial liturgy (hence, a pastoral office in a parish like the rest, though one reserved to the chief pastor of the bishop). The underpinnings of this understanding are related to the original intention of the framers of the prayer book to frame the liturgy simply as a Renewal of Baptismal Vows, albeit in the presence and with the blessing of the bishop.

In recent times, however, some bishops have taken to removing this rite from its parochial celebration and turning it into a diocesan liturgy. I even regret to report that I have heard a bishop say in a diocesan gathering that confirmation is like ordination for the laity. One cannot stress enough that this is the farthest from the theological truth of this rite. If confirmation was ordination for the laity, then it would be listed as the first liturgy in the episcopal services, followed by the ordination rites for the three other orders of ministry. However, baptism is ordination for the laity, and confirmation exists to respond to the pastoral reality and need that those who have been baptized as children might wish to renew those promises and "confirm" them as their own when they are grown up (as the rubric noted above indicates). Thus, the rite of confirmation is closer to the renewal of ordination vows and, as one's baptized ministry is most clearly exercised within the local parish community, the rite of confirmation is also best retained there, as was the intention of the framers of the prayer book.

At the same time, I have been a priest long enough to have a limited amount of hopefulness that the bishops will listen to this plea. Increasingly, our bishops seem to want to justify the importance of the diocese by removing rites and experiences from the parish and placing them within diocesan celebrations. While this *may* make the diocese look more important to the life of those who attend, it has the unfortunate corollary effect of meaning that the average worshipper in the pew never sees these rites performed (and thereby might develop their own sense

---

21. Hatchett, *American Prayer Book*, 424.

of desiring these rites). Thus, the parson is left (as is often the case in the multiple versions of Dearmer's handbook) to long for the bishops to take heed of the prayer book and, absent that, to do the best one can with the episcopal leadership one is given.

If one is blessed enough to have a bishop who understands the proper parochial context for the rite of confirmation, then the following instructions may be helpful. First, the diocesan office should be informed well in advance of whether there will be candidates for confirmation, reception, or the reaffirmation of baptismal vows. The canons require a visitation by the bishop at least once every three years, and so it should be fairly common that there will be a collection of candidates desiring this rite. Most bishops attempt to visit once every other year or, even better, once a year. The canons do allow that "interim visits may be delegated to another Bishop of this Church,"[22] and bishops with larger dioceses are well advised to take note of this allowance so that a bishop may be within a congregation as close to annually as possible.

If regular visits are impossible in a diocese, then larger diocesan offerings a couple times a year for those parishes that may not have a visitation makes sense—but this allowance is best seen in the same manner of the allowance for All Saints' Sunday. The diocesan gatherings should be in addition to confirmation offered at the parochial visit, not in lieu of it. Opportunity should also be given at any episcopal visitation for candidates to attend from a nearby parish, and this may also lighten the load somewhat.

Aware that there may often be candidates from more than one parish at an offering of the rite, the instructions below include how best to accommodate those guests. The instructions are intended to help the parson be an amiable and helpful host, as well as to assist those occasional diocesan or regional offerings of the rite. This in no way, of course, indicates that these are the normative experiences. The offering of the rite in the parish in the context of the bishop's visitation remains the norm of the prayer book.

Those who register for confirmation, reception, or the reaffirmation of baptismal vows, having been duly prepared through a course of study on the catechism of our church and her other points of doctrine as articulated in the prayer book, should have their names forwarded to the diocese for the preparation of certificates. If these are not offered by the

---

22 Episcopal Church, *Canons* (2022), §III.12.3.a.

diocese, then the parson should create them. The bishop will certainly not hesitate to sign them after the liturgy. It is helpful for the names of sponsors to be included in the registration form as well, so that appropriate seating arrangements can be made in advance. During the course of preparation, all candidates should have been given their own copy of the Book of Common Prayer. Here, it would be helpful for the parson not to be parsimonious. A handsome imitation leather copy can be had for between twenty and thirty dollars and will be much more likely to see use than a cloth-bound hardcover edition. Candidates can bring their prayer books to class, study them with the catechists, and them bring them with them to the liturgy for the bishop to sign as a meaningful keepsake of this moment in their Christian life.

The age at which those baptized as children should be confirmed should be determined with consultation of the canons and rubrics of the rite. The rubrics indicate that this is intended to be a "mature public affirmation" of their faith.[23] The canons indicate that those who are sixteen years of age and over are to be considered adult members of the church.[24] Thus, one should not be confirmed until one is at least sixteen years old. Anxious parents should be reminded that this rite is meant to be the candidate's own choice and affirmation of their faith and that if their child does not have that desire as a teenager, they are best left alone from pressure. It could very well be that making this decision on one's own slightly later in life (say, around the mid-twenties, when our brains complete development and we are more accurately adults from a scientific standpoint) is actually better for some people.

This purpose is different than the one given in the first prayer book, where great anxiety existed as to the temptations and sins of adolescence and so the prayer book advised that confirmation "is most meet to be ministered, when children come to that age, that partly by the frailty of their own flesh, partly by the assaults of the world and the devil, they begin to be in danger to fall into sin."[25] But many of the most experienced and successful parsons consider that better permanent results of confirmation are secured by not having young people confirmed too early, and the current rubrics of our prayer book support that approach. There are other forms of formation out there to help children and teenagers

---

23. *1979 Book of Common Prayer*, 412.
24. Episcopal Church, *Canons* (2022), §I.17.1.b.
25. *1549 Book of Common Prayer*, 70.

navigate the experience of adolescence, and navigation of that experience is not the goal of confirmation.

For the service itself, the candidates will come to the church an hour before the commencement of the rite, each accompanied by at least one sponsor. Each should be given in advance (or upon arrival in the church) a name tag with their Christian name, their parish, how many sponsors they have, and what rite they are here to receive (confirmation, reception, or reaffirmation). The parson of the church where the liturgy is to be held, having been informed some days before of the number of candidates and sponsors to be expected from other parishes, will allot seats in the eastern part of the nave for the candidates and some places near them for the sponsors. If candidates from another parish are attending, then a barrier or cord should be thrown across the middle alley at the place where the reserved part ends. Each parish should have its own row or rows, with a label showing to which parish the row belongs.

This part of the church should be corded off all round so that access can only be obtained through the barrier in the middle alley; here one or two ushers will stand to admit candidates, who will show their name tags. The usher will look at their tags to see what parish they are from and will show them to the allotted seats. The verger of the liturgy, or a clergyperson who will serve as a master of ceremonies (often the rector of the hosting parish, if candidates from other congregations are in attendance) should assist so as to answer any questions that might arise.

The candidates and sponsors should be asked to be in their seats and ready forty-five minutes early. This will give time both to prepare them for the logistics of the liturgy and, equally important, enable there to be time for conversation with the bishop. No bishop who gives this extra time is likely to be disappointed. Of utmost importance in preparing people for the logistics of the liturgy itself is the explanation of two things: first, the manner of the presentation (as articulated below) and, second, how one will know when to go forward for the rite itself and the proper route to return. If this is explained by the verger or master of ceremonies as people arrive, there is no need to require everyone to come several hours early to a rehearsal that is really needed mostly by the bishop and the verger. This means that after ten or fifteen minutes of logistical reminders to the group of what the candidates and sponsors will do, the remainder of the time can be reserved for the bishop to get to know the candidates.

The clergy who have prepared the candidates will be present to present them along with the candidate's other sponsors. As each priest arrives, they should be shown into the vestry by the verger. There the priests will put on surplices, hoods, and tippets (not stoles), and the verger will conduct them to the seats reserved for them in choir. If there is not room in the choir, then they should sit with the candidates from their parish in the pews reserved in the nave.

Archbishop Thomas Cranmer in his Outdoor Habit[26]

26. 1546. From a painting by Gerbicus Flicius or Flichs, of Cranmer in cassock, rochet, chimere, tippet of sables, and square cap, now in the National Portrait Gallery, London. The following description is by the Rev. N. F. Robinson, SSJE: "The Archbishop, in a half-length figure, is seated in a richly inlaid chair, at a low table covered with a carpet. His chimere, apparently of a dark olive-green color, with a wide border of black velvet, is open in front, but with one side overlapping the other; and at the breast is seen the rochet; above which appears the neck of a black cassock. The sleeves of the rochet are turned up with cuffs of black velvet, not with fur of sables, like the cuffs in Archbishop Warham's portrait. Over the chimere there is a black velvet furred tippet, scarf, or "collar of sables"; both the black velvet and the dark brown fur being beautifully painted in the original portrait. A signet ring is on the forefinger of the left hand. The ring is of gold, with a very dark stone, on which is an incised coat-of-arms, in colors, and the initials of the archbishop's name inverted. The artist's name appears in the upper part of the portrait—'Gerbicus flicius Germannus faciebat.' A little scroll,

Strictly, the bishop ought to arrive at the church in official outdoor dress—that is, rochet, chimere, tippet, and cap. However, those days are sadly long behind us. When it is time to prepare for the liturgy, which is properly a eucharistic liturgy (though the prayer book does not actually require it to be), the bishop vests accordingly. The cope and mitre may well be worn, as a dignified procession befits the liturgy and the cope is much easier to wear when confirming people. The bishop should still change to the chasuble at the peace in order to preside over the rest of the eucharistic liturgy.

The two altar candles and the two standards will be lit, and the altar, vested in a frontal with a color used according to the feast being observed (if it is an ordinary Sunday, then white should be used). The bishop's chair or, even better, a faldstool[27] will be placed, facing west, at the chancel or sanctuary step, and it will be good have a cushion or decent hassock on this step so that the bishop will be able, without stooping, to lay hands on those who kneel there.

Once all is ready, the bishop and ministers then leave the vestry in the following order: verger, crucifer with cross, taperers with candles, clergy from other parishes (if there are any), the rector or priest-in-charge of the hosting parish, deacon, the bishop's chaplain (vested in surplice and carrying the bishop's staff, the crook turned inwards), and the bishop (if there is no chaplain, the bishop carries the staff). If there are choristers present, it is much better for them to be in choir when the bishop and ministers enter, but if they enter with the bishop, they will walk in their usual order behind the taperers. Similarly, clergy from other parishes might not join the procession but instead be in their stalls or seats when it is time for the liturgy to begin.

The beginning portions of the liturgy are much like that for holy baptism, with the presentation and examination of candidates after the

---

lower down, contains the age of the archbishop at the time the portrait was made, 'Anno aetat. 57, July 20.'" Cranmer wears on his head a square cap of black velvet.

27. The faldstool was a folding chair that used to be the seat a bishop would most commonly use when not occupying the cathedra in the cathedral church of the diocese. The church supply houses were somehow successful in the twentieth century in convincing parishes of the need to purchase a special, often elaborate (and sometimes ostentatious), chair marked with a mitre for the bishop to use when visiting. This is an unfortunate development, as the only chair especially for a bishop is indeed the one in the cathedral. A revival of the faldstool would restore the proper understanding of the seat of the bishop to our church and also bring more beauty to our worship as every faldstool in existence is far more beautiful than any supposed bishop's chair. Armentrout and Slocum, *Episcopal Dictionary*, 199.

CATECHISM AND CONFIRMATION

sermon being the point at which the liturgy shifts. It is customary for the bishop to preach and for this to be a sort of address to the candidates. If the address is not too long, the bishop's words may be very helpful to them. But there has been a tendency to overlay the rite with excessive preaching, a practice which may lead the people to regard the laying on of hands as of little efficacy in itself. The act of confirmation takes some time, and the authors of the prayer book have therefore wisely given us a beautiful liturgy. But some bishops have buried the office under a mass of interpolations and accretions worse than any practiced by lawless priests.

After the sermon, all candidates and sponsors should stand. If it is a small number, they should stand with their sponsors at the chancel steps. If it is a larger number, then all should stand in their pews. Once all candidates and sponsors are standing and ready, the bishop says, "The Candidates will now be presented." The service leaflet should make it clear that the presenters should then speak in order. All sponsors presenting candidates for confirmation shall say in a single voice, "I present these persons for Confirmation." Then, all those presenting candidates for reception should say in a single voice, "I present these persons to be received into this Communion." Finally, all those presenting candidates for the Reaffirmation of Baptismal Vows shall say in a single voice, "I present these persons who desire to reaffirm their baptismal vows."[28] Notice that, unlike the baptismal liturgy, candidates are not presented by name. This is because their Christian name was already given at baptism and there is no need for a further presentation by name.

The candidates are given an abbreviated invitation to renew the baptismal renunciations and affirmations, after which the bishop should invite the rest of the congregation to stand so that they may likewise signal their own support for the candidates. The bishop then invites the renewal of the baptismal covenant for all those who are gathered. After the renewal, the bishop invites the congregation to pray for those who have renewed their commitment to Christ and the prayer book directs us to the prayers for baptismal candidates as a helpful model.[29] After those prayers, the rubrics are clear that "a period of silence follows."[30]

Note that, unlike the baptismal liturgy, there is no provision for a special prayer for the Holy Spirit (that Spirit was already given at baptism and here we are merely asking for the Spirit to strengthen the lives of the

---

28. *1979 Book of Common Prayer*, 415.
29. *1979 Book of Common Prayer*, 305–6.
30. *1979 Book of Common Prayer*, 417.

candidates). To interpolate the *Veni Creator* or any other hymn between the prayers for the candidates and the imposition of hands is an error of the gravest kind.

The rite then begins, the bishop sitting in the chair or faldstool, the chaplain standing by to hold the staff. The candidates will be directed by the verger to come forward one by one with their sponsors and to kneel before the bishop, their sponsors standing on either side. This is the older tradition—but the rubrics do not require this posture and so care should be given to what makes the most sense. Some bishops in our time have taken to confirm while standing, with the candidate likewise standing, to keep the emphasis on the prayer of blessing and invocation of the strengthening of the Spirit instead of an appearance of authority over another. It should be noted that this approach is particularly often appreciated by those who have experienced religious trauma in the past.

Whatever the posture of the bishop and candidate, the bishop's chaplain should stand nearby holding a book and pointing to the proper prayer according to the rite indicated on the name tag of the candidate. If the verger brings the candidates a little down the church as they come out of their seats, and so reverses their order, those who sat farthest from the middle will go up first to the bishop, and thus they will come back in their right order, and be able to return straight to their seats without crossing one another. (This is not necessary when the rows are open at both ends and the candidates can then return by the side aisles.) The priest who prepared candidates comes from the stall when her or his candidates come forward, joining them at the chancel steps and standing alongside the other sponsors as the candidates kneel or stand before the bishop.

The verger may await the newly confirmed as they come into the nave and show them their place, keeping them to one side of the alley (unless they are able to return by the side aisles) so that they do not collide with those who are coming up. The verger will also see to it that the candidates from the next parish are ready when it is their time. The priest who presents any candidates will go back to the stall (unless sitting in the nave with her or his parish) as soon as the last has been confirmed. As one priest does so, the next priest will go to the chancel step to meet the candidates she or he has prepared. A great deal is lost if the candidates are huddled up in one indistinguishable stream, and now that the clergy have so often to take their candidates to a neighboring church, it is important to mark the share each parish has in the confirmation. If there are many candidates, suitable hymns might be sung softly during the laying on of hands, with short intervals of silence, but the organist should not attempt extemporizations, which would distract from the rite itself.

The laying on of hands being finished, the bishop will stand, give the staff to the chaplain, say the concluding prayer, and then invite the exchange of the peace of Christ. Though the rubrics allow the liturgy to continue with the prayers of the people, the prayers for the candidates suffice (just as they do in a baptismal liturgy), and it makes more sense to continue with the offertory of the Eucharist.

DIRECTIONS TO THE CLERGY AND CHURCHWARDENS

It may be a convenience for the parson to have a typical set of episcopal directions. I therefore venture to reprint the following, which marks a great advance on the older methods. As, however, I cannot help hoping that there will continue to be improvement in the future, I have added notes where this seems possible.

The quiet, joyful, orderly, and reverent conduct of the Liturgy of Confirmation, Reception, and the Reaffirmation of Baptismal Vows depends very much upon attention to little details. The following suggestions are therefore offered as an assistance to the clergy and churchwardens:

1. The confirmation service should be prepared carefully, with an eye towards hospitality for those from other parishes if any will be attending.

2. The bishop's chair or faldstool should be placed at the entrance to the chancel.

3. It is best not to direct the candidates to be in church more than one hour before the service begins, or they become weary. There will be brief logistical preparation and explanation and then time for the candidates to have conversation with the bishop. A well-trained (and prepared!) verger or master of ceremonies makes a longer rehearsal for the candidates and sponsors (at which few will likely pay attention or remember what to do) unnecessary.

4. Name tags with the name of each candidate, their parish, and the rite for which they have come, should be available as people arrive. This will also help the bishop (and chaplain) to know which prayer to use.

5. It is well that the bishop's chaplain, if present (or, if not, one of the clergy), should stand near the bishop during the laying on of hands to point to the proper prayer according to the name tag of the candidate and to be ready to take any message for the bishop (if the bishop sees anything requiring notice), as well as to assist infirm candidates in kneeling or rising.

6. If it is thought fit, and there are many candidates, the organ may play or hymns may be sung very softly during the laying on of hands.

7. The candidates should come up very quietly in a continuous stream, roughly a pew full at a time, the next pew being brought out before the previous one is quite nearly ended.

8. The front row on each side should always come first, for then those behind see the arrangements and follow them more easily.

9. A verger, master of ceremonies, or other assisting clergyperson should stand quite in front, taking care that the candidates pass on one side going up and on the other returning and pointing out to them, if necessary, the way by which they should return.

10. The candidates, both in coming up and in returning to their seats, should not be taken past the congregation but only past other candidates; having returned to their seats, they should at once kneel down for a time of quiet prayer.

11. Arrangements should be made so that no candidate, in returning to one's place, should need to push past another who has come back and knelt down. Where the pews are open at both ends, they can come out at one end and return by the other. When the pews are not open at both ends, each pew can be emptied entirely, with those seated at the farther end coming up first so that when they return those seated at the closed end of the pew enter first, thereby avoiding clambering over one another.

12. Each clergyperson should present their own candidates.

13. The clergy should recommend simplicity of dress. The candidates should further be carefully instructed how to employ themselves during the periods of waiting and of silence, and they should be provided, if possible, with some prayers and helps to meditation.

14

The Solemnization of Matrimony

I AM KEENLY AWARE that few of those in leadership in the Episcopal Church are desirous of prayer book revision. And I can understand why, given the deeply important place the prayer book has in the lives of members of our church. And yet, there remain a handful of places where prayer book revision is deeply needed. One of them is the sacrament of marriage. When a person enters one of our churches and picks up the prayer book in the pew, perhaps flipping through it to begin to understand what this church believes (the priest, after all, having said several times that, if you want to know what we believe, you should look at our prayer book), they may very well turn to p. 422, where, in the very first rubric, they will read, "Christian marriage is a solemn and public covenant between a man and a woman in the presence of God."

Now, while this statement is true, it is only partially true. The General Convention of the Episcopal Church has passed numerous resolutions, changes to the canons, and authorizations of liturgy in favor of marriage equality. And yet, until the language in our prayer book regarding marriage is changed to say something like "Christian marriage is a solemn and public covenant between two persons in the presence of God," then the doctrine of the Episcopal Church has not officially changed and marriage equality remains a pious belief (see the explanation of the three types of belief in the previous chapter) instead of the doctrine of our church. And separate but equal is not equal. If the Episcopal Church embraces sacramental marriage equality, then the General Convention of our church must revise the prayer book with the already proposed gender-neutral version of the rite and revise the appropriate section of the catechism accordingly as well. Thankfully, the 2024 General Convention did begin this process of revision, and one is hopeful that it will move forward and be approved expeditiously and not be caught up in wrangling that will further delay this much needed revision.

One must stress that by changing "a man and a woman" to "two people," one does not require those who hold the traditional view of marriage to change. Rather, we engage in the wonderfully Anglican tradition of writing our liturgy broadly enough so that those with different views may come to the same rite without the need to "make windows into men's souls." This phrase is often attributed to Queen Elizabeth I as emblematic of the approach taken after the Act of Uniformity of 1558.[1] After thirty years of tumult, war, and religious strife, her majesty sought to bring Catholic and Protestant factions together with one prayer book. She knew that some people would read the words of the prayer book with a more catholic understanding of Communion, for instance, and others with a more Protestant understanding, and the entire Elizabethan settlement that gave birth to modern Anglicanism was predicated upon the premise of carefully choosing language that could be interpreted differently so as to hold diverse groups together. The same certainly can be done in the area of marriage equality, as those with a more conservative view can read "two persons" and believe they should be a man and a woman while also respecting that others will read "two persons" and believe the sex or gender of those coming to the sacrament is not essential to matrimony.

Thus, in this chapter, I have sought to offer Dearmer's directions for the solemnization of holy matrimony in a manner that will make sense and be intelligible to a parson in today's Episcopal Church where marriage may indeed be offered without respect to the sex or gender of those who come to the altar.

---

1. David Loades attributes this phrase to Elizabeth I in the decade following the settlement. See, Loades, *Elizabeth I*, 137. However, as Benjamin Guyer rightly notes, the phrase actually comes from Francis Walsingham who was describing the queen's approach in a letter to the secretary of France. Though I would take issue with Guyer's interpretation of the Elizabethan Settlement in his essay, this note of historical accuracy is well made. See Guyer, "Elizabethan Apocryphon," para. 3.

THE SOLEMNIZATION OF MATRIMONY

PREPARATION FOR THE RITE

One note must be made at the outset and that is that every sacrament, of course, has the proper minister. Thus, bishops ordain and confirm, priests celebrate Mass and offer unction, and so on and so forth. However, the proper minister of the sacrament of marriage is not the priest but is, instead, the couple. They are the ones who confect the mystery of the grace of this sacrament. The priest's role is to lead them in this sacramental act and to, in the name of the church, pronounce God's blessing on the sacrament itself. This point should be stressed in the preparation with the couple. After all, so much of preparing for a marriage can focus on one's guests that the couple can easily lose sight of the sacramental reality they are creating.

Though the rubrics permit deacons to solemnize a marriage, requiring that they omit the nuptial blessing, this is only when no priest or bishop is available[2] and is further only allowed when civil law would also permit. This is because the solemnization of marriage is a rite performed by the priest as the pastor of a couple. Of course, a marriage solemnized by a deacon is perfectly valid (the blessing not being an essential part of the rite), yet it is very undesirable, as well as irregular, that marriage should be solemnized without the nuptial benedictions.

The priest should have proper registers to record marriages and, upon assuming a cure in a new state, should first inquire what is needed to be able to solemnize marriages in that jurisdiction, as the requirements vary significantly from state to state in our country. Attention should be paid to the legal requirements for obtaining the license, when and how the license is filled out, and what copies are given to the couple and/or sent into the local municipal authority. Following the canons of our church, the priest must ensure that the declaration of intention is signed at least thirty days prior to the solemnization.[3] Prior to solemnization, the priest must also ensure that the marriage is legal and freely chosen, at least one party is baptized, and "that both parties have been instructed by the Member of the Clergy, or a person known by the Member of the Clergy to be competent and responsible, in the nature, purpose, and meaning, as well as the rights, duties and responsibilities of marriage."[4]

---

2. *1979 Book of Common Prayer*, 422.
3. Episcopal Church, *Canons* (2022), §I.18.2.
4. Episcopal Church, *Canons* (2022), §I.18.3.C.

While the parson should certainly meet with the couple to discuss the Christian nature of marriage, to form a pastoral relationship if one does not already exist, and to prepare for the liturgy itself, the parson who knows their own limitations will further require some form of premarital counseling with a licensed and trained therapist. Thankfully, the mistakes of recent times, whereby clergy often thought themselves trained to serve as counselors, have been recognized. Clergy are not therapists and every couple entering into holy matrimony should have some conversation with a trained therapist to ensure that the relationship is beginning from a healthy starting point and that they have adequate tools for building a healthy marriage after their wedding day is over. The confidentiality of the therapeutic relationship is, of course, tantamount, and so there is no need for the therapist to give an opinion on the couple. A simple written statement that the couple participated in sessions (usually four to six) will suffice and ensure that the parson has sought to give the couple the strongest base for their life together.

In those cases where it is not a first marriage for one of the parties, the priest should also follow the guidelines of the bishop in requesting permission to solemnize the rite. Some extra conversation with the couple may be needed in order to request that permission, but this should always be achieved as early as possible so that a couple does not feel to be at the mercy of an ecclesial hierarchy they do not know.

The structure of the rite in our prayer book does not require Communion, though it is clearly laid out to allow for Communion and most devout Christian couples will desire to have that Sacrament as their first meal, as food for their journey together. This also balances the liturgy well, placing the high point not on the celebration of an invented perfect couple as the height of romantic and sentimental bliss, but instead placing the high point as the commemoration of our Lord's sacrifice, his willingness to let go of what could be demanded by right for the purpose of healing and saving the other. There is no better message upon which to center a marriage.

THE MARRIAGE LITURGY

A rehearsal a day earlier, often early in the evening or late afternoon, is customary and helps people know where to go and when. The rehearsal can also teach the participants some of the etiquette of Anglican liturgy (bowing to the altar upon entrance, for example) and give those reading a chance to practice (and for the parson to offer kind advice, if needed, to ensure the readings are heard and edifying to those who gather). All those who are moving or speaking in the liturgy should be present for the rehearsal, which should not take more than sixty minutes (unless those who come to the rehearsal find it to be an opportunity to share their humor throughout—in which case it is likely that all must suffer through ninety minutes). It is often helpful to begin the rehearsal by going through the responses so that all those present can learn the participatory nature of our liturgy and be encouraged to be enthusiastic in their responses. These would include:

- The Lord be with you. ("And also with you.")
- The Word of the Lord. ("Thanks be to God.")
- The peace of the Lord be always with you. ("And also with you.")
- Will all of you witnessing these promises do all in your power to uphold these two persons in their marriage? ("We will"—said heartily and with enthusiasm.)
- Those whom God has joined together let no one put asunder. ("Amen"—said heartily and with enthusiasm as well.)

Instruction for the responses of the Gospel acclamation and conclusion should also be given (though these are the least likely to be remembered and if the others noted above are remembered, the whole liturgy will be a much better experience). The couple should be reminded to bring the wedding license to the rehearsal (new clergy are often surprised how often they are forgotten the day of the service). The license should not, of course, be signed at the rehearsal or before the wedding itself. It can instead be set out at a side place where the couple and parson can sign after the service (which is also a nice moment to document with the photographer).

Before the service, the candles are lit and two cushions may be laid before the altar for the couple, as kneeling is required (and not suggested) at the nuptial blessing.[5] If the service is choral but without Mass, the priest may wear a cope as well as a white stole and surplice. If the priest is to celebrate Holy Communion, then amice, albe, cope, and maniple are appropriate. The chasuble may instead be worn throughout, but it is

---

5. *1979 Book of Common Prayer*, 430.

often easier to do the pieces associated with the marriage rite in a cope and then change into the chasuble to celebrate Eucharist. The priest may be accompanied by an acolyte or verger who will hold the book, wherein Post-it notes with the Christian names of the couple written on them are placed in the book in the proper places, lest one's mind go vacant at precisely the wrong time.

Priest Vested for a Wedding without Communion, in Surplice and Stole[6]

As with all liturgies, the marriage rite begins with the entrance. Here the rubrics are sparse: "At the time appointed, the persons to be married, with their witnesses, assemble in the church or some other appropriate place."[7] But the fact of the matter is that much of the time at the rehearsal

6. 1913. Photograph by V. K. Blaiklock. Surplice and stole by the Warham Guild. The priest is vested not for a choir service but for a wedding or a baptism. If the wedding were to be followed by a bridal Eucharist, in which the priest was to take part as one of the ministers, he would wear an albe instead of a surplice.

7. *1979 Book of Common Prayer*, 423.

is spent getting this entrance straight, at least according to our current marriage customs. As with so much in life, you cannot prepare for where you are going without knowing your destination. Thus, at the rehearsal, first, the final ending of the entrance is arranged. The priest stands at the top of the chancel steps with the couple below on the floor of the nave (if it is an opposite-sex couple, the rubrics indicate the woman stands to the right of the priest and the man, to the left). The attendants of each person in the couple form a line from there, moving across the chancel wall. The line may either be parallel to the seats in the nave or may arch slightly to form a semicircle. If it arches, those at either end should be instructed to match the position of the person across from them. All attendants should stand in what is known in theater as a one-quarter cheat during the entrance. This is accomplished through having one foot face where the couple will stand and one foot face those gathered in the nave. When the couple has arrived, the couple faces the priest and the attendants should do likewise, now taking a three-quarter cheat with one foot facing the altar and one foot facing the couple. Once all are lined up at the front for where they will be after the procession, then they may be "backed out" to where they will be at the start of the entrances.

First, there is the entrance of the ministers: verger with mace, thurifer, crucifer, taperers, choir, assisting clergy, eucharistic minister, [deacon,] and priest. All follow the normal actions for the entrance of Holy Communion, except that, after the entrance, the priest goes to stand at the top of the chancel steps and off to the side. Often, though, a smaller entrance is desired, consisting solely of verger and priest. If this is the case, the entrance need not go to the altar but may instead simply go to the chancel steps. In opposite-sex liturgies, the groom will often enter with the ministers (directly before the [deacon and] priest) and take his place at the foot of the chancel steps. One of the individuals to be married in a same-sex rite may also choose this option. If this approach is taken, the attendants for this member of the couple may also enter at the same time and take their place. Or, if one wants to follow the more liturgical entrance, then after the choir, all the attendants can follow and then both members of the couple can fall into the procession directly in front of the deacon or priest, as they are, once more, the ministers of the sacrament.

After the entrance of the ministers (and, perhaps, the groom and his attendants) comes the entrance of the attendants and couple (or whichever attendants and member of the couple did not already enter). The attendants walk in (customarily with the groomsmen escorting the bridesmaids, though those rules for gender roles are not kept as strictly anymore). If the attendants are coming in two by two, then, when they reach the chancel steps, they bow to the altar and then split to take their places. A flower girl and/or ring bearer can either be the first of the attendants to enter or the last of the attendants before those to be married.

For the entrance of the bride (or the couple), often a different piece of music is chosen—however, the parson must stress that in a church liturgy the rubrics are quite clear: "The words of anthems are to be from Holy Scripture, or from this Book, or from texts congruent with them."[8] If instrumental music is substituted, it also should come from a context congruent with Scripture or the prayer book. For instance, it is inappropriate to use music such as Wagner's "Bridal Chorus" from *Lohengrin* or Mendelssohn's "Wedding March" from *A Midsummer Night's Dream* as both have pagan—not Christian—settings. For a worship service, Wagner seems particularly inappropriate: the bridegroom in the opera is attacked in the bridal chamber and finally banished from the earth because the bride breaks a promise not to ask his identity; she, in turn, dies![9] The Mendelssohn march is not much better. It was composed for the wedding of Theseus, the Duke of Athens, to Hippolyta, the mythological queen of the Amazons, along with the other two reconciled couples at the end of the play, all of whom have gone through an experience of forced engagements, magical love potions, and the transformation of one of the characters into a man with the head of a donkey.[10] This is surely not the atmosphere appropriate for a Christian wedding. Thankfully, there are several wonderful pieces of music that can be used for a wedding that also fit with the expectations of the prayer book.

If only one member of the couple enters at this point, that person is customarily escorted by a parent or other supportive friend or family member. If both parents wish to enter at this point, then one parent walks in front and the other escorts the person to be married. It is tradition for the people to stand at this entrance and a fine approach is to invite the parents already seated to stand when they see the person (or couple) entering, which signals for all else to stand.

Once all are assembled, the priest steps to the center of the chancel steps, with the verger or other assistant holding the book, and begins with the exhortation and declaration of consent. At the words "this man

---

8. *1979 Book of Common Prayer*, 14.
9. This is a summary of act 3 of the opera. See Wagner, *Lohengrin*, 57–77.
10. See Shakespeare, *Midsummer Night's Dream*.

THE SOLEMNIZATION OF MATRIMONY

and this woman," the Sarum Manual has the note "*Hic respiciat sacerdos personas suas*," indicating the priest might turn the head slightly to each of the parties as they are mentioned. The charge "I require" is said in a serious voice to the couple coming to be married and not in a voice that would indicate the question is a foolish jest. Nor is it said to all those gathered like the earlier part of the exhortation. In our prayer book, the declaration of consent not only asks each individual if they wish to be married but further asks those who witness the vows if they will "do all in your power to uphold these two persons in their marriage."[11] The response should be a hearty "we will," and the attendants (having been instructed during the rehearsals) can lead that response.

If there is a presentation or giving in marriage, it happens at this point, according to the instructions on p. 437. Every effort should be made so that this feels like the joyous presentation of a loved one, similar to the role a sponsor plays in confirmation, and not the exchange of property. Those responding to the presentation or giving away should be clearly instructed that the response is "I do," as we always speak for ourselves in liturgy and never for others (unless sponsoring someone who cannot speak for themselves). For an exuberant father to respond, "Her mother and I," not only is contrary to the rubrics but is a usurpation of the mother's own voice. After the presentation, a greeting in the form of an embrace is most appropriate. There is no need for a convoluted placing of the bride's hand in that of the groom—if she does not yet know how to hold his hand, then clearly they are not yet ready to be wed! A hymn, psalm, or anthem may follow here, if the couple wants extra music, though it often works best to move directly to the ministry of the word, which begins with the salutation and collect of the day.

The couple then faces the altar, holding hands (at this point if they are wearing gloves, they will have been removed), as the priest says the salutation and turns to the altar to say the collect of the day. After this prayer, all should go to their places for the readings and sermon. If there is room in the choir stalls, this is an ideal choice. Otherwise, the attendants can file into the first pews of the nave and the couple can take special chairs set up for them at the front of the nave. If the wedding is a shorter one—say, with one lesson and a brief homily—then all may remain standing throughout. Interestingly the rubrics do not require a sermon

---

11. *1979 Book of Common Prayer*, 425.

in the marriage rite and permit an "other response to the Readings."[12] However, most couples will prefer a brief homily. This should, like all sermons, be focused on the grace of God as made manifest in the sacrament, in the context of the couple and the readings selected. The homily at a wedding is an excellent opportunity for the parson to address a room full of people who often have little experience of the church (or, perhaps more accurately, very little positive experiences of the church). This opportunity should not be squandered by a homily that is over long, sentimental, or clearly canned. Rather, if one speaks authentically and persuasively about the grace of marriage as an example of the self-giving love of God displayed in Christ, those gathered will be grateful and perhaps even curious to learn more.

After the sermon, the priest leads the couple in a small procession to the altar for the marriage proper. If there is room, the attendants may join them at the altar. If there is not much room, then just the primary legal witnesses of the couple should go with them. They face each other and, in turn, take the right hand of the other and say the vows. They should be instructed that the hand is extended, palm down, for the other to take and grasp. One is not shaking hands to buy a used Toyota. The priest leads the vows, using short phrases that each individual can easily repeat. They loose hands after each vow to emphasize the equality of the couple, as each takes hands and makes vows. The priest generally has to whisper "loose hands" after each vow, or the couple will forget.

If there is a blessing of rings (which almost always is the case), the rings may be set on the open prayer book of the priest, who can then go to the altar, place the rings upon it, and pronounce the blessing. The rings are then returned to the book and held out to the couple for the exchange. Whoever spoke first in the vows, the other should speak first in the giving of rings. The couple should be advised in the rehearsal to put the ring on the ring finger as far as it will easily go (generally, up to the middle knuckle) and then when they drop hands, the person who received the ring may discretely push the ring the rest of the way on. Fingers have been known to swell slightly with anxiety and the picture of one pushing a ring on their beloved's finger is far from ideal.

The priest then joins the right hand of the couple (one palm up and one palm down, remembering that we are not buying a car) and traditionally wraps the joined hands with a stole. This is where the term

---

12. *1979 Book of Common Prayer*, 426.

"tying the knot" comes from. The couple is pronounced as married and the people respond, once more, with a hearty amen, led by the attendants.

The priest then takes the stole back from the couple, puts it back around her or his neck, and invites the people to stand. The priest then steps to the side and invites the beginning of the prayers with the introduction to the Lord's Prayer (unless Communion is to follow, in which case the Lord's Prayer is omitted here and the rite proceeds immediately to the prayers for the couple). At that point, it is fitting for all to face the altar, including the couple who may hold hands as they recite the words our Lord has taught us to say. After the Lord's Prayer, the person leading the prayers for the couple should immediately go to the lectern to lead those prayers.

After the prayers, the priest returns to the center of the altar and the couple kneels for the nuptial blessing. They then stand as the priest invites the exchange of peace, which the couple customarily begins with a kiss. However, all should be instructed at the rehearsal to greet one another with a sign of Christ's peace at this point, after the couple have kissed.

If there is no Communion following, the priest may make brief announcements, present the couple (using whatever form the couple requests, noting that few will want the older traditional Mr. and Mrs. John Smith) after which they exit the church, often to a joyous postlude or anthem. The couple should have the entire aisle to exit, after which the attendants form up, couple by couple, reverence the altar and turn to exit, giving each couple within the attendants roughly half the aisle before the next goes. Last to exit will be the ministers and priest, who will go to whatever place is set aside for signing the marriage license.

If Communion is to follow, then announcements should still be made, which should include instructions about Communion for those who are unfamiliar. It is fitting that the couple bring forward the bread and wine at the offertory and also are the first to receive the Sacrament after the ministers at the altar. The rest of the liturgy is according to the Communion rite, with the note that after the dismissal there may be a presentation of the couple and an exit in the order described above.

If there are three priests, the best plan is, perhaps, for one to take the marriage rites, the second to celebrate Holy Communion (the first and third acting as deacon and eucharistic minister), and the third to give the sermon. If there is no Eucharist, it would be best for one priest to take the first part of the service and for the other to go to the altar to take the last part. The first priest would then precede the second to the sanctuary and would stand to one side, facing across the sanctuary, for the marriage proper. The third priest would give the sermon in the middle part of the service and may also join the other two in the sanctuary for the marriage proper, standing on the other side of the sanctuary so that the priest leading the marriage proper is in the center, with an assisting cleric on each side.

THANKSGIVING FOR THE BIRTH OR ADOPTION OF A CHILD

The original *Parson's Handbook* included instructions for the rite of the "Churching of Women."[13] This rite has its origins in the Levitical requirements that considered a woman unclean after childbirth for forty days after the birth of a male child or eighty days after the birth of a female child, after which an offering for purification was made according to the rules in Lev 12. (Thus, the origin of the Feast of the Presentation of our Lord in the temple, commonly known as Candlemas, always falls forty days after Christmas day for this reason). However, in the Christian sense, the worry was not ritual defilement—sin having been washed away in baptism—but a blessing of the mother after a time of rest when she is finally ready to rejoin the community. This has not always been clear or agreed upon and, indeed, the Canons of Hippolytus from the fourth century refer to a rite of purification after childbirth.[14] This distinction was drawn as early as the sixth century, though, by Pope Gregory I, who insisted that defilement was not caused by childbirth and that the churching of women should not, thus, be about separating them from the church but blessing them after the experience of giving birth to a child.[15] It should further be noted that this rite was kept regardless of whether the child survived childbirth or not.

Dearmer's original instructions for this rite placed it after the instructions for the ministration to the sick. Our current prayer book, however, sets the new rite, with a clearer name articulating the true purpose, after the rite of holy matrimony. It also broadens the rite to be used in the case of the adoption of a child as well. The rubrics on p. 439 indicate a preference for this rite to be observed on a Sunday Eucharist, ideally the first one the new parents attend with their new child.

---

13. Dearmer, *Parson's Handbook*, 423–25.
14. Hippolytus, *Canons of Hippolytus*, 20.
15. Bede, *Ecclesiastical History*, 81–83. See also Hatchett, *American Prayer Book*, 441.

After the prayers of the people, the family should join the priest at the altar. The priest addresses the congregation first, with a different address given for the birth of a child than for adoption. The address for an adoption is followed by an official taking of the child as their own, with the child also being invited to speak, if old enough to do so, taking the parents as their own. The priest, then, "holding or taking the child by the hand, gives the child to" the parents, using language that connects the adoption of the child to our own adoption as children of God by grace.[16] Afterwards, whether thanksgiving for a birth or for an adoption, the rite continues with an act of thanksgiving, with both the *Magnificat* and Ps 116 or 23 being suggested. The priest then says a concluding prayer and may add other prayers among those offered on pp. 444–46 that fit the specific circumstance. The rite concludes with a blessing of the family, after which the priest invites the exchange of the peace.

One of the unfortunate choices in the revision of the rite to its current form is the elimination of a ritual acknowledgment following the loss of a child during pregnancy or through childbirth. Though this was likely done because the desire was to place the rite within the joyous context of the return to the community with a new child, by eliminating the ritual return after a mother has lost a child through miscarriage or stillbirth, the prayer book has, as a result, made that profound grief all the more invisible and unspoken to the faith community.

Thankfully, thirty years after the revision of the prayer book, volume 5 of *Enriching Our Worship* was published with supplemental liturgical materials related to childbearing, childbirth, and loss. While this handbook has generally focused on the rites of our prayer book, as the quality of the supplemental materials our church has authorized is, shall we say, uneven at best, in the area of the loss of a child, these supplemental materials are absolutely essential for giving a ritual context through which grieving parents can pray to receive God's grace and loving care in the prayers of the church. This slender volume includes the following:

- A liturgy for healing after any kind of painful or challenging experience related to pregnancy or childbirth, as would be experienced with a small gathering at home, in the hospital, or in another private setting[17]

---

16. *1979 Book of Common Prayer*, 441.
17. *Childbearing, Childbirth, and Loss*, 11–13.

The Twenty-First-Century Parson's Handbook

- Private devotions for individuals, couples, families, or small groups on, which could be printed out and shared with the family[18]
- Prayers of blessing for a pregnant woman[19]
- A specific rite for mourning the loss of a pregnancy that does an admirable job of carrying the grief of this moment and offering comfort through prayer and Scripture[20]
- A liturgy for repentance and reconciliation for an abortion intended for those who might have regret for an abortion they wish they had not had[21] —though it must be stressed that in no way should this be used to shame those who went through this tragic and difficult experience, it's existence is for women who may desire it of their own accord
- A more public service of lament and remembrance for loss through miscarriage, stillbirth, abortion, placing for adoption, or inability to conceive[22]

The remaining parts of the book have other liturgies and prayers with which the parson should be familiar. The more painful side of childbirth—including infertility, miscarriage, stillbirth, and adoption—remains largely hidden and out of sight of the community in our own time. These rites enable the priest to gently envelop the experience with the prayers of the church so that those who walk this path know they do not walk alone.

Here, perhaps, a word should be said as well about the observance of Mother's Day and Father's Day. Neither of these days are feasts of the church and yet they have become so very common in our culture that the priest can hardly ignore them. At the same time, modern customs like giving a rose to each mother should be studiously avoided. After all, that mother could be sitting near another person whose mother was abusive

---

18. *Childbearing, Childbirth, and Loss*, 14–18.
19. *Childbearing, Childbirth, and Loss*, 19–21.
20. *Childbearing, Childbirth, and Loss*, 21–26.
21. *Childbearing, Childbirth, and Loss*, 27–30.

22. Though a more public liturgy at the church, this is not the same as the Sunday celebration of the thanksgiving for the birth or adoption of a child. It has similarity in that it would be an appropriate rite for the first time the family returns to the church building but, given the grief and pain, would best be observed with the family alone (along with any invited friends) rather than at a Sunday morning liturgy. *Childbearing, Childbirth, and Loss*, 31–38.

or someone struggling with infertility who has longed to be a mother and cannot. Simply to celebrate mothers or fathers, without pastoral attention to the multiplicity of experiences people bring to these days, can make the church seem uncaring and unaware. The priest then loses an opportunity to speak words of healing grace. The following prayers are ones I have adapted from a variety of resources over the years:

> *A Mother's Day thanksgiving*: Knowing that Mother's Day touches everyone differently, we offer this thanksgiving: To those who gave birth this year to their first child—we celebrate with you. To those who lost a child this year or those who still feel the ache of loss from years before—we weep with you. To those who are in the trenches with little ones every day and wear the badge of food stains—we appreciate you. To those who experienced loss this year through miscarriage, failed adoptions, or running away—we mourn with you. To those who walk the hard path of infertility, fraught with pokes, prods, tears, and disappointment—we walk with you. Forgive us when we say foolish things. We don't mean to make this harder than it is. To those who are foster moms, mentor moms, and spiritual moms, no matter your gender identity—we need you. To those who have warm and close relationships with your children . . . or your own mother—we celebrate with you. To those who have disappointment, heart ache, and distance with your children . . . or your own mother—we sit with you. To those who lost their mothers this year or who still feel the hole in their lives from loss long ago—we grieve with you. To those who experienced abuse at the hands of your own mother—we acknowledge your experience. To those who lived through driving tests, medical tests, the testing of arguments impossible to win, and the overall testing of motherhood—we are better for having you in our midst. To those who will have emptier nests in the upcoming year—we grieve and rejoice with you. And to those who are pregnant with new life, both expected and surprising—we anticipate with you. This Mother's Day, we walk with you. Mothering is not for the faint of heart and we have real warriors in our midst. We remember you and we ask God's blessings upon you, through the name of Jesus Christ, our Mother, who nourishes us with pure milk and gathers all children to God's heart. Amen.[23]

---

23. The original version of this is lost to my memory, but I have also adapted it several times over the years.

A Father's Day prayer: We give our thanks, Creator God, for the fathers in our lives. Fatherhood does not come with a manual and reality teaches us that some fathers excel while others struggle. We ask for your blessings for fathers of all types—and for your forgiveness where it is needed. This Father's Day we remember the many sacrifices fathers make for their children and families, and the ways—both big and small—they lift children to achieve dreams those children thought were beyond reach. So too, we remember all those who have helped fill the void when fathers pass early or are absent—grandfathers and uncles, brothers and cousins, teachers, pastors and coaches—and the women of our families whose love so often fills in the gaps others may leave behind. For those who are fathers, whether through blood or through love, we ask for wisdom and humility in the face of the task of parenting. Give them the strength to do well by their children and by you. For those who long to be fathers, we ask for your strength as they dream the dream of Abraham—lead them to the joy of children in the way you would have them serve, whether through birth, adoption, or the choice to love and mentor others with wisdom and grace. For those whose fathers were abusive or absent, whose failings—whether through choice or disease—left wounds that are deep, we pray for your healing grace. Bring us the balm from Gilead. For those who have lost their fathers, and those fathers who have lost their children, we ask for your peace and the confidence of the resurrection. Keep our fathers who have died in your care until we see them again. Above all, help us rejoice in your fatherhood toward us, your adopted children through Christ, and give us grace to spread that love in a broken and hurting world. In Your Holy name, O God, we pray. Amen.[24]

Both birth and death are transient and challenging experiences—the church walks alongside people at times when the line between life and death can seem as slender as a knife's edge. The parson should seek to walk that line faithfully, not shirking from people in their grief or joy because of uncertainty about what to say but instead claiming the rites of the church and bringing them to bear on whatever pastoral situation arises.

---

24. This prayer is an adaptation and expansion of an originally shorter prayer for the day written by Rev. Dr. Chuck Currie. See Currie, "For Father's Day."

15

Confession, Unction, and Last Rites

THERE IS A DEEP connection between physical and spiritual health that is often missed in our own time. When the paralytic's friends brought him to Jesus for healing in the Gospels,[1] our Lord's first act was to forgive the man's sins, not to heal him. Related to this is the reality that in ancient times there was often a desire to connect sinfulness with a lack of health. Jesus, though, would resist those absolute connections. Thus, for example, when Jesus and his disciples encounter a man born blind in John 9, the disciples ask whose sin—that of the man or of his parents—caused the blindness. But Jesus responds, "Neither this man nor his parents sinned; he was born blind so that God's works might be revealed in him" (v. 3).

In the history of the church, the focus has gone back and forth. In the ninth century, there was an effort to revive anointing with oil—but for remission of sins instead of healing.[2] In the centuries that followed, rites of penitence multiplied, and unction began to be reserved only to the end of life in what is known as extreme unction. By the late Middle Ages, the Sarum office included an exhortation with the essential theme that "sickness is God's chastisement to correct sinful humanity."[3] In modern times, the movement has been to remove the connection between illness and sin, and in the twentieth century, there was often a strong desire to separate the medical from the spiritual.

---

1. A version of this story is found in all three Synoptic Gospels, speaking to its meaningfulness to the early Christian community. It can be found in Matt 9:1–8, Mark 2:1–12, and Luke 5:17–26.

2. Hatchett, *American Prayer Book*, 460.

3. Hatchett, *American Prayer Book*, 461.

As is so often the case, we may have swung too far in favor of a complete separation. The medical profession is increasingly aware of the spiritual dynamics of illness, just as we are more aware of physical ailments that can result in behavior formerly called sin but for which there is likely a decreased level of culpability and choice involved. Thus, in navigating these rites, both pastoral sensitivity and perspective are needed. Sometimes a person might be desirous of the sacrament of healing but, as the rubric allows, might also need to make a special confession related to that healing. Other times a person might arrive for the reconciliation of a penitent and, in the course of confession, speak of things that are not truly sins but are forms of sickness of body, mind, or spirit (for example, the illness of addiction). In those cases, the sacrament of healing might be needed as well.

In the end, healing takes a variety of forms and can be needed in different ways. Judicious use of these rites can be a great aid in the spiritual life of the members of our churches and the parson should work to ensure people know these rites exist for them when they are hurting, struggling, or burdened.

CONFESSION—THE RECONCILIATION OF A PENITENT

The earliest forms of penitence and restoration in the church were likely communal experiences, given what we read in Scripture and of the early church. In the Middle Ages this had increasingly become an individual rite with the priest, and confession increasingly became required before Communion. During the Reformation, some reformers sought to remove private confession and restore public forms of penance. In the English Reformation, the practice of private sacramental confession with the priest remained articulated as an option in the exhortation. The exhortation in the current book continues that invitation and should be read at least at the beginning of Lent and perhaps at the beginning of Advent as well. The key section for our purposes is as follows:

> If, in your preparation, you need help and counsel, then go and open your grief to a discreet and understanding priest, and confess your sins, that you may receive the benefit of absolution, and

spiritual counsel and advice; to the removal of scruple and doubt, the assurance of pardon, and the strengthening of your faith.[4]

The key here is twofold: First, that private confession is not required in our church but is intended for those who may need help and counsel as they examine their lives. Here the current adage for confession, "All may, some should, and none must," is likely inaccurate and should be banished from our vernacular. After all, surely almost every Christian, at some point in her or his life, will find themselves burdened and could benefit from opening their "grief to a discreet and understanding priest." To say otherwise is to tell our people that the grief or struggle they are feeling is abnormal, something only some people experience. Surely this is not only far from the truth but is pastorally unwise and unkind. Second, unfortunately not all priests are "discreet and understanding" and so the penitent should be judicious in determining who to choose as a confessor. Questions of the familiarity of the priest with the rite, how often the parson hears confessions, and whether the rite is a regular spiritual discipline in the life of the priest will help the penitent suss out whether a cleric would be suited to this important work and ministry.

The current prayer book is the first in the American church to offer specific forms for private confession. The first form offered is similar to those used in other Anglican provinces and has much in common with the older Roman version of the rite. The second fuller form is drawn from material from the Byzantine form and also aligns with the current Roman revision.[5] The parson should stress, of course, in preaching and teaching, that mutual confession to one another has long been a part of the life of the Christian church since her outset. The forms provided in the prayer book are for when people are specially burdened and could benefit from hearing someone trained in the Christian life offer their own godly admonition and advice.

In preparation for this rite, there are two books to commend to the parson. For years, *Reconciliation: Preparing for Confession in the Episcopal Church* by Martin Smith, published in 1985, has proved an invaluable resource for those who are penitent and desirous of a more fulsome preparation for this rite.[6] Recently, Smith has also worked with Julia Gatta, professor of pastoral theology at the School of Theology at the University

---

4. *1979 Book of Common Prayer*, 317.
5. Hatchett, *American Prayer Book*, 452–453.
6. Smith, *Reconciliation*.

of the South in Sewanee, Tennessee, to prepare a book to guide clergy on the art of hearing confessions, the fruit of which is *Go in Peace: The Art of Hearing Confessions*.[7] The word used in the subtitle is important, because hearing confessions well truly is an art learned with practice and care. One who would like to become a "discreet and understanding priest" well capable of hearing confessions, should prepare appropriately, not only by reading books like those by Father Smith and Mother Gatta, but also by making one's own confession regularly as well.

It is wise to advertise times for regular confession, particularly in the seasons of Lent and Advent, and to include within the listing the note that the sacrament may also be scheduled by appointment with the parson. Though the rubrics are clear that the rite may take place anywhere, the rubrical suggestion is that it be done with the priest sitting within the altar rail and the penitent kneeling nearby. The priest should sit perpendicular to the penitent, with the penitent facing the altar, so it is clear that the confession is one that is made to God, with the priest, on behalf of the church, listening in so as to be able to provide godly counsel. The priest should ask which form the penitent prefers, with the first form being briefer and intended for regular use and the second form being longer and intended for use as a first confession or after some significant life event.

Once the rite is chosen, the priest dons the stole, sits wherever has been decided, and invites the penitent to kneel in quiet prayer and to begin the rite whenever she or he feels ready, using the opening words (which, in both forms, are spoken by the penitent—with the priest joining with the penitent in the second form after the penitent begins).

Within the rite, the rubrics require two things: confession of "all serious sins troubling the conscience" along with "evidence of due contrition."[8] After the confession, the first form invites the priest to "offer counsel, direction, and comfort."[9] The second form invites the priest to "offer words of comfort and counsel."[10] This is a difference without a distinction and what is key is to offer counsel that will help make manifest and concrete the repentance of the penitent. What should be considered are actions that could make right a relationship one has wronged, a

---

7. Gatta and Smith, *Go in Peace*.
8. *1979 Book of Common Prayer*, 446.
9. *1979 Book of Common Prayer*, 447.
10. *1979 Book of Common Prayer*, 450.

situation in which one has caused harm, along with acts of thanksgiving, such as the recitation of a psalm or prayer, in gratitude for forgiveness granted.

The priest must always bear in mind that the seal of confession is morally absolute and is different from the requirements for mandatory reporting in confidential counseling sessions. The absolute nature of the seal is intended so that there is always an entirely safe place where someone who is struggling can come and talk to the priest. If things are told to the priest in the context of the rite that would fall under the requirements for mandatory reporting were this an ordinary pastoral conversation, care should be taken. The priest should pause at the portion where counsel is given and urge the penitent to report their wrongdoing to the authorities as "evidence of due contrition." An extended conversation may be needed but absolution must not be given until the penitent has reported the wrongdoing to the proper authorities. If the penitent refuses, then absolution should not be pronounced, the rite should end immediately, and the penitent implored to make right the wrong that was done. That said, if the penitent will not, the seal must still be maintained.[11]

The essentiality of the seal also means it is important for the parson to be careful who to give one's own confession to and whose confession one should or should not hear. A good rule of thumb is that those in a role of authority and subordinate (such as diocesan bishop and parish priest or parish priest and employee) should seek someone else to hear confession when it is needed. This ensures that what is heard in confession doesn't create issues with multiple relationships and responsibilities.

If someone who has done something that would require mandatory reporting in other circumstances comes to a priest, hopefully the godly counsel of the clergy can be the final tipping point to turning themselves in. If not, perhaps talking with a priest has created an opening in their conscience that drives them later to make the right decision. At the same time, one should be perfectly clear. While seminarians and those in confirmation classes relish this debate and discussion, the experienced parson knows that rarely, if ever, are these the matters brought to confession. After several years of hearing confession, the priest will learn

---

11. This is the teaching of the Episcopal Church and also of other catholic traditions that maintain the sacrament of confession and this teaching is generally affirmed by law in most states. The parson will want to check to ensure when taking a cure in a new state. For more exploration of the seal of the confessional and its application, see Gatta and Smith, *Go in Peace*, 53–55.

that most parishioners share all the same sorts of sins. This can create an attitude of gentleness and humility on the part of the parson, along with an encouragement for all Christians to trust in the loving grace of God.

All words of counsel concluded, the priest then returns to the rite in either form. When pronouncing God's absolution, the priest should place both hands on the head of the penitent (or one hand, if the priest needs to continue holding the book), and make the sign of the cross on the penitent's forehead. Having reminded the penitent that their sins are forgiven, the priest then sends the penitent on their way.

The first time a priest hears someone's confession, it is wise to give them advice for preparation, to remind them of the seal of the rite and why that seal is essential, and also to let them know that this seal means matters disclosed in confession will never, under any circumstances, be brought up to the penitent again after the rite has concluded. The priest is called to practice a blessed forgetfulness. If the penitent should wish to discuss any of the matters again with the priest, either in another offering of the sacrament of reconciliation or in a pastoral conversation, they may of course be instructed that this is their prerogative. However, the priest will always keep it "under the stole" unless the penitent invites otherwise.

UNCTION—THE MINISTRATION TO THE SICK

This fine order has not been known enough by our clergy; even more, though, it is not often enough known by our people. For the very first rubric for the order is clear, "In case of illness, the Minister of the Congregation is to be notified."[12] The prayer book here is gently reminding parishioners that no parson, no matter their gifts, can read minds, and the people should be taught that, if they are ill and desire prayers, they need to notify the minister of the congregation. This rubric dates back to the 1662 prayer book and, apparently, has never ceased being needed.

The idea of the sacraments being precisely seven in number was first formulated about 1150 by Peter Lombard.[13] Our current prayer book keeps to that number by naming the two great sacraments of the gospel as baptism and Communion,[14] and then including the other five traditional sacraments by describing them as "other sacramental rites [that] evolved

---

12. *1979 Book of Common Prayer*, 453.
13. Armentrout and Slocum, *Episcopal Dictionary*, 452.
14. *1979 Book of Common Prayer*, 858.

CONFESSION, UNCTION, AND LAST RITES

in the Church under the guidance of the Holy Spirit."[15] The distinction the catechism draws is that baptism and Communion are a part of the life of every Christian, but, while the other sacramental rites may be a means of grace, they are not necessary in the same way for every person as the sacraments of the gospel.

That this scriptural rite of unction should have been omitted in former times in deference to the prejudices of those reformers who followed Scripture only so far as it pleased them is undoubtedly to be regretted. But it must be remembered that there was some justification for the reaction; for the conversion of unction into a rite only for the dying was a serious abuse. In primitive times it was used for the healing of the sick, and prayers for the recovery of the sick person have not entirely disappeared from any rite, though the purpose of the rite of unction has been lost sight of. It is not to be wondered at that this confusion should have led to the rise of new faith-healing sects.

In earlier ages unction was regarded simply as one of the means of helping people to recover by the use of spiritual power, with the laying on of hands being another. This is in accord with both the New Testament and modern science. There can be little doubt that the ministry of healing will be desired by devout Christians in proportion as this is understood. We sometimes wonder at our small success in recovering to the church great numbers of people who are earnestly looking for the help of religion. It might be worthwhile to remember that the disciples were ordered to convert people by helping them both in body and soul.

Nearly all the prayers and rubrics for the original version in the 1662 prayer book are to be found in the Sarum Manual. Many of those are also retained in the current rite. Some of the prayers can be traced to almost primitive times. It is a solemn rite that should be used, if possible, as a preparation for Communion, which is the greatest grace and nourishment a sick person can receive (remembering, of course, that Communion always follows unction and never precedes it). The rite is divided into three sections and the parson can choose which ones are needed and appropriate to the context.

The fourth rubric allows for the laying on of hands or anointing to take place in the context of a public service of Holy Eucharist. When this happens, the rubric is clear, once more, that this should precede the distribution of Holy Communion and not follow it. To receive the

---

15. *1979 Book of Common Prayer*, 860–61.

sacrament of unction after having received the Sacrament of Holy Eucharist is to receive the lesser after the greater and most important sacrament of healing—the body and blood of Christ. The prayers and laying on of hands of unction is meant to be preparatory to coming to the altar for the Sacrament of Eucharist and not to occur afterwards. The rubrics recommend that unction take place immediately before the exchange of the peace and this makes good sense at a midweek service of Holy Eucharist and healing. If it is desired to be offered at Sunday liturgies, it can be done during the anthem the choir sings while the alms are collected, either in a side chapel or at the altar. If offered at an early Sunday morning liturgy without music, it can be offered at the rail or in a side chapel in the five minutes before the liturgy begins. When used for a stand-alone offering in the middle of the week, the public version of the rite as provided in the *Book of Occasional Services* is the preferred resource.

Dearmer suggested that when a priest arrived at the house of the person who was sick, as the door was opened, the priest would immediately begin the rite, saying, "Peace be to this house (place), and to all who dwell in it."[16] A more friendly (and likely less jarring) greeting at the door makes sense in most cases. Then, after all are settled, a moment of silent prayer or recollection is needed before the priest begins with the words of peaceful greeting. If the service is to be of a more formal character, the priest puts on a surplice, and a stole also if there will be Communion. A cross may be set up in the room so that the sick person can look upon it. It is generally most convenient for the priest to sit for most of the rite so as to be on the same level as the person being visited.

If the full rite is used, the priest begins with the ministry of the word, selecting from the suggested Scripture readings which ones may be most helpful to the person in need of healing prayer. In particular, Ps 91 is excellent and can well be recited by the parson or by all those gathered in unison. A comment is permitted after any of the readings and is a good time to share why the priest chose the ones that were read. The rubrics then invite prayers according to the occasion. While extemporaneous prayer is, of course, appropriate, the parson will be grateful for the many fine prayers suggested in the prayer book, beginning on p. 458. A few may be selected that fit with the pastoral situation.

The rubric about confession has been sometimes neglected and sometimes overstrained in the past. In the older rubric, the priest is

---

16. Dearmer, *Parson's Handbook*, 415.

directed to "move" those who are troubled in conscience.[17] Pastoral sensitivity and instinct should be one's guide.

If the priest does not travel with an oil stock containing oil previously blessed for healing, a small amount of pure olive oil from the household can now be put into a very small bowl (no more than a teaspoon or so is needed), and the oil is then blessed using the form provided. In the same way that there is much benefit to recognizing the bread and wine at Eucharist to be the same that is found at table at home, it is good to see that the healing oil is the normal oil of everyday use, blessed by the rites of the church and set apart for healing.

It may be helpful to have a small card with this rite printed upon it to give to those that one visits or to hand them a small prayer book with which to follow along. Much of the rite will include language that is familiar to the average churchgoer (the general confession and the Lord's Prayer can often both be said from memory). However, items like the anthem,[18] which begins the laying on of hands, is unlikely to have been memorized and so help in knowing what to say when will likely be appreciated. The Psalm *In te, Domine, speravi*, with its antiphon *Salvator mundi salva nos*, was the beginning of the office of unction in the older books as well. That is maintained here in the anthem (which the astute person will recognize from the Good Friday liturgy as well).

Following the anthem, the priest chooses one of the forms of prayers for the laying on of hands and then, if using anointing oil, dips a thumb in the oil and makes the sign of the cross on the forehead while saying the words for unction. If the forehead is injured in some way that the anointing would cause pain, then other traditional places are the chest or the back of a hand.[19] The final prayer is optional but, if used, is a good time to use a small tissue or cloth to wipe any excess oil off the thumb. If the rite is not continuing with Holy Communion, the priest invites all to say the Lord's Prayer and then says a final concluding prayer.

COMMUNION WITH THE SICK

If it is desired to commune the sick person, the rubrics permit two options. Either the Sacrament may be consecrated in a service of Holy

---

17. *1662 Book of Common Prayer*, 183.
18. *1979 Book of Common Prayer*, 455.
19. Hatchett, *American Prayer Book*, 465.

Eucharist that begins with the peace and/or the offertory, naturally using bread and wine from the home of the person being visited for the eucharistic elements. The current book was the first American prayer book to restore reservation of the Sacrament for the purpose of communing those who are sick, as well as being the first to allow for Communion in one kind. Thus, the second option is to bring the Sacrament that has been consecrated at a previous eucharistic celebration of the parish.

As to the rubrical allowance for Communion in one kind, a bit more should be said. Theologically, the church has long believed that Christ's full presence subsists in both the bread and the wine. The former requirement of always communing in both kinds was in response to the withholding of the chalice prior to the Reformation. The allowance of Communion in one kind only in this rite is not to restore that refusal but, rather, to give latitude for times "when it might be difficult or impossible for the sick person to receive one or the other of the eucharistic elements."[20] The rubric should not be used by an overly anxious parson to revive the medieval withholding of one of the forms of the Sacrament from God's people.

If celebrating Eucharist in the home, then the proper vestments should still be worn (amice, alb, and stole being the minimum). The chasuble may be dispensed with. If desired, a simple set of vestments, such as a linen chasuble and stole, could be kept apart for celebrating Communion in the home of a sick person. A table should be made ready in the house, covered with a clean white cloth (according to the rubric) that the parson may provide, and on it should customarily be stood a cross and two lighted candles (though these are not, of course, rubrically necessary). The eucharistic vessels should then be placed upon the home altar, with bread and wine (ideally from the person's home) set nearby. Care should be taken only to set out as much bread and wine as is necessary for the number of people who will receive. All those in the home, including those visiting—family members and any caretakers—should be invited to join in the service and to receive Communion, if they would like.

It is often best for someone from the altar guild to join in this visit and to take responsibility for setting up the home altar. This has several benefits. The person who is ill gets another visitor from the church. The altar is prepared by someone with real regular understanding. And one will find that, when invited, members of the altar guild see this as a great

---

20. Hatchett, *American Prayer Book*, 467.

honor and not a burden. Then when the priest arrives, there can be time for some pastoral conversation and a period of quiet prayer instead of the hustle and bustle of getting things set up. The first two parts of the ministration of the sick can then be said, followed with the eucharistic rite, as noted above. One should not worry about elaborate ceremonial here, but focus on a plain, reverent, and meaningful celebration.

Since the restoration of reserving the Sacrament for the sick, the practice of celebrating Communion in a person's home has largely gone out of practice. Many a priest will be surprised to be reminded that this is permitted and even preferred (as is generally indicated by listing something first in the rubrics) by the framers. Furthermore, the rubrics of our prayer book make it quite clear that "when persons are unable to be present for extended periods, it is desirable that the priest arrange to celebrate the Eucharist with them from time to time on a regular basis."[21] While bringing the reserved Sacrament is absolutely acceptable, when the sickness is significant or a person has been absent from the community's celebration for quite some time, celebrating the full rite itself can give great meaning and comfort to the Christian.

When the reserved Sacrament is brought to someone, it is preferred to be brought directly after service in which the Holy Mysteries were celebrated. The priest (or lay person who is authorized as a eucharistic visitor) should go straight from the church to the sick person's house. In the case of a visitation by a eucharistic visitor, the best rite to use is the one provided in the 2022 *Book of Occasional Services*.[22] Leaflets with this rite can be prepared in advance and kept near the kits used to prepare Communion for a home visit. The rubrics for that rite suggest that, following the Communion of the people in the church, the eucharistic visitors come forward and be commended with the words:

> In the name of this congregation, I send you forth bearing these holy gifts, that those to whom you go may share with us in the communion of Christ's body and blood. We who are many are one body, because we all share one bread, one cup.[23]

The eucharistic visitor should then respond with amen, as a symbol of their own assent to this charge. They then step to the side for the rest of

---

21. 1979 *Book of Common Prayer*, 396.
22. This rite begins on p. 278.
23. *Book of Occasional Services*, 278.

the liturgy's conclusion and then join the procession at the end of the service, walking in front of the altar ministers.

This practice has much to commend it, as it makes manifest to the congregation the care that we give to one another. Many a lay person has expressed a desire to be trained and licensed for this ministry because they have seen the sending out of a eucharistic visitor on Sundays enough times to feel the Spirit prod them in that direction. The rubrics in the *Book of Occasional Services* also suggest that "it is desirable that other parishioners, relatives, and friends also be present to communicate with the person visited."[24] This can also heighten the sense of connection with one's community when suffering from illness. After all, the isolation created by illness can be one of the most painful aspects of the experience and every effort should thus be made to ensure that those who are sick still feel that they are very much a part of their faith community.

If the priest will be the one to make the visit, the priest will then wear a stole. In many cases it will be found convenient to keep a plain stole of blue or violet silk or linen in the vestry for taking out to people's houses. The color of the vestment is a small consideration, but it may be worthwhile to state that violet or blue is the color for the visitation, and red, the color for the reserved Sacrament, while the color of the day or feast is likely more suitable for chronic cases. Thus, practically any color may be used.

The practice of intinction, i.e., the dipping of the species of bread into the chalice, is sometimes the most convenient way of administering the Blessed Sacrament to the sick. It was not discontinued in the West till the chalice was withdrawn from the laity, and it is still the universal method of communicating the laity in the East, where the clergy always intinct for the laity. Indeed, intinction is sometimes necessary when the celebration of the Eucharist is in the sick person's room, especially if there is danger of infection from the chalice, or if the patient cannot move his head. As noted earlier, intinction by the laity, where multiple person's hands are going in and out of the chalice is by far more infectious than the common cup. In cases of virulent infection, when the common cup might carry a risk it would not have in normal situations, then the priest intincting the bread in the wine and administering the sacrament may be preferred. Sometimes, however, when the sick person cannot receive from the chalice, she or he can still be communicated

---

24. *Book of Occasional Services*, 278.

from it by means of a spoon. And, as noted earlier, the person may also receive in one kind only.

For Communion with the reserved Sacrament, the first two parts of the Ministration to the Sick are followed as laid out above. When it is time for Communion, then a table should be prepared with a clean cloth, at least one candle, and the cruets for the ablutions. The priest lays the pyx or other vessels containing the reserved Sacrament upon the linen cloth. The rite continues using the form provided in Communion under Special Circumstances, beginning with the peace (as there will have already been a reading from Scripture and an opportunity for confession).[25] After leading the recitation of the Lord's Prayer, the priest administers the Sacrament using the same form as in the eucharistic liturgy. The post-communion prayer in Communion under Special Circumstances is identical to the one in Ministration to the Sick, and both rites then conclude with a blessing or dismissal.

The following precautions should be observed with highly infectious cases or during times of pandemic. Avoid visiting dangerous cases of illness with an empty stomach or with lungs exhausted by a quick ascent of stairs. It may be good to take some small food before going out, but above all things the priest should go in a spirit of calmness and faith. In infectious cases, therefore, it is obvious that Communion except with the reserved Sacrament is unsafe. In all infectious cases, the sick person should consume all that remains of the species of wine, and should also, in accordance with the wise ancient practice, consume the ablutions. When the sick person cannot, then any that remains of the Sacrament and also the ablutions should be burnt on the fire or poured into the earth. In all sickness, whether infection is declared or not, the sick person should be communicated last, as the rubric directs, and no one should touch the chalice after that person. Afterwards, care should be taken that the chalice is washed at once inside and out with hot soapy water.

The cassock is an ideal protective garment from the medical point of view, but it should be of silk or other close material. Immediately on leaving a highly infectious patient, it should be taken off, given a good shake, and hung in the air for six hours, and the parson should air the rest of her or his clothes by a short walk. Indeed, priests should never enter their own, or any other house, until their clothing has aired out sufficiently. In cases of virulent infection, the cassock and any other

---

25. *1979 Book of Common Prayer*, 398.

vestments should be promptly laundered. It is best to dispense with a burse altogether and to boil the corporals and purificator or, instead, to use a white paper cloth that can afterwards be burned. The vestments should be of linen, for preference white or blue, and always washed after use. In virulent infections, the priest should take care not to inhale the breath of the patient and may wear a medical grade face mask and keep her or his hand from contact with the hand of the patient. It may be wise to do the entire rite outdoors and with some distance between the priest and the patient. The priest should never eat any food in an infectious house. No matter the virulence of the illness, after leaving the sick room, the priest should wash hands at once (and should, of course, have washed hands before visiting as well, to protect the patient). Soap and water, used thoroughly, scrubbed for a good half minute, then thoroughly rinsed with water, is appropriate.

These precautions are not, of course, only to protect the priest but are particularly important because clergy often visit many people who are immunocompromised. For a priest to be the source of transmission of infection would be contrary to everything essential to pastoral ministry. It is also for this reason that the priest should take care regularly to ensure one is up to date with vaccinations, especially the influenza vaccine, the vaccine for the COVID-19 virus, and any other vaccines currently recommended by medical professionals.

LAST RITES—MINISTRATION AT THE TIME OF DEATH

As Christians who believe, as the prayer book says in the proper preface for Eucharist at a funeral, that at death "life is changed, not ended,"[26] it is a primitive part of Christianity to accompany those who die with appropriate rites and prayers for this change. As Hatchett notes, the practice of communing those who are dying "as a means of *viaticum* (sustenance for the journey) seems to have been regarded as an ancient custom."[27] It also must be acknowledged that the form of last rites provided in the prayer book's Ministration at the Time of Death lacks the fullness of the church's tradition, when seen on its own and not put together with the other prayer book rites that would rightfully form the full liturgies offered on the deathbed. While the church has thankfully recovered the

---

26. *1979 Book of Common Prayer*, 349, 382.
27. Hatchett, *American Prayer Book*, 472.

sacrament of unction from its older use only as extreme unction at death, the need for extreme unction has not disappeared, and to restore one form of unction while now neglecting the other would simply be to repeat the mistakes of the past.

A proper understanding of Christian healing will help in this area and will also clarify the intent of the prayers and rites that are normally offered in the Ministration to the Sick; that is, there is a difference between "healing" and "cure." While it cannot be denied that the ministrations and prayers of the church have, at times, resulted in inexplicable cure and recovery, that is often the exception and not the norm. Thus, most of our prayers for those who are sick understand healing as being the infusion of God's strength and a sense of God's care during the course of an illness. And, in the end, there are circumstances where the true healing event would be for the individual to pass from this mortal life into the next—death being the final healing of the body. It is with this in mind that the last rites are offered, with an understanding that the healing we are now asking for is no longer the recovery of the individual (though it is curiously common for someone to rally after receiving last rites before they succumb to an illness) but for God's grace to suffuse this person and strengthen them as their life is changed from what it was here on earth to that which it will be after they die.

Similar to when a person is ill, the first rubric requires that the parson be notified when a person is near death "in order that the ministrations of the Church may be provided."[28] The fullest form of these ministrations, though, do not consist only of the prayer, litany, and concluding prayer that follows on those pages. Rather, the parson should instead offer the full version of Ministration to the Sick, including the third part of Communion, as instructed above. The prayers that begin on p. 462 are then what are offered during the section of Ministration to the Sick where the rubric reads, "Prayers may be offered according to the occasion."[29] Given the way this is structured in the prayer book, those participating should either be given a card or leaflet with everything placed together, or a small prayer book can be given to each, with the priest directing those gathered to the proper page, as needed, throughout the ministrations. Thus, the full form of the rite would be as follows:

---

28. *1979 Book of Common Prayer*, 462.
29. *1979 Book of Common Prayer*, 454.

- Words of greeting to begin Ministration of the Sick are said.[30]
- Next comes the ministry of the word, using any of the Scriptures suggested on pp. 453–54, or others that may be appropriate. The opportunity for brief comment should not be avoided, though brevity is often key in this moment as the rite and the Sacrament is where the deepest comfort is found.
- At this point the rite turns to the prayer, litany, and concluding prayer in the Ministration at the Time of Death, beginning on p. 462. The litany found in the second volume of *Enriching Our Worship* may be easier for use than the one found in the prayer book, as it has a consistent response that can be easily taught and remembered.[31]
- Time is then given for a general confession,[32] or an invitation for a last confession, using the rite for the reconciliation of a penitent.[33] If the reconciliation of the penitent is used, all should exit the room except for priest and penitent until that rite is concluded.
- The rite then returns to the laying on of hands and anointing, beginning on p. 455. Here the opening anthem sharing a use on Good Friday, when our Lord died, makes the power of that connection most manifest. After the anointing, the priest says the concluding prayer of that portion of the rite.
- For the Holy Communion, if the person near death has strength for a full celebration of the eucharistic prayer, this can be deeply meaningful and comforting to all involved. However, at this point, that is often unlikely and the sense of exhaustion and grief by those sitting near the deathbed may be profound. Thus, in most circumstances the priest will continue with Communion using the form for Communion under Special Circumstances, beginning with the peace on p. 398. Care should be taken that enough bread and wine is brought for all those gathered to commune with the person near death. If the person near death is unable to eat or drink, or is now unconscious, then a small drop of wine is placed on the lips or in the open mouth—taking care that it is a small enough drop not to

---

30. *1979 Book of Common Prayer*, 453.
31. *Enriching our Worship*, 102–3.
32. *1979 Book of Common Prayer*, 454.
33. *1979 Book of Common Prayer*, 447, 449.

cause further difficulties. The priest then says the appointed post-communion prayer and concludes with a blessing or dismissal.

If those keeping watch at the deathbed do not have a prayer book handy, then one should be left with them marked to the commendatory prayer on p. 465 to be said when the person dies. Of course, the priest will repeat those prayers at the funeral itself, but friends and family saying them at the time of death often provides a helpful ritual container to hold the grief of that moment.

If the priest was unable to visit before the person died, according to the rubrics, it is still appropriate for the priest to come together with friends and family prior to the funeral.[34] Then the litany at the time of death or the prayers for a vigil may be used.[35]

---

34. *1979 Book of Common Prayer*, 465.
35. *1979 Book of Common Prayer*, 465.

16

The Burial of the Dead

IN DEARMER'S TIME, HE believed nothing needed more reform than the manner of conducting funerals. I would daresay that in our own time much advancement has been made thanks to the revisions of the current prayer book and capable instruction of clergy in formation. Dearmer's key principle to all who live among the poor, as well as to those who live among the rich, is the reduction of secular pomp. To secure this, he added a second principle—the increase of sacred pomp. Something meaningful must be offered on these sad occasions. If the church does not supply what the mourners crave, the world will step in with the miserable trappings of its pride. It must be within the experience of every parson that even those who dislike "ritual" on other occasions are most grateful for its comfort at this time, when comfort is so much needed.

At the same time, the church's pomp should not be copied from that of the world, as still happens from time to time in our churches and even more commonly in the broader culture, where the undertakers are allowed practically to take over the church for the day. The church must assert her duty to, in a paraphrase of the title of Tom Long's excellent book, accompany their deceased siblings in Christ to the grave with singing.[1] What is essential at every funeral is that one would be hard pressed to tell whether the deceased was a guest in the church's kitchen ministry

---

1. See Long, *Accompany Them with Singing*. Though not a book on Anglican traditions surrounding funerals, Long does admirable service to the broader church in charting the history and, even more important, the essential points and goals of a Christian funeral. Much of it can well be applied in our own tradition, using the rites of the prayer book as a guide.

or a wealthy and longtime member and benefactor of the congregation. What truly matters in the end is our state as a baptized Christian, and just as death is the great equalizer of all people, baptism is what should mark every person's funeral as the most important identifier.

PREPARATION FOR THE RITE

When a member of the parish dies, the priest has hopefully already been informed, the prayer book having instructed Christians to inform the minister both upon illness and upon the approach of death. However, sometimes death strikes at times that are unexpected. Regardless, the first rubric at the beginning of both rites for the burial of the dead reiterate that the minister should be informed and that arrangements should be made in consultation with the minister of the congregation. Once informed, time should be found for the parson and family of the bereaved to meet and plan for the funeral rites of the church. Doing this as soon as possible avoids the awkward times when a family might form plans for a funeral liturgy that are actually outside of what is permitted and envisioned by the rites of the church.

Whereas earlier prayer books had understood that burial may happen either in the church or at the grave, the new book stresses not only that "baptized Christians are properly buried from the church" (and not, it should go without saying, from a funeral home) but also that the funeral should be held at a time when the congregation can be present.[2] Even families who might desire a smaller funeral should be gently reminded that no liturgy is a private event and that those who wish to join them in mourning and prayer should be allowed and enabled to attend.

The current prayer book was also the first to recognize cremation, and it should be noted that permission is given for the funeral and committal to take place prior to cremation. As any priest will tell you, a funeral with a body present is a very different experience from a funeral with ashes present. To bring the body to the church for the funeral and committal and then afterwards to cremate the body before placing it in its final resting place is not only expressly permitted by the rubrics, but it also helps the mourners feel they have truly said goodbye to the person they love and not the ashes that remain after that person was cremated.

---

2. *1979 Book of Common Prayer*, 468, 490.

When the priest meets with the family, it is helpful to clarify that our culture has confused three distinct aspects of saying goodbye to someone who died: the time of remembrance, the commendation to God in a funeral, and the time of celebration. The current "Celebration of the Life" style of funeral is far from the proper Christian funeral and often has more to do with a premature hagiography than it does with marking someone's death by commending them to God through Scripture, song, and prayer.

And yet, of course, human nature usually requires all three for a full grieving process. The best time for sharing of memories is at the visitation before the service or the reception or wake following the service. This has the benefit of giving more than just one or two people a chance to speak. It also has the added benefit of the family hearing much more than they would if one (or several) of their number gave remembrances within the rite of the funeral. Furthermore, the prayer book does not permit a eulogy or remembrance within the rite for the Burial of the Dead. If the family is insistent, then it could be suggested that a very brief remembrance might make up a part of the sermon (as that is at the discretion of the parson) or that one or two brief remembrances could be offered from the lectern before the liturgy begins (as the rubrics do not govern what happens before the rite). Both of these, however, should be discouraged so that a fuller and better way of remembering the deceased can be practiced at a more appropriate time.

One often wishes to celebrate the person who has died and the impact they have had on the lives of others. Once more, this celebration is best kept to the reception or wake. Along those lines, enthusiastic family members may desire special music or poems that are not Christian in nature and therefore not appropriate to the funeral rites of the church. Those are best shared as celebrations and reminders at the reception, which may have a more joyous atmosphere.

The funeral itself is a proclamation of the gospel and a commendation of the deceased to the grace of God revealed in that gospel. The framers of the current prayer book structured the rite as an Easter liturgy, thus marking a change from the former practices of black vestments and requiems with the *Dies irae*. However, in their desire to return funerals to a focus on the hope of the resurrection, the unintended result has sometimes been the denial of grief with the expectation of white vestments and joyous Easter hymns. And yet, a denial of grief was far from their intention in making this liturgical shift. As the note at the end of the rites states:

> This joy, however, does not make human grief unchristian. The very love we have for each other in Christ brings deep sorrow when we are parted by death. Jesus himself wept at the grave of his friend. So, while we rejoice that one we love has entered into the nearer presence of our Lord, we sorrow in sympathy with those who mourn.[3]

Thus, when meeting with a family, it is pastorally sensitive to suss out whether this particular funeral is one that is celebratory and joyful in nature or one that is loaded with a sense of grief and loss, particularly when the death was not the falling asleep of a faithful Christian who lived a full life but actually the robbing of life because of the brokenness of sin, violence, illness, or the world in which we live.

If possible, each parish should have both a set of white or gold vestments (which are already used for Easter) and a set of black or violet vestments (the black which may be kept especially for more somber funerals, along with the Commemoration of all Faithful Departed on All Souls' Day, or the violet which may already be on hand for Lent if the Lenten array is not used). If an alternative set of a more somber tone is not available, the parson will discover that securing a set is the easiest fundraiser ever undertaken. A pall should always be used, and the coffin ought never to be carried into church uncovered. The rubric in this regard is suggestive, saying "it is appropriate" for the pall to be used. However, the rubric requiring the casket to be closed before the service and after the service's conclusion is clear and without doubt.[4] This naturally also means photos should not be set out near the casket. It is doubtful anyone has forgotten who the deceased is and their attention should be on the actual body of the deceased lying in the church, not a photo from another time.

The use of a multiplicity of flowers in church is to be deprecated and should be discouraged in every possible way, short of hurting the feelings of mourners. The best approach is for the same standards used for flowers upon the altar on Sundays to be kept for funerals. This is one of the clear ways of creating a sense of equality in the burial rites of the church. The fashion of covering the coffin with flowers seems to have come in because of the absence of the pall—the natural desire to provide the coffin with some sort of veil found its outlet in this way. Thankfully, the coffin pall frees us from this need. Few people will desire to use flowers once they have seen the beautiful colored pall every church ought to possess.

3. *1979 Book of Common Prayer*, 507.
4. *1979 Book of Common Prayer*, 468, 490.

In church all will be ready—the altar-candles lit (whether there is to be a Eucharist or not) and the funeral candlesticks standing in their places before the chancel steps. The paschal candle is close by where the reception of the body will take place so that it may be lit and accompany the body into the church (see the next section for details). Incense may, if it is desired, be used at funerals. The crucifer will have the funeral cross ready if there be one; if not, then the Lenten cross for a solemn funeral using dark vestments or the ordinary processional cross for a festive funeral using white or gold vestments in appropriate. (Unless, of course, there is but one processional cross in the church, in which case that is the one used.) The taperers will use their ordinary tapers, unless they have lanterns, which are more convenient for outdoor processions and might be used if the procession after the funeral will take the casket outdoors and to the hearse or place of burial.

If there is no administration of the Lord's Supper, the surplice is worn. If there will be a celebration of Eucharist (which there should be and which, thankfully, is now more common in our times), then the priest should wear the amice and albe, along with the other proper eucharistic vestments. At Sarum the canons used to wear the *cappa nigra*, or black choir cope, over their surplices, and the priest might wear the same, or a silk cope (of white, gold, black, or blue), for protection over the albe. Apparels of matching color may be worn with the amices and albes or the albes may be without apparels. A cope for the procession, which is changed into a chasuble for Communion, is most fitting. If proceeding from the burial rite directly to the final resting place of the deceased, then after the dismissal, the priest may exchange the chasuble for the *cappa nigra*, which will be needed at the grave outside. The canterbury cap should be nearby so that it can be carried in procession and donned once the procession exits the church. All may wear their caps for that part of the service that is out of doors, but whenever prayers are said, the cap may be taken off and the head left bare or covered with the coif or skullcap only.

THE BURIAL OF THE DEAD

A Funeral: The Procession to the Church[5]

The prayer book notes that the priest customarily will meet the body and lead it into the church (or towards the grave).[6] The rite for the reception of the body at the door of the church, which begins on p. 466, is essential

---

5. British Museum MS. Add. 35313, f. 159. In this Flemish miniature of the fifteenth century, the herse, covered with pall of bright crimson ornamented with a cross of figured gold, is borne by mourners wearing black hoods; on the torches are scutcheons emblazoned with a coat of arms. Officiant, holding book, in purple cassock, surplice, red stole with a series of gold crosses, crimson cap; over his left arm a gray fur almuce. On his left a figure, also with almuce, in crimson cassock, surplice, bright blue stole with a series of gold crosses. The cap of the figure behind the officiant is black, and he wears a surplice. On his right, at the edge of the picture, a figure in blue cassock, surplice, red stole with gold crosses like the others. The official in the foreground carries a wand and is dressed in rose color and green.

On the right, two banner bearers, and clerk with cross, the latter wearing a crimson cassock and a surplice (or rochet); his cross is golden on a red or brown staff. Both the banner poles are red, and both the banners are of green, bordered with gold rings and edged with red and gold; the oblong picture in the middle of each banner is on a gold ground. The nearest banner bearer is in a blue cassock and a surplice; the farther one is in a green cassock and a sleeveless rochet. The absence of black, with the exception of the mourners' hoods, is conspicuous. In the background are two modest grave crosses.

6. *1979 Book of Common Prayer*, 468.

from a pastoral, theological, and historical standpoint. After saying the prayers of welcome, the paschal candle is lit and placed near the body, unless the procession is to begin immediately.

The procession will go in the usual order: verger, thurifer, crucifer with cross, taperers with candles, choir, eucharistic minister, [deacon,] priest, a member of the congregation bearing the lighted paschal candle, and the body of the deceased. If desired, the family may walk in procession after the priest and before the paschal flame and the body. Often one of them may very well wish to carry the paschal flame for the person who died.

During the procession into the church, the rubrics allow for either the burial anthems appointed in the prayer book or some other hymn, psalm, or suitable anthem at the entrance. Whichever is chosen, the verger will take care that the family is duly seated while the procession continues in the customary manner. The choir will go straight into the chancel, and the crucifer will place the cross in its appropriate place. When the body is placed at the position it will occupy for the liturgy, the lighted paschal candle is placed near it. Normally, the coffin will be laid on the bier outside the chancel gates between the candles, its foot to the east, and the bearers will go to the side. If a hymn is sung at the entrance into the church, then the rubric seems to give permission for the burial anthems to be said as well "by the celebrant standing in the accustomed place" before the liturgy continues.[7]

Once all are in place, the rubrics invite the celebrant to address the congregation and bid their prayers, but this often seems unnecessary as everyone in the church is well aware of the purpose of their gathering. Thus, the liturgy should best continue with the salutation and one of the collects of the day, which can be chosen by the family. After the collect of the day, the priest may add the collect for the bereaved, inserting the names of immediate family members of the deceased, if so desired.

For the liturgy of the word, the scripture readings should be selected by the family and are appropriately read by the laity, as at all celebrations of Eucharist. This is an excellent way to channel the desire to participate away from the multiplication of eulogies and towards the real substantive needs of a Christian funeral. The *Dies irae* was sometimes used as a sequence before the Gospel and may be appropriate at more somber liturgies. The rubrics in Rite Two are gentler with regard to the homily,

---

7. *1979 Book of Common Prayer*, 468, 490.

allowing it to be given either "by the Celebrant, or a member of the family, or a friend."[8] This does give possible allowance for someone other than the priest to speak, but any who speak should be reminded that they are called to give a homily and not a eulogy. That is, it must be someone capable of proclaiming the gospel in the context of the person who died. Following the homily, the priest may invite the recitation of the baptismal creed, that of the holy apostles.

If there is no Communion, the liturgy continues with the Lord's Prayer, the proper prayers of the people, and then one or more of the prayers at the end of the rite.[9] If there is to be a Eucharist, which is most desirable, the liturgy continues with the prayers of the people. Though the form on pp. 480–81 and p. 497 are not required, one doubts whether one of the other forms could be better. The priest says a concluding collect; often the family is invited to choose the one most meaningful among those provided. The priest then invites the exchange of peace and, after the peace is exchanged, begins the offertory with one of the offertory sentences (or, perhaps, a sentence from one of the Scriptures chosen for the day).

If the priest was formerly wearing a cope, then the priest should change into a chasuble after the offertory sentence, while the offertory takes place. There should not, of course, be a collection of alms and gifts during the offertory. However, it is fitting for the family of the deceased to carry forward the bread and the wine for the celebration of Communion. If incense is used in the funeral, the coffin should have been censed by the deacon during the entrance, before the Gospel, during the procession, and after the censing at the offertory.

---

8. *1979 Book of Common Prayer*, 495. Interestingly enough, the rubrics in Rite One on p. 480 aren't as explicitly broad, saying only, "A homily may be preached." However, they can be interpreted similarly to the ones in Rite Two as they don't restrict the homily to the parson.

9. *1979 Book of Common Prayer*, 487–89, 503–5.

The Twenty-First-Century Parson's Handbook

A Funeral: The Lord's Supper[10]

After the eucharistic prayer and Communion of the people, which occur in the normal manner, the priest leads the post-communion prayer and, unless the committal follows immediately in the church, the ministers take their place at the body for the commendation. The crucifer and taperers should stand at the west end of the body, facing the casket (this is an echo of the position they take at baptism and intentionally so). The verger and eucharistic minister should stand on either side of the body, hands folded in prayer. The priest should stand at the chancel steps, with

---

10. British Museum MS. 2468, f. 115. Priest in bright red and gold chasuble, gold apparels; frontal and dorsal of blue and gold, frontlet of gold; embroidered fair linen reaches nearly to the ground at the end of the altar but does not hang over in front; single large corporal of the earlier shape turned back over chalice; two golden candlesticks on altar; no cross; missal on wooden desk. The clerk holds a third taper, and wears a surplice over a red cassock. A chanter wears a rich blue and gold cope; with two other singers in surplices he reads from a large wooden desk fixed on the choir stalls. Herse cloth of blue and gold with red and gold cross, surrounded by seven golden candlesticks. Behind the herse are the mourners, wearing the usual black cloaks and hoods.

the deacon on the right, and, once all are in place, should then begin the commendation.

Afterwards, the priest pronounces the blessing, the deacon pronounces the dismissal, and then the body is born from the church in the same order that the procession came in. Though a hymn is allowed by the rubrics, the congregation will often file out after the family and so the singing will be less than ideal. Thus, the concluding burial anthems during the procession from the church or an appropriate instrumental postlude are the best choice. The funeral pall is removed from the coffin at the church doors.

The priest should walk at the head of the body all the way to the hearse, if used, and then to the grave, constantly saying the prayers of the church, which is why three canticles are offered in addition to the concluding burial anthems.

For those who are veterans, military honors may be desired. If so, those should take place either outside the church or, with a larger congregation, perhaps in the parish hall. They should be clearly separate from the rites of the church. When military honors are used, it is essential that the priest go with the family to the cemetery for the burial so that the church has the last word over a baptized child of God during the committal.

At the grave, it seems generally most convenient for the crossbearer to stand at the foot of the grave, looking west, and the priest to stand at the head, looking east, with the torchbearers holding their torches on either side of the priest's book, the thurifer standing near the grave, and the choir and the mourners grouping themselves as may be most convenient.

It is helpful to bring the committal liturgy on leaflets to the grave. Before it begins, the priest might invite final remembrances or last words, this also being a good time to remember or share items important to the bereaved at that moment. Once all who desire have had a chance to speak, the body is lowered into the ground while the priest says the committal anthems. In some areas, it may be necessary to consult with the funeral home and cemetery in advance to ensure they will be prepared to lower the body at the start of the burial. Unfortunately, many in the previous century have grown accustomed to a burial in a cemetery where the dirt is covered by AstroTurf and any sense of actual burial is strenuously avoided. Christians, however, do not shy away from that which is true, and so we lower the body into the ground comforted by words of anthems. We cast earth upon the grave while the priest confesses our hope in the resurrection.

Anciently the earth was strewn in the form of a cross. It is still the custom to cast it in thrice. If casting the earth in the form of a cross, the dirt is first along the coffin from the head to the midst, then from the foot to the midst, and the third time completing the cross by sprinkling the earth across the coffin in the midst. The rubric does not say this is to be done at the words "earth to earth," but rather implies that it is to be done in such a slow and deliberate manner as to last during the whole commendation.[11]

The Lord's Prayer is then said once more and other prayers may be added. At those times the parson is asked to do a burial at the graveside without the full Christian funeral of the prayer book having already occurred, these other prayers might include the prayers for the departed in our funeral rite. The additional prayers beginning on pp. 487 and 503 also give helpful suggestions, according to context. There is a concluding versicle and response and then two options given for the dismissal.

The people should then be invited to join in casting earth upon the grave as they depart, which is often a helpful concluding act.

MONUMENTS

There are few churchyards or cemeteries that have not been spoiled by ill-chosen monuments. In the Middle Ages (when, by the way, the dead were more carefully commemorated than at the present day) there were few monuments in the churchyard, and those few were generally of a simple kind, such as a small wooden cross with a plain coping. In more recent times plain headstones have appeared, at first often of a beautiful type, but also a few monuments of great ugliness and pretension.

This is mainly due to the fact that people will not be contented with the use of the local stone but desire memorials of marble or polished granite. Now, any polished stone is bad enough as a rule, but marble is worst of all. It is utterly out of character with its surroundings, and stands out in glaring consequence, refusing to blend with the stone of the church behind it. As it is nearly always ill-proportioned, clumsy, and badly lettered, this wretched prominence is the more unfortunate. Furthermore,

---

11. *1979 Book of Common Prayer*, 485, 501.

in a northern climate, marble becomes harsher and more dismal in color every year.

A modern churchyard gives the most wretched impression of competitive self-advertisement, and is, I venture to think (in spite of the obtrusive use of the cross in our monuments), far more out of harmony with the Christian spirit than were the quiet headstones and occasional square enormities of our ancestors. There should be a large churchyard cross in every burial place, and when this is done, there is no need to repeat the sacred symbol over every grave. The older type of carved headstone is much to be recommended, and I am inclined to question the propriety of using any but wooden crosses or panels (or, at the most, small stone crosses, not of the conventional shape) for individual graves. Panels fixed between two low posts are the best of all, and the cross or crucifix that belongs to the churchyard should stand sovereign and significant as the one cross of the Redeemer round which all the graves are clustered. In any case white marble should not be used if it can be avoided. If the church is of stone, then the stone of the cross should be the same as that of which the church is built.

Nearly every old church, and every cathedral, has run the risk of being ruined by the garish setting of white monuments that is creeping round it. There is now and then good cause for monuments, but respectability and death are not in themselves sufficient reasons for a prominent *siste viator*.[12] Often the best memorial is something of real use or beauty for the church. Yet even in such cases one often cannot but notice with pain how loudly some voice of brass advertises the family of the deceased. Brasses need not be hideous, and some modern ones are good. A very great deal can be done with incised brass—and far more if it is treated with colored enamels by a real artist. Tombstones, tablets, and memorials of all kinds should not be articles of commerce.

---

12. This phrase means "stop, traveler" and was often used on Roman roadside tombs. *Merriam-Webster*, s.v. "siste viator," last updated Dec. 6, 2024.

17

Notes on the Seasons

THE NOTES IN THIS chapter are intended to supplement the directions given in a good liturgical kalendar and the remarks as to variations in the service offered in other chapters of this book. Consequently, where there is nothing special to be said from this point of view about a day, all mention of it is omitted.

For other information the reader is referred to a sound kalendar. The Episcopal Church Year Guide Calendar, published by Ashby Company and sold by Church Publishing, is a decent choice—though it often, strangely enough, does not include the feasts in the most recent revision of *Lesser Feasts and Fasts*. That said, one still might be hung in the sacristy or vestry. Next to it the actual schedule of the parish should be placed. An online resource that is often much more up to date and which follows both the *Revised Common Lectionary* and the current version of *Lesser Feasts and Fasts* is the "Lectionary Page."[1] For hymns, the series *Liturgical Music for the Revised Common Lectionary*, published in each of the three lectionary years, is an excellent resource. It has further been republished in a second edition to include music from Lutheran and Moravian hymnals—churches with which our church is now in full communion—along with the hymnal of the Anglican Church of Canada.

As Leonel Mitchel and Ruth Meyers aptly stated, "The liturgical year has its roots in the early centuries of the church's life and turns the mystery of life in Christ like a fine jewel so that we see it reflected and refracted through different windows as we pass from Advent through

---

1. The Lectionary Page can be found at http://lectionarypage.net.

Christmas to Epiphany and then from Lent through Holy Week to Easter and Pentecost and the season following."[2] The practice of seasonal observance is the turning of that fine jewel so that we might perceive salvation from a variety of angles.

ADVENT

During the season of Advent (and previously from Septuagesima to the end of Lent), the deacon and subdeacon sometimes wore a special kind of chasuble instead of their tunicles. The use of this sort of chasuble is, however, confusing, and rather elaborate, and there is plenty of evidence that tunicles were worn, although the earlier custom at Salisbury had been to wear chasubles.[3] But on Good Friday, and also on all vigils and Ember Days, at all times of the year, neither chasubles nor tunicles were worn by the ministers—except on Easter Eve, the vigil of Pentecost, Christmas Eve (when on a Sunday), and the Whitsun Ember Days, on which days tunicles were worn.[4] There was much diocesan variety.

The tendency at one time had been to make another Lent of Advent, a tradition that is much to be deprecated. The O Antiphons in the hymnal remind us of the spirit of joyful expectation, which is the liturgical characteristic of Advent. And, yet, that is not to say that penitence is absent from the season. There is a clear penitential theme, as is readily apparent when considering the collects for each Sunday:

- Advent I—"Almighty God, give us grace to *cast away the works of darkness*, and put on the armor of light, now in the time of this mortal life in which your Son Jesus Christ came to visit us in great humility; that in the last day, when he shall come again in his glorious majesty to judge both the living and the dead, we may rise to the life immortal; through him who lives and reigns with you and the Holy Spirit, one God, now and for ever. Amen."[5]

---

2. Mitchell and Meyers, *Praying Shapes Believing*, 4.

3. It seems that it was not until the thirteenth century that the use of chasubles was reserved only to priests and bishops and yet even in the fourteenth century there remains evidence of chasubles for deacons and subdeacons in Norfolk. See Mayo, *Ecclesiastical Dress*, 40, 55.

4. "Per totum adventum et a septuagesima usque ad Cenam Domine [also called Pascha/Easter in the Consuetudinary] diaconus et subdiaconus ad missam casulis induantur." Legg, *Sarum Missal*, 14. See also Dearmer, *Parson's Handbook*, 441–42.

5. *1979 Book of Common Prayer*, 211 (italics added).

- Advent II—"Merciful God, who sent your messengers the prophets to *preach repentance* and prepare the way for our salvation: Give us grace to *heed their warnings and forsake our sins*, that we may greet with joy the coming of Jesus Christ our Redeemer; who lives and reigns with you and the Holy Spirit, one God, now and for ever. Amen."[6]

- Advent III—"Stir up your power, O Lord, and with great might come among us; and, because we are *sorely hindered by our sins*, let your bountiful grace and mercy speedily help and deliver us; through Jesus Christ our Lord, to whom, with you and the Holy Spirit, be honor and glory, now and for ever. Amen."[7]

- Advent IV—"*Purify our conscience*, Almighty God, by your daily visitation, that your Son Jesus Christ, at his coming, may find in us a mansion prepared for himself; who lives and reigns with you, in the unity of the Holy Spirit, one God, now and for ever. Amen."[8]

So, while Advent is a time of hopeful preparation, we are still called to turn from our sins as one of the particular ways in which we prepare for the Nativity Feast. It is simply a different sort of penitence than the kind practiced in the Lenten season. Furthermore, this is a busy season in the secular world and in the church as we prepare for Christmas (clearly each in its own way), but the parson must take care not to let the roar of activity crowd out our spiritual experience of the season as we make ready to celebrate the mystery of the incarnation at Christmastide.

The altar hangings may be changed to either a deep blue or purple, according to the tradition of the church. If an Advent wreath is used, it is hung or set out before the first Sunday of Advent. However, no matter the push of sentimentality in Advent, the parson must insist upon abiding by the rubrics of the *Book of Occasional Services* which remind us that the wreath is primarily a domestic (i.e., household) devotion to count down the Sundays until Christmas.[9] Giving each candle symbolic meaning is, as the rubrics note, "a more recent innovation" and should be avoided. Finally, there is no authorized rite or ceremony for the lighting of the wreath. Indeed, the rubrics in the *Book of Occasional Services* actually

---

6. *1979 Book of Common Prayer*, 211 (italics added).
7. *1979 Book of Common Prayer*, 212 (italics added).
8. *1979 Book of Common Prayer*, 212 (italics added).
9. *Book of Occasional Services*, 20.

forbid such a practice, saying, "When the Advent Wreath is used in the worshiping community at morning services, the appropriate number of candles on the wreath are lighted, without prayer or ceremony, with the other candles."[10] Seasonal blessings may be used in place of the normal blessing at the end of Communion and specific ones are appointed in the 2022 *Book of Occasional Services*.[11]

During Advent, it is wise to advertise the availability of baptism on the first Sunday after the Epiphany in January of the coming year. This will give ample time for preparation of candidates, if needed. At some point near the end of Advent, before it gets forgotten in the movement of Christmastide through Epiphany, the parson should see that candles for the coming year have been ordered so that they will be available to be blessed on Candlemas on February 2. These would include beeswax altar candles, a new paschal candle, new Advent candles, and whatever votive or handheld candles are needed for liturgies during the coming year.

CHRISTMASTIDE

Festal evensong on the fourth Sunday of Advent is a fitting preparation for the coming Christmas celebrations and a convenient way of imposing a time for the work of decoration, which can occur either after the Sunday services that day or before evensong. For this service, the color of Advent may be changed for the festival white in light of the approaching holiday.

The Christmas (or Advent, if used on the fourth Sunday of Advent and so desired) festival Lessons and Carols, as found in the *Book of Occasional Services* may also be used. Carols were sung in church on Christmas Day in the eighteenth century, and sometimes on Christmas Eve, with the parish clerk wishing the congregation a Merry Christmas at their conclusion.[12] The Christmas festival of Lessons and Carols comes from this tradition and has much to commend it. However, this liturgy should not replace the liturgy of the word in a celebration of Holy Eucharist. This was not the design of Lessons and Carols, and the rubrics of the *Book of Occasional Services* discourage it.[13] (In the initial version

---

10. *Book of Occasional Services*, 20.
11. *Book of Occasional Services*, 10–11.
12. Dearmer, *Parson's Handbook*, 444.
13. *Book of Occasional Services*, 22, 37.

proposed to the General Convention, it was expressly forbidden, but the committee gave into the pressure of some well-meaning—though clearly mistaken—clergy in recommending that General Convention permit it, albeit with reservation).

The decoration of the church with boughs of evergreens has come down to us from the Middle Ages, although between the seventeenth and the nineteenth century it became generally obsolete except at Christmas. The medieval custom of strewing sweet-smelling herbs on the pavement also lasted long after the Reformation and would be well worth revival in our time. Holly, ivy, and bay have long been used at Christmas, and it is a pity that rosemary is now forgotten. It was used in honor of the Lord's mother.[14]

The parson will often have to use her or his authority to protect the altar from misguided attempts at over decoration. In the rest of the church, it does not matter so much, and the parson may not have to interfere, beyond forbidding absolutely the driving in of nails and the encumbering of altar rails, stalls, font, or pulpit. But if the priest does not look after the altar, it will lose its dignity under the inroads of a multitude of good people who do not know what an altar is. Flower vases on the altar should be used sparingly, if at all, and are best put on the retable behind the altar or on two stands in the chancel. All decorations should be restrained, following the broad architectural lines of the building. Festoons and wreaths are generally best; and artificial materials are to be avoided. Lettering is one of the most difficult branches of design; and it is useful to remember that a text is not the more sacred for being illegible. The greenery may, in accordance with old custom, remain up till the Epiphany (the day after the twelfth day of Christmas) or its octave, but the flowers should all be removed after a day or two. Decaying vegetable matter in church is very objectionable. Great reverence and quietness must be observed.

The creche, if used, should be set up near the front of the church where it is visible to the people. It should be of handsome design and a size fitting the space of the nave. A small household creche from a local department store often looks worse than simply forgoing the creche entirely. It is customary at the entrance for the Christmas Eve Mass to carry the Christ child from the creche in procession and place the babe in the

---

14. Dearmer, *Parson's Handbook*, 444.

manger, after which the prayer for the station at the creche may be used.[15] The magi are not yet placed in the creche but may be set up along the nave, moving each day of the Christmas season closer to the Christ child.

In many parishes, there will be two masses on Christmas Eve. Care should be taken that there is one very early celebration on all the great feasts, for the benefit of families with small children and others. As a general rule it may be said that the more celebrations there are on these days, the more communicants there will be. The custom in many parishes is for the earlier celebration on Christmas Eve to be geared towards families while the later celebration is often described as the midnight Mass. This name is customary even though it rarely ends (and even more rarely starts) at midnight. No matter the name, the latest service will often be the one that is more solemn with full use of chant, incense, and all the solemnity of great liturgical worship. Seasonal blessings, if desired, may be used.[16]

EPIPHANY AND THE OCTAVE

The Feast of the Epiphany falls on January 6 of each year and care should be taken that it is observed properly as one of the principal feasts of the church. According to our prayer book, this feast cannot be transferred, and the expectation of the prayer book is that a service of Holy Eucharist (befitting that of a principal feast) will be offered. The magi are finally placed at the creche and the use of incense on this day is greatly desired. Frankincense was one of the three gifts given to the holy family, and it follows that we should offer it up on Epiphany as well. Seasonal blessings, if desired, may be used.[17]

It has been a custom in the church since ancient times to bless chalk on Epiphany so that the faithful can ask God's blessing upon their house in the coming year. The prayer for the blessing of chalk and the instructions for using it are found in the *2022 Book of Occasional Services*.[18] It is a good idea to print out the instructions for how the chalk is used so that people do not go home with a piece and find themselves confused and

---

15. See *Book of Occasional Services*, 35–36.
16. See *Book of Occasional Services*, 11.
17. See *Book of Occasional Services*, 12.
18. *Book of Occasional Services*, 211–12.

unsure. When done regularly, this quickly becomes a beloved tradition in the parish.

The first Sunday after the Epiphany is the celebration of the Feast of the Baptism of the Lord (it is not "Epiphany Sunday" because, once more, principal feasts may not be transferred in our church). One sees clearly the problem with the unlawful, unauthorized transfer of feasts because if a priest attempts to transfer Epiphany to the following Sunday, then the church loses the celebration of our Lord's baptism (which is perhaps the oldest incarnational celebration of them all, actually). It is much worse when they seek to rectify this by transferring it to the Sunday before the Epiphany, thus shortening the full twelve days of Christmas as though the proper celebration of the incarnation was simply inconvenient. Of course, it is still the first Sunday after the Epiphany and so Epiphany-themed hymns and choral music are certainly appropriate.

The first Sunday after the Epiphany, properly observed, is one of the four baptismal days in the prayer book and so the invitation for baptisms (hopefully having been made during Advent) may have produced candidates. If there are no candidates, then the Renewal of Baptismal Vows may be used, and the people may be sprinkled with baptismal water during the entrance.

CANDLEMAS

Both the name of Candlemas and the ceremonies associated with it were long a part of the traditions of the English Church. John Donne (d. 1631), in one of his sermons, defended the "solemnizing" of this day by admitting "candles into the church," "because he who was the light of the world was brought into the temple" on "this day of lights."[19] It was still a grand day at the Temple Church ninety years later, and at Ripon, so late as in 1790, on the Sunday before Candlemas Day, the Collegiate Church was one continued blaze of light all afternoon, by reason of an immense number of candles.[20] This seems still to be the best way of observing the day, so long as the extra lights are not put on the altar itself.

Candles for the upcoming year should be set on a table at the entrance of the church and members of the parish should be invited to bring candles from home to be blessed as well. A form is provided for

---

19. Donne, *Sermons*, 80, 112.
20. Walcott, *Customs of Cathedrals*, 199.

the Candlemas procession in the *2022 Book of Occasional Services*.[21] The procession includes the traditional station at the chancel steps and it is wise to offer a helpful reminder to the people that they may extinguish their candles after the collect of the day, lest they grow drowsy and burn the church down.

THE SEASON OF LENT

This season of penitence begins on Ash Wednesday, often preceded by a festal celebration known as Shrove Tuesday the previous day. Ashes may be prepared at Shrove Tuesday by burning the palms leftover from the previous year's Palm Sunday liturgy. If desired, this activity could also take place after the Candlemas or Epiphany liturgy. Regardless, there are several other preparations to be made if this season will be a holy journey for the priest and people.

If the Lenten array is used, ample time must be given to hang it properly. The veils are hung up before the crosses, pictures (such as are not removed), and such images that are not of an architectural character. Where there is a triptych, or other reredos with leaves, it is closed. If the reredos has no leaves, it should be covered by a white veil. The veils should be of unbleached linen, brown holland, or silk. But nothing whiter than the toned white of homespun linen should be used; the white linen of which surplices are made (especially when the mellowness is spoiled by the blue of most detergents) does not have a good effect. The beauty and significance of the Lenten array will be at once appreciated if this is remembered: with the walls of the church being distempered in a toned white (as they should be), the veiling of pictures, reredos, and the like causes them to be lost in the general background till Easter comes again. For the same reason, the leaves of a triptych should be painted the same white on the outside.

---

21. *Book of Occasional Services*, 47–50.

The Lenten Array[22]

The frontals and dorsals give excellent opportunities for appliqué or painted work in red on rough white linen, but these, of course, must be most carefully designed. Generally, the great rood was veiled in linen, and the Lenten veil that hung in front of the sanctuary (a relic of the primitive custom of hiding the altar within curtains during the Holy Mysteries) was often made in strips of various colors; though this too was often white like all the rest. The vestments should be like the frontal. A special processional cross was usually reserved for Lent. It was generally of wood, painted red, and it was without the image of our Lord.

22. British Museum MS. Add. 25698. Showing the Lenten array in a Flemish church, ca. 1492. Rood and attendant figures veiled in white with red crosses; white dorsal, riddels, and hangings behind altar; the dorsal with red crosses; frontal, frontlet, and apparels red with gold fringe (this combination of red frontal with white hangings and veils would be for Passiontide); two candlesticks on altar. Priest hearing confession, vested in blue-gray cassock and coif, surplice, cappa nigra, gray almuce on shoulders. The two kneeling men wear a blue lay dress.

Eucharistic vessels made of precious metal may be exchanged for those of pewter or a very simple glass. As this whole project requires a good deal of work, parishioners should be invited to assist with it after the Shrove Tuesday celebrations that may take placer earlier on in the evening.

The Ash Wednesday liturgy on the next day should not begin with any sort of hymn or special entrance rite. A small procession may be made of only those ministers needed, in their normal order. After they reverence the altar, they go to their places and the liturgy begins with the salutation ("The Lord be with you" / "And also with you") and moves directly to the collect of the day. There is no *Kyrie* or other part of the entrance rite in this liturgy. After the collect, all sit for the lessons, Gospel, and sermon, which occur in their normal way (though the mood may be more subdued for the day).

Then, after the sermon, the celebrant goes to the chancel steps or the altar and issues the invitation to a Holy Lent, perhaps with the assistant (either the verger or eucharistic minister) holding the book. The priest and assistant then kneel at the altar rail or directly before the altar for the moment of silence (which should be fulsome), after which the priest goes to the altar to say the prayer over the ashes (which, one will notice, is not actually worded as a blessing). The priest then imposes ashes on the assistant, who in turn imposes them on the priest, using the words in the prayer book. The people should then be instructed by the usher to come up in a similar manner as they do for receiving Communion so that the ashes may be imposed on them.

After all who desire have received ashes, the priest and assistant return to their previous position kneeling while Ps 51 is sung or said. The celebrant then leads the Litany of Penitence. Though normally an invitation to confession is led by the deacon, on this day it is fitting for the priest as parson and pastor to lead it, as the rubrics indicate. The priest then stands and pronounces forgiveness from the position where absolution is normally pronounced (noting, once more, that the prayer in the prayer book is actually not an absolution). The peace is then exchanged, and the liturgy continues with the offertory and Eucharist.

During the season of Lent, the Great Litany may be sung or said on the first Sunday, the exhortation and penitential order on the second Sunday, and the penitential order without the exhortation on the remaining Sundays (of which there are three, which makes it convenient as one of the three short sentences of Scripture in the penitential order may be used on each of those Sundays). Whenever the exhortation is used, an insert or announcement should make clear when confession will be offered and also how to schedule an appointment for confession at other times.

It is a wise idea during Lent to carefully consider the schedule of offerings for Holy Week. If one begins in Lent with a plan, then even a single parish priest need not be overwhelmed during that sacred time. I once heard a bishop describe Holy Week as "Hell Week" when he was in active pastoral ministry—and if that is the experience of the priest, the priest absolutely must find a different way to prepare and lead the observance of this most sacred time. In my own experience, by writing two sermons and preparing two liturgies each week during Lent, one is able to reach Palm Sunday with all liturgies prepared and all sermons written for Holy Week through Easter Day and perhaps even the second Sunday of Easter. Though this suggestion may at first seem onerous to others in the parish, once it has been tried and everyone has had the opportunity of simply being present during Holy Week—able to respond to pastoral needs, to sit and talk with people, or to say one's prayers and focus on liturgy, and then fully to rest on Easter Week—the wisdom will quickly be seen and appreciated.

PASSIONTIDE AND THE START OF HOLY WEEK

The services of Holy Week of old were many and elaborate. The almost universal tendency to supplement those given in the prayer book—sometimes by new services (traditions such as the Three Hours or hymns and dissolving views) or sometimes by old services (such as a modified version of the old Reproaches or Tenebrae)—shows that there is a keen want of more observances during this solemn week. Permission should be obtained, of course, before offering any rites not authorized by the church, though several of the traditions of Holy Week are now fully authorized in the *2022 Book of Occasional Services* (this would include the Way of the Cross, a Scriptural Way of the Cross, Tenebrae, and an Agapé for Maundy Thursday). However, no parson should add any of these extra services until the full Holy Week liturgies of the church as articulated in the prayer book are first observed.

Whereas Passiontide used to begin on the fifth Sunday in Lent, which was known as Passion Sunday, the start of Passiontide in our prayer book is "The Sunday of the Passion: Palm Sunday." In accordance with old custom, red is used, marking it off from the rest of Lent. To omit the change is to miss a valuable opportunity of teaching our people.

The procession of palms on Palm Sunday, the first day of Holy Week, is as old as the fourth century, and anciently every village had this ceremony at least. Dried date palms are not a beautiful decoration for the altar, and the appropriateness of using bleached and dead leaves of this kind may be questioned. If they are used at all, fresh palms should be ordered, but the rubrics clearly allow for the use of the branches of "other trees or shrubs."[23] Thus, local branches may be used (and could be desirable when compared to the ecological effects of the massive ordering of palms each spring). Willow and yew, for instance, look much better about the altar and screen than the long palms which one often sees propped in awkward curves against the reredos. The word "palm" was anciently applied to willow and yew indifferently, and their use, at least outside of the church, has never been dropped entirely. If palms are chosen, particularly if they may be gotten locally and are native plants to the area, then Sago or other larger palms may be attached to the pews to create a sense of an archway through which the people may walk.

The procession takes place before the Eucharist only, and not at evensong. Before the procession, the veils of the altar cross (both on the high altar and on minor altars) should be untied so that they can be easily removed. Assistants should be prepared to lower the veil covering the rood at the station at the chancel steps. The palms for distribution should be set out at the place where processions begin. Whereas formerly the blessing of palms often took place at the altar, the current rubrics prefer that "when circumstances permit, the congregation may gather at a place apart from the church, so that all may go into the church in procession."[24] In many ways, the Candlemas blessing and procession functions as a helpful reminder—usually with a much smaller congregation—of how this is done in advance of Palm Sunday. Thus, the palms are set where the candles were set on Candlemas and the procession makes a station at the chancel steps, as it did at Candlemas.

The priest, wearing a red cope over the vestments, enters the place where the procession will begin, along with the ministers (who do not wear their tunicles). Standing near the palms, the priest says the opening, "Blessed is the king," with the people responding. The priest then leads

---

23. *1979 Book of Common Prayer*, 270.
24. *1979 Book of Common Prayer*, 270.

the short prayer. The palms Gospel is then read. It should be noted that this is not the Gospel of the Mass, and so the normal Gospel acclamation and conclusion should be omitted. It is unfortunate that the editors of the Gospel book one may order from Church Publishing missed this point. That this is not the Gospel of Mass is made further clear with the allowance that it may be read by the deacon "or other person appointed."[25] There is no requirement that it be read by the priest and, indeed, it could be read by a lay person. The priest then says the blessing of the palms and concludes with the final anthem, after which the deacon says the dismissal (which actually is the invitation for the procession to begin). The older tradition, once more, of having the people walk last in the procession is affirmed by J. Neil Alexander for practical and historical reasons.[26]

The cross should be carried as usual, and one or two banners may be used also—preferably of red, with a dark blue or black cross, in linen or silk. The procession may go around the church building and then enter the building in the normal fashion, pausing, as noted earlier, for the station at the chancel step. At this station, those appointed unveil the cross on the rood loft and others unveil the altar cross, and the procession continues the rest of the way in the normal fashion.

After the collect of the day and lessons, the passion Gospel is read with the introduction given in the prayer book and without the customary response. The rubrics allow it to be read or chanted by lay persons, with various roles being assigned and the congregation playing the role of the crowd. This can be a stirring practice, if it is done well and with practice. After the Gospel, the sermon is preached (as noted earlier, it may not be omitted), but the Nicene Creed and confession may be omitted if there has been a liturgy of the palms to begin the service.[27]

On Monday, Tuesday, and Wednesday of Holy Week, a simple service of Holy Eucharist should be offered. Though the attendance will likely not be great, each day's Gospel and readings move us through this most sacred time and the priest will be grateful for the grounding, as will any who attend.

---

25. *1979 Book of Common Prayer*, 270.
26. Alexander, *Celebrating Liturgical Time*, 103–4.
27. See the rubric on p. 273 in the *1979 Book of Common Prayer*.

NOTES ON THE SEASONS

THE SACRED TRIDUUM

Maundy Thursday is the birthday of the Eucharist and was also most appropriately the day of the reconciliation of penitents, in accordance with that "godly discipline" of older times.[28] It marks the beginning of the Triduum, the Great Three Days of the church, and after the opening acclamation from Maundy Thursday, there is not a dismissal until the end of the Great Vigil of Easter. Christians should be encouraged to observe the entire Triduum to get the fullest experience of the breadth and movement of the story of our salvation.

From the fifth century on, the ceremony of consecrating the chrism was fixed for this day also. The very early ceremony of washing the feet of twelve or thirteen poor men was confined to bishops and other great ecclesiastical and secular personages. Cranmer practiced and defended the custom. Queen Elizabeth kept it up with great ceremony, herself washing and kissing the feet of as many poor persons as corresponded with her age.[29] The Hanoverian sovereigns deputed the office to the royal almoners, who soon dropped the washing (in 1737), but retained the custom of giving alms, which is still done at a cathedral or royal peculiar of the Church of England with some ceremony, including the processional use of a towel, each year.[30] It is to this practice of foot washing that we owe the name of Maundy Thursday; maundy comes from the Latin *mandatum* (commandment) and refers to the commandment from Christ that we wash one another's feet as a symbol of love and service.[31]

The Holy Eucharist should be observed with much solemnity on this day. The red Passiontide color is best continued. While it is true that white may be worn for the Lord's Supper, red was more generally in England the color for a mass in commemoration of the Blessed Sacrament.

---

28. "Brethren, in the primitive Church there was a godly discipline, that, at the beginning of Lent, such persons as stood convicted of notorious sin, were put to open penance, and punished in this world, that their souls might be saved in the day of the Lord; and that others, admonished by their example, might be the more afraid to offend. Instead whereof (until the said discipline may be restored again, which is much to be wished,) it is thought good, that at this time, in the presence of you all, should be read the general sentences of God's cursing against impenitent sinners, gathered out of the seven and twentieth chapter of Deuteronomy, and other places of Scripture; and that ye should answer to every sentence, Amen." 1662 *Book of Common Prayer*, 193. See also Dearmer, *Parson's Handbook*, 457–58.

29. Staley, *Hierugia Anglicana*, 263.

30. Staley, *Hierugia Anglicana*, 250.

31. Armentrout and Slocum, *Episcopal Dictionary*, 325.

It also keeps Maundy Thursday rooted in Holy Week and allows for a greater experience of change when the festal white comes out again, first at the Great Vigil of Easter.

The liturgy begins "in the usual manner,"[32] which means using the opening acclamation for Lent "and other penitential occasions."[33] After the sermon, the prayer book gives a liturgy for the washing of feet, and another alternative is provided in the 2022 *Book of Occasional Services*. Though Episcopalians are generally anxious about being barefoot in church, the rite should continue to be encouraged as an act of humility. In no way should a substitute rite, such as a mutual washing of hands as is seen in some places, be considered. It is contrary to our Lord's explicit command and not authorized by the rites of the church.

During Communion, the people might sing *Pange lingua gloriosi corporis mysterium*, hymn 329, as an excellent hymn extolling the Sacrament. It also has the benefit of echoing the tune for the next day, on Good Friday, in the hymn sung during the veneration of the cross. After Communion and the post-communion prayer, the Sacrament may be carried to an altar of repose, with the rubrics allowing that "the sacrament may be reverently carried to its place of reservation immediately before the Stripping of the Altar."[34] For a processional hymn at this point, if desired and if the hymn *Pange lingua* (hymn 329) was not sung earlier, it is best sung now and is quite traditional. The rubrics further suggest that "any devotional activities should not distract from the principal focus on the proper liturgies of Maundy Thursday and Good Friday."[35] That said, the popular custom of keeping watch with the Sacrament all night at the altar of repose surely does not distract from but rather heightens the principal focuses of the proper liturgies, providing a devotional bridge between Maundy Thursday and Good Friday.

In the older traditions of the church, the altars were then stripped and washed by two priests, a deacon, a subdeacon, and a taperer, assisted by two other ministers carrying the wine and water, all vested in albes. Each altar was washed, with wine and then water being poured on its five crosses, dried with a branch of box or other tree, and then the collect was said of the saint in whose honor the altar was dedicated.[36] The rubrics in

---

32. *1979 Book of Common Prayer*, 274.
33. *1979 Book of Common Prayer*, 323, 355.
34. *Book of Occasional Services*, 108.
35. *Book of Occasional Services*, 108.
36. This rite was called "Ablution of the Altar." Pearson, *Sarum Missal*, 140–41.

the 2022 *Book of Occasional Services* instruct that if the stripping of the altar is a public ceremony it should take place after the Maundy Thursday liturgy and may be done in silence or while Ps 22 is being recited or sung.[37] An antiphon for the psalm is also given.

Some have the custom of removing all vestments and simply wearing the black cassock for the stripping of the altar, but that is to perform a public rite of the church without a vestment (for the cassock is, of course, clothing and not a vestment). It is better to keep to the old tradition of wearing only the albe. The altars should remain stripped till Easter Eve. Furthermore, the albe having been maintained at the Stripping of the Altar, the priest will not choose the equally misguided current custom in some places of officiating at the liturgies of Good Friday in cassock alone. Once more, the cassock is not a vestment and the proper vestment for the Good Friday offices is that of any office of the church: surplice and tippet (or stole, if Communion is distributed). We commemorate our Lord's death on Good Friday; let us not also see the death of proper liturgical etiquette by clergy eschewing the garment that connects us to our baptismal rites.

All the church bells should be silent during the last three days of Holy Week after the Maundy Eucharist. Therefore, we have no precedent for the objectionable and morbid practice of tolling a bell at 3 p.m. on Good Friday.

The services essential to Good Friday are the regular daily offices of the church and the appointed Proper Liturgy of the Day in the prayer book. The most practicable arrangement at an ordinary parish will probably be something like this:

- At 8:30 a.m., morning prayer may conclude the all-night watch, with the prayer book rite of Communion from the reserved Sacrament after morning prayer, at which the remainder of the Sacrament is consumed.

- At noon, the Proper Liturgy of the Day may be used as found in the prayer book.

- If the Way of the Cross from the *2022 Book of Occasional Services* is desired, it can be offered as a private devotion after the proper liturgies for Good Friday.

---

37. *Book of Occasional Services*, 108.

- The day may close with evensong (though only monotoned, if it is sung)—or, better yet, a simple service of evening prayer.

The ancient tradition of the church is that mass is not celebrated on Good Friday, other than "mass of the presanctified."[38] By pairing Communion to morning prayer, an appropriate liturgical conclusion is given to the all-night watch and the people are also given the opportunity to receive Communion, if they desire. This also enables the proper liturgy to stand on its own as a service of Scripture, prayers for the world, and devotion to the cross.

For the proper liturgy, the priest may vest in surplice and tippet (or cope, if desired). The ministers enter in silence, according to the prayer book's rubrics, and then kneel in silent prayer.[39] This time of prayer should be fulsome and not simply a closing of one's eyes but a time of true prayer by the ministers. The officiant should then stand and may say a short versicle or proceed directly to the collect of the day, which is said without the salutation, in accordance with the tradition of the church.[40] The lessons are then read in the normal manner (though the conclusion of "hear ends the reading" may function as a more somber conclusion fitting to the day), followed by the passion Gospel, announced according to the rubrics of the prayer book and ended without any of the customary responses.

The sermon follows and, as on Palm Sunday, it may not be omitted. If a parson cannot find words for a short homily on our Lord's crucifixion, then that person should begin the process of discerning a different vocation. Following the sermon the rubrics allow for a hymn and there is scarcely one better than "O Sacred Head," with the setting found as hymn 168 in our hymnal being the superior one.

A great feature of the old service was intercession, and some of the solemn collects then used have been preserved in our service. The biddings are said or sung by the deacon or other appointed minister, with the priest responding with the collects. After these collects, the liturgy may end with a hymn or anthem, the Lord's Prayer, and the final prayer.[41]

However, the prayer book also allows for the liturgy to continue with the veneration of the cross. As this is one of the most ancient

---

38 Attwater, *Catholic Dictionary*, 401.
39. *1979 Book of Common Prayer*, 276.
40. Hatchett, *American Prayer Book*, 239.
41. *1979 Book of Common Prayer*, 282.

liturgies of Holy Week, first observed by Egeria in Jerusalem in the late fourth century, it is a tradition best maintained.[42] Assistants may bring in a wooden cross and set it up in the sight of the people.

After the cross enters the church, though, the rubrics generously state that "appropriate devotions may follow."[43] For those unfamiliar with the traditions of the church, they may feel at a loss. One traditional devotion would be for the cross to be brought to the door of the church while the priest goes to the back entrance in a simple quiet procession (there is no rush, for this is a day for prayer). The priest may then carry the cross into the church. Stations may be made three times (at the same locations where the stations at the Great Vigil of Easter will be made on the following day), with the priest standing up the cross, all kneeling, and then the priest saying, "Behold the wood of the cross, upon which hung the world's salvation." The people respond, "Come, let us adore him," or "O come, let us worship,"[44] and the procession continues until the cross is set up in its place. Customarily the priest kisses the cross and then goes to the priest's stall so that the people may make their devotions.

If another minister carries in the cross, the priest should make devotions first as a model—ascending the chancel steps, bowing, walking to the middle, bowing, walking to the cross, bowing a third time, and then kneeling and kissing the base of the cross. If the priest carries in the cross, another minister should be assigned to go first to model this approach. The people may, of course, approach the cross making whatever devotions they desire, but many will appreciate an example from which to draw. The prayer book invitation for "appropriate devotions" also suggests that any or all of three traditional anthems are appropriate. That said, what devotions are best fitting at this sacred moment has been the subject of some debate.

As the work was being done to restore the Triduum liturgy in the 1979 prayer book, there was significant debate about the Reproaches or *Improperia*.[45] These are texts developed between the seventh and eleventh century for use alongside the veneration of the cross. After the Draft

---

42. Armentrout and Slocum, *Episcopal Dictionary*, 162–63.

43. *1979 Book of Common Prayer*, 281.

44. A form of this is found in the Sarum rites for Good Friday, including this specific versicle and response. See Pearson, *Sarum Missal*, 152–53.

45. Louis Weil helpfully lays out the story of this debate and his own participation and perspective as one of the framers of the 1979 prayer book in his article "The Solemn Reproaches of the Cross."

Proposed Book of Common Prayer was published in 1976, there was a movement to remove the Reproaches from the book due to a perspective that they had anti-Semitic elements and had been a part of historical violence against the Jewish people.[46] For example, the older version before the one authorized by Pope Pius XI included a prayer for the conversion of the Jews. Though liturgist Louis Weil, one of the architects of the 1979 prayer book, was raised in a Jewish family, he did not find the current revised version to be anti-Semitic and raised his confusion with John Townsend, a professor at Episcopal Divinity School in Cambridge, who was one of the key forces arguing for their elimination. As Weil articulated to Townsend, in his own experience of the Reproaches, "it had never occurred to me that the texts were addressed to the Jews. I had always heard them as words addressed to the Christian people, indicating that we, like the Jews, fail to live up in our daily lives to the great acts and promises of God."[47] Unconvinced, Townsend continued his work and was successful in having them removed.

Those who continue to use the Reproaches do so under the expansive permission of the rubric, which says, "Appropriate devotions may follow, which may include any or all of the following, or other suitable anthems."[48] The safest approach, of course, is simply to follow the rites of the authorized book and leave them out entirely. However, if there is a desire to use them, then care must be taken (particularly by the parson, who must teach about the dangers of anti-Semitism, stressing that anti-Semitism has a dark history with Good Friday and reinforcing Weil's reminder that we all bear culpability for the death of Christ). While some parishes have used the Roman version authorized by Pope Pius XI, most use either the updated versions found in the Anglican Church of Canada's *Book of Alternative Services* or the Evangelical Lutheran Church in America's *Evangelical Lutheran Worship* instead.

Whatever devotions are used, the prayer book suggests that they conclude with the congregational singing of *Pange lingua gloriosi proelium certaminis*, in the hymnal as 166. As noted, this can echo the other *Pange lingua* that can be sung on Maundy Thursday. All then say the Lord's Prayer and the liturgy concludes with a final collect, after which the ministers rise and exit.

---

46. For a contemporary criticism of the Reproaches, see Joslyn-Siemiatkoski, "Good Friday."
47. Weil, "Solemn Reproaches."
48. *1979 Book of Common Prayer*, 281.

On Holy Saturday, there is a small office that can be said between the Triduum liturgies of Good Friday and the Great Vigil of Easter. The liturgy begins directly with the collect (which is, as on Good Friday, not preceded by salutation). Though it only occupies a single page in the prayer book, observance of this liturgy is, as Hatchett notes, almost uniquely Anglican and it functions as a sort of burial liturgy for Christ.[49] The appointed Gospel is from the burial itself and, as this is not a eucharistic liturgy, the normal acclamations before and after are not included. Instead, it can be introduced as "the conclusion of the Passion of our Lord Jesus Christ according to . . ." There should be a brief homily, with this day being an excellent opportunity to preach on the harrowing of hell. In accordance with ancient liturgies, we then read a portion of the burial rite (the anthems from our prayer book) and conclude with the Lord's Prayer and the grace.

It is particularly appropriate to invite the altar guild and any who will assist with preparing the church for the Great Vigil to attend the Holy Saturday liturgy. They will likely resonate with the disciples who do the quiet and unseen work of burying Christ. The liturgy also then provides a helpful marker from which they can begin the preparations for the Great Vigil, decorating the church and changing the hangings accordingly in anticipation of the great feast that will be celebrated that night.

Easter Eve, called in Latin Holy Saturday or the Great Sabbath, was anciently marked by the blessing of the new fire and paschal candle, and by the hallowing of the font. The Great Vigil of Easter was restored by the current prayer book and should be marked as the single most important liturgy of the church year, with the parson bringing to bear all the musical and liturgical resources of the church for the commemoration of Christ's passing over from death into life. It is the best day in the year for the celebration of holy baptism with special solemnity, and, whenever possible, baptisms should be arranged for this day. Adults who seek admission to the church should, if convenient, be prepared throughout Lent and baptized on Easter Eve.

In addition to decorating the church for the Easter celebrations, there is much to do to prepare for the Great Vigil of Easter itself. Of all the days, this is one where a rehearsal of all the ministers in advance of the liturgy is wise, during which notes may be taken and outstanding tasks

---

49. Hatchett, *American Prayer Book*, 238–39.

assigned. In addition to a full complement of ministers, a second verger to assist during the liturgy will be much appreciated. The priest vests in cope, since this is the most formal procession of the church year, and the chasuble should be set inside for changing at the appropriate time.

A place should be determined where the new fire will be lit, usually outside of the church. If the church has a cemetery, columbarium, or memorial garden, these are particularly fitting places. The new fire should be prepared in such a way that it will light easily when lit by a flame—small dry pieces of wood, tinder, and kindling are essential. The addition of some lighter fluid is not a bad idea if one is outside. If the fire needs to be lit indoors, either due to weather or the specific context of a building and property, then a small metal vessel (either a fire pit or a vessel the size of a good-sized pot) should be lined with a goodly amount of aluminum foil. Three boxes of ordinary rock salt (the sort used to make ice cream) are poured in the center and a small divot is made in the middle. Then, three bottles of isopropyl rubbing alcohol (70% alcohol content is sufficient) are poured on in the middle and around the salt, fully saturating it. Some should be pooled in the center to catch the flame when lit, along with some along the outside of the mound of salt. Flint and steel or a long match can then be used to light the fire. It will burn without smoke for about fifteen to twenty minutes. Particularly when lit inside, someone with a fire extinguisher should be nearby to step in, if needed.[50]

Near the new fire should be the five grains of incense, encased in wax and nails, to be used in preparing the new paschal candle. It is helpful to use a small bit to drill the five holes into the candle in advance (otherwise too much pressure on inserting them will often cause the wax nails to break). A candle follower that can be fitted with a glass cover to break the wind is much desired for the paschal candle. Coals for the incense should either be lit from the new fire (using long matches) or lit in advance of the procession to the new fire. The tapers used for this liturgy should be fitted with covers to keep the wind from extinguishing them—or, better yet, lanterns with an enclosed flame can be used.

The liturgy for the Great Vigil should be scheduled to occur very close to sunset, which may vary by geographic location. It need not be fully dark when the liturgy begins, but the feel of twilight should have already descended. The inside of the church should be entirely dark (unless the new fire will be lit inside, in which case it should be darkened but

---

50. My gratitude to Father Steve Rice, rector of St. Timothy's Episcopal Church in Winston-Salem, North Carolina, for this recipe and approach.

still visible for walking and finding a place). When people arrive at the church, they should be given a service leaflet and a small handheld unlit candle and invited to gather wherever the new fire will be lit. Then, at the appropriate time, the procession forms in the usual manner, with the deacon carrying the unlit new paschal candle to the new fire. Once all are in position, it is wise to offer some words of greeting and introduction, especially letting the people know that when they light their handheld candles in the church, the person with the lit candle holds it straight up and the person with the unlit candle holds it perpendicular to light it. This approach keeps wax from dripping all over the floor.

Once all is ready, the priest kindles the new fire using flint or a long match (flint is ideal and traditional, a long match is acceptable, but a mechanical lighter is to be eschewed). With the verger holding the book, the priest then begins the liturgy with "Dear friends in Christ . . ." The priest then says the prayer of blessing for the new fire and prepares the incense, censing the new fire with three swings. The paschal candle is then presented to the priest, held by the deacon or another minster. The priest, tracing the thumb over the appropriate parts, says the customary prayer:

- Christ yesterday and today (tracing the vertical arm of the cross),
- the beginning and the end (tracing the horizontal arm),
- Alpha (tracing the "Alpha" above the cross)
- and Omega (tracing the "Omega" below the cross),
- all times belongs to him (tracing the first numeral of the year, upper left)
- and all the ages (tracing the second numeral, upper right),
- to him be glory and power (tracing the third numeral, lower left)
- through every age for ever (tracing the final numeral, lower right).[51]

The priest then takes the five wax nails from the verger and inserts them into the predrilled holes, saying the customary prayer, "By his holy and glorious wounds may Christ our Lord strengthen us and make us whole," and the people respond, "Amen."[52] Using a long match, the paschal flame is then lit from the new fire and the glass cover is fitted over it

---

51. See, for example, Scottish Episcopal Church, "Vigil of Easter," 16.
52. Scottish Episcopal Church, "Vigil of Easter," 9.

to protect it from the wind. If there are covers for the tapers, these may be removed and the tapers lit; or if lanterns are beings used, these may be lit at this time as well. Otherwise, the tapers are lit when inside the church and away from the wind. The ministers then lead the procession into the church, with the people following the priest, taking the most important position in the traditional manner, just as they did on Palm Sunday.

Once in the church, the procession pauses three times (at the doors, in the middle, and at the chancel steps), just as it did for the procession of the cross on Good Friday. Each time the deacon sings, "The light of Christ," and the people respond, "Thanks be to God."[53] The first time, the deacon should then turn west, allowing the taperers or the first worshippers with candles to light their candles from the paschal flame. Other candles or lamps may be lit at this time—though those lighting them should never move ahead of the paschal flame. The candles at the altar are explicitly not yet lit. The deacon should wait until the first few candles are lit and then proceed, at a slow and solemn pace, to the center of the nave for the next station and then to the chancel steps for the final station. At the chancel steps, the paschal candle is placed in its holder and the deacon stands at the lectern or ambo, or alternatively, a small legilium set near the paschal flame, for the *Exsultet*.

The priest then censes the paschal candle before going to the priest's stall. Once all are in place, and the people standing in their seats, the deacon sings the *Exsultet*. This ancient song of the church really must be sung and should be sung well. If a deacon is not able to sing it, then a priest should. If no clergy are able to sing it well, then a cantor should be appointed. The rubrics stress that the paschal flame will burn at all liturgies during the Great Fifty Days from Easter Day to the Day of Pentecost. At all remaining liturgies during Eastertide, it should be lit (usually by the parson) before the people arrive, and all other candles should be lit from its flame. This gives the sense of it burning perpetually.

After the *Exsultet*, the priest gives the brief address in the prayer book, which begins the series of vigil readings and responses that comprise the liturgy of the word. After that address, an acolyte should light candles by the lectern or ambo to provide extra light for the readers. The lights may also be raised to a lower level. The people may be invited to extinguish their own candles or to keep them burning throughout the readings and responses. The rubrics require at least two of the nine possible

---

53. *1979 Book of Common Prayer*, 285.

lessons, and the psalms and canticles, which function as responses, are optional; others may be selected. Ideally, the responses increase in strength, beginning from a recitation of a psalm and building to fully sung responses with accompaniment. A homily may be preached after any of the lessons, but that is best left until later in the liturgy.

If there is a baptism, the liturgy then moves to the presentation and examination of the candidates. Otherwise, it moves to the Renewal of Baptismal Vows as found on p. 292 of the prayer book.[54] If the Renewal of Baptismal Vows is used, then the priest still might bless new baptismal water, using the Thanksgiving over the Water from the baptismal liturgy, and then inviting the renewal of vows. After the baptism or renewal, the candles at the altar are lighted, the priest sings the Easter acclamation, and all other lights in the church are lit or brought to their normal full level. The prayer book suggests three possible canticles,[55] and any of the three are fine choices for the Great Vigil. While the canticle is being sung and the acolytes are lighting candles and raising lights, the priest may take the newly blessed baptismal water and walk among the people, asperging them liberally.

The priest then dons the chasuble (or, if the custom is for the change from cope to chasuble to take place after the homily at the offertory, it may be done at that time). The altar should be censed, and all should eventually find themselves in the normal place for the beginning of a eucharistic rite. It should be noted that the canticle may not take enough time for all that is to be done; further celebratory music (such as organ, bells, or trumpets) may be used before or after the canticle, if needed, to stretch out the musical celebration until all are ready for the liturgy to continue.

The priest then continues with the salutation and one of the appointed collects, after which all sit for the Epistle reading. As is normal, a psalm, hymn, or anthem is permitted for the sequence between the Epistle and Gospel, but the "resurrection of the alleluia," where it is sung and repeated sequentially on a higher pitch is an excellent tradition and is suggested by the rubrics.[56] Unless the parson has perfect pitch, however, it would be best for the organist to intone the two notes each time, lest the alleluia reach the stratosphere before the Gospel of the resurrection is proclaimed. For the homily that is preached here (if it was not preached

54. *1979 Book of Common Prayer*, 292.
55. *1979 Book of Common Prayer*, 294.
56. *1979 Book of Common Prayer*, 295.

earlier), I would commend the ancient and venerable practice of using St. Chrysostom's paschal homily. If it is truly preached, and not merely recited, it can be a stirring invitation to Easter joy.

The liturgy can then continue with holy baptism or the renewal of vows, if those were not done earlier (though one can hardly imagine why they would be placed here instead of being used as the way to move from the vigil into the paschal celebration). Then the liturgy continues with the prayers of the people and the rest of the service is according to the normal practices of the church. After the reception of Communion, when the remaining Sacrament is once more placed in the tabernacle, the sanctuary light (if used) may be lit once more, having been extinguished since the removal of the Sacrament on Mandy Thursday.

EASTER SUNDAY

After the journey through Holy Week, reaching its climatic conclusion in the Great Vigil of Easter the night before, Easter Sunday can find the clergy and ministers exhausted. However, while the devout will surely attend the liturgies of Holy Week and the Triduum, the vast majority of Christians will show up on Easter Sunday without any awareness of what has taken place in the past few days. Those who attend on Easter should be seen as Christ himself, who approached the disciples on the walk to Emmaus in Luke 24, expressing uncertainty over what has occupied their attention. The parson might feel like one of the disciples, "Are you the only stranger . . . who does not know the things that have taken place there in these days?" (v. 18). Thus, the Easter Day liturgies should be opportunities to open the Scripture and break bread, only to realize that Christ has already risen and come among us in the faces of those who arrive to the Easter celebration. Every opportunity ought therefore to be given by providing as many celebrations as are needed so that the fullness of the paschal joy may be amply celebrated by all.

After Easter Sunday, the parish should be informed that the next opportunity for baptisms will be the Day of Pentecost, so that time is given for applications to be made and preparation given. The parson should then nap.

ROGATION DAYS

The tradition of the Rogation Days on the Monday, Tuesday, and Wednesday before the Feast of the Ascension has much to commend it and comes from a long and venerable tradition in the English Church. They should still be carefully kept as days of intercession for God's blessing on the fruits of the earth.

As late as about 1675, at Wolverhampton, "the sacrist, resident prebendaries, and members of the choir, assembled at morning prayers on Monday and Tuesday in Rogation Week, with the charity children, bearing long poles clothed with all kinds of flowers then in season, and which were afterwards carried through the streets of the town with much solemnity, the clergy, singing men and boys, dressed in their sacred vestments, closing the procession, and chanting in a grave and appropriate melody the Canticle *Benedicite omnia opera*."[57] The boundaries of the parish were marked at many points by Gospel trees where the Gospel was read. Here, then, we touch hands with tradition, and the parson may easily accommodate it to one's own opportunities.

The *2022 Book of Occasional Services* has several helpful suggestions for observing the Rogation traditions in our own time, and in the context of the Episcopal Church. It notes that "anciently, the observance consisted of an outdoor procession which culminated in a special celebration of the Eucharist. In more recent centuries, the procession has frequently taken place on a Sunday afternoon, apart from the Eucharist."[58] The rubrics then go on to clarify that this would happen in addition to the Eucharist of that day, as the celebration of Rogation Days should not supplant the sixth Sunday of Easter or Ascension Day.

The rubrics of the *2022 Book of Occasional Services* instruct the procession to begin in a suitable place and for "hymns, litanies said or sung, bells, instrumental music, or silence"[59] to be what fills the space between the various stations. The choir and clergy leave the church, preceded by the churchwardens, verger, and the crucifer with the cross (taperers and thurifer being optional), with the servers all wearing surplices over their cassocks and the clergy (including the officiant), surplices, hoods, tippets, and caps. Banners may be carried. The choir may be followed by the schoolchildren carrying flowers and garlands. In our current version of

---

57. Brand, *Popular Antiquities*, 109; for more details on the celebration, see 107–13.
58. *Book of Occasional Services*, 113.
59. *Book of Occasional Services*, 113.

this rite, the stations are not just for agriculture but for a variety of concerns and vocations. The procession rightly ends with the Great Litany, which is said as a part of the entrance into the church. If the procession is said on a Sunday afternoon, one should take advantage of the rubric that says the liturgy concludes with one of the appointed collects, the peace, and the blessing and dismissal. If the rogation procession takes place on Monday, Tuesday, or Wednesday of the week, then it should very well continue with a celebration of Holy Eucharist, following the rubrical instructions given.

ASCENSION DAY

Always falling forty days after Easter, on a Thursday, the Feast of the Ascension of our Lord into heaven is one of the seven principal feasts of the church and, like All Saints' Day and Epiphany (the other two lesser-observed principal feasts, when they do not fall on a Sunday), should still be celebrated with all the liturgical trappings of a great feast. Everything should be done to make Ascension Day, always a Thursday, as much a holiday as Christmas, and the people should be strongly urged to observe it according to the custom of the church. There should be a sung Eucharist if possible, and the use at least of a small schola of singers can heighten the liturgy for the (likely small) congregation. The rubrics of the prayer book are clear in the Great Vigil that "it is customary that the Paschal Candle burn at all services from Easter Day through the Day of Pentecost."[60] The extinguishing of the paschal flame at the Ascension liturgy is a tradition from before the current prayer book sought to restore the integrity of the Great Fifty Days and should be put aside in our own time. That said, the rubric is written by stating a fact of custom and not a hard and fast requirement, and so those churches that choose to ignore the prayer book's custom cannot be said precisely to be violating the rubric. That said, the parson who seeks to abide by the ideals of the prayer book will follow the book's ideal of keeping the candle burning.

THE DAY OF PENTECOST: WHITSUNDAY

The Day of Pentecost is the fiftieth Day of Easter and, as a principal feast of the church, should be celebrated with great solemnity. It is also one of

---

60. *1979 Book of Common Prayer*, 287.

the days given for baptism and, the invitation for applicants having been made, there will perhaps be candidates. If there are none, then the Renewal of Baptismal Vows is used. Even when baptisms are celebrated, Pentecost red is still used, as the baptism is being observed because of Pentecost, not to supplant it. Following this liturgy, the paschal flame is extinguished and only lit again when there are other baptisms and at funerals.

TRINITY SUNDAY

The final principal feast of the "program year" in many places is Trinity Sunday. Though it is the second in a row to fall on a Sunday, it should still be observed with the care and attention befitting a principal feast of the church. In some churches there has arisen a habit of using the Athanasian Creed in place of the Nicene, but this is contrary to the rubrics of our church and not permitted. Though it is common for the parson, having been exhausted by the celebrations of the Great Fifty Days and ready for some vacation, to have an assisting priest or seminarian preach on this day, it is far better for the parson to preach on this day. And while the homily should be sound theologically when it comes to the doctrine of the Trinity, the parson might also consider the wise advice of Thomas á Kempis at the beginning of *Imitatio Christi*—"What doth it profit thee to enter into deep discussion concerning the Holy Trinity, if thou lack humility, and be thus displeasing to the Trinity?"[61]

THE SEASON AFTER PENTECOST

A good half of the church year is experienced as the season after Pentecost. A long green season (both outdoors—in most places—and indoors, with the vestments), the focus is on the regular life of the church and what it means to follow the teachings of Jesus. An effort might be made to alter the liturgy after the first half of the season—that is, after Labor Day—to add a bit more variety, rather than using the same prayers of the people and mass settings throughout the six months, which can run from Trinity Sunday until the first Sunday of Advent. As most parishes begin their program year after the Labor Day holiday, one can have a more "summer" approach to the first half of the season and then a more "autumn" approach to the second half. Attention should be paid to the

---

61. Thomas á Kempis, *Imitation*, 15.

way the readings and collects in the final Sundays of this season begin to draw us towards the eschatological themes of Advent, during which all things are made new once more.

ALL SAINTS' DAY (OR, THE LESSER TRIDUUM)

The final principal feast of the liturgical kalendar falls on All Saints' Day, November 1. As already mentioned, the rubrics do permit this day to be celebrated as well on the following Sunday, as "All Saints' Sunday," but the rubrics are also clear that this is only ever done "in addition to its observance on the fixed date."[62]

The parson may consider this feast, and the observances surrounding it, as a lesser or fall triduum, with the sweep of three holy days: All Hallows' Eve (commonly known as Halloween), All Saints' Day, and All Souls' Day (known as the Commemoration of All Faithful Departed in our kalendar). The 2022 *Book of Occasional Services* includes a "Service for All Hallows' Eve" and the observance of the service can provide great delight (and instruction!), particularly to the young people in the church.

All Saints' Day should then be a festal observance of the great saints of the church. The Litany of Saints can be used for the entrance, beginning with the *Kyrie* and "O Christ, hear us" before continuing with the litany itself. A version of the litany is provided in appendix 1 of this book. As with the other principal feasts that do not fall on a Sunday, the use of a small schola to sing the mass settings, along with incense, can add to the solemnity of this day.

All Souls' Day on November 2 is an optional observance of the church, but the parson will find the people very grateful for the opportunity to remember those loved ones who have died. The priest should invite names for the necrology, which may be read as a part of the prayers of the people or during the offertory. Included in the necrology should be any parishioners who have died in the previous year. The appropriate color is black, and a catafalque may be set up, draped with the black funeral pall, and surrounded by six candles at the chancel steps.

The liturgy for an All Souls' Day requiem is largely the normal one for Holy Eucharist with a few exceptions. As this is not a major feast, the *Kyrie* or the *Trisagion* is used in place of the *Gloria*. A collect of the day is appointed in *Lesser Feasts and Fasts*, along with eucharistic readings

---

62. *1979 Book of Common Prayer*, 15.

and other propers. The prayers of the people might use the form in the Burial Rite, substituting "all faithful departed" in the places where the name of the deceased would be said. I would discourage the omission of the confession because the grief of loss is often paired with a sense of regret, and the people will be grateful to hear the words of God's absolution pronounced over them. Before the post-communion prayer, some sort of commendation might be sung (either the *Kontakion*, hymn 355, or "May Choirs of Angels Lead You," hymn 356). Then any of the additional prayers for the departed may be said, along with the "Rest eternal grant," and the response, followed by the words, "May their souls, and the souls of all the departed, through the mercy of God, rest in peace." The post-communion prayer, blessing, and dismissal may then end the rite.[63]

---

63. I have taken these prayers from the Burial Rite and adapted for them for All Soul's Day. See *1979 Book of Common Prayer*, 486.

APPENDIX 1

The Most Common Rubrical Violations

As DEARMER OFTEN NOTED, when it comes to fidelity to the prayer book, usually all that is needed is intentionality and care to see that the rubrics are not onerous but that they actually carefully shape the worship of our church. In the decades since the 1979 prayer book was published, there are some unrubrical practices that persist. They have already been noted throughout this book but I'm aware that few clergy possess an eidetic memory and so have listed below the most common as a hopefully helpful resources for the observant parson.

- "In all services, the entire Christian assembly participates in such a way that the members of each order within the Church, lay persons, bishops, priests, and deacons, fulfill the functions proper to their respective orders, as set forth in the rubrical directions for each service" (BCP 13). Each of the four orders of ministry have their place in the worship of our church. The laity should read the first and second lessons and may read the prayers (after the prayers are introduced by a deacon, if there is one). The bishops are the normative celebrants at Holy Eucharist. The priests celebrate in the bishop's place in parochial celebrations. Deacons should read the Gospel, invite the prayers and confession, set the table, and assist in the administration of Communion. Each of these are the rights and prerogatives of each order and they elucidate the purpose of the ministry of each. Laity should only ever distribute Communion when there are not sufficient clergy. Seminarians who are not ordained should not "practice" by assuming the role of a deacon. The

APPENDIX 1

place of the bishop is in front of the altar of a parish church and not the seat of a CEO's desk in a diocesan office.

- "These [principal] feasts take precedence of any other day or observance. All Saints' Day may always be observed on the Sunday following November 1, in addition to its observance on the fixed date" (BCP 15). Holy Eucharist must be celebrated on all seven principal feasts of the church and this must be done on the day the feast falls. There is no provision for transferring Epiphany, Ascension, or All Saints' Day to the following Sunday. All Saints' Sunday may only be observed "in addition" to All Saints' Day.

- "When the Advent Wreath is used in the worshiping community at morning services, the appropriate number of candles on the wreath are lighted, without prayer or ceremony, with the other candles" (BOS 20). There is no provision for special ceremony or prayers when lighting an Advent wreath in church.

- "Holy Baptism is especially appropriate at the Easter Vigil, on the Day of Pentecost, on All Saints' Day or the Sunday after All Saints' Day, and on the Feast of the Baptism of our Lord (the first Sunday after the Epiphany). "It is recommended that, as far as possible, Baptisms be reserved for these occasions or when a bishop is present" (BCP 312). This rubric is instructed to be kept "as far as possible," it is not permission for the parson to refuse baptism on other Sundays during the year when the family has a good reason for making such a request.

- "Where practicable, the font is to be filled with clean water immediately before the Thanksgiving over the Water" (BCP 313). The reason this rubric is "when practicable" is because a baptismal pool for immersion would naturally be filled in advance. There is no provision for filling the font during the Thanksgiving over the Water. The focus at that point is the prayer itself, not the action of pouring water.

- "The Sermon" (BCP 326 & 358). There is no provision for eliminating the sermon from a celebration of Holy Eucharist, neither on the Sunday of the Passion: Palm Sunday nor on Good Friday.

- "On Sundays and other Major Feasts there follows, all standing, the Nicene Creed" (BCP 326 & 358). The Nicene Creed is not used at celebrations of Holy Eucharist which are not on a Sunday or some other major feast of the church. That said, it must be used on Sundays and major feasts unless noted otherwise, such as on Palm Sunday.

THE MOST COMMON RUBRICAL VIOLATIONS

- "Representatives of the congregation bring the people's offerings of bread and wine, and money or other gifts, to the deacon or celebrant. The people stand while the offerings are presented and placed on the Altar" (BCP 333 & 361). The bread, wine, and alms are all brought together in a single procession and placed on the altar. There is no provision for then removing the alms basin from the altar before the Great Thanksgiving (and it is expressly against the rubric for an acolyte to receive the alms and then carry it off instead of placing it on the altar). The people's gift of money is just as holy as their gift of bread and wine.

- "The Celebrant breaks the consecrated Bread. A period of silence is kept" (BCP 337 & 364). The silence after the fraction of the bread is absolutely required by the rubric. Anthems are only said or sung after the period of silence has been kept.

- "From the Easter Vigil through the Day of Pentecost 'Alleluia, alleluia' may be added to any of the dismissals" (BCP 340 & 366). The addition of the alleluias is to mark the profound joy of the Great Fifty Days, to set Eastertide off as something different from the rest of the year. To use them year round just because people are (or, more usually, the deacon is) excited not only violates the rubric but it also destroys one of the key ways the Great Fifty Days are marked off in our prayer book.

- "During the Great Thanksgiving, it is appropriate that there be only one chalice on the Altar, and, if need be, a flagon of wine from which additional chalices may be filled after the Breaking of the Bread" (BCP 407). There is no provision for multiple chalices on the altar during the Great Thanksgiving.

- "The following anthem [the *Agnus Dei*] may be used at the Breaking of the Bread" (BCP 407). The purpose of this and any other anthem after the fraction and silence is to give time for the bread to be broken sufficiently for the first group of communicants and for additional chalices to be filled, if needed. Following this rubric enables the next to be followed.

- "While the people are coming forward to receive Communion, the celebrant receives the Sacrament in both kinds. The bishops, priests, and deacons at the Holy Table then communicate, and after them the people" (BCP 407). If the bread has been broken, chalices filled,

APPENDIX 1

and all made ready for the distribution during whatever fraction anthems are used, then after the priest gives the invitation the people can immediately come forward while the ministers are receiving Communion themselves. All receive as equals and the people should not gaze at the ministers receiving but should be walking forward or be in a time of prayerful preparation until it is their turn to go forward. Even worse is the violation that has the ministers receive last. As noted in this book, this is not only a violation of the rubric and good meal etiquette, it all but guarantees that the Communion of the ministers becomes a show the people watch—entirely destroying the purpose of the rubric.

- "A hymn may be sung before or after the postcommunion prayer" (BCP 409). There is no provision for dividing the blessing and dismissal by placing a hymn in between them. The blessing is the priest's final words, and the dismissal is the deacon's final words. The rubrics require them to be said one after another. If a hymn is desired for the exit, it is sung after the postcommunion prayer (which would have both the blessing and dismissal said from the back, a truly bizarre choice) or (far better) it is sung after the deacon speaks the dismissal from the altar. The liturgy having been concluded according to the rubrics, all are certainly welcome to sing another song while the ministers depart.

- "A period of silence follows" (BCP 417). After the bishop invites the prayer for the candidates for confirmation, reception, and the Reaffirmation of Baptismal Vows, and then the petitions (usually on pp. 305–306) are prayed, a period of silence is rubrically required before the concluding collect on p. 418. This is one of only a very few times that silence is required in the prayer book.

- "When the Laying on of Hands or Anointing takes place at a public celebration of the Eucharist, it is desirable that it precede the distribution of Holy Communion, and it is recommended that it take place immediately before the exchange of the Peace" (BCP 453). People should not be directed to go to a side chapel or some other place for the sacrament of unction after they have received Communion. Unction precedes Communion, it never follows it, for Communion is the church's great sacrament of healing.

- "The Psalter is a body of liturgical poetry. It is designed for vocal, congregational use, whether by singing or reading. There are several traditional methods of psalmody. The exclusive use of a single method makes the recitation of the Psalter needlessly monotonous" BCP 582). There is no need to only ever recite or sing the psalter in a singular way and the rubrics are clear (and correct) that only one way of engaging with the psalms is "needlessly monotonous." Diversity is to be desired.

APPENDIX 2

A Litany of Saints for the Episcopal Church

THE FOLLOWING LITANY OF the Saints comes from the sources traditional to the church but has been updated to be brought into closer alignment with our understanding of sanctity in the Episcopal Church and our church's sanctorale kalendar. The following are some note on the adaptations we have made at my own parish.

We always begin with the *blessed Virgin Mary*. According to tradition, our Lady appeared in a vision to Lady Richeldis in England, showing her a vision of the house where the Holy Family once lived. Lady Richeldis built the house, which became both a shrine and the focus of pilgrimage to Walsingham.

In the list of *holy angels*, St. Michael is mentioned in Daniel and Revelation; St. Gabriel is the announcer of the annunciation to our Lady and is also in Daniel; St. Raphael is mentioned in the book of Tobit.

To the list of *holy apostles*, we have added Mary Magdalene, who, in the Eastern Church, is called the apostle to the apostles, as she was the first to bear witness to the resurrection. We have also added the women who remained with Christ at the cross after the men fled, along with the myrrh-bearing women who came to anoint him on Easter morning.

To the list of *patriarchs*, we have added the *matriarchs* Sarah, Rebekah, Rachel, and Leah (the wives of Abraham, Isaac, and Jacob) along with Bilhah and Zilphah (the handmaids of Rachel and Leah, who are matriarchs each of two of the tribes of Israel). After the disciples, the

Holy Innocents are named, the male babies of Palestine that were killed in Herod's mad raging to rid himself of the foretold Christ child.

With the *martyrs*, we have added Jonathan Myrick Daniels, an Episcopal Seminarian who was martyred in Selma, Alabama, outside of a gas station, as he was protecting a young black girl; Janani Luwum, an Anglican archbishop of Uganda, martyred in 1977 by Idi Amin; Oscar Romero, a Roman Catholic archbishop of San Salvador, an advocate for the poor, who was martyred while celebrating Eucharist; and Constance and her companions, Episcopal nuns attached to the St. Mary's Cathedral in Memphis, Tennessee, who stayed behind to minister in a Yellow Fever outbreak.

With *bishops and doctors*, we have added William Laud, a friend of St. Charles—king, martyr, and opposer of Puritanism. Laud himself was martyred in 1645. We have also added William White, the first bishop of the Episcopal Church; John Henry Hobart, a bishop with great missionary zeal and the founder of General Theological Seminary; and Barbara Clementine Harris, the first woman bishop in our church.

Doctors of the church are those who made significant theological contributions. We have added Austin Farrer and Frederick Denison Maurice, just two of the greatest theological minds of modern Anglicanism, along with Teresa of Ávila and Catherine of Siena, the first two female doctors recognized by the Roman Church.

The sixth section includes all remaining orders of the church: *priests, deacons, and laity from history*. I have included again, for reasons noted above, John Keble, who preached what is known as the Assize Sermon in 1833, which effectively launched Anglo-Catholicism in England. James DeKoven was a seminary professor and a leader in the Anglo-Catholic movement in the Episcopal Church. He was elected several times as bishop but never took the mitre due to others contesting his eucharistic theology. George Herbert and John Donne are both deeply loved English authors and Anglican priests. Florence Li Tim-Oi was the first woman ordained as an Anglican priest in 1944; the Episcopal Church remembers her day of ordination. Monica was the mother of St. Augustine, whose tears and prayers helped convert her son to Christianity. Hildegard of Bingen was a medieval mystic and composer; her music is still performed today. Evelyn Underhill was an Anglo-Catholic mystic and writer of the book *Mysticism*, which is considered one of the foundational works on the subject. At the end, we have included those faithful who were marginalized by the church in their time but are no less faithful. The traditional response of the litany is "pray for us," but some with an allergy to things catholic may find "pray with us" to be easier; and what matters most is not adherence to old forms but encouraging the faithful to join those prayers with those of the saints of the church.

V Holy Mary, R Pray with us.

V Holy Mother of God, R Pray with us.

V Our Lady of Walsingham, R Pray with us.

V Michael, Gabriel, and Raphael, R Pray with us.

V Seraphim and Cherubim, R Pray with us.

V All you holy angels and archangels, R Pray with us.

V John the Baptist, R Pray with us.

V Abraham, Isaac, and Jacob, R Pray with us.

V Sarah, Rebekah, Rachel, Leah, Bilhah, and Zilpah, R Pray with us.

V Moses and Miriam, R Pray with us.

V All you holy patriarchs, matriarchs, and prophets of God, R Pray with us.

V Mary Magdalene, apostle to the apostles, R Pray with us.

V Paul, Peter, and Andrew, R Pray with us.

V James, the brother of our Lord, R Pray with us.

V Thomas, the doubter, R Pray with us.

V James and John, sons of Zebedee, R Pray with us.

V Philip, Bartholomew, Matthew, and Simon the Zealot, R Pray with us.

V Thaddeus, Matthias, and Barnabas, R Pray with us.

V Mark and Luke, R Pray with us.

V The faithful women who stayed at the cross, R Pray with us.

V The holy myrrh-bearing women, first witnesses of the resurrection, R Pray with us.

V All you apostles and evangelists, R Pray with us.

V All you holy disciples of our Lord, R Pray with us.

V Stephen and Lawrence, R Pray with us.

V Polycarp, Perpetua, and Felicity, R Pray with us.

A LITANY OF SAINTS FOR THE EPISCOPAL CHURCH

V Janani Luwum and Oscar Romero, R Pray with us.

V Jonathan Myrick Daniels and Martin Luther King Jr., R Pray with us.

V Constance and her companions, R Pray with us.

V All you holy martyrs, R Pray with us.

V Augustine, Gregory, and Ambrose, R Pray with us.

V Augustine of Canterbury, Cuthbert, and Athanasius, R Pray with us.

V John Chrysostom and Nicholas, R Pray with us.

V William Laud and William White, R Pray with us.

V John Henry Hobart, R Pray with us.

V Barbara Clementine Harris, R Pray with us.

V Austin Farrer and Frederick Denison Maurice, R Pray with us.

V Teresa of Ávila and Catherine of Siena, R Pray with us.

V All you holy bishops and doctors, R Pray with us.

V Anthony, Benedict, and Bernard, R Pray with us.

V Dominic, Francis, and Bede, R Pray with us.

V James DeKoven and John Keble, R Pray with us.

V George Herbert, John Donne, and Florence Li Tim-Oi R Pray with us.

V Agatha, Lucy, Agnes, Cecilia, and Helena, R Pray with us.

V Julian, Bridgit, and Hildegard, R Pray with us.

V Monica and Catherine, R Pray with us.

V Clare of Assisi and Evelyn Underhill, R Pray with us.

V All you priests of God, R Pray with us.

V All you monks and hermits, R Pray with us.

V All you holy abbesses and nuns, R Pray with us.

V All you baptized, given unto God, R Pray with us.

V All you servants of God, throughout all time, R Pray with us.

V All you faithful, marginalized by the church, R Pray with us.

V All you whose faith is known to God alone, R Pray with us.

The litany then picks up in the Great Litany with "remember not, Lord Christ, our offenses . . ." When sung or said in procession, the litany should be timed to end at the altar, according to the instructions given earlier in this book for the Great Litany.

Bibliography

Alexander, J. Neil. *Celebrating Liturgical Time: Days, Weeks, and Seasons*. New York: Church Publishing, 2014.
Armentrout, Don S., and Robert Boak Slocum. *An Episcopal Dictionary of the Church: A User-Friendly Reference for Episcopalians*. New York: Church Publishing, 2000.
Attwater, Donald, ed. *A Catholic Dictionary*. 3rd ed. New York: Macmillan, 1948.
Bede. *Ecclesiastical History of the English People: With Bede's Letter to Egbert and Cuthbert's Letter on the Death of Bede*. Edited by D. H. Farmer. Translated by D. H. Farmer et al. Rev. ed. New York: Penguin, 2003. Kindle.
Beeson, Trevor. "The Master of Ceremonies: Percy Dearmer, Westminster." In *The Canons: Cathedral Close Encounters*, edited by Trevor Beeson, 98–111. London: Student Christian Movement, 2006.
Bishop, Edmund. *The Genius of the Roman Rite*. London: Beaufort House, 1899.
Blair, John. *Church in Anglo-Saxon Society*. Rev. ed. Oxford: Oxford University Press, 2006.
Blunt, John Henry, ed. *The Myroure of Oure Ladye: Containing a Devotional Treatise on Divine Service*. London: Early English Text Society, 1873.
Bond, Francis. *Fonts and Font Covers*. Oxford: Oxford University Press, 1908.
Bradshaw, Henry. *Statute of Lincoln Cathedral*. Edited by Charles Woodworth. Cambridge: Cambridge University Press, 1897.
Bradshaw, Timothy. "Macquerrie, John (1919–)." In *The SPCK Handbook of Anglican Theologians*, edited by Alister E. McGrath, 166–69. London: SPCK, 1998.
Brand, John. *Observations Popular Antiquities: Chiefly Illustrating the Origin of Our Vulgar Customs, Ceremonies, and Superstitions*. London: Chatto & Windus, 1913.
Bray, Gerald, ed. "The Elizabethan Injunctions, 1559." In *Documents of the English Reformation*. 3rd ed. Cambridge: Lutterworth, 1994.
Brightman, Frank Edward. *The English Rite: Being a Synopsis of the Sources and Revision of the Book of Common Prayer*. 2 vols. London: Rivingtons, 1915–21.
Buchanan, Colin. *The Savoy Conference Revisited: The Proceedings Taken from the Grand Debate of 1661 and the Works of Richard Baxter*. Gorgias Liturgical Studies 52. Piscataway, NJ: Gorgias, 2010.
Cayley, David. *Ivan Illich: An Intellectual Journey*. University Park, PA: Pennsylvania State University Press, 2021.
Church of England. *The 1549 Book of Common Prayer*. Satucket Software. http://justus.anglican.org/resources/bcp/1549/BCP1549.pdf.

———. "The Authorised Liturgy for the Coronation Right of His Majesty King Charles III." May 6, 2023. https://www.churchofengland.org/sites/default/files/2023-05/23-24132-coronation-liturgy-commentary_v4.pdf.

———. *The Book of Common Prayer and Administration of the Sacraments and Other Rites and Ceremonies of the Church.* Cambridge: Baskerville, 1662. http://justus.anglican.org/resources/bcp/1662/Baskerville.pdf.

———. *Constitution and Canons Ecclesiastical.* London: Robby Barker, 1640.

———. *Constitutions and Canons Ecclesiastical.* 1604. Anglican.net. https://www.anglican.net/doctrines/1604-canon-law/.

———. *The Second Prayer Book of Edward the Sixth and the Liturgy of Compromise (1552).* Edited by George W. Sprott. London: William Blackwood and Sons, 1905.

Cicero. *On the Orator: Books 1–2.* Translated by E. W. Sutton and H. Rackham. Loeb Classical Library 348. Cambridge: Harvard University Press, 1942.

Cobb, David, and Derek Olsen, eds. *Saint Augustine's Prayer Book.* Rev. ed. Cincinnati: Forward Movement, 2012.

Collier, Jeremy. *An Ecclesiastical History of Great Britain, Chiefly of England: From the First Planting of Christianity, to the End of the Reign of King Charles the Second; With a Brief Account of the Affairs of Religion in Ireland.* Vol. 2. London: William Straker, 1840.

Cramer, Jared C. *Percy Dearmer Revisited: Discerning Authentically Anglican Liturgy in a Multicultural, Ecumenical, Twenty-First-Century Context.* Eugene, OR: Wipf & Stock, 2020.

Currie, Chuck. "A Prayer for Father's Day." *Rev. Dr. Chuck Currie* (blog), June 18, 2011. https://chuckcurrie.blogs.com/chuck_currie/2011/06/a-prayer-for-fathers-day.html.

Cuthbert, E. G., and F. Atchley. *A History of the Use of Incense in Divine Worship.* New York: Longmans, 1909.

Cyril of Jerusalem. *The Catechetical Lectures.* Translated by Edwin Hamilton Gifford. In vol. 7 of *The Nicene and Post-Nicene Fathers of the Christian Church*, Series 2. Edited by Philip Schaff and Henry Wace. Grand Rapids: Christian Classics Ethereal Library, 1886–89. https://ccel.org/ccel/schaff/npnf207/npnf207.

Davies, J. G. *The Architectural Setting of Baptism.* London: Barrie & Rockliff, 1962.

Dearmer, Nan. *The Life of Percy Dearmer.* London: Alden, 1940.

Dearmer, Percy. *The Art of Public Worship.* London: A. R. Mowbray, 1919.

———. *The Cathedral Church of Oxford: A Description of Its Fabric and a Brief History of the Episcopal See.* London: George Bell & Sons, 1899.

———. *The Cathedral Church of Wells: A Description of Its Fabric and a Brief History of the Episcopal See.* London: George Bell & Sons, 1899.

———. *Christianity and Art.* New York: Association Press, 1926.

———. *The Ornaments of the Ministers.* 2nd ed. London: A. R. Mowbray, 1920.

———. *The Parson's Handbook: Containing Practical Directions Both for Parsons and Others as to the Management of the Parish Church and Its Services According to the Anglican Use, as Set Forth in the Book of Common Prayer.* 12th ed. London: Oxford University Press, 1932.

———. *A Short Handbook of Public Worship in the Churches of the Anglican Communion.* London: Oxford University Press, 1931.

———. *The Story of the Prayer Book in the Old and New World and Throughout the Anglican Church.* London: Oxford University Press, 1933.

BIBLIOGRAPHY

Dicastery for Promoting Christian Unity. "Guidelines for Admission to the Eucharist Between the Chaldean Church and the Assyrian Church of the East." July 20, 2001. http://www.christianunity.va/content/unitacristiani/en/dialoghi/sezione-orientale/chiesa-assira-dell-oriente/altri-documenti/testo-in-inglese.html.

Ditchfield, P. H. *The Parish Clerk*. New York: Dutton, 1907.

Donne, John. *LXXX Sermons*. London: Richard Royston & Richard Marriot, 1640.

Episcopal Church. *The Book of Common Prayer and Administration of the Sacraments and Other Rites and Ceremonies of the Church*. New York: Church Publishing, 1979.

———. *The Book of Occasional Services: Conforming to General Convention 2022*. New York: Church Publishing, 2022.

———. *Constitution and Canons, Together with the Rules of Order: For the Governance of the Protestant Episcopal Church in the United States of America, Otherwise known as the Episcopal Church*. Adopted and Revised in General Conventions 1785–2022. New York: Office of the General Convention, 2022.

———. *Enriching Our Worship: Ministry with the Sick or Dying Burial of a Child*. Vol. 2. New York: Church Publishing, 2000.

———. *Journal of the 79th General Convention*. New York: General Convention, 2018. https://www.episcopalarchives.org/sites/default/files/publications/2018_GC_Journal.pdf.

———. *Resolutions of the 81st General Convention*. New York: General Convention, 2024. https://extranet.generalconvention.org/staff/files/download/32550.

Fenwick, John R. K., and Bryan D. Spinks. *Worship in Transition: The Liturgical Movement in the Twentieth Century*. New York: Continuum, 1995.

Frere, Walter Howard, ed. *The Use of Sarum: I. The Sarum Customs as Set Forth in the Consuetudinary And Customary*. Translated by Walter Howard Frere. Cambridge: Cambridge University Press, 1898.

Fulton, Charles N., et al. *The Church for Common Prayer: A Statement on Worship Space for the Episcopal Church*. New York: Episcopal Church Building Fund, 1994.

Galley, Howard E. *The Ceremonies of the Eucharist: A Guide to the Celebration*. Lanham, MD: Cowley, 1989.

Gatta, Julia, and Martin Smith. *Go in Peace: The Art of Hearing Confessions*. New York: Morehouse, 2012.

Glibetic, Nina. "Passion of Christ in Byzantine Vesting Rituals: The Case of the Epitrachelion." In *Studies in Oriental Liturgy: Proceedings of the Fifth International Congress of the Society of Oriental Liturgy*, edited by Bert Groen et al., 265–76. Eastern Christian Studies 28. Leuven: Peeters, 2019.

Goffine, Leonard. *Devout Instructions on the Epistles and Gospels for the Sundays and Holydays*. New York: Benzinger Brothers, 1896.

Gray, Donald. "The British Museum Religion: Percy Dearmer in Context." Lecture given to the Anglo-Catholic Historical Society, London, May 8, 2001.

———. "Percy Dearmer." In *They Shaped Our Worship: Essays on Anglican Liturgists*, edited by Christopher Irvine, 71–76. London: SPCK, 1998.

Groves, Nicholas. "The Use of the Academic Hood in Quire." *Transactions of the Burgon Society* 8 (2008) 98–105. https://doi.org/10.4148/2475-7799.1065.

Gunn, Scott, and Melody Wilson Shobe. *Walk in Love: Episcopal Beliefs and Practices*. Cincinnati: Forward Movement, 2018.

BIBLIOGRAPHY

Guyer, Benjamin. "+Robinson and an Elizabethan Apocryphon." *Covenant*, Feb. 17, 2012. https://livingchurch.org/covenant/robinson-and-an-elizabethan-apocryphon/.

Haddon, Arthur West, and William Stubbs, eds. *Councils and Ecclesiastical Documents Relating to Great Britain and Ireland*. Vol. 3. Oxford: Clarendon, 1871.

Hatchett, Marion J. *A Manual of Ceremonial for the New Prayer Book*. Sewanee, TN: St. Luke's Journal of Theology, 1977.

———. *Commentary on the American Prayer Book*. New York: Seabury, 1980.

Henderson, W. G., ed. *Processionale ad Usum Insignis ac Praeclarae Ecclesiae Sarum*. Leeds: M'Corquodale, 1882.

Hendrickson, Robert. "Cassock Albs Are Destroying the Church." *A Desert Father* (blog), Mar. 26, 2024. https://adesertfather.org/2014/05/21/cassock-albs-are-destroying-the-church/.

Hooker, Richard. *Of the Laws of Ecclesiastical Polity: The Fifth Book*. London: Macmillan, 1902.

Inter-Lutheran Commission on Worship. *Lutheran Book of Worship*. Minneapolis: Augsburg, 1978.

Joslyn-Siemiatkoski, Daniel. "How Christians Made Good Friday Bad for Jews—and What's Changed." *Sojourners*, Apr. 3, 2023. https://sojo.net/articles/how-christians-made-good-friday-bad-for-jews-and-whats-changed.

Justin Martyr. *First Apology*. In vol. 1 of *The Ante-Nicene Fathers*. Edited by Alexander Roberts and James Donaldson. Grand Rapids: Christian Classics Ethereal Library, 1885. https://ccel.org/ccel/schaff/anf01/anf01.i.html.

Kiraz, George Anton, ed. *Memorial Services: Extracted by Permission from "A Prayer Book Revised" as Issued in 1913*. Analecta Giorgiana 536. Piscataway, NJ: Gorgias, 2010.

Lambert, Malcolm. *Christians and Pagans: The Conversion of Britain from Alban to Bede*. New Haven: Yale University Press, 2010.

Lang, Uwe Michael. *Turning Towards the Lord: Orientation in Liturgical Prayer*. San Francisco: Ignatius, 2009.

Legg, J. Wickham, ed. *The Sarum Missal: Edited from Three Early Manuscripts*. Oxford: Clarendon, 1969.

Liddell, Henry George, and Robert Scott. *A Greek-English Lexicon*. 7th ed. New York: Harper & Brothers, 1883.

Liguori, Alphonsus. *Dignities and Duties of the Priest or Selva: A Collection of Materials for Ecclesiastical Retreats; Rule of Life and Spiritual Rules*. Translated and edited by Eugene Grimm. The Complete Works of Saint Alphonsus de Liguori 12. New York: Benzinger Brothers, 1889.

Littlejohn, Brad. "The Word Made Flesh for Us: Richard Hooker on the Sacraments." *Ad Fontes*, Apr. 10, 2024. https://adfontesjournal.com/web-exclusives/the-word-made-flesh-for-us-richard-hooker-on-the-sacraments/.

Loades, David. *Elizabeth I: A Life*. London: Hambledon Continuum, 2006.

Long, Thomas G. *Accompany Them with Singing: The Christian Funeral*. Louisville: Westminster John Knox, 2013.

Macquarrie, John. "In Memoriam: The Reverend Dr. John Macquarrie, 1919–2007." Church of Saint Mary the Virgin. https://www.stmvirgin.org/benediction.

Malloy, Patrick. *Celebrating the Eucharist: A Practical Ceremonial Guide for Clergy and Other Lay Ministers*. New York: Church Publishing, 2007.

Mascall, E. L., and H. S. Box, eds. *The Blessed Virgin Mary: Essays by Anglican Writers.* London: Darton, Longman & Todd, 1963.

Maskell, William. *The Ancient Liturgy of the Church of England, According to the Uses of Sarum, York, Hereford, and Bangor, and the Roman Liturgy Arranged in Parallel Columns with Preface and Notes.* 3rd ed. Oxford: Clarendon Press, 1882.

Mayo, Janet. *A History of Ecclesiastical Dress.* New York: Holmes & Meier, 1984.

Michno, Dennis G. *A Priest's Handbook: The Ceremonies of the Church.* Wilton, CT: Morehouse-Barlow, 1983.

Micklethwaite, J. T. *The Ornaments of the Rubric.* 3rd ed. London: Longman, Green, 1901.

Milavec, Aaron. *The Didache: Text, Translation, Analysis, and Commentary.* Collegeville, MN: Liturgical Press, 2003.

Mitchell, Leonel L., and Ruth Meyers. *Praying Shapes Believing: A Theological Commentary on the Book of Common Prayer.* Rev. ed. Weil Series in Liturgics. New York: Seabury, 2016.

Narsai of Nisibis. *The Liturgical Homilies of Narsai.* Translated by Dom R. H. Connolly. Cambridge: Cambridge University Press, 1909.

Nockles, Peter B. *The Oxford Movement in Context: Anglican High Churchmanship 1760–1857.* Cambridge: Cambridge University Press, 1997.

Oakley, Mark. "The Pity and the Glory." *Church Times*, Apr. 18, 2019. https://www.churchtimes.co.uk/articles/2019/18-april/faith/faith-features/the-pity-and-the-glory.

Olsen, Derek A. "'Traditional' Office Hymns." *St. Bede Blog*, May 23, 2007. http://www.stbedeproductions.com/traditional-office-hymns.

Paul VI. *Ministeria Quaedam.* Apostolic letter. Vatican website. Aug. 15, 1972. https://www.vatican.va/content/paul-vi/la/motu_proprio/documents/hf_p-vi_motu-proprio_19720815_ministeria-quaedam.html.

Pavlechko, Thomas, and Carl P. Daw Jr. *Liturgical Music for the Revised Common Lectionary: Year A.* 2nd ed. New York: Church Publishing, 2022.

Pearson, A. H., trans. *The Sarum Missal in English.* Reprint, Eugene, OR: Wipf & Stock, 2004.

Pontifical Council for Promoting Christian Unity (PCPCU). "Guidelines for Admission to the Eucharist between the Chaldean Church and the Assyrian Church of the East." July 20, 2001. http://www.christianunity.va/content/unitacristiani/en/dialoghi/sezione-orientale/chiesa-assira-dell-oriente/altri-documenti/testo-in-inglese.html.

Price, Matthew J., et al. *The Hymnal Revision Feasibility Study: A Report to the Standing Commission on Liturgy and Music.* https://prod.cpg.org/globalassets/documents/publications/report-hymnal-revision-feasibility-study.pdf.

Procter, Francis, and Walter Howard Frere. *A New History of the Book of Common Prayer: With a Rationale of Its Offices.* Rev. ed. London: Macmillan, 1908.

Reed, John Shelton. *Glorious Battle: The Cultural Politics of Victorian Anglo-Catholicism.* Nashville: Vanderbilt University Press, 1996.

Ritual Conformity: Interpretations of the Rubrics of the Prayer-Book, Agreed Upon by a Conference Held at All Saints, Margaret-Street, 1880–1881. Oxford: Parker, 1881.

Schwartz, Victoria. "The Theological Differences Between Godly Play and Catechesis of the Good Shepherd." *Center for Children & Theology* 25 (July 2018). https://cctheo.org/godly-play-cgs-theological-differences/.

BIBLIOGRAPHY

Scottish Episcopal Church. "The Order for Solemn Evensong and Benediction of the Blessed Sacrament." Old Saint Paul's, Edinburgh. May, 2021. https://www.osp.org.uk/wp-content/uploads/2021/05/Evensong-sine-Lucernarium-2021.pdf.

———. "The Vigil of Easter." https://www.scotland.anglican.org/wp-content/uploads/Easter-Vigil.pdf.

Shakespeare, William. *A Midsummer Night's Dream*. Edited by Barbara A. Mowat and Paul Werstine. Washington, DC: Folger Shakespeare Library, 2024.

Shaver, Stephen R. "*O Oriens*: Reassessing Eastward Eucharistic Celebration for Renewed Liturgy." *Anglican Theological Review* 94.3 (Summer 2012) 451–73.

Smith, Martin L. *Reconciliation: Preparing for Confession in the Episcopal Church*. Lanham, MD: Cowley, 1985.

Spinks, Bryan. "The Prayer Book 'Crisis' in England." In *The Oxford Guide to the Book of Common Prayer: A Worldwide Survey*, edited by Charles Hefling and Cynthia Shattuck, 239–43. Oxford: Oxford University Press, 2006.

Staley, Vernon, ed. *Hierugia Anglicana: Documents and Extracts Illustrative of the Ceremonial of the Anglican Church After the Reformation*. Vol. 1. London: De La More, 1902.

Stielau, Allison. "The Censer in and After the Reformation: Authority, Rebellion, and Transgression." In *Holy Smoke: Censers Across Cultures*, edited by Beate Fricke, 207–50. Munich: Heamer, 2024.

Stuhlman, Byron D. *Prayer Book Rubrics Expanded*. New York: Church Publishing, 1987.

Temple, Frederick, and William Dalrymple Maclagan. *The Archbishops on the Lawfulness of the Liturgical Use of Incense and the Carrying of Lights in Procession*. London: Macmillan, 1899.

Terrien, Samuel. *The Elusive Presence: Toward a New Biblical Theology*. San Francisco: Harper & Row, 1978.

Theodore of Mopsuestia. *Commentary on the Lord's Prayer, Baptism and the Eucharist*. Translated by Alphonse Mingana. Cambridge: W. Heffer & Sons, 1933. https://www.tertullian.org/fathers/theodore_of_mopsuestia_lordsprayer_01_intro.htm.

Thomas á Kempis. *Imitation of Christ*. Translated by William Benham. New Prague, MN: FaithPoint, 2006.

Thomas, Zachary. "The Amice and Papal Fanon." *Liturgical Arts Journal*, Apr. 6, 2018. https://www.liturgicalartsjournal.com/2018/04/the-amice-and-papal-fanon.html.

Tribe, Shawn. "The History and Development of the Mitre." *Liturgical Arts Journal*, Jan. 16, 2023. https://www.liturgicalartsjournal.com/2022/09/the-history-and-development-of-mitre.html.

Turrell, James F. *Celebrating the Rites of Initiation: A Practical Ceremonial Guide for Clergy and Other Liturgical Ministers*. New York: Church Publishing, 2013.

United States Conference of Catholic Bishops (USCCB). "The Requisites for the Celebration of the Mass." In *General Instruction on the Roman Missal*. Washington, DC: USCCB, 2011.

Wagner, Richard. *Lohengrin: Son of Parsifal*. Translated by Oliver Huckel. New York: Thomas Y. Cromwell, 1905.

Walcott, Mackenzie E. C. *Traditions and Customs of Cathedrals*. London: Longmans, 1872.

Weil, Louis. "Challenges and Possibilities in the Anglican Liturgical Future." Lecture, University of the South, Sewanee, TN, June 18, 2016.

———. "The Solemn Reproaches of the Cross: The Debate about Anti-Semitism in the Good Friday Liturgy with Special Reference to the Reproaches." 2005. https://static1.squarespace.com/static/56ed844ea3360c829bb8da2d/t/5772bdea15d5dbae58edd7be/1467137514408/The+Solemn+Reproaches+of+the+Cross.pdf.

Wilkins, David, ed. *Concilia Magnae Britanniae et Hiberniae*. Vol. 3. London, 1740. https://archive.org/details/bim_eighteenth-century_concilia-magnae-britanni_wilkins-david_1737_3/page/n13/mode/2up.

Wood, James. *Dictionary of Quotations*. New York: Frederick Warne, 1899.

Wright, J. Robert. *Readings for the Daily Office from the Early Church*. New York: Church Publishing, 2000.

Xenophon. *Memorabilia*. Edited by E. C. Marchant. Perseus Digital Library. http://www.perseus.tufts.edu/hopper/text?doc=Perseus%3Atext%3A1999.01.0208%3Abook%3D4%3Achapter%3D1%3Asection%3D3.

Yates, Nigel. *Anglican Ritualism in Victorian Britain: 1830–1910*. Oxford: Oxford University Press, 1999.

Index

Ablutions, 83, 156, 203, 243, 266, 246–47, 329, 360
Absolution, 55, 99, 150, 151, 185, 187, 193, 240, 247, 258, 318, 321, 322, 355
Academic Hood. *See* Hood.
Acolytes, 12, 27, 126, 194, 209, 212–15, 241, 243–44, 254, 256, 306, 368–69, 379. *See also* Crucifer *and* Taperer.
Advent, 41, 42, 80–81, 86–89, 91, 93, 125–26, 129, 155, 156, 173, 180, 183, 187, 204, 213, 233, 318, 320, 346–49, 352, 373–74, 378
Advent Wreath, 42, 348–49, 378
Administration of Communion, 151, 166, 264, 338, 377
Agnus Dei, 152, 243, 262, 379
Alb. *See* Albe.
Albe, 8, 10, 25, 96–97, 100, 112–15, 134, 171, 213–15, 249, 253, 279, 306, 361
All-Night Watch, 360–62
All Saints' Day, 88, 91, 93, 156, 221, 269, 292, 372, 374, 378
All Souls' Day, 129, 337, 374–75
Alms, 25, 46, 55, 57, 83, 195, 211, 241, 248–49, 259–60, 324, 341, 359
Alms Basin. *See* Basin, Alms.
Almuce, 43, 105, 107, 339, 354
All Night Watch. *See* Watch, All Night.
Altar, 5–8, 38, 40–41, 42–47, 55, 57, 60, 64–84, 100, 104, 108, 112, 116, 120, 124–26, 132, 159, 164, 167, 170–74, 193–96, 201–3, 206, 209, 211–12, 214–16, 218, 225, 227, 239–67, 281, 296, 302, 305, 307, 309–11, 313, 320, 324, 326, 328, 337, 342, 350, 352, 354–55, 360–61, 369, 378, 380, 386. *See also*
Book, 80, 151, 158, 256. *See also* Missal.
Bowing to, 162, 163, 170, 196, 305, 308, 311
Canopy, 8, 43, 66, 68
Candles. *See* Candles, Altar.
Censing of, 99
Cross, 11–12, 26, 76, 125, 161, 167, 225, 255, 326, 357–58
Eastward Facing, xi, 16–17, 42, 45, 51
English. *See* English Altar.
Hangings. *See* Hangings.
Lights. *See* Candles, Altar.
Rail, 7, 12, 55, 65, 71, 83, 193, 194, 214, 227, 230, 238, 241, 243, 264, 266, 281, 320, 324, 350, 355
Steps, 71, 170, 240, 247, 261
Ambo, 45–50, especially 49
Amen, Great. *See* Great Amen.
Amice, xi, 69, 95–97, 100, 110–16, 119, 133, 224, 25–53, 268, 305, 326, 338
Announcements, 221, 234, 240, 259, 272, 311, 356
Anointing. *See* Unction.

395

INDEX

Ante-Communion, 143–45
Anthem
   Burial, 340, 343
   Choral or Sung, 39, 45, 150, 152, 160, 182, 185, 192, 194, 209, 210–11, 233, 243, 256, 260, 264, 276, 308, 309, 311, 324, 325, 340, 362–63, 369, 379
   Spoken, 332, 362–63, 365
   Fraction. *See* Fraction Anthem, *also* Agnus Dei.
Antiphon, 153, 158, 162, 184, 186, 203, 207, 325, 347, 361
Apparels, 43, 74, 95, 96, 97, 100, 110–15, 118, 133–34, 137, 224, 252, 338, 342, 354
Apostles' Creed, 15, 182, 184, 274, 288, 289, 341
Ascension Day, 76, 91, 93, 128, 153, 155, 204, 217, 222, 233, 275, 371, 372, 378
Ashes
   at Burial, 355
   on Ash Wednesday, 353, 355
Ash Wednesday, 23, 86, 91, 173, 199, 217, 353, 355
Asperges, 352
Aumbry, 7, 82. *See also* Tabernacle.

Banners, 127, 214, 215, 217, 339, 358, 371
Banns, 259
Baptism, ix, xxiv, 4, 17, 25, 42, 50–52, 94, 111–12, 116, 126, 128, 141, 146, 155, 168–69, 195, 210–12, 269–82, 288, 290–92, 296–97, 299, 306, 322–23, 335, 342, 349, 352, 361, 365, 369–70, 373, 380
Baptismal Covenant, 274–76, 288, 297. *See also* Renewal of Baptismal Vows.
Baptismal Font. *See* Font.
Baptismal Garment, 25, 111–12, 279
Baptismal Pool, 17, 51–52, 279, 378
Baptismal Sponsors. *See* Sponsors, for Baptism.
Baptismal Water, 50–51, 210, 275–82, 325, 352, 369, 378

Basin
   Alms, 46, 83, 195, 241, 248, 259, 379
   and Ewer (for the *lavabo*), 7, 124, 137, 236, 260
   at Baptism, 51, 281. *See also* Baptismal Pool.
   for Censer, 140
Bell, 58, 61–62, 123, 130, 178, 180, 201, 203, 361, 369, 371
Benediction of the Blessed Sacrament, 196–203
Benedictus, 192
Bible, 18, 21, 25, 27, 30, 47, 49, 56, 188, 209
Biddings, 192, 214, 225, 235, 275, 340
Bier, 129–30, 338, 339, 340, 342, 343
Bishop, xxiv, 2, 8, 9, 12, 14, 17, 19–20, 23–26, 32, 41, 50, 65, 69, 83, 90, 92, 97–100, 104, 108, 110, 112, 119, 122, 128, 144, 159, 164, 167, 173, 175–76, 179, 198, 200, 205, 211, 214–15, 217, 224, 225–26, 228, 231, 246, 253, 265, 269, 270, 276, 286, 290–300, 303–4, 347, 356, 359, 377–80, 383, 385
   choir habit, 26, 98, 101, 104, 112, 119, 215, 217, 295
   eucharistic vesture, 69, 97–99, 100, 110
Blessed Virgin Mary, 22, 44, 77, 86, 88, 93, 125, 162, 197, 203, 251, 290, 382, 384
Blessing, 179, 216, 223, 254, 267, 291, 298, 313, 314–15, 329, 333, 343, 372, *also*
   at Benediction, 198, 202
   at Eucharist, 99, 144, 156, 169, 195, 244, 249, 349, 351, 375, 380
   of a Marriage. *See* Nuptial Blessing.
   of a Paschal Candle, 42
   of New Fire, 367
   of Palms, 357–58
   of rings, 310
   of water at Baptism, 210, 214, 277
   Nuptial, 64, 165, 303, 305, 311
Boat, incense, 125, 135–36, 193, 252, 254
Bookmarkers, 49, 80, 194

INDEX

Book of Common Prayer, 1662, 5, 7, 14, 18–21, 24–25, 28–30, 49, 64, 86–87, 157–58, 162–63, 165, 168, 178–79, 188, 195, 205, 209, 211, 222, 224, 227–28, 246, 259, 266, 269, 274, 278, 283–84, 322–23, 325, 359

Book of Occasional Services, x, 42, 53, 214, 270, 324, 327–28, 348–49, 251, 353, 356, 360–61, 371, 374

Bow, 104, 163–67, 166–67, 170, 194, 196, 201–2, 215, 218, 238–39, 242–43, 247–49, 254, 257, 260–62, 267, 279, 308, 363

Bread. *See* Communion Bread.

Bread Box, 86, 123, 201, 229

Breaking of the Bread. *See* Fraction.

Burial Anthems. *See* Anthems, Burial.

Burial of the Dead, 129, 141, 192, 210, 334–45, 375

Burse, 121–22, 133, 241, 244, 247, 251, 259, 330

Candlemas, 22, 126, 173, 312, 349, 352–53, 357

Candles, 41–42, 48, 130, 134, , 139, 140, *Also*
  Altar, 3, 5, 6, 8, 26–27, 41–42, 46, 64, 71–72, 75–79, 90, 100, 134, 138, 139–40, 172–74, 184, 187, 193, 215, 221, 247, 249, 251, 263, 296, 305, 326, 329, 338, 342, 349, 352–54, 368, 369
  Around the Altar, 77, 201, 296
  Baptismal, 280
  Paschal. *See* Paschal Candle.
  Processional. *See* Tapers.
  Riddle, 6, 46, 82

Candlestick, 6, 75–79, 126–27, 130, 139, 172, 174, 263, 342, 354

Canon of Mass, 80, 160, 165, 167, 250, 261

Canons of 1604, 26, 45, 50, 72, 160, 161, 162, 163, 169, 257

Canons of 1640, 161, 163

Canopy, Altar. *See* Altar Canopy.

Cantor, 32, 41, 104, 160, 181, 205, 206, 207, 276, 368

Cappa nigra, 105, 109, 164, 338, 354

Carol, 349

Carpet, 7, 84, 121, 221, 295

Cassock, x 43, 98, 100–103, 112–15, 120, 140, 193, 217, 329, 339, 354, 361

Cassock-albe, 114–15

Catechist, 283, 286, 293

Celebrant's Chair. *See* Sedilia.

Celebration of a New Ministry, 65

Censer, 27, 124–25, 136, 140, 170, 176–77, 193–94, 201–2, 215–18, 220, 254, 256, 260

Censing, 99, 164, 176, 193–94, 254, 260, 276, 341, 367, 369

Cerecloth, 75

Chair 117, 193, 205, 296, 298–99

Chair for the Bishop, 41, 296. *See also* Faldstool.

Chalice, 7, 25, 74, 100, 116, 121–24, 139, 165–66, 201, 225–26, 228, 231, 236, 241–44, 247–49, 251, 260, 262–63, 265–67, 281, 326, 328–29, 342, 379

Chalice Bearer. *See* Eucharistic Minister.

Chalice Veil, 122, 243, 266

Chancel, xix, 6, 8, 24–25, 36–39, 41–45, 49, 54, 57, 66, 67–68, 71–72, 83, 132, 161, 195, 206, 208, 212, 214, 215, 216, 218, 226–27, 235, 247, 259, 268, 273, 276, 280, 296–99, 307–8, 338, 340, 342, 350, 353, 355, 357–58, 363, 368, 374

Chapel, xi, xii, 27, 38, 44, 50, 57, 70, 82–83, 132, 161, 178–79, 217, 241, 251, 266, 324, 380

Chapter (as in short Scripture reading), 186

Chant, 39, 48–49, 100, 120, 149, 153, 158, 188, 194, 205–6, 208, 224–25, 256, 276, 342, 351, 358, 371

Charcoal, 27, 135–36, 138, 170, 252, 366

397

INDEX

Chasuble, 3, 8, 9, 13, 25, 27, 43, 88, 95–100, 109–11, 116–19, 129, 133–34, 202, 214, 224, 235, 236, 247, 251, 252–54, 263, 272, 278, 296, 305–6, 326, 338, 341, 342, 347, 366, 369

Chests (for storage), 73, 132, 137

Chimere, 26, 98, 104, 119, 217, 252, 295, 296

Choir
   as in a group of singers, x, 33, 39–41, 45, 58, 61, 120, 131, 140, 148, 150, 152–53, 159, 160, 164, 176, 180, 187, 188, 192, 194–96, 204, 207, 209, 214–17, 247, 253–55, 257, 260–61, 267, 307, 340, 343, 371
   as in a habit of dress, 98–99, 101–9, 110, 306, 338
   as in a location in the Church, 8, 25, 42, 43, 49, 116, 170, 193, 205, 212, 295, 309, 342

Choir Vestry, 131, 140, 196

Chrisom. *See* Baptismal Garment.

Chrism, 25, 92, 280, 282, 359

Christmas, 23, 41, 81, 88, 97, 93, 139, 155, 174, 214, 221–23, 258, 312, 347–52, 372

Churching of Women. *See* Thanksgiving for the Birth or Adoption of a Child.

Church Warden, 26, 61–62, 127, 131, 141, 299, 371

Churchyard, 57, 61, 344–45

Ciborium. *See either* Altar Canopy *or* Bread Box.

Cincture. *See* Girdle.

Clerk, xix, 8, 26, 43, 104, 112, 113, 119, 126, 148, 172, 178, 188, 195, 205–6, 236, 251, 263, 278, 339, 342, 349

Clock, 47–48

Collection. *See* Offering.

Colors, Liturgical. *See* Liturgical Colors.

Comfortable Words, 151

Commemoration of All Faithful Departed. *See* All Souls' Day.

Commination, 205

Communion. *See* Eucharist.

Communion Bread, xii, xiv, 12, 68, 83, 121, 121, 124, 137, 163, 165–66, 182, 199–203, 211, 228–32, 241–43, 248, 251, 259–62, 266, 281, 311, 325–28, 332, 341, 370 379

Communion Under Special Circumstances, 329, 332

Compline, 184, 185, 200

Confession, Private. *See* Reconciliation of a Penitent.

Confession, General, 99, 149–51, 157, 165, 180, 183, 185, 187, 193, 240, 247, 251, 258, 325, 329, 332, 355, 358, 375, 377

Confirmation, 94, 128, 283, 287–94, 296–99, 303, 309, 321, 380

Confirmation Sponsors. *See* Sponsors, for Confirmation.

Consecration
   of bishop, 26
   of a church, 65, 210
   of chrism, 92, 164, 359
   of Eucharist, 145, 151, 165–68, 177, 225, 230, 248, 261, 266, 325–26

Cope, 8, 10, 25–26, 43, 69, 88, 96, 98–99, 104, 108–10, 118, 120, 129, 133–34, 164, 177, 187, 193–94, 201–2, 209, 215, 217, 225, 252, 254, 272, 281, 298, 305–6, 348, 341, 342, 357, 362, 356, 369

Corporal, 25, 70, 72, 120–22, 137, 139, 236, 244, 247–48, 251, 259, 261, 266, 267, 330, 342

Corpus Christi, 197, 217

Cotta, 105, 120

Coverlet, 75, 247, 249, 251

Creche, 350–51

Credence, 7, 25, 82, 84, 170, 195, 243–44, 247, 251

Creed. *See* Apostles' Creed *or* Nicene Creed.

Cross
   Altar. *See* Altar Cross.
   Processional. *See* Processional Cross.
   Sign of. *See* Sign of the Cross.

398

INDEX

Veneration of. *See* Veneration of the Cross.
Crozier, 97, 99, 100, 110, 225, 299
Crucifix, 43–44, 55, 76, 90, 345
Crucifer, xiv, 125, 170, 176, 213, 215, 216, 238, 252, 254, 256, 259, 260, 267, 277, 296, 307, 338, 340, 342, 371
Cruet, 7, 83, 124, 136–37, 139, 236, 247–49, 251, 329
Cupboard, 57, 73, 132–37, 140, 215
Cushion
for Altar, 6, 71, 76, 79, 238, 244, 251
for Kneeling, 41, 52, 84, 193, 296, 305

Daily Devotions for Individuals and Families, 186
Daily Office, 22, 98, 106, 145, 150, 152, 154–59, 165, 172–74, 178–203, 204, 205, 207, 225, 270, 361
Dalmatic, 8, 96, 98, 100, 110–11, 118–19, 129, 134, 224, 236, 253
Day of Pentecost, 81, 86, 89–90, 92–94, 127–28, 154, 156, 223, 269, 275, 347, 368, 370, 372–73, 378–79
Days of Special Devotion, 23–24, 174
Deacon, 7–8, 14, 31–32, 40, 49, 71, 100, 104, 108, 110, 112, 116, 118–19, 134, 144, 156, 168, 170, 178, 187, 200–201, 203, 211, 214, 220–21, 224–26, 232, 236–44, 246, 249–50, 253–60, 262, 265–67, 277, 296, 303, 307, 311, 340–41, 343, 347, 355, 358, 360, 362, 367–68, 377, 379, 380, 383
Decalogue. *See* Ten Commandments.
Dedication of a Church, 23, 94, 173
Devotions, 4, 17, 20, 23–24, 29, 40, 42, 54, 56, 151–52, 160, 169, 171, 174, 185–86, 197–204, 263, 314, 348, 360–64
Diaconate. *See* Deacon.
Dies irae, 336, 340
Dismissal, 49, 143–44, 156–57, 180, 182, 185–87, 196, 203, 244, 249–50, 267, 311, 329, 333, 338, 343–44, 359, 372, 375, 379–80

Distribution of Communion, 32, 121, 123–24, 225, 227, 265, 323, 380
Dorsal, 6, 8, 26, 46, 69–71, 81–82, 90, 342, 354
Dossal. *See* Dorsal.
Doxology, 185–86

Easter, 42, 64, 86, 91, 93, 126–29, 144, 153, 164, 173, 180, 210, 222, 258, 269–70, 272, 275, 336, 347, 353, 356, 361, 363, 365, 368–72, 378–79, 382
Easter Vigil. *See* Great Vigil of Easter.
Eastertide, 23, 81, 87–88, 93, 155, 174, 180, 203, 222, 233, 368, 379
Eastward Position, xi, 67–68, 70–71, 159, 172, 215, 235, 238–41, 257, 258
Elements, Eucharistic. *See* Eucharistic Elements.
Elevation of the Bread, 167–68, 242
Ember Days, 347
Embroidery, 6, 73–74, 80, 91, 100, 115, 117–18, 121, 127, 129, 133, 137, 217
Emergency Baptism, 281–82
English Altar, 6, 69, 78, 82, 90, 174, 251, 354
Entrance, 126, 156, 176, 187, 193, 209, 212–14, 253–54, 296, 305–8, 340–41, 352, 355, 357, 362–63, 372
Epiclesis, 242, 262
Epiphany, 88–91, 93, 153, 155, 221–22, 233, 269, 347, 349–53, 372, 378
Episcopal Chair. *See* Chair for the Bishop *also* Faldstool.
Epistle, 48–49, 136, 156, 173, 184, 191–92, 222, 231, 255–56, 369, 389
Eucharist, ix–xi, 5, 15, 19, 22, 25, 32, 37, 57, 64, 68, 71, 83, 98–99, 102, 106–7, 109–16, 121–22, 129, 133, 136, 144–47, 151, 153, 156, 159, 165–68, 172–73, 176, 180–81, 183, 187–89, 192, 195–202, 204, 207–15, 219–68, 270, 272–73, 277, 281–82,

399

INDEX

Eucharist (continued), 288–89, 296, 299, 306–7, 311–12, 323–28, 329–30, 332, 338, 340–42, 351, 355, 357–59, 361, 369, 371–72, 374, 377–78, 380, 383

Eucharistic Canopy. *See* Altar Canopy.

Eucharistic Minister, 32, 71, 110, 168, 213–14, 225–27, 236–43, 246–54, 257–61, 265, 267, 277, 281, 307, 311, 340, 342, 355. *See also* Subdeacon.

Eucharistic Elements, 121–22, 163, 209, 231, 243, 260, 266, 289, 326

Eucharistic Vestments, xiii, 5, 7, 12–13, 15, 18, 20, 25, 27, 50, 59, 69, 84, 85–89, 91–100, 101–2, 107, 109–20, 121, 129, 131–34, 138, 172, 201, 206, 220, 238, 246–49, 252, 268, 326, 330, 336, 338, 354, 357, 361, 373

Eulogy, 336, 341

Evening Prayer, 24, 77, 98, 145, 147, 150, 154–56, 164, 172, 176–78, 180, 182, 183–85, 186, 192–96, 195, 200–203, 204–5, 212, 215, 220–21, 267, 283–84, 349, 357, 362

Evensong, 98, 147, 150, 164, 176–77, 185, 192–96, 199, 200–203, 212, 215, 220, 267, 284, 349, 357

Ewer, 7, 124, 137, 251

Exhortation
before Eucharist, 55, 150, 200, 318, 355
in marriage, 308–9
in unction, 317

Exsultet, 368

Extreme Unction. *See* Ministration at the Time of Death.

Faldstool
as in the folding chair a bishop sits on, 41, 205, 296, 298–99
as in the litany desk, 205

Fair Linen, 26, 72, 74–75, 100, 120–21, 137, 139, 251, 266, 342

Fasting Communion, 145–46

Fasts, 21, 173–74

Feast, Transferring of a. *See* Transferring of a Feast.

Festal Vestments, 91–94, 129

Fifty Days of Easter. *See* Eastertide.

Fire, Blessing of New. *See* New Fire.

Flagon, 97, 124, 260, 282, 379

Flowers, 59, 77, 80–81, 91, 308, 337, 350, 371

Font, 17, 25, 50–52, 126, 139, 208, 210, 212, 272, 276–77, 279–82, 350, 365, 378

Footpace, 57, 71–72, 84, 100, 201–2, 236

Foot washing, 96, 359–60

Fraction, 124, 199, 225, 229–30, 243, 258, 260, 262–63, 379–80

Frontal, 6, 8, 26, 43, 46, 59, 69, 70, 72–74, 77, 81, 86, 90–91, 94, 100, 137, 138, 221, 225, 251, 296, 342, 354

Frontlet, 6, 8, 74–75, 90, 100, 137, 221, 251, 342, 354

Funeral. *See* Burial of the Dead.

Funeral Pall, 129, 337, 339, 343

General Confession. *See* Confession, General.

General Thanksgiving, 154, 157, 180, 182, 185, 187

Genuflection, 163–67

Girdle, ix, 96, 103, 110, 112–13, 115, 118, 134, 171, 252–53

Gloria in excelsis, 20, 152, 153, 158–59, 164, 169, 215, 232–33, 238–39, 247, 255, 273, 374

Gloria Patri, 159, 162, 179, 185, 203

Godparents. *See* Sponsors, for Baptism.

Gold Vestments, 43, 91–92, 100, 116, 202, 220, 224, 337–39, 342

Good Friday, 23, 86, 93, 173–74, 325, 347, 360–61, 363–65, 368, 378

Gospel, xix, xx, 20, 48–49, 80, 99, 129, 156, 161, 169, 173, 175–76, 181–82, 184, 191–92, 200

Gospel Book, 80, 238–39, 256, 358

Gospel Procession. *See,* Procession, Gospel.

INDEX

Gown
    Academic, 46, 96, 101, 102, 109, 235
    Baptismal. *See* Baptismal Garment.
    Vergers, 57, 119–20, 213, 215
Gradine, 70, 72, 75–77
Gradual, 181
Great Amen, 167, 176, 222, 242, 262
Great Fifty Days. *See* Eastertide.
Great Litany, 158, 165, 204–7, 209–10, 355, 37, 385–86
Great Thanksgiving, 124, 232, 241, 260–61, 379
Great Vigil of Easter, 42, 64, 94, 126, 127, 210–12, 269–70, 275, 278, 359–60, 363, 365–66, 369, 370, 372, 379
Greening of the Church, 41, 350
Green Vestments, 87–90, 92–93, 373
Greeting. *See* Salutation.
Gum olibanum, 135

Hands
    position of (for minister), 46–47, 117, 158, 171, 218, 257, 261–62, 267, 342
    for reception of communion, 7, 227–28
Hangings, xiii, 3, 26, 60, 72–74, 78, 81, 82, 88, 91, 93, 129, 132–33, 348, 354, 365
Hassock. *See* Cushion, for Kneeling.
Healing, 241, 271, 274, 304, 313, 315, 317–18, 323–25, 331, 380. *See also* Unction.
Hearse. *See* Bier.
Herse cloth. *See* Funeral Pall.
High Mass. *See* Solemn Eucharist.
Holy Baptism. *See* Baptism.
Holy Communion. *See* Eucharist.
Holy Eucharist. *See* Eucharist.
Holy Saturday, 365
Holy Spirit, 98, 375–76, 280, 297–98, 328
Holy Table. *See* Altar.
Holy Thursday. *See* Maundy Thursday.
Holy Water. *See* Baptismal Water.

Holy Week, 155, 173–74, 210, 347, 356, 358, 360–61, 363, 370
Homily. *See* Sermon.
Hood
    Academic & in Choir, 8, 10, 25, 43, 96, 98, 106–9, 187, 193, 214, 295, 371, 389
    On Cope, 118, 217
Host. *See* Communion Bread.
Humble Access, Prayer of. *See* Prayer of Humble Access.
Humeral Veil, 202
Hymn, ix, 14–16, 36, 56, 57, 134, 144, 151–57, 160, 164, 176, 182, 183–87, 194, 196, 199, 201–2, 204, 209–16, 218, 233–34, 239, 256, 260, 264, 267, 276, 298–300, 309, 336, 340, 343, 346–47, 352, 355–56, 360, 362, 364, 369, 371, 375, 380
Hymnal 1982, x, 14, 151, 153–54, 156, 185, 199, 201, 204, 276, 347, 362, 364
Hymn board, 56

Images, 52–54, 76–77, 90–91, 95, 174, 177, 221, 251, 353–54, 382
Immersion, 17, 51, 279
Imposition of Ashes, 355
Imposition of Hands. *See* Laying on of Hands.
Improperia. *See* Reproaches.
Incarnation, xii, 23, 91, 159, 198, 203, 222, 239, 257, 348, 352
Incense, 27, 125, 133, 135–36, 140, 170, 175–77, 193, 213, 215–16, 218, 252, 254, 260, 276, 338, 341, 351, 366–67, 374
Inclination. *See* Bow.
Inscription of the Paschal Candle, 367
Instrumental Music, 44, 182, 209, 211, 217, 308, 343, 371
Intercession, 150, 154, 182, 185–86, 196, 206, 258, 362, 371. *See also* Prayers of the People.
Intinction, 265, 328
Introit. *See* Entrance.
Invitatory, 180–81, 183–84, 188

401

INDEX

Jubilate Deo, 180

Kalendar, 21–24, 141, 154, 156, 173–74, 180, 222, 346, 374, 382
Kindling of the New Fire. *See* New Fire.
Kissing the Altar, 238
Kissing of the Cross, 252, 363
Kiss of Peace. *See* Peace, The.
Kneeling, 8, 20, 41, 52–53, 55, 61, 65, 71, 83–84, 108, 139, 157–58, 160–61, 163–65, 167–70, 187, 192–94, 196, 202, 204–7, 216, 236, 239, 240, 247–49, 257–58, 267, 279, 296, 298, 300, 305, 311, 320, 354–55, 362–63
Kontakion, 375
Kyrie eleison, 152, 185–86, 190, 206–7, 215, 233, 238, 355, 374

Lace, 11, 74–75, 106, 113, 116, 120
Lamp, 41, 90, 139, 225, 368
Lavabo, 241, 244, 248, 260, 267
Laity, v, xxiv, 2, 4, 16–17, 32, 32, 39, 49, 86, 98, 104, 108, 110, 112, 120, 122, 131–32, 141, 146, 149, 165, 179–80, 187, 188, 200, 205–6, 225–26, 234, 237, 239, 249–50, 255, 261, 281, 282, 291, 327–28, 340, 358, 377, 383
Last Rites. *See* Ministration at the Time of Death.
Laying on of Hands
  at Confirmation, 290, 296–300
  at Ordination, 179
  at the Sacrament of Reconciliation, 322
  at Unction, 323–25, 332, 380
Lectern, 8, 26, 41–43, 45, 48–50, 100, 176, 193, 209, 239–40, 247, 255–58, 311, 366, 368
Lection. *See* Reading.
Lectionary, 19, 22, 141, 188–91, 256, 346
Lector. *See* Reader.
Lent, 7, 23, 47, 50, 53, 76, 80–82, 86–92, 125, 137, 155, 164, 173–74, 180, 183, 187, 199, 204, 213, 222, 233, 318, 320, 337–38, 347–48, 353–58, 359, 360
Lenten Array, 47, 90–93, 337, 353–54
Lenten Cross, 125
Lenten Veil, 90–91, 137, 164, 353–54, 357–58
Lesser Feasts and Fasts, 23–24, 141, 174, 222, 234, 346, 374
Lesson. *See* Reading.
Licensed Ministry, 32, 104, 179, 225, 253, 328
Light, 26–27, 41–42, 46, 48, 61, 64, 73, 76–79, 115, 126–27, 172–75, 177, 183–84, 193–94, 210, 212, 215, 247, 268, 277, 280, 326, 340, 348–49, 352, 366–70, 378
Linen, 7, 26, 50–51, 72–75, 79, 82, 86–87, 90–91, 96, 100, 113, 115, 118, 120–22, 133–34, 137–40, 225, 251, 263, 266, 281, 326, 328–30, 342, 353–54, 358
Litany. 26, 98, 143, 150, 152, 158, 165, 201, 204–7, 209–10, 212–13, 218, 331–33, 355, 372, 374, 382–86. *See also* Great Litany.
Litany Desk, 26, 205
Litany of the Saints, 382–86
Liturgical Colors, xii, 6, 12, 19, 47–50, 73, 75, 81, 85–94, 95, 99, 115, 117, 118–21, 129, 193, 202, 221, 228, 282, 295–96, 328, 337, 338, 339, 359, 374
Liturgical Year. *See* Kalendar.
Lord's Prayer, 149–51, 157–58, 169, 179, 182, 185–86, 194, 203, 206, 236, 243, 262, 274, 282, 311, 325, 329, 344, 362, 364, 365
Lord's Supper. *See* Eucharist.
Lucenarium. See Service of Light.

Magnificat, 176, 184, 192–93, 313
Major Feast, 23–24, 174, 221, 223, 233, 256, 374, 378
Maniple, 95–98, 134, 235–36, 252–53, 305
Marriage, 64, 94, 116, 141, 165, 190, 211, 259, 301–12

INDEX

Mary the Virgin. *See* Blessed Virgin Mary.
Mass. *See* Eucharist.
Matins. *See* Morning Prayer.
Maundy Thursday, 76, 92–93, 146, 164, 356, 359–61, 364
Mediation, 185, 201, 234–35. *See also* Sermon.
Memorial Acclamation, 262
Ministration at the Time of Death, 210, 317, 330–33
Ministration to the Sick. *See* Unction.
Missal, 10, 30, 76, 79–80, 83, 87–88, 125, 151, 158, 164, 166–68, 223, 232, 241–42, 251–54, 263, 342
Missa Cantata. *See* Sung Eucharist.
Mitre, 69, 97–100, 104, 110, 224, 296, 383
Monstrance, 201–2
Morning Prayer, 5, 15,, 24, 143, 145–47, 150, 154–56, 172, 178, 180–83, 184–87, 190, 192–93, 204–5, 221, 361–62, 371
Music, x, xii, 13, 15, 23, 36–37, 39–41, 44–45, 96, 104, 140, 145–48, 150–53, 161, 170, 174, 179, 182, 196, 204, 209, 211, 213, 217–18, 220, 235, 243, 256, 262, 308, 324, 336, 346, 352, 365, 369, 371, 383

Nativity of Our Lord Jesus Christ. *See* Christmas.
Nave, 37–41, 42–43, 45, 49, 52, 62, 67–68, 83, 132, 210, 212, 259, 294, 298, 307, 309, 350, 351, 368
New Fire, 127, 365–67
Nicene Creed, 15, 159, 169, 223, 269, 288–89, 358, 373, 378
Noonday Prayer, 185–86
Nunc dimittis, 184, 186, 195
Nuptial Blessing. *See* Blessing, Nuptial.

Oblation, 68, 241, 260
Offering of Gifts, xii-iii, 83, 179, 195, 211, 220, 241, 248, 259, 341, 379

Offertory, 156, 159, 163, 176, 195, 209, 211–12, 231–32, 237, 240–41, 247, 259, 272, 299, 311, 326, 341, 355, 369, 374
Office. *See* Daily Office.
Office Hymn, 154–57, 182, 185–86, 194, 196
Officiant, 157–58, 178–85, 187, 193–94, 201–3, 215, 282, 339, 362, 371
Oil of Chrism. *See* Chrism.
Oil of Healing. *See* Unction.
Orans, 158
Ordinary Time, 81, 85, 89, 93, 125–26, 154, 233, 296, 373–74
Ordination, 28, 65, 94, 165, 179, 212, 253, 291, 383
Organ, 39, 44, 61, 132, 217, 256, 300, 369
Ornaments of the Church, 7, 9, 25, 120–30
Ornaments Rubric, 5–10, 12, 25–26, 29, 42, 87, 107
Orphrey, 8, 43, 92, 95, 100, 117–19, 129, 224
O Salutaris Hostia, 201
Osculate. *See* Kissing the Altar.
Our Father. *See* Lord's Prayer.
Oxblood Red Vestments. *See* Passiontide Red Vestments.
Oxford Movement, 36

Pall, 121, 129, 337, 339, 343
Palms, 209–10, 353, 357–58
Palm Sunday. *See* Sunday of the Passion: Palm Sunday.
Pange lingua gloriosi corporis mysterium, 360
Pange lingua gloriosi proelium certaminis, 364
Parents, 147, 252, 270–71, 273, 280–81, 283, 288, 293, 308, 312–13, 316–17
Pascha Nostrum, 180
Paschal Candle, 42, 127–29, 210–12, 277–78, 338, 340, 349, 365–68, 372–73

INDEX

Passion, 53–54, 87–88, 92–93, 115, 202, 234–35, 354, 356, 358–59, 362, 365, 378
Passion Gospel, 358, 365
Passion Sunday. *See* Sunday of the Passion: Palm Sunday.
Passiontide Red Vestments, 88, 92–93, 115, 354, 356, 359
Pastoral Offices, 290
Paten, 7, 12, 25, 100, 123–24, 139, 201, 225, 236, 241–42, 244, 247–48, 251, 260–61, 263–64, 266–67
Patronal Feast, 23, 94, 173
Pavement, 7, 61, 71, 78–79, 83–84, 170, 176–77, 193–94, 196, 216, 238, 253, 256, 260, 350
Pavement Lights, 7, 78–79, 170
Peace, The, 232, 240, 274, 258, 280, 296, 299, 305, 311, 324, 326, 329, 332, 341, 355
Penance. *See* Confession, Private.
Penitential Order, 232–33, 239, 355
Pentecost. *See* Day of Pentecost.
Pentecost Red Vestments, 92–94
Pew, 26, 39, 52, 54, 57, 61, 139, 147, 218, 291, 295, 297, 300–301, 309, 357
Phos hilaron, 183, 194
Pictures, 53–54, 60, 73, 76, 91, 104, 109, 130, 134, 142, 158, 167, 263, 353
Pink Vestments. *See* Rose Vestments.
Piscina, 7, 83, 121, 136, 236, 249, 282
Plainsong, 153–56, 184, 204
Pool, Baptismal. *See* Baptismal Pool.
Postcommunion Prayer, 380
Prayer of Humble Access, 151, 165
Prayers of the People, 149, 151, 165, 225–26, 238–40, 257–58, 276, 299, 313, 341, 370, 374–75, 377
Preaching, 12, 26, 45–48, 98, 106–7, 109, 116, 145, 149, 171, 179, 194, 225, 235, 239, 256–57, 297, 319, 341, 348, 358, 365, 369, 370, 373, 383
Preparation of Gifts, xii, 83, 195, 211, 225, 232, 241, 248, 259–60, 341, 379

Presentation. *See* Candlemas.
Principal Feast, 22–24, 78, 91, 153, 173–74, 192, 213, 223, 258, 351–52, 372–73, 378
Private Confession. *See* Reconciliation of a Penitent.
Procession, 45, 56, 170, 175, 177, 195–96, 208–19, 385–86. *See also*
    at Ash Wednesday, 355
    at Baptism, 272, 276, 28–81
    at Burial, 338–40, 343
    at Candlemas, 352–53
    at Christmas, 350–51
    at Confirmation, 296
    at Good Friday, 363
    at Marriage, 307, 310
    at Maundy Thursday, 360
    at Palm Sunday, 209, 357–58
    at the Great Vigil of Easter, 366–68
    Entrance, 26, 132, 134, 187, 253–54
    Gospel, 80, 204–7, 239, 247, 256
    for Great Litany, 98–99, 158
    Offertory, 209, 211–12, 241, 379
    Retiring, 157, 328
    Rogation, 371–72
Processional Cross, 26, 125–26, 130, 252, 254, 338, 354
Psalms, 39, 45, 56, 134, 148, 150, 152, 157, 160, 162, 179–81, 183–86, 190, 203, 209–10, 239, 273, 276, 309, 321, 325, 340, 361, 369, 381
Pulpit, 25, 42, 45–49, 109, 139, 171, 235, 239, 256–57, 350
Purificator, 83, 121–23, 136–37, 139, 247, 251, 267, 281, 330
Purple Vestments, 87–89, 91–93, 129, 217, 328, 337, 348
Pyx, 8, 43, 123, 266, 329

Rail, Altar. *See* Altar Rail.
Reader, xix, 48–49, 104, 149, 178, 188, 191, 247, 255, 257, 368
Reading, 19, 21, 26, 48–49, 56, 99, 148–49, 177, 179–81, 184–85, 188, 225, 234, 239, 256–57, 273, 305, 309–10, 320, 324, 329, 340, 358, 362, 368–69, 374, 381

404

INDEX

Reaffirmation of Baptismal Vows, 292, 294, 297, 299, 380
Reception (from another communion of the church), 292, 294, 297, 299
Reception of the Body, 338–39
Reconciliation of a Penitent, 54–55, 64–65, 314, 318–22, 324, 332, 356, 359
Red Vestments. *See* Pentecost Red Vestments *or* Passiontide Red Vestments.
Register, 132, 137, 141–42, 281–82, 303
Renewal of Baptismal Vows, 269, 291–92, 294, 352
Reproaches, 356, 363–64, 393
Requiem, 129, 336, 374
Reredos, 6, 26, 43, 60, 69–72, 75–77, 81, 100, 236, 251, 263, 353, 357
Reservation of the Blessed Sacrament, 123, 197, 218, 230, 326–29, 360–61
Reverence, 31, 39, 50, 83, 161–63, 165–67, 170, 174, 192, 195, 199, 229, 239, 244, 246, 253, 262, 266–67, 311, 350
Riddels, 6, 69, 78, 82, 90–91, 100, 174, 221, 236, 251, 354
Ritualist, xii, xxiii, 5, 9–10, 12, 16, 30, 33–34, 88, 102, 165, 168, 175, 236
Rochet, 8, 25–26, 96, 98, 104, 111–12, 215, 217, 295–96, 339
Rogation Days, 93, 204–5, 217, 371–71
Rogation Procession, 371–72
Rood, 43–44, 61, 69, 76–77, 164, 206, 208–9, 212, 214, 216, 354, 357–58
Rood Screen, 42–44, 68–69, 83, 132, 357
Rose Vestments, 221

Sacristan, 56, 89, 138, 177
Sacristy, xviii, 57, 120, 124, 126, 131–34, 194, 196, 211, 216, 215, 249, 251–54, 267–68, 346

Salutation, 179, 182, 185, 207, 215, 239, 241, 255, 261, 273, 309, 340, 355, 362, 365, 369
Salve festa dies, 213
Sanctuary, 36, 43, 57, 66, 71–72, 78, 82–83, 90, 193, 216, 296, 311–12, 354, 370
Sanctuary Light, 90, 370
Sanctus, 152, 242, 248, 261
Sarum, xiii, 28–30, 39, 77, 87–88, 125, 161, 164, 166–68, 172–74, 223, 253–54, 261, 263, 309, 317, 323, 338, 363
Scarf, 10, 26, 96, 107, 109, 295
Scripture, 14–15, 19, 30, 53, 145, 180–82, 184–88, 223, 226, 248, 255–57, 259, 286–87, 289, 308, 314, 318, 323–24, 329, 332, 340–41, 355, 359, 362, 370
Savoy Conference, 8, 50, 144, 159, 173
Second Vatican Council, xxi, xxiii, 16, 55, 66, 86, 96, 110
Secrecy of Confession. *See* Reconciliation of a Penitent.
Sedilia, 7, 84, 170, 215
Sequence Hymn, 176, 239, 256, 340, 369
Sermon, 45, 48–49, 145, 161, 179, 192, 194–95, 234–36, 239–40, 247, 256–57, 259, 273, 275, 297, 309–12, 336, 352, 355–56, 358, 360, 362, 378, 383
Service of Light, 42, 183–84
Short Lesson. *See* Chapter.
Shrove Tuesday, 54, 353, 355
Sign of the Cross, 168–69, 169, 198, 242, 254, 257, 262, 267, 322, 325
Silence, 10, 140, 179, 185–87, 199–203, 240, 243, 258, 262–63, 297, 299–300, 324, 355, 361–62, 371, 379–80
Sitting, 39–41, 46, 52, 55, 65, 67, 117, 122, 141, 157–58, 160–61, 170, 192–93, 194, 226, 239, 295, 298, 314–15, 320, 322, 324, 332, 355–56, 369
Solemn Bow, 166, 242, 262

405

INDEX

Solemn Collects, 362
Solemn Liturgy, 98, 104, 213, 351
Solemn Eucharist, 351
Solemn Evensong, 199–200
Song of Mary. *See* Magnificat.
Song of Simeon. *See* Nunc dimittis.
Song of Praise, 196, 255
Song of Zechariah. *See* Benedictus.
Sponsors
    for Baptism, 126, 212, 270–71, 273–76, 278, 280–81, 309
    for Confirmation, 293–95, 297–99, 309
Stabat Mater, 155
Stains, how to remove, 136, 139–40
Standing, xi, xix, 40, 49, 64, 83–84, 144, 148–49, 157–58, 160–61, 165, 168, 170–71, 188, 192–96, 206–7, 211, 215–16, 225, 227, 235, 238–44, 248–49, 254–62, 267, 271, 273, 275, 279–80, 294, 297–300, 307–8, 311–12, 340, 342–43, 355, 357, 362–63, 368, 378–79
Stations in Processions, 206, 209, 212–14, 216, 254, 351, 353, 357–58, 363, 368, 371–72
Stations of the Cross, 53–54
Statutes, 88, 89, 162
Staves, 120, 126, 193, 225
Steps, Altar. *See* Altar Steps.
Stole, 10, 69, 94–96, 98–99, 108–11, 116, 118, 134, 187, 214, 235, 249, 252–53, 278, 279, 281–82, 295, 305–6, 310–11, 320, 322, 324, 326, 328, 339, 361
Stripping of Altars, 70, 73, 360–61
Subdeacon, 8, 31–32, 71, 100, 110, 112, 119, 220–21, 224, 236–38, 253, 347, 360
Suffrages, 157, 182, 184, 194, 206, 207
Summary of the Law, 233
Sunday of the Passion: Palm Sunday, 92–93, 164, 210, 213–14, 217, 353, 356–57, 362, 368, 378
Sunday, 22, 24, 42, 85–89, 91–93, 138, 144–47, 150, 156, 164, 172–74, 178, 182–83, 187, 195–96, 204–5, 207, 210, 213–14, 217, 219, 221–23, 229, 232–33, 246, 269, 272, 283–85, 287, 292, 296, 312, 324, 328, 337, 347–49, 352–53, 355–57, 362, 368, 370–74, 378
Sung Eucharist, 133, 175, 237
Superfrontal. *See* Frontlet.
Supplication, 206–7
Surplice, x, 8, 10, 12, 25–26, 39–40, 43, 96, 100, 104–10, 112, 116, 119–20, 134, 140, 187, 193, 214–15, 217, 225, 235, 249, 263, 278, 281, 295, 296, 305–6, 324, 338–39, 342, 353–54, 361–62, 371
Sursum Corda, 80, 99, 104, 110, 160, 241, 248, 261–62

Tabernacle, 82, 201, 203, 370. *See also* Aumbry.
Table, Holy. *See* Altar.
Tantum ergo Sacramentum, 202
Tapers
    Baptismal, 126
    Handheld, 130
    Processional, 126, 130, 193–94, 215, 220, 343
Taperer, 138, 170, 176, 193–94, 213, 215, 237, 343
Te Deum, 156
Ten Commandments, 46, 165, 239, 274
Tenebrae, 356
Thanksgiving for the Birth or Adoption of a Child, 312–14
Thurible. *See* Censer.
Thurifer, 136, 138, 170, 176–77, 193–94, 201–2, 209
Time of services, 146–47, 223
Tippet, 107–9, 187, 193, 214, 295–96, 361–62
Tolling, 178, 361
Torches. *See* Tapers.
Towel, 7, 96, 100, 122, 134, 139, 249, 251, 260, 279
Tract, 56, 107
Tractarian, 10, 16, 165
Transferring of a Feast, 22–23, 221–23, 351–52, 378

INDEX

Transfiguration, 22, 93, 173
Triptych, 90, 221, 353
Trinity Sunday, 86, 91, 93, 156, 373
Trisagion, 152, 215, 233, 238, 374
Tunicle, 8, 25, 88, 96–98, 110, 119, 129, 134, 213–14, 224, 235–36, 253, 347, 357

Unction, 240–41, 303, 317–18, 323–25, 331–32, 380
Usher, 227, 248, 259, 294, 355

Vase, 80–81, 350
Vatican II. *See* Second Vatican Council.
Veil, 68, 137, 337. *See* Lenten Array, *also*
    Chalice. *See,* Chalice Veil.
    Humeral. *See,* Humeral Veil.
    of the Cross or Rood, 90–91, 164, 353–54, 57–58
Veneration of the Cross, 360–63
Veni Creator Spiritus, 156, 164, 298
Venite, 180
Verger, xi, 26, 56–57, 62, 96, 119, 127, 138, 170–71, 194, 202, 206, 208, 210, 213–16, 218, 226, 235–36, 241, 244, 251–52, 254–55, 268, 277, 295–96, 298–300, 306–8, 340, 342, 355, 366–67, 371
Versicle and Response, 151, 185–88, 214, 260, 344, 363
Vespers. *See* Evening Prayer, Evensong.
Vestments. *See* Eucharistic Vestments.
Vestry, 61, 94, 99, 113, 126, 131–32, 134, 137, 140–41, 177, 187, 193, 196, 209, 217, 238, 244, 268, 281, 295–96, 328, 346

Vigil, 94, 333, 347. *See also* Great Vigil of Easter.
Violet Vestments. *See* Purple Vestments.
Virge, 26, 57, 127, 217

Wafers, 198, 228–29, 230–31
Warden. *See* Church Warden.
Washing
    of Feet. *See* Foot washing.
    of Hands. *See* Lavabo.
    of Altar, 360
Watch, All-Night. *See* All-Night Watch.
Water, 25, 47, 83, 124, 136, 139–40, 229–30, 231, 241, 243, 260, 329–30, 360. *See also,* Ablutions, Baptismal Water, Preparation of Gifts.
Wax, 42, 75, 78, 121, 139–40, 349, 366–67
Way of the Cross. *See* Stations of the Cross.
Weddings. *See* Marriage.
Weekday Eucharist, 23, 57, 221–23, 233–34, 272
White vestments, 81, 86, 88–94, 99–100, 129, 202, 224
Whitsunday. *See* Pentecost.
Wine, xii, 25, 79, 83, 97, 124, 136–67, 139–40, 163, 166, 199, 211, 228, 231–32, 241–43, 248, 259, 260, 262, 265, 267, 281, 311, 325–26, 328–29, 332, 341, 360, 379
Witness, 226, 274–75, 305–6, 309–10, 382, 384
Words of Institution, 166, 262, 289
Wreath, Advent. *See* Advent Wreath.

www.ingramcontent.com/pod-product-compliance
Lightning Source LLC
Chambersburg PA
CBHW071435300426
44114CB00013B/1448